THE
MARKETING
CODE

Stephen Brown is no relation to Dan Brown, though he wishes it were otherwise. He is hopeful, however, that *The Marketing Code* will benefit from its shameless attachment to Dan Brown's coat-tails. Written as a thriller, it reveals that *The Da Vinci Code* was a marketing conspiracy from start to finish.

THE MARKETING CODE

Stephen Brown

CYAN

Marshall Cavendish
Business

Copyright © 2006 Stephen Brown

First published in 2006 by:

Marshall Cavendish Business
An imprint of Marshall Cavendish International (Asia) Private Limited
A member of Times Publishing Limited
Times Centre, 1 New Industrial Road
Singapore 536196
T +65 6213 9300
F +65 6285 4871
E te@sg.marshallcavendish.com
Online bookstore: www.marshallcavendish.com/genref

and

Cyan Communications Limited
119 Wardour Street
London W1F 0UW
United Kingdom
T +44 (0)20 7565 6120
E sales@cyanbooks.com
www.cyanbooks.com

*This book is a work of fiction. Names, characters, places, incidents and brands are either
a product of the author's imagination or are used fictitiously. Any resemblance to actual
people living or dead, companies, events or locales is entirely coincidental.*

A CIP record for this book is available from the British Library

ISBN-13 978 981 261 842 9 (Asia & ANZ)
ISBN-10 981 261 842 2 (Asia & ANZ)
ISBN-13 978-904879-88-6 (Rest of world)
ISBN-10 1-904879-88-8 (Rest of world)

Printed and bound in Great Britain

Everything is connected.

−Umberto Eco, *Foucault's Pendulum*

People of the same trade seldom meet
together, even for merriment and
diversion, but the conversation ends
in a conspiracy against the public.

−Adam Smith, *Wealth of Nations*

Fact

This book is a work of fiction. Apart from the true bits, that is. The places are exactly as described, with one obvious exception. The conspiracy theories are accurate in almost every detail, even the weird and wonderful ones. The marketing principles, though exaggerated, are as close to gospel as makes no difference. The characters, however, are either entirely fictional or, in the case of actual persons, fictionalised representations of those persons. They bear no resemblance whatsoever to anyone living or dead.

The characters in this novel may be imaginary, but the plot most definitely isn't. There *really is* a conspiracy at the heart of marketing. As one of its prime movers recently made clear, "Sometimes you have to kill to make a killing."

Chapter One

How Now Cash Cow

The room buzzed with anticipation as the speaker strode towards the imposing podium. Conservatively dressed and carefully coiffed, she looked much like any other middle-aged marketing professor. Only the smart Paul Costelloe suit betrayed her country of origin, as did a tiny twist of emerald ribbon on her Irish linen lapel. To all intents and purposes, she was indistinguishable from the three previous presenters, Professor Bland, Professor Boring, Professor Blowhard.

Professor Emer Aherne was different in one important respect, however. Unlike the earlier presenters, she had rehearsed and polished and buffed up her speech. She didn't believe in inarticulacy, considering it a sign of professional weakness. She was an educator, someone who earned her living from standing and delivering. She regarded ums, ahs, ers, and analogous stuttering utterances as an affront, an indicator of the presenter's scholarly laxity, of their failure to appreciate that conference papers are professors' moments of truth, the instant when the intellectual sale is made.

Nor did Emer Aherne believe in beginning with banal bromides of the nice-to-be-here, thank-you-for-coming, you're-a-wunnerful-wunnerful-audience variety. She subscribed to the showbiz notion of starting with a bang and building things up from there. This was true of all her presentations, but it was especially true of the one she had rehearsed so assiduously. Not only did it deal with an important aspect of the entertainment economy, but it was being delivered in the very apogee of showbusiness, Las Vegas.

She stood silently behind the podium, waited for the room to settle and, fixing the audience with an imperious stare, proceeded to give them rhetorical hell.

"Tahiti. The beach. A lone figure strolls disconsolately along the shoreline. It is Dan Brown, a jobbing musician whose career is going nowhere. Several years in and he's sold next to nothing, apart from a theme song for the Atlanta Olympics. It's time to try something new, possibly related to his passion for art history. Turning back to his hotel, he stumbles over a tattered blockbuster novel, devoured and discarded by a departed holidaymaker. It's *The Doomsday Conspiracy* by Sidney Sheldon. Brown starts reading. Engrossed, he can't put it down. He swallows it whole and, in a moment of inspiration, decides, 'I can do that.' And do that he does.

"His first conspiracy-propelled thriller, *Digital Fortress*, is published in 1998. No one notices. His second and third novels, *Angels & Demons* and *Deception Point*, follow *Digital Fortress* to paperback Palookaville. The music-business pattern is starting to repeat itself.

"Dan moves to Doubleday. He writes *The Da Vinci Code*. Expectations are low, since its irreligious stance is deemed inappropriate in the post-9/11 climate. But his editor, Jason Kaufman, can't put Brown's manuscript down. Nor can Kaufman's editorial colleagues. Nor can Barnes & Noble's chief fiction buyer, Sessalee Hensley. Collectively, they take a chance on the risky property, even though the market signals are discouraging. A record number of advance reader copies are produced in order to build some much-needed buzz. Barnes & Noble, facing fierce price competition from supermarket chains, especially on brand-name blockbusters by Grisham and King, backs the no-name author to the hilt. *The Da Vinci Code* is released on 18 March 2003 and, thanks to the pre-publication marketing campaign, shoots straight to the top of the *New York Times* bestseller list.

"Beginning as it means to go on, the book barnstorms bestseller lists worldwide. Brown's back catalogue follows suit. Special editions are issued. Books about the book sell like hot cakes, even the Da Vinci Diet Book. Grail trails around the locations mentioned in the book are promptly pulled together and prove extremely popular, much to the clergy's dismay. A big-budget, Ron Howard–

helmed movie starring Tom Hanks is put into production. Meanwhile, Dan the Man has gone into hiding, writing his next thrilling novel, a sequel to *The Da Vinci Code* called *The Solomon Key*. The world awaits. Agog."

In the bowels of the auditorium, a member of the hitherto somnolent audience sat up, intrigued by what he was hearing. Barton Brady II glanced at his associate, Yasmin Buonarroti, and raised an inquiring eyebrow. Yasmin replied with a slight frown. It was difficult to make out what the presenter was saying, due to her impenetrable Irish accent and quickfire delivery. But the slick slides more than compensated.

Images of Dan Brown, interspersed with video clips of his TV appearances scrolled impressively across the screen. And just when the sight of Dan's doe-like stare was becoming unbearable, the slide-show segued into shots of Leonardo's *Mona Lisa*, the Louvre's glass pyramid, Saint-Sulpice Church, Chateau Vilette, Westminster Abbey and Rosslyn Chapel, the key locations in Brown's better-than-bestselling thriller. These were followed by video inserts of Dan's fans taking the tie-in tours of Paris and vox-pop interviews with exasperated church officials who daily deal with hordes of loud-mouthed, Coke-chugging, plaid-clad Langdon-lovers whose enthusiasm was surpassed only by their ignorance.

PowerPoint this wasn't.

It was a shame there were so few people in the audience. A lot of time and effort had obviously gone into Professor Aherne's presentation. But it was the last day of the American Marketing Association conference, and the majority of delegates were making their weary way to McCarran Airport. Having delivered their own words of wisdom and paid sycophantic obeisance to those in power – principally Professor Kate Phillips, the guru of gurus, who had deigned to attend the bacchanal – most conference-goers didn't feel the need to listen to yet another yawn-inducing speech.

Only Barton Brady, Yasmin Buonarroti and a smattering of die-hard delegates, all with later planes to catch, were in the Bordeaux Room of the Paris Hotel & Casino for the turbo-charged presentation. You'd have thought a title like "The Marketing Code:

11

How Brown's Bestseller Holds the Key to Business Success" would have packed them in. However, the dead-zone scheduling, plus the raging hangovers of hard-partying marketing professors, militated against it. The Las Vegas Strip has a lot to answer for, as indeed the delegates would, once they got home to their unforgiving partners.

Brady glanced again at his associate, who sat across the aisle of the unspeakably ostentatious conference room, where vast paintings of Versailles Palace and the Tuileries Gardens dominated the side walls, and where the chandelier was bigger – and brighter – than most of the audience. He raised both eyebrows querulously. Yasmin responded with a "not sure" shake of the head.

"So, what are the secrets of Dan Brown's staggering marketing success?" Professor Aherne went on. "Are there lessons for others and, if so, what are they?"

The audience, such as it was, looked up expectantly.

"Well, it seems to me that there are four crucial factors. The first of these is entertainment. Entertainment is the key ingredient here. For all its alleged literary faults, *The Da Vinci Code* is a rattling good read, a veritable roller-coaster ride. It is a wonderful, unforgettable, page-turning, thrills-and-spills–filled story. It epitomises today's entertainment economy, our fast-moving, hit-driven, fad-fuelled world of show-stopping, knock-em-dead, next big things.

"This very venue," she went on, opening her arms to embrace the thinly populated auditorium, "is testament to entertainment's central place in the contemporary marketing cosmos. The thrill we get staring up at the Paris Hotel's imitation Louvre façade, or its scaled-down Arc de Triomphe, or its half-size replica of the Eiffel Tower, is similar to the thrill we get reading about Robert Langdon's adventures in the 'real' Louvre, the real Arc de Triomphe, the real Eiffel Tower, all of which feature in Brown's book."

At this precise point, a shiny-suited slick of self-importance, the conference-session chairperson, leapt to his feet and, with more than a hint of East Coast condescension, announced that the presenter had five minutes remaining.

Aherne ignored the interruption.

"The second factor is determination. Dan didn't give up, even though his first three books were failures, near enough. He kept plugging away, as did his support team at Doubleday. Business history shows that it's those who persevere despite repeated failure, abject failure, heart-wrenching failure are those who win through in the end. Thomas Edison, Henry Ford, Walt Disney, Ted Turner, Steve Jobs, James Dyson, Oprah Winfrey, Martha Stewart, Mary K. Ash and so on exemplify this never-say-die attitude. Dan Brown, indeed, is a personification of the philosophy of Samuel Beckett, the Nobel Prize–winning Irish playwright, who urges us to 'fail better.' That is, to accept failure, to learn from failure and, eventually, to overcome failure. Brown failed better!"

Yasmin Buonarroti nodded enthusiastically. Brady was too preoccupied with the creases in his Armani pants to notice his associate's change of heart.

"The third factor is obscurity. People like puzzles, mysteries, enigmas, secrets – the more head-scratchingly cryptic the better. And *The Da Vinci Code*, with its arcane amalgam of esoteric symbology and cranky conspiracy theory, attractively wrapped up in a thrill-a-minute detective story, pressed all the right buttons. Better yet was Brown's post-publication withdrawal from public life. His refusal to give interviews, save in exceptional circumstances, and his 'strictly no comment' stance served only to ramp up interest in the increasingly intriguing author. As J. D. Salinger, Thomas Pynchon and Don DeLillo remind us, there's nothing more newsworthy than a newswary celebrity."

The slick insect stood up with a one-minute warning.

"Fourthly and finally," the presenter said forcefully, "Controversy proved vital. There's nothing like a little controversy to attract attention, especially in today's world of superabundant similitude. There are so many brands out there, all functionally indistinguishable, all ably marketed, all vying for consumers' attention, that it's very difficult to stand out from the crowd. The commercial clamour is deafening these days, and controversy helps cut through the cacophony. The Vatican's official disapproval was the best thing that ever happened to Brown. The wrath of Opus Dei, the harrumphing of hidebound historians, and the legal action brought by outraged authors, who claimed that Dan had stolen their ideas, also helped move the merchandise. Madonna's been doing it for years. Eminem's no slouch either."

Glaring at the session chair, with a don't-dare-interrupt expression, Emer Aherne continued, "In conclusion, Brown's success is down to Controversy, Obscurity, Determination and Entertainment. Or CODE for short. CODE is the key to the *Code*!"

As the audience chuckled appreciatively, the presenter pressed home her advantage, "However, a code without a well-trained operator is useless, and Dan Brown is a very well-trained, very astute operator. He is what I call an 'authorpreneur,' a writer with an exceptionally strong sense of what the market wants. Charles Dickens, Mark Twain, L. Frank Baum, Edgar Rice Burroughs, Norman Mailer and, of late, J. K. Rowling all qualify as authorpreneurs. Dan Brown is an authorpreneur and a half. He has discovered, dare I say it, the Holy Grail of modern marketing. He . . . "

Slick had had enough, even if the audience hadn't. "Thank you, Professor Aherne, thank you very much. Perfect timing! Are there any questions?" he went on quickly, hoping that his disapproving tone would discourage the curious and he'd be on his way as expeditiously as possible. Inevitably, his attitude had the opposite effect. An arm shot up to slick's obvious annoyance. It was an eager doctoral student attending her first academic conference and determined to savour every moment. "Is Brown's CODE applicable outside the bookselling business?"

"Oh very much so. As I said in my presentation, we live in an entertainment economy where there's no business *without* showbusiness – not even in the business-to-business business – and CODE applies there too. Marketers often treat the cultural industries as if they are a benighted backwater where the principles of modern marketing have yet to penetrate. I believe the opposite is true. The entertainment industry is the toughest, most competitive business around, and while its marketing ideas are incompatible with mainstream Kate Phillips–style marketing, it seems to me that the 4Ps brigade have much to learn from Brown's marketing code."

"But it's not very scientific, is it?" interjected slick, assuming that the ultimate academic put-down would close the discussion.

"No, it's not," conceded Professor Aherne. "But then, I don't believe marketing is a science. Never has been, never will be."

"If it's not a science, what is it?"

"It's a belief system, just like religion, or magic, or indeed science for that matter. If you believe in marketing, it works. And if you don't believe, no amount of fancy analysis or hypothesis testing or marketing-metric measurement will help you."

Slick rolled his eyes. Another hand flew up, an older hand this time, the hand of an ageing tenured professor, with ponytail. "Aren't we talking about two different marketing approaches here?" he inquired. "The left brain and the right brain, the artistic and the scientific, the feminine and the masculine? Brown's basic approach is feminine, is it not? Doesn't he talk about the 'eternal feminine' in *The Da Vinci Code*? Isn't his marketing premised on it too?"

"That's an interesting one," Aherne answered, choosing her words carefully. "Brown has been criticised by many feminists. The 'eternal feminine' stuff is regarded as a veneer, a thin cover for what some regard as antediluvian sexism. His books, especially *Angels & Demons*, the prequel to *Da Vinci*, are full of references to rape, sadomasochism, and the brutal degradation of women generally. The comedic books Brown wrote before he tried his hand at thrillers are equally misogynistic. One of the songs on his debut album was a ballad about the dubious pleasures of telephone sex. Even his hero, Robert Langdon, is a love-'em-and-leave-'em kind of guy, an unreconstructed chauvinist. So, I think the jury is out on the feminine angle."

"What you're really saying, Professor Aherne, is that the acronym CODE is inappropriate. The keywords surely are Chauvinist, Reactionary, Androcentric and Patriarchal. Or CRAP for short!"

"An awful lot of people have swallowed it, though," the quick-witted presenter retorted.

Slick seized the day. His moment of glory had arrived. "If anyone wants to continue talking CRAP, Professor Aherne will be around after the session. Unfortunately, we've run out of time. Thank you all for attending. Have a safe journey home."

Barton Brady II stood up. He straightened his Hermès tie, shot the cuffs of his Brooks Brothers button-down, checked the time on his vintage Rolex Oyster, and sauntered across the aisle. He leaned over his Prada-clad colleague, who was busy pulling a Moleskine notebook and Mont Blanc pen from her Miu Miu purse. "Get her," he whispered. "Take Aherne out! Make her an offer she can't refuse."

Chapter Two

The Ginger Man

Simon Magill wasn't a symbologist. But he knew a man who was. For two years now he'd been acquainted with, and occasionally worked for, Professor Pitcairn Brodie, Scotland's foremost religious symbologist. And some of it was starting to rub off.

Sitting on the steps of the Scott Monument, Edinburgh's efflorescent tribute to its greatest literary genius, Magill found himself wondering about the symbology of Scotland, his adopted home. Why, he mused, do Scots abhor the stereotypical images that adorn countless picture postcards and biscuit tins – roamin' through the gloamin' with tartan-wearin', shortbread-bakin', bonnie Highland lassies – when they are so crucial to Scotland's USP, its international brand image? Hatred of being pigeonholed, he suspected. What on earth, he further pondered, persuaded the Scots to opt for their dirge-like national anthem *Flower of Scotland*, when the red-blooded, heart-stirring skirl of *Scotland the Brave* was readily available? A congenital need to suffer, presumably.

Scotland was a profoundly paradoxical place. That's why Simon Magill loved it so much. That's why he decided to study there, rather than in the south of England, where he was brought up. That's why he stayed on in Scotland when he dropped out of the University of Edinburgh after discovering a degree in divinity wasn't for him, nor was his second choice, English literature. That's why he moved thirty miles up the road to Stirling, where he took courses in marketing and computer science, and graduated with distinction. That's why he went into business back in Edinburgh, though his many and varied e-commerce ventures had proved unsuccessful thus far. And *that's* why he renewed his acquaintance with Professor Pitcairn Brodie – having attended a couple of his lectures prior to dropping out – and worked for him occasionally on a freelance basis. Nothing special, just maintaining his website, helping with the odd consultancy report and doing menial clerical jobs from time to time. He was a McGofer really, albeit a well-qualified one.

But that was set to change, and that's what today's meeting with the prodigal professor was about. He hadn't seen the revered symbologist for several weeks, because Brodie had been off on one of his clandestine consulting projects. However, a lot had happened in the interim, and Magill was planning to bring the great man up to speed.

Uncharacteristically, the Caledonian colossus was late. Although years of post-divorce dissipation had taken their toll, Professor Brodie continued to take pride in his time-keeping. He set enormous store by the self-symbology of punctuality – if not quite next to godliness, it was next to next to godliness, goddammit – and it wasn't like him to miss an appointment.

Magill wasn't the worrying type, luckily, so he was quite content to watch the passing pedestrians, studying hats, hairstyles, fashion and footwear, gradually acquiring the social symbology skills that Pitcairn Brodie perfected long ago. Perhaps his symbologic antennae were defective, but Magill couldn't help thinking that people in the mass were pretty acquiescent, largely content to follow prevailing fashions, styles, trends. As he'd discovered in his marketing classes at Stirling, most consumers are conformist, not creative, be it for low-rider Levi's jeans, furry Ugg boots or those ubiquitous charity wristbands. Despite all the talk about "anything goes," "unlimited choice," or "have it your way," there was very little consumer individuality as far as he could see.

Professor Pitcairn Brodie was a spectacular exception to the rule. As indeed was Simon Magill. Magill knew all about exceptionalism. Gangly, gawky and giraffesque, with a massive shock of bright ginger hair, he'd hit 6' 4" by the age of fourteen and was teased mercilessly by his Aylesbury Grammar School chums. Nicknames, he'd had a few, but more than enough to be getting along with. The one that stuck was Fido Dido, the elongated cartoon mascot of 7UP soda, and, to be fair, he could see the resemblance. The major difference was that Simon Magill was

18

more pale and less interesting than the original, spiky ginger hairdo excepted. He looked, as one of his "friends" memorably remarked in the school magazine, like someone who's seen a ghost while falling down a lift shaft.

"Well, laddie! Well, well, well!"

Magill jumped, catapulted out of his reverie by Pitcairn Brodie bellowing in his ear. He wasn't the quietest of men. Simon smiled broadly at his sixtysomething mentor, who was resplendent as ever in his Brodie royal tartan trews. He'd grown a bushy beard since Magill last saw him, and it wasn't a flattering look. In the topography of facial topiary, it was situated somewhere west of Gandalf, north of Dumbledore and east-southeast of ZZ Top. Still, it softened his craggy face, which ordinarily cast more shadows than Arthur's Seat in late-autumnal sunshine.

Brodie laid a massive hand on Magill's right shoulder. "How did the interview go, laddie?"

"I got it!" he replied, clenching his fist in a mock victory salute.

"Excellent news, Simon. Excellent news. I knew you'd carry the day."

"Well, I'm not so sure about that," Magill said modestly. "I suspect it was your reference that swung things my way. The name Pitcairn Brodie means an awful lot over there."

Brodie shrugged, affecting what passed – barely – for bashfulness. "Oh, they've long forgotten about me, laddie. Hustler University has changed a lot since my day. It wasn't called Hustler, for starters. They didn't even have a business school back then. I was in a different faculty, furthermore."

"Yes, but your work is very well known. Virtually everyone I met mentioned your landmark study of the Orange Order's marketing strategy."

The prodigious professor settled his not inconsiderable bulk on the steps beneath the florid sandstone monument. "Did they now?"

"I didn't know Orangemen were marketing-strategy types," Magill went on, oblivious to the wary look in the symbologist's strabismic eye. "I just thought they swaggered around Northern Ireland in funny costumes, marching up hill and down dale

19

whistling their flutes, battering their big drums and intimidating innocent Roman Catholics."

Brodie removed his scarlet eye-patch and turned it slowly in his massive hands, something he only ever did when deep in thought, or roaring drunk. Or both. "No, laddie, no. It's not like that at all. There's a lot more to the Orange Order than street parades, lambeg drums and bonfires on the eleventh of July."

Brodie exhaled slowly. It was as if something subterranean, a painful or deep-seated memory perhaps, was struggling to the surface. He quietly explained that his report was supposed to be provocative. It was designed to stir the Orange Order up and force it out of its lethargy. But his well-meaning study only succeeded in provoking certain people – certain influential people. When Magill inquired about the individuals concerned, Brodie merely replied that they were, "People you don't want to know about. Or have any dealings with. Keep your nose clean over there."

"I'll try, Pitcairn," Magill replied politely, refusing to take his words of wisdom seriously.

"I'm serious, Simon. Ulster's a very funny place, and I don't mean funny ha-ha. It's fairly quiet now, but there's a lot going on below the surface. Be careful, young man. Remember what happened to your brother."

An awkward silence settled between them: one lost in the world as it was, the other in a world that might be. Magill felt as far as he had ever been from Brodie, even though they'd been working in close proximity for the past two years.

"Enough!" exclaimed the hyperbolic academic, rubbing his hands with exaggerated glee. "This is supposed to be a celebration, not a wake. Let's go for a gargle to celebrate your success, laddie. It's almost time."

Simon Magill smiled, knowing that this might the last time he'd enact Pitcairn Brodie's midday ritual: meeting at the Scott Monument around 12.45, discussing matters in hand for fifteen minutes or so, listening for the one o'clock gun from the battlements above, and repairing to a nearby hostelry for a tincture or two. Dozen, that is. But only after the professor had called out his alliterative incantation.

"Crag! Castle!! Cannon!!! Cocktail!!!!"

All academics, they say, affect some kind of eccentricity, but some are more affected than others. Professor Pitcairn Brodie went all the way up to eleven on the academic affectometer. Unfailingly attired in Harris tweed or Brodie tartan, he was probably the last lecturer in the land to wear a single-breasted hunting jacket with purple corduroy elbow patches. His overgrown eyebrows, extravagant whiskers – now with shaggy sandy beard attached – and less than artfully disguised male pattern baldness made him an unforgettable sight. Not only did his orotund comb-over put Donald Trump to shame, especially on a windy day when it lifted like a cranial trapdoor, but his swaggering gait, military bearing and windblown air of Caledonian bonhomie made Pitcairn Brodie nothing less than a walking, talking advert for himself. A one-person tourist attraction, in effect. Complete strangers bought him drinks in bars. Holidaymakers posed for photographs with him. Restaurateurs, hoteliers and nightclub owners cultivated the great gregarious granite hulk, since a single word of recommendation could do wonders for business. More importantly, generations of Edinburgh University undergraduates aped his sartorial idiosyncrasies. Generations of postgraduate students admired his staggering erudition, carefully hidden behind the hail-fellow façade. Generations of post-doc divinity students benefited from his kindness, encouragement and unerring ability to pull the levers of power when it came to job applications, grant submissions and the rest of the academic subjugation process. They worshipped the ground he walked upon. And rightly so.

The university, however, felt differently.

"The drinks are on me, laddie," Brodie roared, and set off at a breakneck pace, double-double time or thereabouts. He marched out of Princes Street Gardens, pausing only to greet passers-by with unsolicited salutations and write autographs for bewildered little boys, whether they wanted them or not. He turned heads, stopped traffic and attracted awestruck finger-pointers all the way to the Dome, a garish watering-hole in nearby George Street. He strode across the gleaming checkerboard lobby of the fabulous former bank, made a grand entrance into the vaulted main bar –

a monument to the magnificence of money, money, money – and, taking advantage of the expectant hush that greeted his arrival, bellowed cheerfully at the startled barman, "Hello Hector. Heet us wi' a Heidbanger!"

Brodie's order raised smiles among the Dome's regular clientele, a mixture of prominent local businessmen who considered the mad professor good for Edinburgh's image, top-dollar American tourists who'd heard of Auld Reekie's characters but never expected to meet one in the flesh, and xtra-chic New Town trendies who disdained their clichéd Caledonian heritage but considered Brodie so far over the top that he qualified as an ironic comment on the cod-Celtic claptrap that surrounded them.

"What are you havin', Simon? Will you join me in a celebratory cocktail? What about one of my own creations? A Hummin' Lum? A Reekin' Keek? A Manky Hanky? A Hissin' Thistle? A Skanky Sporrin? A Highland Sling, Lowland Sting, Borders' Disorder?"

"No, Pitcairn, a half of Guinness is fine."

"Not even," he paused to ensure the bar's full attention, "a Fartin' Tartan?"

"Once was quite enough, Professor Brodie."

Magill caught the barman's eye and, with a semaphoric wiggle of his splayed right hand, silently mouthed, "Just a half of Guinness, please."

"Comin' right up," Hector answered. "I'll bring them over to your table."

They took their seats in the corner of the nouveau neoclassical extravaganza. With its Doric columns, delightfully domed ceiling and circular central bar, a sol invictus for worshippers at the shrine of the ancient Celtic god, Narcissus Cirrhosis. It was the place to be and the place to be seen in. Pitcairn Brodie basked in the attention of the still-buzzing imbibers while his proprietary Heidbanger was prepared. A mephitic mixture of Old Navy rum, Irn-Bru and Buckfast fortified wine, it looked like coke but tasted like anthracite. It wasn't so much a pick-me-up as a pick-me-up, throw-me-down and dance-on-my-head-in-Doc-Martins.

Professor Brodie sipped the fetid beverage, winced as his gold fillings felt the frigid impact, and, after it finally hit the spot, smiled serenely at his newly ennobled gofer. "So, Simon, have you told your parents the good news?"

Magill shook his head. "Not yet, Pitcairn. My father's not interested and my mother's past caring. I'll tell them later, when I get settled over there. I don't want another scene with my father. He has issues with Northern Ireland, as you know."

"He's not the only one, laddie. He's not the only one."

Chapter Three

Wizard of the North

Sometimes Simon Magill didn't know what to make of Pitcairn Brodie. Much as he owed him, much as he admired him, much as he loved his hubba-hubba chutzpah, especially in full tartan jacket mode, there was something about Brodie – something symbological – that he couldn't comprehend. Maybe it was Paspi.biz, the bizarre website that Brodie had developed for budding self-publicists; maybe it was the clandestine research projects he disappeared off on for weeks at a time; or maybe it was the whoppers he told gullible tourists about himself, everything from being Miss Jean Brodie's secret love child to his alleged descent from the city's most infamous burglar, sometime businessman and pillar of the community, dirty Deacon Brodie.

But whatever it was, there was something about Professor Pitcairn Brodie that wasn't quite right. It wasn't so much a case of still waters running deep, as a case of gushing, rushing, turbulent waters bursting the banks and braes o' bonnie Doon.

Not long after overhearing Brodie claim Sir Water Scott as a direct ancestor, Simon Magill did a bit of genealogical cyber-grubbing on the University of Edinburgh's finest. Far from being related to the Great Unknown, let alone the Laird of Abbotsford, the Great Well-Known had been brought up on a council estate in Clackmannanshire. His assertion that family tradition dictated he'd enter the church, while his two elder brothers managed the property and joined the regiment respectively, was a bit of an exaggeration too. One brother was a lance-corporal in the territorials; the other did odd jobs round Livingstone while signing on the 'broo.

Pitcairn Brodie was nevertheless a testament to the Promethean spirit of the lowland Scots. By studying hard, making connections, seizing opportunities and never stinting on endeavour, the canny symbologist had made something of himself, something to take pride in. He might not have been a blood relation of Walter Scott, Deacon Brodie, J. M. Barrie, Robbie Burns, or Burke and Hare – or anyone else who took his fancy – but he didn't need to be. Brodie was part of a great Scottish tradition. Like the inimitable Sir Walter, he was a Wizard of the North.

Happily ensconced in his Dome from home, Pitcairn Brodie was on a well-oiled roll. He exuded more good cheer than a Wal-Mart greeters' convention whose drinks have been spiked with Prozac. He doled out impromptu pleasantries, merry quips and hilarious yarns to all within earshot, and if not quite a Scottish Shangri-La, the grill bar was within spitting distance of Elysium.

When his Gaelic glad-handing act was over, Brodie turned back to the University of Hustler's latest recruit and roared, "How did the interview go, laddie? Tell all, tell all!"

"Oh, the usual. It started with a ten-minute presentation to assess my latent lecturing skills."

"A presentation, eh?" He shook his head vigorously, though not so vigorously as to disturb his carefully arranged comb-over. "It wasn't like that in my day."

"It was a bit unnatural, I must say."

"And what did you dazzle them with, laddie?"

"I didn't have a choice, Pitcairn. The topic was selected for me. 'Wither marketing?' would you believe. I covered the standard Kate Phillips stuff, the customer-oriented marketing concept, but said that it had become so commonplace these days that it failed to confer competitive advantage. Every organisation is customer oriented, every company is marketing led, every executive has read Kate Phillips from cover to cover, and consumers have grown wise to marketers' wiles. I also said that marketing has nowhere left to go, and it's starting to feed on itself, recycling old ideas, old products, old ad campaigns. Buzz marketing is just another word for word-of-mouth, viral marketing isn't a million miles from publicity stunt pulling, and, as your website demonstrates, self-branding has been around for donkey's years."

Brodie smiled at Magill's gratuitous yet welcome injection of flattery. Not that his ego was Himalayan or anything. "Did you venture a solution to marketing's manifold ills?" he asked, with more than a touch of irony.

"Not really," Magill replied truthfully. "I kind of bluffed my way. I claimed that what we really needed was sustainable marketing."

"Sustainable marketing? Remind me, laddie."

Magill smirked like the overgrown teenager he remained beneath the twenty-something sophistication. "There's nothing to remind you of, Professor. I made it up on the spot. I just thought that, as 'sustainability' seems to be the latest buzzword, applied to everything under the sun from ecosystems and erections to pizzas and politics, it might be worth adapting the idea to marketing. We need to sustain Kate Phillips's ideas of customer orientation and the traditional marketing concept, otherwise the discipline is doomed. Don't we?"

A roar of laughter echoed round the Dome's singular signature feature. Not everyone can get away with using a word like erection in a job interview, and fewer still appreciate the immensity of the achievement. Instantly inspired, the great man suggested his Ulster-bound acolyte should apply the principles of sustainability to the Orange Order, which was sorely in need of them. But Magill's jocular rejoinder was not well chosen. He quipped that he might get run out of the country just as Brodie himself once was. He instantly regretted what he'd said. He knew he'd overstepped the mark. It was too late, however.

Taken aback by the nerve of the flame-haired, pasty-faced, wet-behind-the-ears whippersnapper, Pitcairn Brodie reacted with stunned silence. His once-handsome physiognomy, now sadly raddled by rum and Rogaine, clouded over as long-repressed memories resurfaced. "That report," he replied, regaining his composure, "was the best thing that ever happened to me, though I didn't appreciate it at the time. If it hadn't been for the Orange Order study, I'd never have heard from Procter & Gamble about their allegedly satanic logo."

"I didn't know you worked for P&G, Professor," Magill responded, in a desperate attempt to regain lost ground.

"Nor," the strangely softly-spoken symbologist went on, "would I have heard from McKinsey, KFC, Snapple, Disney, Lucent, Citroën or any of the other organisations that've had to cope with conspiracy nuts, New Age cranks and Satan-fixated symbol seekers."

"Citroën?" Magill asked incredulously. "I'd heard of the others, but I didn't know Citroën had conspiracy seekers on its case. Since when?"

"Ever since that execrable book *The Da Vinci Code*. Thanks to Desperate Dan Brown, people have been plaguing Citroën about its double chevron logo. Some think it's a reference to the Priory of Sion; others see two pairs of masonic compasses; yet others suspect it has something to do with the eternal feminine. Heaven help us!"

Magill was about to protest, having read and enjoyed the Brown books. But after the previous indiscretion, he didn't want to offend his mentor again. In any event, Brodie was in full flow. "So you see, laddie, the Orange Order debacle worked out well for me in the end. I left Hustler, moved to Edinburgh, and lived happily ever after." He motioned to the barman. "Must be time for another, Hector. Add a bit more Buckfast this time," he bellowed. "When, oh when, will they invent sustainable cocktails, eh, laddie?"

Despite the maladroit means by which the topic had been brought up, Magill was fascinated by the turn their conversation had taken. He'd never heard Brodie talk so openly about his clandestine consultancy work, and he wasn't about to let the opportunity slip. "The thing I can't quite understand," he said, choosing his words carefully, "is why the Orange Order would seek advice from a specialist in the symbology of the early Christian church – the Catholic Church."

Pitcairn Brodie took the bait. "Orangeism doesn't have a problem with Catholicism, Simon, only Roman Catholicism. The early Christian church wasn't Roman Catholic, it was closer to, well, Coptic Catholicism, an entirely different tradition of belief. It was only after the Council of Whitby in 664 AD that Rome acquired the Irish church. Prior to that, Ireland looked to the Middle East. You must understand that after the Fall of Rome in 406 AD, the whole of Europe was overrun by barbarians. The only places

28

where Christian civilisation clung on by its fingernails were the Middle East on the one hand, and the recently converted Celtic fringe on the other. The Celts, what's more, were great traders. They were the travelling salespersons of prehistory. Ireland has always had very close links with the eastern Mediterranean, Simon, especially in the aftermath of the Roman Empire. If it weren't for Ireland's commercial connections to the Holy Land, the fruits of Indo-European civilisation would've been lost forever."

"They don't tell you that in the citybreak brochures."

"And that," Brodie continued, rightly disregarding Magill's ignorant remark, "is why the Irish often claim to be one of the Lost Tribes of Israel, or confidently assert that Ireland was the final resting place of Noah's Ark. And that's why many Irish people, Ulster Protestants in particular, maintain that they are nothing less that God's chosen people."

"Mentally disturbed people, more like."

"That too, Simon. That too. Sigmund Freud is on record as saying that the Irish were the only race who couldn't be helped by psychotherapy."

"Their talking cure comes from Arthur Guinness."

"So, Simon, to cut a long story short, I was the obvious choice to write the Orange Order report. Asking me to do the report wasn't the problem, laddie. It was my marketing strategy for the Orange Order and its offshoots that proved problematic."

"But how . . . "

"*Sláinte*, Simon," Brodie interjected, his confessions at an end. "Many congratulations on your appointment."

"Here's to you, Pitcairn."

They clinked glasses. The professor drank deeply, and smoothly steered the conversation back to his protégé's laudable performance. "So, what happened after your ten-minute presentation? You still haven't told me, laddie. Were Hustler so impressed with sustainable marketing that they offered you the job on the spot?"

Magill laughed and snorted Guinness simultaneously. Then laughed again at his embarrassment. His face went bright red, a perfect complement to his gargantuan ginger mane. He looked like a genetically modified carrot in the throes of strangulation. "'Fraid not, Professor," he spluttered. "They grilled me about my qualifications, job experience, research interests and stuff. They even asked if I had any special talents, a self-branding USP of some kind."

"What, a special talent beyond setting up short-lived e-commerce companies?" Brodie could be a terrible tease when he put his mind to it.

Magill played along. "Yes, Professor, even more special than that. They were looking for evidence of creativity, apparently."

"And what did you do as your creative party-piece, laddie?"

"I couldn't think of anything special, Professor, so I demonstrated my piphilology skills."

"Piphilology?"

"Memorising the span of digits of pi. You know, the mathematical constant that measures the ratio of the circumference of a circle to its diameter. There's no pattern to the digits. More than a trillion decimal places have been calculated. Even the biggest supercomputers can't find a pattern."

"So?"

"So . . . piphilologists memorise the places. They run competitions and stuff. My mother used to enter me for them when I was a kid. She liked that kind of thing: spelling bees, Trivial Pursuit, backgammon, piphilology. I used to be able to 'do the digits' for hours. I've forgotten most of it now, but I remembered enough to give the Hustler interview panel a taste of the old 3.14159265358979323846264338327950288419716939937510. They said they were very impressed. Very impressed."

"Don't believe everything they tell you at Hustler," Brodie teased. "Have you time for another, laddie, or are you heading back to work?"

"Subtle as ever, Professor," the ginger man replied wryly, draining his Guinness with a single swallow. "I'll bring the last of your books over later, my liege, my lord, my Lochinvar. I'll be doing the rest of your packing this afternoon."

"No rush, laddie. Tomorrow's OK. Lunchtime's best. I might be having a wee lie-in after tonight's celebrations. You are coming, aren't you?"

"Wouldn't miss it, Pitcairn. But I'll have to do the last delivery first thing tomorrow. I'm booked on a lunchtime flight to Belfast. Semester's already started. Hustler want me on board ASAP."

"Tomorrow morning it is then, laddie."

"Tomorrow it is. Ah . . . thanks for everything Professor Brodie. I can't begin to tell . . . "

"None of that, laddie. None of the soft stuff. It's the hard stuff I want. Buy me a drink this evening." Brodie extended an enormous rough-hewn hand and said with sincerity, "Well done, Simon, I'm very proud of you."

Magill felt his throat constrict with sorrow and gratitude. Farewells pained him. He'd grown immensely fond of the Great Dissimulator. He shook the symbologist's calloused hand and turned to leave.

"Oh, Simon," Brodie called out as Magill made his way through the crowded bar, "Don't forget to clear out the Hubbard cupboard."

Chapter Four

The Future's Bright

New College glowers down on central Edinburgh like a Calvinist with haemorrhoids. Its twin towers – four-square and fiercely pointed – frown daily on the shopping frivolities of Princes Street, the impudent exhibitionism of the National Galleries, and the half-cut Hibernian hordes each and every Hogmanay. Fortunately, it isn't forced to look at Enric Miralles' Scottish Parliament building, a £431 million monument to the late architect's vaunting ambition and Auld Reekie's boundless self-importance. Godless, feckless, shameless spendthrifts have inherited the earth. Or Edinburgh, at least.

Built in the mid-nineteenth century, as a youthful rival to the ageing if photogenic Old College, New College's once fresh-faced features have settled into angry senior citizenship. Dark, dour and dismal, New College is Scottish hospitality set in stone. Aptly, it plays annual host to the General Assembly of the Church of Scotland, and for seventy-odd years has been the home of the university's School of Divinity, one of the premier centres of theological excellence in the United Kingdom. Though some call it a boot camp for bigots.

New College isn't the sort of place you'd expect to find a larger-than-life lecturer, especially one with wardrobe malfunctions, bibulous inclinations and a braying laugh that rattled rafters in the college's vaunted vaulted library. But just as the General Assembly Hall drops its spinsterish petticoats every August when the sin-ridden Edinburgh Festival commandeers the sacred space, so too New College accommodates a professor who proves raucous exception to the rule. Albeit with considerable reluctance and not a little embarrassment.

Pitcairn Brodie's days were numbered, however. After thirty

years ministering to trainee ministers at the School of Divinity, including spells as Director of Studies, Senior Director of Studies and, for two unforgettable months, Head of School, Brodie was finally vacating his second-floor office, the weather-beaten windows of which looked down on the college's flagstone courtyard. It was from these windows that the sainted scholar loudly chided dilatory undergraduates, mercilessly mocked misbegotten colleagues, poured seditious scorn on narrow-minded General Assembly delegates, and, when drink had been taken to excess, earnestly debated finer points of theology with John Knox, whose statue stood in the courtyard, arms outstretched, directly opposite Brodie's book-lined lair.

Rustication is not a word normally applied to professors, but when universities want to get rid of a disruptive employee, they can rusticate like nobody's business. Deeply loved though Pitcairn Brodie was by the student body, his barely tolerated idiosyncrasies finally became too much for an institution increasingly enmeshed in quality audits, research-assessment exercises and analogous bureaucratic impositions. Inseminated by the demon seed of New Labour, UK universities had become unwitting victims of focus-group think and remade in the grisly image of their league-table-obsessed paymasters. They had no more time for the weird, wacky or wilful. Exuberant eccentrics were especially unwelcome and, when push came to shove, UK unis shoved with gusto.

Professor Brodie was put out to pasture on trumped-up charges. In the good old days, it would have been gross moral turpitude. In the good old bad old days, it would have been creedal infractions, schismatic inclinations or consorting with Roman Catholics. These days, though, the most heinous academic crime, apart from failing to publish unreadable articles in unread journals, was doing undeclared consultancy work, or indeed anything on the side. With his background in early Christian symbology, and the consecration of P&G, Professor Pitcairn Brodie was in constant demand. In addition to the occasional corporate exorcism, such as the Citroën chevron kerfuffle, he provided bespoke branding services for countless arts and crafts companies on the wild and woolly Celtic fringe, as well as personal coaching programmes for wannabe self-publicists. "Be a brand" was his watchword, "Outsource, demons, outsource" his magical management mantra.

The fruits of Brodie's labours in the Augean stables of management consultancy had put his children through university, paid for an extremely messy divorce and purchased a pleasant villa in Corstorphine, a middlebrow suburb four miles from New College. It had also earned him the enmity of the university's manifold mean-spirited bean-counters, as well as the ire of innumerable envious colleagues. When one of them dished the dirt, the university seized its opportunity and, ever mindful of the institution's unsullied scholarly reputation, promptly pensioned off the troublesome titan with an emeritus professorship, gold-plated library card and lashings of hail-fellow, back-slapping, beat-it-buster bluster. Meanwhile, the lock on his office was changed, his college key was sequestered and, to add insult to injury, he was officially stripped of his photocopying privileges, the academic equivalent of a dishonourable discharge.

But what did Brodie care? He was glad to be out of it. He cared nothing for the epaulettes of office or the fact that he'd been cashiered so conspicuously. He'd repair to his Corstorphine villa and write the book on brand symbology he'd always wanted to write. Rainy Hall, the college refectory, would be a much duller place without him. The flagstone courtyard would no longer echo to his full-force greetings and drunken debates with Iron John Knox. The Mound would have to do without his one-person procession into the New Town's fleshpots. The Scott Monument would have to entertain the tourists by itself, no easy task with today's copious competing attractions and diminishing attention spans.

Yet for all his defiance, Pitcairn Brodie couldn't bring himself to go back into college, not even to clear his desk, remove his accumulated possessions or discard the detritus of thirty years in scholarly shackles. He asked Simon Magill to do it instead. And Simon was happy to oblige.

It was a small price to pay for Brodie's support, Magill thought, as he made his way into the sulking professor's former office. Brodie's glowing reference had definitely swung the Hustler job his way. Several post-docs had applied for the post, or so he'd heard on the QT, and there was absolutely no way he should have got it, even with his e-commerce experience. His teaching experience was non-existent and his research experience way too limited, though they'd responded surprisingly enthusiastically to his background in English and divinity. How odd was that? The theologically inclined don't get jobs in business schools, though God knows B-schools could do with a bit of faith, hope and charity. Charity especially. Still, there's a first time for everything.

There's a last time for everything as well. And Simon's clapped-out 2CV, if not quite on its last legs, was certainly feeling the worse for wear. Professor Brodie's books, papers and general paraphernalia had played havoc with its back axle, and the big end was at the end of its tether. Edinburgh is built on seven hills – seven very steep hills – where the stress of ascending in an ancient, overloaded Citroën is counterbalanced by an unstoppable descent in an ABS-less, airbag-free, crumple-zone–challenged death trap. A week into the removal operation, the 2CV's brake pads were a distant memory and its engine was making noises like a Magimix during household-appliance mating season. It kept cutting out at the most inopportune moments, such as the junction of Lothian Road and Princes Street during rush hour. Mortification . . .

There was only the Hubbard cupboard to do. Professor Brodie was a bit of an antiques buff, as Magill's aching arms bore witness, and he had a thing about the Arts and Crafts movement, as well as its many and varied American offshoots, Roycroft especially. The brainchild of Elbert Hubbard, a larger-than-life dandy during America's gilded age, Roycroft had produced ostentatiously branded furniture that was once considered irredeemably vulgar, but now fetched tidy sums in the antiques aftermarket. Simon suspected Professor Brodie's interest in Roycroft had more to do with the creator than the creations: Elbert Hubbard was one of the role models featured on Brodie's bizarre website. The parallels between the two were more than coincidental. Hubbard was famous for his bestselling self-help books, and Magill was convinced that Brodie had not only read every word but returned to them repeatedly for inspiration.

The Hubbard cupboard was ugly, if undeniably solidly built. Simon unlocked the double doors only to be greeted with a scene of devastation. This had obviously been the dumping ground for Pitcairn Brodie's offprints, handouts, reading lists and teaching aids. It was like a history lesson in office-equipment ancillaries: 5.4" computer disks, bulky Betamax cassettes, handwritten OHP slides, never-ending sheaves of computer print-out, dozens of sticky Roneo templates, manifold microfiche acetates still smelling of chlorine, and piles upon piles of Tippex–touched-up typescripts. Bet the secretarial staff loved him.

Much of this could be dumped, Magill reckoned, but he didn't have time to sift the gold from the dross. He had to do his own packing before tomorrow's flight to Belfast, and there was also Brodie's informal farewell to attend. The best he could do was pile it willy-nilly into boxes and make the final delivery next morning, en route to the airport. The professor could sort it out for himself.

He began busily boxing up the disks, the printouts and the mountainous manuscripts. Rather too hurriedly, as it happened. A pile of top-shelf typescripts avalanched to the floor. When the paper cascade slithered to a stop, Simon swore loudly and stooped to scoop them up. A yellowing report caught his eye: *From Bands to Brands: On the Orange Order's Options (Draft Discussion Paper, August 1971)*.

Magill made to box it with the others, only for curiosity to get the better of him. He started skimming the report that had changed Pitcairn Brodie's life so dramatically. Far from being incendiary, as the great symbologist insinuated, it read like a standard marketing analysis of a not-for-profit organisation. Perhaps it was pioneering for its time. Magill vaguely recalled from his Stirling lectures that marketing concepts weren't normally applied to not-for-profits back in 1971. But basically it was a straightforward summary of the Orange Order's strategic positioning.

The organisation, apparently, was founded in 1795 and named after William III, the Protestant Prince of Orange who supplanted his Roman Catholic father-in-law, King James II, when he defeated him at the Battle of the Boyne in July 1690. The Order was dedicated to maintaining the Protestant Ascendancy. It was implacably opposed to what it alleged were the iniquities of Roman Catholicism. It had a membership of approximately 100,000 people who were affiliated to 1,300 lodges in Ireland and many other countries, Scotland especially.

To commemorate the victories of King Billy, the order held large parades on the twelfth of July and other salient occasions during the summer marching season. The marchers wore distinctive regalia – orange collarettes, white gloves, bowler hats – and carried elaborate banners depicting scenes from the Order's illustrious history. Led by bombastic pipe, flute, brass or accordion bands, they paraded along a series of "traditional" routes, often through Roman Catholic residential areas.

As he read on, however, Magill began to see how Brodie's report could have ruffled a few feathers back in the early seventies, when Northern Ireland was plunging from crisis via chaos into conflict. In a section titled "Image," the symbologist stated that the Orange Order was seen as a highly secretive society, similar to the Freemasons. Its various sub-brands – the Royal Black Institution, the Royal Arch Purple, the Apprentice Boys of Derry – only added to the confusion that the institution then aroused. It was widely regarded as anachronistic and out of touch with contemporary life. Worse, despite its undeniably noble ideals, it was seen as a repository of sectarianism, intransigence, obduracy and intemperance, as well as a front for pernicious Protestant paramilitaries like the Ulster Volunteer Force. Its parades, far from being Northern Ireland's answer to Mardi Gras, were widely condemned as inflammatory, triumphalist and confrontational. It was losing members hand over fist, particularly among the middle and upper social classes.

The order's fatal marketing flaw, however, was its excessive customer orientation. The more the organisation swore undying loyalty to its ultimate customers, the British establishment, the less those customers appreciated it. The only exception was when it played hard to get, most notably in the constitutional crisis of 1912, when Irish Home Rule was on the cards and the Orange Order stood four-square against it. The obvious inference was that ever more heartfelt declarations of fidelity served only to heighten customers' disdain. Customer orientation, paradoxically, was undermining the brand.

Utter nonsense, Magill thought to himself. Surely Kate Phillips teaches us that customer orientation is all, that it's impossible to be too customer oriented. The problem with the Orange Order, he suspected, was that it wasn't customer-focused enough. Pitcairn Brodie had clearly never been properly trained as a marketer. Magill flicked through the rest of the misguided marketing report before turning to the last few pages.

The brand, Brodie's document concluded, was approaching the end of its natural life. The future wouldn't be Orange unless radical steps were taken. The existing customer base – Britain's empurpled establishment – should be abandoned. The Orange Order should appropriate Ireland's pre-Christian heritage, its Celtic heritage. The organisation should look to Tara rather than the Houses of Parliament. Ulster men and women could pension off King Billy, forget the Battle of the Boyne, and celebrate instead the achievements of mighty Celtic warriors like Cú Chulainn, the indomitable, indefatigable, indestructible Hound of Ulster. This was a brand image that the entire community could buy into, one that predated Protestantism and Catholicism alike. The alternative was a slow and painful death.

After a report like that, Magill reflected, as he threw *Bands to Brands* into a chock-full cardboard box, Pitcairn Brodie was lucky to get out of Northern Ireland alive. His parents were almost killed for less. His brother *was* killed for less.

Chapter Five

Divide and Rule

It was mid-morning by the time Simon Magill loaded the last of Brodie's boxes into his recalcitrant Citroën, illegally parked in the compact courtyard of New College. He slipped the 2CV into gear, glanced in his rear-view mirror (only to see a curtain of cardboard), and carefully released the stuttering clutch. With the automotive equivalent of a Gallic shrug, Magill's clapped-out chariot clattered across the cobblestones outside the college, accelerated rapidly around and down the Mound, turned hard left into Princes Street, shuffled through four sets of traffic lights, and eventually veered down Shandwick Place, past Haymarket Station and out along Roseburn Terrace, towards the heights of Corstorphine.

Pitcairn Brodie lived in a tree-girt gingerbread house at the confluence of Kaimes Road and Gordon Road, immediately adjacent to Edinburgh's renowned zoological gardens. The villa was surprisingly nondescript, given the flamboyance of its occupant. But it served as Brodie's back stage, a low-key place where the mask could be dropped, some serious research could get done and the larger-than-life figure who held court in Oloroso, Vermilion, the Dome and similar look-at-me locales could revert to something approaching human scale.

Of course, Brodie wouldn't be Brodie without a bellow or two. Every so often, when he couldn't stand the silence of the suburbs, he'd climb on top of his flat-roofed garage and, fortified by a Buckfast or several, perform high-decibel Tarzan yells for the zoo's mammalian inhabitants. Not only did his yodel cause pandemonium among unsuspecting visitors to Edinburgh's peerless animal collection, but the critters responded in kind. The gorillas thumped, the baboons shrieked, the gibbons gibbered, the painted dogs howled, the warthogs grunted, the penguins honked in unison and the tapirs wondered what the hell was going on, as the big cats roared aristocratic disapproval at their uppity neighbour. Brodie roared back and, on a good night, a bestial call-and-response would echo up and down Kaimes Road, terrifying tourists in the Holiday Inn and petrifying patients in Corstorphine Hospital alike.

Magill chugged past Murrayfield Stadium, idly noting that in the four years he'd lived in Edinburgh, he'd never once attended a rugby international. Nor had he been to the castle, or the City Observatory, or even the Camera Obscura, even though it was right beside Brodie's office. He'd done exactly the same thing in Stirling, where he studied for his marketing and IT degree. The incomparable castle, Bannockburn battlefield and even the Wallace Monument, which was less than a mile from the university campus: he had roundly ignored them all during his three-year stay. He'd always intended to visit the local attractions, but they were so close, so convenient, so easily available that he never quite got round to it. There's a marketing issue there somewhere, he thought to himself. Latent demand. Lazy consumers. Tourism for non-tourists. Whatever.

At least he had a good excuse for his less than incisive thinking. He'd rushed out with nothing to eat and his head still fuzzy from the night before, a night that had turned into something extraordinary even by Pitcairn Brodie's extraordinary standards. The evening began quietly enough at the Beehive, an ancient Grassmarket inn a couple of minutes' walk from New College. Very few of Brodie's former colleagues turned up, though the tarnished titan affected indifference. The presence of numerous past students and many admiring postgraduates, who were still hoping to benefit from his intellectual largesse, more than compensated for the absence of erstwhile academic acquaintances.

Brodie had dominated proceedings as usual, telling fantastic tales of the ghosts that haunted the Beehive's cellars, interspersed with grisly stories of the executions that used to take place outside, when Grassmarket marked the edge of the old town and its gibbets were in constant use. A raconteur of spellbinding ability, Pitcairn Brodie kept the entire bar enthralled, until several stragglers from a literary tour turned up unbidden. They'd done the rounds of Conan Doyle's Edinburgh, Muriel Spark's Edinburgh, J. M. Barrie's Edinburgh, Irvine Welsh's Edinburgh and Robert Louis Stevenson's Edinburgh. Yet despite witnessing the wonders of the world's inaugural City of Literature, the loudly dressed and even more loudly mouthed Americans were decidedly disgruntled. It seems they'd been out to nearby Rosslyn Chapel, where their tour guide stressed Rosslyn's starring role in the works of Sir Walter Scott and Ian "Rebus" Rankin. Yet she hadn't mentioned the single most important writer on the chapel's extraordinary architecture, Dan "the Man" Brown!

This contention, needless to say, was like a Glasgow kiss to the Heidbanger-fuelled symbologist. An argument concerning Brown's literary merits rapidly ensued, with the professor asserting that Dan Brown wasn't fit to tie Pa Broon's boots. After much splenetic debate on either side, Brodie put Magill on the spot. As the Beehive's only resident authority on English literature, Simon was invited to adjudicate. Naturally he tried to evade the unwanted responsibility by emphasising that his expertise consisted of one year's undergraduate study, when his attendance at lectures was patchy to say the least. However, the professor insisted he make the literary call. "Don't diss the Danster, dude," one of the Americans shouted out, and, to his eternal shame, young Magill admitted he much preferred reading Dan Brown to Walter Scott. He'd told the truth but, in doing so, he'd betrayed his mentor, his city, his home from home.

Luckily Brodie laughed it off and bought everyone drinks. The party accelerated from there. By the time Magill left, Pitcairn Brodie had not only removed his scarlet eye patch and performed his legendary eye-rolling routine, but was preparing to lead the bar in a chorus of "Flower of Scotland," sung to the tune of "The Star-Spangled Banner." What a night!

As he spluttered past the zoological gardens on his right, Magill vowed he'd turn over a new leaf in Northern Ireland. There'd be no more drinking for starters, and he'd make a point of visiting Ulster's tourist attractions, if only to get a feel for the place. He'd heard so much about the province, most of it unfavourable, that he'd been pleasantly surprised during his recent flying visit for the Hustler job interview. Far from being bomb-blitzed or derelict, Belfast's neat and tidy streets exuded affluence. Brand new BMWs were two a penny; the sleek shops put Princes Street to shame; and gleaming office blocks, concert halls, sports arenas and international hotel chains peppered the pristine urban fabric. There were even open-topped tourist buses, packed to the gunnels with Germans, Americans and Australians, all taking stock of a city where sightseers were sufficiently rare to warrant a warm welcome. If this was the Northern Ireland peace process, he was looking forward to a piece of the action.

Simon's 2CV swung hard right into Kaimes Road, and on hitting the very steep hill, its 602 cc engine promptly expired. "Not again," muttered Magill as he manoeuvred the stricken car to the side of the road. Brodie's abode was about 75 metres away, just too far to carry the last of the heavy packing cases. He could either wait for the Citroën to get its wind back, which usually took about 40 minutes, or see if he could borrow the professor's most precious possession, a souped-up Mini Cooper with Brodie tartan paint job. It would certainly speed things up, and he did have a plane to catch.

As Magill walked briskly round the bend at the bottom of Kaimes Road, it was easy to tell which house was Brodie's. The triangular front garden was badly overgrown, and the bow-fronted building was in a sorry state of repair. "Life," he'd often heard the prodigious professor proclaim, "is too short to worry about planting, pruning, pointing or painting, much less plumbing, plastering or papering." And it showed.

No amount of next-door-neighbour nagging could get Brodie to fix the roof, or excavate the overgrown front path, much less amputate the magnificent Scots pine whose mighty arms embraced the front of the house and whose fingernails scratched "clean me" messages on the great man's grubby dormer windows. Yet, for all the evident neglect, when the professor's splendid silver birch shimmered in the duck-egg blue of the mid-October Corstorphine sky – striated with go-faster cirrus – Simon couldn't help concluding that Edinburgh was the most beautiful city on earth. By far.

Magill knocked on the door, knowing that the bell was out of order. It swung open. That's odd, he thought. Brodie's a lock, stock and two smoking deadbolts kind of guy, mainly to keep out the neighbourhood's buzzing busybodies, who took it upon themselves to take the titan to task for lowering the tone of the suburb. Escaped animals had also been known to pay him a visit when they broke out of their cages with a view to sorting out old yeller. Many a night Brodie had rolled home to find meerkats camped in his front garden. Pink elephants weren't unknown either.

"Hello. Hello. Anyone there?" shouted the freckled ferryman.

Silence.

"Hello, Pitcairn, are you in? It's Simon. I'm here with your stuff."

Deeper silence.

"Pitcairn. I'm borrowing the Mini. I'll only be a couple of minutes. My car's corpsed at the bottom of the hill."

Magill searched around for Brodie's car keys, but there was no sign of them. It looked as though he'd have to disturb the occupant, who was likely sleeping things off. He quickly mounted the book-lined stairs, checked both book-lined, box-filled bedrooms and wormed his way down a short book-and box-lined corridor to Brodie's airy study, nestling under the Scots pine–scratched eaves. The buckled door was stiff. A ziggurat of boxes, some full, most empty, hindered its full extension. Simon shoved the door open as best he could and squeezed though the gap, only to see Professor Brodie asleep at his rolltop Roycroft desk, which was also piled high with manuscripts and books. The room beyond was a depository of unpacked, half-packed and fully packed packing cases. The walls were crawling with books of all shapes and sizes. Only the professor's priceless Art and Crafts carpet was free of academic flotsam and jetsam.

The slumberer's Harris tweed jacket hung on the back of the door and, hoping he could avoid disturbing the symbologist's drunken repose, Magill went through its pockets. To no avail. He dreaded waking Brodie up, because when he'd done so once before, the testy tartan titan thrashed uncontrollably as he surfaced, striking Simon on the temple, nearly knocking him out cold.

45

"Professor Brodie. Professor Brodie. Professor Brodie," he whispered, turning up the volume with each iteration.

No response.

He shook the recumbent scholar, gently at first and then harder and harder.

Still no response.

Magill composed himself and reached out to try again. Suddenly, and with a noise like a felled sessile oak, the prodigal professor toppled onto the floor. His cradling captain's chair crashed down beside him.

"Oh sweet Jesus," Simon swore. "He's had a heart attack. I knew that godforsaken lifestyle would get him." But as Magill turned Brodie's great hulking bulk over, hoping there was still time for CPR, he saw that it was much, much too late. And that a coronary wasn't the cause of death.

Pitcairn Brodie's lifeless eyes stared up at him. Or rather, his blood-filled eye-sockets did. A pair of what looked like compasses or dividers or, surely not, Citroën chevrons had been rammed into his face . . . into his eyes . . . right through the pupils . . . a point in each brimming socket. Rivulets of vermilion blood ran down his raddled face, channelled by the creases, folds and wrinkles of his craggy countenance, diverted by the rococo moustache, dammed by the bushy beard. There was blood oozing from under his comb-over as well, and, inexplicably, a hank of rope was wrapped roughly round his neck. The great man had been murdered. Brutally murdered.

Simon Magill felt the room close in on him. He was sure he was going to faint. His head swam. His legs shook. He felt weak. He had never seen a dead body before, not even his brother's, which had come home in a sealed coffin. He thought he was going to be sick. He could hear the blood pounding in his ears. He could hear thumping in the distance, a strange banging noise that got louder and louder and louder and eventually shook him out of his catatonic torpor.

There was someone in the house! More than one of them. They were rummaging down below. They were climbing up the creaking stairs. They were turning into the corridor outside Pitcairn Brodie's study. He could hear them talking.

It was the killers. Brodie's killers had returned. They had come back for more . . .

Chapter Six

O Captain! My Captain!

Barton Brady II was a lucky man. He'd always been lucky, exceptionally lucky. He had simply no conception of how lucky he'd been. A descendent of Mathew Brady, the celebrity photographer who snapped just about anyone who was anyone in the mid-nineteenth century – including, infamously, the Civil War dead – Barton Brady II had been brought up in the bosom of inordinate good fortune. He was pampered as a youngster in salubrious Westchester County. He was the youngest child, and moreover the only boy, in a well-heeled family of four. He studied literature at Yale, like his father and grandfather before him, where he was "tapped" by Scroll and Key, one of the three most exclusive secret societies, alongside Skull and Bones and Book and Snake. He graduated *magna cum laude* and, after taking a course in creative writing at the University of Chicago, published two preternaturally slim volumes of sub-Whitman poetry, *Leaves of Absence* and *Spinal-Taps*, to considerable critical acclaim and commendably insignificant sales.

If he'd wanted, Barton Brady II could have made it as an American man of letters. He had the family background. He had the connections. He had the private income. He had the way with words. He also had the looks that literary celebrity increasingly demands: tall, athletic, handsome, impeccable orthodontics and an ever-ready gigawatt grin. Brady wasn't so much a walking, talking, all-American cliché as an embodiment of John Winthrop's "shining city on a hill." He was red, white and blue through and through.

But Brady had grown bored with poetry and publishing and pretension and paternalism, the essential ingredients of latter-day literary life. A firm believer in the American dream, tarnished though it was in the post-Clinton epoch, he aspired to be a self-

49

made man like the frontiersmen of yore. This admirable aspiration, admittedly, didn't prevent him using the old-boy network as a leg-up on the greasy career ladder of life.

However, his heart was in the right place. He started near the bottom at BBDO and, with his natural flair for copywriting, was soon the talk of Madison Avenue, as were his Westchester- and Yale-honed schmoozing skills. Blue-chip clients loved him; wannabe blue-chips loved his blue-chipped experience, blue-blood background and true-blue, can-do attitude. He segued effortlessly from the creative to the client-handling side of BBDO, and from there to the obligatory Harvard MBA, and from there to the inevitable vice-presidency, and from there to a number of other top-tier agencies, which paid top-dollar salaries to secure his scintillating, Ivy League– embossed services.

Brady had it made.

Or so it seemed.

Everything in the Barton Brady garden was rosy until he had his Damascene moment. It had occurred in Las Vegas of all places, at the annual American Advertising Association convention. Brady had bumped into another delegate during a coffee break at the Bellagio, and, ever the smarm-oozing networker, he struck up a conversation with the woman who changed his life.

Yasmin Buonarroti was a second-generation Italian African American. Her grandparents met in north Africa during Il Duce's vainglorious campaign against Abyssinia. The star-crossed couple – Berber beauty and Tuscan sharpshooter – fell instantly in love and, feeling the inevitable familial heat, fled to the land of opportunity. They never looked back. They brought up their kids in the belly of the Bronx, and their kids did exactly the same. Life was tough, assimilation took time, pennies were pinched and blue-collar hardscrabble was their constant lot.

But Yasmin, the Buonarroti firebrand (as her grandfather fondly called her), wouldn't put up with it. Unencumbered with easy interpersonal skills or even good looks – her nose was Roman, all seven hills – she did the night school, no-name college, bottom-rung battler thing, and, after a series of dead-end telemarketing jobs shifting rancid real estate, dubious insurance policies and questionable investment services, she ended up managing the want ads section of the *New York Post*. A hard-headed, hard-assed, hard-driving, hard-working, hard-luck-buddy ball-buster, Buonarroti was the Bronx in a bottle. Not only could she sell ice to Inuit entrepreneurs, but she could get them to take out full-page ads for hurry-while-stocks-last promotions.

Inevitably, it was Yasmin who seized control when she bumped into Brady in Vegas. He had what she wanted – class, charm, charisma, contacts – and she had what he needed: drive, determination, desire and doughty down-to-earthiness. Over coffee, she sold him a vision of independence, adventure, self-made success and everything he'd ever yearned for. And, over coffee, Brady bought the bill of Buonarroti goods, while erroneously assuming that Serendipity Associates was his own idea.

As management consultants go, Serendipity Associates went like a Lamborghini Diablo. It lucked out with its first corporate concept, which followed the classic trajectory of *HBR* article, book of the article, executive training roadshow and, the money-shot killer app, tailored coaching sessions for CEOs. One on one. Candy from babies. Ka-ching, ka-ching, ka-ching.

SA's big idea, ironically enough, involved luck management: the simple fact that success in business often boils down to luck, fluke, fortune, fate, contingency, chance and basically being in the right place at the right time. A battery of bedazzling well-I-never case studies – Apple, McDonald's, Disney, P&G, Sony, Microsoft, Kellogg's, Citroën – and a battalion of brilliantly successful brands that owed their existence to serendipity, everything from Viagra, Velcro and Kevlar to penicillin, Post-it Notes and Dom Perignon champagne, convinced their corporate clientele that luck was worth looking at. The fact that good fortune had been all but ignored by ivory-tower academics and B-school gurus, who seemed to believe that business was rational, right-brained and readily modelled, meant that Brady and Buonarroti had the field to themselves.

Luck, they maintained, could be not only managed but increased by judicious use of their proprietary training techniques.

In essence, these comprised an update and rebranding of the how-to, self-help, auto-suggestion methods that had long played an important role in the cut-throat world of American commerce, though they kept that to themselves. Perhaps it was old wine in new bottles, but then packaging is all-important in the beverage business, as Blossom Hill bears witness.

Better yet, they were both extraordinarily lucky individuals, Brady thanks to his impeccable family background and Buonarroti on account of her astonishing ability to pick winners. In almost every game of chance she entered – craps, slots, roulette, wheel of fortune, to name but a few – she invariably scooped the pool, much to the gaming industry's disquiet. Be that as it may, Brady and Buonarroti were living, breathing commercials for their own corporate concepts, and they shilled them very successfully.

Serendipity Associates rode the luck bandwagon for several seasons, but like all corporate cure-alls, "Chance Would Be a Fine Thing" eventually ran out of steam. Copycats, competitors and full-service consultancies who offered luck training as part of a pan-management package soon drove SA's gravy train into the ground. They scrambled for a knock-'em-dead alternative, one with a suitably snappy title. They tried Postmodern Marketing, but no one could understand a word of "the ism that isn't," Brady and Buonarroti included. Then they turned to Retro-marketing, a canny attempt to cash in on the nostalgia boom that accompanied the millennial transition, only to find that clients expected to pay good old-fashioned retro prices for the good old-fashioned retro advice that SA disbursed.

Next up was Marke*tease*, an approach that advocated tantalising consumers, thereby making them ever more desperate to get their hands on an organisation's delectable, delightful, near-enough irresistible offerings. However, in an era of rampant corporate malfeasance and CSR *mea culpas*, tormenting the customer via Marke*tease* was about as welcome as a shower-curtain salesman at Tyco. Beaten but unbowed, they then bet the farm on Pushmi-pullyu Branding, a copycat attempt to capitalise on American companies' boundless fondness for animal metaphors: purple cows, dancing elephants, rabid rats, querulous squirrels, floundering fish, cheese-eating surrender monkeys, to name but a few. Unfortunately, the notion that brands should pull together in opposite directions was rather too much for SA's conservative clientele.

With four bombs in a row, it looked as though luck was running out for the Las Vegas–based luck hucksters. Then they had a second serendipitous stroke of good fortune. Just as General Electric discovered that the real money is made not in products and tangibles but in services and intangibles, Serendipity Associates reinvented themselves as a corporate-concept hotshop. That is to say, instead of hawking their own ideas around the management consultancy circuit, they'd develop ideas for other organisations, which did the heavy lifting. Such was the size of the management fad market, and such was the rate of turnover – garden variety ideas lasted a couple of years at most, real showstoppers like excellence, reengineering or good-to-great had a lifespan of ten years tops – that there was an almost insatiable demand for gee-whiz ideas, super-snazzy concepts and knock-'em-dead notions, to say nothing of jaunty metaphors, sizzling similes, feel-good formulae, anthropomorphism a gogo and, not least, all singing, dancing acronyms (aka ASDA).

So Serendipity Associates put their heads together, hired a bunch of left-brain barnstormers – symbologists, semioticians, sitcom writers, Sudoku solvers – and quickly carved out a richly remunerated niche for themselves. Virtually every aspect of cultural life was grist to their marketing mill. You name it, they stuck it in front of "marketing," "accounting," "organization," "management" or "branding." They were prefix providers, in effect, conceptual Kleenex vendors for executive suites worldwide. Instant insights, disposable ideas, throw-away concepts, no-fuss frameworks, wash 'n' go solutions, boil-in-the-bag bullshit were their stock in trade.

Nano-marketing was one of theirs, as was New Marketing, New new Marketing, Nearly-new Marketing, Nearly nearly-new Marketing, New and improved Marketing, As-good-as-new Marketing, Nova Marketing, Neue Marketing, Nü-marketing and, naturally, New-Age Marketing.

Feng Shui Marketing was one of theirs too, as were I-Ching Marketing, Tai-Chi Marketing, Kung-Fu Marketing, Chin Na Marketing, Dim Mak Marketing, Yin-Yang Marketing, Bullshido Marketing, McDojo Marketing, Zen-Buddhist Marketing and, inevitably, the Tao of Marketing.

They also came up with Make-'em-Laugh Marketing, Razzle-Dazzle Marketing, Razzamatazz Marketing, Hubba-Hubba Marketing, Hocus-Pocus Marketing, Brand X Marketing, X-Rated Marketing, X-Ray Marketing, XL-Marketing, XXL-Marketing, XXXL-Marketing, X-treme Marketing, X-Marks-the-Spot Marketing and, it almost goes without saying, X-Factor Marketing.

They then turned their hands to Hardball Marketing, Softball Marketing, Curveball Marketing, Balls to the Wall Marketing, Pedal to the Metal Marketing, Hole in One Marketing, Bottom of the Ninth Marketing, Blitz-Defence Marketing, Home-Run Marketing, Home-Stretch Marketing, Home is Where the Heart is Marketing, Home on the Range Marketing and Home from Home Marketing.

Inevitably, they added an American idiom series: Have a Nice One Marketing, Missing You Already Marketing, You're Welcome Marketing, Way Cool Marketing, Catch You Later Marketing, Don't Go There Marketing, Swivel on It Marketing, Right Back At Ya Marketing, Blow it Out Your Ass Marketing, What Have You Done for Me Lately Marketing and, for the aesthetically inclined, I Don't Know Much About Marketing But I Know What I Like Marketing.

As if that weren't enough, they cooked up Mickey Mouse Marketing, Minnie Mouse Marketing, Mom's Apple Pie Marketing, Marilyn Monroe Marketing, Mahatma Gandhi Marketing, Mother Theresa Marketing, Martha Stewart Marketing, Wishful Thinking Marketing, Tough Love Marketing, Make My Day Marketing, You Talkin' to Me Marketing, Show Me the Money Marketing and Somewhere Over the Rainbow Marketing.

Such was their shamelessness, Serendipity Associates even got a turn out of Twelve-Step Marketing, Ten-Commandment Marketing, Cloud-Nine Marketing, Seventh-Heaven Marketing,

Sixth-Sense Marketing, Five-Star Marketing, Four-Square Marketing, Three Times a Lady Marketing, Two to Tango Marketing and One for the Road Marketing.

Yet for all their infinite inventiveness, Barton Brady was getting bored with SA's bespoke brandstanding. He was fed up, frustrated and, frankly, resentful. Like a songwriter or scriptwriter who seethes with jealousy when the singer/stand-up gets all the acclaim, he was sick and tired of seeing others make their undeserved reputations with his management ideas. He'd had enough. It was time for Barton Brady to get back on the road. It was time to knock 'em dead once more. It was time to barnstorm the battlements of boardrooms worldwide.

And Professor Emer Aherne, the Dan Brown analyst he'd discovered by chance, was going to be his unwitting battering ram.

Barton Brady loved serendipity...

Chapter Seven

Carve His Name With Pride

Edinburgh is an immodest city, with much to be immodest about. The hauteur of the castle on the rock; the rambunctiousness of the redoubtable Royal Mile; the supercilious streets of the noble New Town; the money-no-object exuberance of the Scottish Parliament Building, all bear witness to Auld Reekie's implacable imperiousness. From the heights of Corstorphine Hill to the depths of the underground city, Edinburgh knows its place in the world. And that place is on top.

Auld Reekie's arrogance isn't confined to its setting, however. The criminal classes are arrogant too. Much of their conceit is attributable to Ian Rankin's Rebus novels, which have done for the burgh's criminal underbelly what Walter Scott's Waverley books did for the Heart of Midlothian in the early nineteenth century. Just as the Scottish tourist industry is eternally indebted to Sir Walter for inventing the roaming gloaming branding, so too the city's criminal industry has become big-headed on the back of Rankin. Every gangland boss considers himself the model for "Big Ger" Cafferty, Inspector Rebus's nemesis, and every other lowlife lords it like he's Crook of the Walk.

That was certainly true of the criminals who burst into Professor Brodie's study, where Simon Magill was trying to cope with the murder of his magnificent magniloquent mentor. The criminals were so arrogant, in fact, that they hadn't even bothered to change out of their police uniforms. One was an inspector, the other a constable. Both were braggarts.

Magill could just make them out from the gap at the top of the empty cardboard box he'd squeezed himself into. It hadn't been easy compressing his gangly frame into a compact carton, but fear can make people do things they thought impossible. Like unleash the inner contortionist. The top flaps didn't quite meet, and Simon could see some of what was going on through the narrow aperture.

When he saw the policemen pushing their way through Professor Brodie's study door, his first thought was to reveal himself. The cavalry had arrived, thank God, though they were suspiciously quick off the mark, especially as a crime hadn't been reported. Not by Magill, anyhow. It was only apprehension about the cops' likely reaction to his sudden emergence, like a giant ginger jack-in-a-box, that kept him stuck to the sides of his container. He might have got himself shot or badly beaten up for frightening the constabulary. And hiding in a box beside a murder victim – a murder victim he'd had a public disagreement with the night before – might not come across well when read out in court.

As he scrutinised the policemen, however, Simon soon realised that this was no ordinary crime-scene investigation. One of the cops, a pustular ferret-faced constable called Cowan, or something similar – it was difficult to hear, their voices were muffled – aimed a vicious kick at Brodie's sanguinary corpse.

"Why do we aye huv tae clean their bloody mess?" he spat, his heavily accented voice as vicious as his behaviour.

"Because the Order of Solomon says so," the older officer, a crumple-faced, bulbous-nosed, late-middle-aged man who went by the name Sinclair and looked as though he'd seen everything but rather wished he hadn't, answered in a nonchalant manner.

"It's aye us. Why cannie they clean up their ain mess? Bastards!" Cowan kicked the body again. It sounded like someone extracting their foot from a peat bog. Magill felt sick.

"We just do what we're told. And we keep our mouths shut. Got it?" There was a hint of menace in Sinclair's world-weary voice, and Cowan responded accordingly.

"Gottit, sir," he said sullenly.

"Check the body," the inspector went on. "Wrap it up in that rug. Make it quick. Let's get this over and done with."

Cowan couldn't resist a third vicious swing at the cadaver. "Order of bloody Solomon. It's aye Order of bloody bastard Solomon," he muttered.

Magill was torn between fury and fear, with confusion in close attendance. Brodie's battered, brutally murdered body was being maltreated by a uniformed criminal – two uniformed criminals – who had some kind of connection to another criminal gang. He'd never heard of the Order of Solomon, though it sounded like one of the many offshoots of Orangeism that the professor had mentioned the previous day. In the Dome.

Was it only yesterday that they were celebrating the professor's retirement and toasting his own new job at Hustler University? Was it only yesterday that the prodigious Pitcairn Brodie was glad-handing Edinburgh's great and good in the city's premier pitstop? Was it only yesterday that the incomparable raconteur held an entire bar spellbound with eerie stories of the Beehive in days of yore, when Rabbie Burns was a regular customer and Covenanters were being executed in the Grassmarket? Was it only yesterday that the Great Well-Known was buying his assistant drinks and insisting that not only did he owe his own success to the Orange Order, but he'd live happily ever after?

The memories of Brodie at his bedazzling best made Simon Magill profoundly ashamed of himself. He wondered what the professor would do in his situation. He wouldn't be cowering in a carton, that was for sure. Magill took a deep breath and steeled himself. He was going to face the sons of bitches, regardless of the consequences.

"C'mere, sir, c'mere. Come an' huv a jook at this." Even from inside his cardboard refuge, Simon could detect the astonishment in the constable's whiny voice.

"What is it, Cowan?" Inspector Sinclair's reply was curt. Clearly he'd had enough of his colleague's contempt for the Order of Solomon, to say nothing of his disrespect for the dead. Icons deserve to be treated with dignity, even fallen ones. Especially fallen ones.

"There are stanes in the pocket o' his breeks. There's somethin' in the ither pocket as well. Looks like a wee ruler."

Evidently the professor's compass-perforated irises and accompanying hank of rope hadn't surprised him. Jesus, Magill thought.

"Don't you know anything, Cowan?" Sinclair snapped. "It's

59

ritual. It's tradition. It's Roberto Calvi."

Taken aback, Magill aborted his breakout. Roberto Calvi? He'd heard that name before. Not so long ago. He'd read something about him in the newspapers. The Calvi affair, wasn't it? Yes, that was it! He remembered it now.

Calvi was the Italian banker found hanged under Blackfriars Bridge back in the early eighties. They said it was suicide, but there was no way a prominent banker would have committed suicide in such a strange manner. He had hard cash and harder concrete in his pockets, and a lanyard round his neck. He also had connections to the Vatican Bank, and the Mafia, and Opus Dei, and the CIA, and was mixed up in money laundering, and planning to spill the beans. He never got the chance, though it took twenty years to find his killers and put them on trial in Italy.

"I ken whit the stanes mean, sir," the constable said gruffly. "It's his heid I'm talkin' aboot. There's somethin' carved on his cranium. Looks like wurds o' some kind. A message maybe. I canna make it oot. There's blood everywhere."

Magill couldn't see anything, but he could sense the inspector's stunned reaction. He heard him walk quickly across the room and crouch down beside Brodie's body.

"Give it a wipe," Sinclair commanded.

"Do I huv to?" Cowan wheedled. "I've only got a wee hankie."

"Do it! Use that paper over there!"

"Bloody bastard Order of Solomon," the constable grumbled, wiping vigorously by the sound of it. Only horrible scrubbing noises broke the rapt silence.

"Bloody bastard Order of Solomon," the gob-smacked inspector echoed softly. "I've never seen anything like that before. They must have used a Stanley knife. Jesus bloody bastard Christ."

"Whit duz it say, sir?"

"I'm not sure. KILL THE something or other. KILL THE PROFS, perhaps."

"Bloody students," Cowan joked, trying to hide his nervousness. "Gie them a bad mark nowadays and they whack their lecturers."

"That's enough. Show some respect." Sinclair said.

"Lighten up, sir. It's only a stiff."

"Hold on, son, it doesn't say PROFS."

"Looks like PEPSI to me, sir. KILL THE PEPSI. Maybe it's Coca-Cola's latest marketing campaign. I've heard o' knockin' copy but this is ... "

"This isn't a joke!" Sinclair barked. "These people don't mess around. Remember that, sonny."

"Aye, they're sick bastards right enough," the chastened constable replied.

"Anyway, it's not PEPSI. It's more like KILL THE PAPISH."

"Protestant bastards. Sick Orange bastards. Those Ulster bastards'd pop anybody. They're mad dugs over there, sir."

"Their spelling's not very good either," the inspector said. "They've misspelled PAPISH. Ignorant Irish bastards."

Cowan must have thought Sinclair had made a joke. He started to chuckle, only to be cut off by a curt, "Wipe his head again, sonny. I want to be sure about this."

The excruciating rubbing sound started up again, even more loudly this time. Brodie's lifeless cranium was squeaking. Magill felt his gorge rising. The previous night's imbibing was coming back to haunt him. If he didn't keep quiet, he'd be giving up the ghost before long.

"Any clearer, Cowan? What does it say?"

"Aye, I ken it noo, sir," the constable answered. "It's PASPI. It says KILL THE PASPI."

"Are you sure?"

"Certain, sir." Cowan stood up, his knees cracking loudly. "Take a jook fir yersel'. Dis PASPI mean anythin' tae you?"

"No. Nothing. Nothing at all. Never heard of it."

It was all Magill could do to stop gasping out loud. He wasn't so much surprised as staggered. Paspi.biz was the name of Brodie's quirky website – the one Simon set up and maintained for the great eccentric. He was killed because of Paspi? It didn't make sense.

PASPI stood for Protean Association of Self-Promoting Inimitables. It featured stories of successful self-publicists. It was where Brodie expounded his "Be a Brand" theories. It contained

61

marketing advice for icons and would-be icons. Simon Magill was baffled. Pitcairn Brodie's website was innocuous. Or so he thought. The policemen were no less bemused. They were talking about running the term through their databases and Googling it for good measure. At least that would keep them busy, Magill thought. The web was full of Paspi-like sites, not least the Porn and Sex Portal Interface, a Spanish clearing-house for the most loathsome pornography imaginable. That should divert them for a while. Quite a long while, by the look of ferret-faced Constable Cowan.

Magill had to make his escape somehow. He'd lie low and do a runner when the coast was clear. By the sound of things, they didn't intend to hang around, thankfully.

With a series of sickening thuds, Brodie's body was roughly rolled up in the priceless Arts and Crafts carpet, one of his prize possessions. Suddenly Sinclair spoke sharply. "Any sign of the other one?"

"Ither wan? Whit ither wan? There's only wan stiff here."

"The Order said two'd be taken out. There must be another one somewhere. I'll look downstairs. It might be in the garage. You check the top storey again. Make sure you do both bedrooms. We need to get a move on. Let's go."

Magill burrowed deeply into his carton. He might just get out of this crazy situation alive. He could hear the policemen manhandling Brodie's body down the narrow book-lined stairs. Chillingly, he also heard the inspector say, "Check the boxes as well."

Chapter Eight

Who's the Paddy?

The "fasten seatbelts" sign flicked off with a ping. Not that Simon Magill noticed anything. He was still in a state of shock as EasyJet flight 486 soared into the cloudless sky above Edinburgh Airport, heading west for Belfast International. He couldn't get the morning's events out of his mind. He kept replaying them over and over again, each time with a different outcome. The murder of his mentor was bad enough, but the cruel mutilation beggared belief. Death by dividers? KILL THE PASPI? It was like something out of a Dan Brown novel. *Angels & Demons*, if memory served.

Unbelievable as the great man's demise undoubtedly was, there was something even more disconcerting about the morning's unspeakable events. Yes, Pitcairn Brodie was the PASPI that got killed. But Simon Magill was PASPI, too. Not only had he precipitated the professor's execution – he must have done, it could only have been something he'd posted on the website – but if the etch-a-threat was to be taken literally, he was next in line for the cranial incision treatment. They said that two were to be taken out, Magill recalled with a shudder. The Orange Order assassination squad was probably waiting for him in Arrivals, bowler hats akimbo.

At least he was alive. That was something. He still didn't know how he'd managed to escape from Brodie's study. Thank God for lazy policemen.

Not long after they'd struggled downstairs with Brodie's body, Ferret Face started checking out the top storey. However, he must have been unsettled by the sight of so much reading material – top-shelf magazines were his staple diet, Magill had surmised – and box after box after box of books, some full, some half-full, some empty, could well have reminded him of his sluggardly

63

schooldays. Or perhaps he was just a skiver. By the time he got back to Brodie's study, he'd settled on a time-efficient system. Kick the box. If it's full, ignore it. If it's empty, or almost empty, look inside.

When Cowan kicked Magill's box, it registered full. Its occupant was tempted to leap up and use the advantage of surprise to let fly at the ferret. However, Sinclair was down below, and he seemed as hard-bitten as they come. Discretion might not be better than valour, but it had kept Simon Magill alive. Better a live coward than a dead hero, no?

After the police car drove off, he crept down the stairs, simultaneously fearing that one of them had stayed behind and hoping that it was Ferret Face. He owed the cretinous constable a kick or three. But there were no signs of life. There were only signs of death. Pitcairn's Arts and Crafts sarcophagus lay in the centre of the lounge, presumably destined for later collection and disposal under cover of darkness. The arrogance of the bastards was so far beyond belief it was well-nigh supernatural.

He'd said his final farewells to the Wizard of the North, slipped out Brodie's back door, sidled down the silent suburban street, sped to the nearby airport and, with minutes to spare, boarded EasyJet 486 for Belfast International.

Jesus, he thought, as the plane commenced its steep descent after the thirty-five-minute flight, this can't be happening. Paspi was supposed to be a bit of fun. It was simply a cyber-resource for self-publicists, that tiny cadre of rampant egomaniacs who spend their lives trying to be larger than life or, as often as not, larger than larger than life. It issued advice, shared experiences and discussed tactics. Its Ego of the Week feature focused attention on protean self-publicists past and present: P. T. Barnum, Richard Branson, Elbert Hubbard, Lillian Russell, Robbie Williams, Frank Lloyd Wright, Larry Ellison, Liberace, Madonna, Paganini, Digby Jones, Salvador Dalì, Damien Hirst, Donald Trump, Michael Jackson, Steve Jobs, Oscar Wilde, Andy Warhol, Thomas Lipton, Martha Stewart, Sarah Bernhardt, Kate Phillips, Walter Scott and so on. Paspi.biz was password-protected, what's more. It was for egotists' eyes only. Membership was strictly restricted. It was a Band Aid for the Brand Me brigade. A phoney secret society for phoneys.

As the wheels of EasyJet's Airbus hit the runway with a chiropractor-friendly shudder, Simon Magill vowed to get to the bottom of this mystery. Brodie's memory deserved nothing less. He'd report for duty at Hustler, get his bearings, beetle back to Edinburgh, and confess all to the police. The proper police. Tell the truth, Simon, he told himself. It was the only way. In life, as well as marketing.

Or was it? British police forces, his big brother once told him, were as corrupt as they come, little more than fronts for secret-handshakers and back-scratchers beyond number. He'd need to be very careful. Careless talk costs lives, his brother also said. Unfortunately, Peter failed to act on his own advice.

Lost in thought, Magill was standing at the baggage reclaim carousel, waiting for the spin cycle to start and for his battered suitcase to appear (it was always last), when someone tapped him on the shoulder. Half expecting a sash-wearing hitman, he whirled round to see a smiling half-pint Ulsterman. An overflowing half-pint.

"Hello, Simon," half-pint said merrily. "You look like shit. Good going-away party, was it?"

"Sorry? I . . . er . . . I don't think we've met."

"Of course we've met," half-pint replied in a basso profundo Belfast brogue. "I drove you to the airport after your interview. I'm not surprised you don't remember, mind you. You were a wee bit shell-shocked. You babbled about Dan Brown's books the whole way. That piphilology performance must've taken it out of you. The whole place was talking about it for days – 3.14159 days, to be precise. I'm Ian Kane, by the way."

"Oh yes, yes. Of course. Ian Kane. I remember you now," Magill bluffed. "It's just that I wasn't expecting anyone to meet me. I was going to get a taxi."

"The university doesn't usually bother with pick-ups," rumbled Kane. "It's nice like that. But the school secretary told me you were due in on this flight and I thought you could do with a hand. As it's your first day and all that." Ian Kane grinned. His porcine face lit up, little piggy eyes agleam with mischievous glee.

He looked like a cheeky cherub that had gone to seed. Seed potatoes, that is. Chipped, boiled, mashed, sautéed. Several sacks per sitting.

Ian Kane was one of those people that other people feel they've known all their lives, even when they've just met. He had a warmth that everyone warmed to. It wasn't that he was particularly prepossessing. On the contrary, he evidently loved the good things in life – the love that dare not speak its weight – though the good things didn't care for him in return. However, he exuded such natural bonhomie that he could doubtless charm the proverbial birds out of the proverbial trees. Then eat them.

"The car's outside, Simon. Let me carry your bags," the chubby grub-lover suggested.

Fearing that his new-found friend might have a cardiac arrest on the way to the car park – he seemed to be in training for the "before" shot in a heart disease prevention leaflet – Magill demurred and picked up his forlorn Samsonite suitcase. It had finally escaped from the bowels of the baggage handlers' holding tank, ostensibly intact.

"Is this all the luggage you've brought?" Kane asked.

"Yes, Ian. That's my lot. I'm only here for a day or so. Then I go back to Edinburgh to pick up the rest of my stuff and come back for good on the ferry."

"What do you drive, Simon?"

"An ancient 2CV, 1990 vintage. I don't think it'll last much longer. It's been under a lot of strain lately." As indeed have I, Magill thought to himself. He felt like confessing all to his collegial colleague, but held back. He didn't want to burden citizen Kane with his Paspi problem. At least not yet.

As they roared off in Kane's top-of-the-range Range Rover, its diminutive driver pulled out a packet of Pall Mall and, with the look of someone who's been cruelly deprived of their constitutional cigarette-smoking rights, promptly lit up, dragged deeply, and exhaled with a sigh of contentment. This was one cherub who was going to hell in a duty-free–filled hand-basket.

"So, what's your area of expertise, Ian?" Magill probed politely.

"Expertise? Hah! You shouldn't use swear words like that over here. This place doesn't take kindly to experts. Especially if they have English accents," Kane answered, with a laugh that morphed into a cough, then a wheeze, then a disconcerting croak from the depths of his diaphragm.

Magill glanced round nervously, wondering if the Range Rover carried a first-aid kit. Ideally with defibrillators as standard. "OK, what are you working on, then?"

"The quantum theory of branding."

"*What*?" the pole-axed passenger exclaimed in spite of himself. "I've never heard that one before. How does it work?"

"Weeeellll," Kane said with obvious relish, extending the syllables as he spoke. "You know the way that in quantum theory subatomic particles can occupy two different states simultaneously?"

"Wave and particle, isn't it?" Magill ventured, desperately trying to remember what little he'd learned about quantum mechanics from the Discovery Channel.

Nodding his assent, Kane sucked deeply on his second cigarette, possibly his third, Magill had lost count already. "It is. It is. And it seems to me that successful brands these days combine two mutually incompatible propositions. JetBlue offers outstanding customer service and rock-bottom prices. Starbucks gets premium prices for the ultimate commodity. Target, the American housewares retailer, sells exclusive products to a mass market. The Toyota Yaris is a big car in a small car's body. Movies like *Shrek* and *The Incredibles* are pitched at adults and children alike. Nokia shifts cellphones that double as cameras, PDAs, MP3 players, and more besides. The old idea of one and only one image or strategy or proposition or positioning or message or attribute or function is passé, Simon. Consumers are sophisticated nowadays. They can cope with complexity. We've got to stop talking down to them. Quantum branding is going to be big, big, big."

He sucked on his cigarette again and examined Magill with an expression that didn't suggest the cat that got the cream so much as the cat that swallowed the cow that supplied the cream.

"But quantum theory applies only at the subatomic level, doesn't it?"

"Exactly," Kane replied. "Exactly. And the marketing equivalent of the subatomic level is the individual consumer. Consumers possesses highly individual, near enough unique, images of today's brands. And that's true of even the most monolithic brands like Coca-Cola or McDonald's. At the most fundamental level, consumers' feelings about brands are inherently contradictory: love and hate, attraction and avoidance, push and pull, pro and con, desire and detestation. That's why anti-capitalist protesters wear Nike trainers while trashing Niketown. That's why they throw rocks at Starbucks and then relax with a Frappuccino Grande."

Magill nestled back into the luscious leather of Kane's fully loaded Range Rover, his troubles temporarily forgotten. He thought for a moment, glanced at his grinning chauffeur and, after careful consideration, said "You're bullshitting me, right?"

"Right!" Kane guffawed. "But I had you going for a while." The laughing, coughing, wheezing, croaking rumble started up again, even louder than before.

The passenger joined in. He couldn't help himself. It felt good. "What do you really do, Ian?"

"SOS, Simon."

"Yeah, right. Save Our Souls?"

"Not quite. Storytelling Outreach Service. I run Hustler Business School's storytelling outreach service. The big problem we have here in Northern Ireland, particularly among small businesses and in the agri-food sector, is that our companies produce fantastic products, among the best in the world, but we're no good at getting the message out. We're useless when it comes to weaving compelling stories around the goods and services we produce. If good branding boils down to good storytelling – and I believe it does – then the real challenge is to improve companies' storytelling skills. End of story."

Magill looked sceptically at Kane, though he couldn't deny that he was speaking the truth. The situation was exactly the same in Scotland. They'd discussed it during his marketing degree at Stirling, though nobody mentioned storytelling as a solution.

"The irony," Kane continued, enthusiasm suffusing his

resonant voice and lifting it a semitone or two, " is that this place is stuffed with storytellers, yarn spinners, dream weavers and bullshitters. The bars are full of them. Every night of the week. It's time Ulster's businesses and bullshitters got together. That's where SOS comes in. We bring together the storytellers and storysellers. Story*less* sellers, rather. SOS runs workshops, training courses, conferences and so on."

"Amazing."

"We even have a hotline, Simon."

"What, an 0800 number that marketing executives can ring when they're in need of a bedtime story?" Magill asked incredulously.

"Whaddya mean, 0800? It's 0870, sunshine. Premium rate, compadre. We're running a business school, not a charity."

Magill shook his head, wondering what on earth he was getting himself into. He didn't know the half of it.

"SOS also runs field trips to storytelling hotspots, Simon."

"Pubs, you mean?"

"Pubs, I mean. Fancy a pint? There's a wee place on our way. We've plenty of time and you look like you need a drink. You're in Ulster now, Simon. We take things easy round here. You've got to learn to relax."

Chapter Nine

The Hound of Hustler

The Crown Bar's long-standing claim to fame is that it is one of the few pubs in the British Isles owned and operated by the National Trust. Unlike most National Trust properties, however, there's no entry fee, nor are its opening hours restricted, nor is it stuffed with stuffy display cases. There is nevertheless something of the museum about the Crown. Its exuberantly tiled exterior, ornate moulded ceiling, polychromatic stained-glass windows, intricately carved wooden snugs, and elaborate partitions interspersed along the burnished granite bar have been replaced, renovated and refurbished on so many occasions that almost nothing of the original remains. Far from being an authentic Victorian gin palace, Belfast's Crown Bar is a pseudo-Victorian tourist trap. Disneyland for the drinking classes.

Tourists, of course, are relatively few and far between in Northern Ireland, so there's usually plenty of room in this admittedly brilliant replica of an imitation of a pastiche of an echo of the original. The bar snacks aren't bad either, if rather too close to comfort food for comfort. The Crown Bar may be a bit of a stereotype, but for first-time visitors to Belfast it synthesises and symbolises the craic-, cholesterol- and cigarette-fuelled culture of the city. A pint in the Crown is a kind of local initiation rite, one that most new arrivals readily undergo.

Dr Kane selected a snug, one of ten semi-private booths that cling to the outer walls like confessionals, and set about initiating Mr Magill. He ordered two pints of Guinness, plus Bushmills whiskey chasers, and without so much as a glance at the menu prescribed two plates of home-made Irish stew. He lit another Pall Mall and wheezed with happy anticipation while waiting for the culinary clichés to appear. Simon suspected this wasn't his first lunchtime sitting that day.

"I enjoyed your presentation at the job interview," Kane said nonchalantly. "It was very . . . hmmm . . . challenging. Shook some people up. Are you planning to develop your sustainable marketing idea at all?"

"Am I planning to sustain it, you mean?"

"If you like." Kane drew on his cigarette and studied Magill carefully, his puffy pale-blue eyes narrowed to a slit. He must have been about thirty-five, though his grizzled grey hair and triple-ripple chins made him look at least fifteen years older. Dr Kane might have been young at heart, but his heart would surely beg to differ.

"I'm not sure how best to develop it, Ian. I think I'd need to move beyond the basic sustainability concept. Maybe flesh it out with some empirical research. I've been toying with a couple of case studies." Magill was new to Northern Ireland, and his bullshitting ability had yet to be fully honed. But he'd made a good start.

Kane took a big bite out of his Guinness. "Oh aye? What have you got in mind? Companies? Products? Markets? Brands?"

"People, actually. I was thinking of looking at people. We need to put people back into marketing. All the talk is about disembodied brands and products, or at least it was on my degree course. But marketing is really about people, isn't it? And, as I said in the interview, if marketing is starting to turn back on itself . . . "

"Eating its young!" Kane interrupted. "That's how you described marketing, Simon. Interesting choice of phrase. I've heard of cannibalised sales and shoot-to-kill strategies, but then I probably haven't played as many computer games as you." He chortled, dewlaps flapping in the non-existent breeze.

"Did I really say that?" Magill flushed at the memory of his atypically ebullient interview performance. "Anyway, if marketing is starting to repeat itself, as it were, maybe we should look back to the people of the past, the great marketers of bygone years, and find out if they've any lessons for us. I suppose it's a sort of people-based conservation strategy."

"Sustainability through conservation, Simon?"

"It's recycling, I suppose."

"Resurrection, surely."

In light of what happened earlier that morning, Magill was disconcerted by the turn the conversation was taking. Resurrection, cannibalism, eating uncooked children . . . it was all too close to home. He downed his firewater in one and gasped as his oesophagus ignited.

"Bushmills is better with ice or a wee drop of water," Kane said solicitously. "Any thoughts on your case studies, Simon?"

Still gasping, Magill exhaled an answer of sorts. "I was thinking," gasp, "of Thomas Lipton and," gasp, "John Henry Anderson."

Kane paused for a second, seemingly processing the names. Or perhaps he was struggling with trapped wind. It was hard to tell. He lit yet another Pall Mall, coughed up a storm, and wheezed as if his life depended on it. Which it probably did.

"I've heard of Lipton," he croaked. "He was the tea baron, wasn't he? But who's Anderson?"

"The Great Wizard of the North, they called him. He was a stage magician in the middle of the nineteenth century. His tricks were fairly routine – magic cabinets, mesmerism, mind reading, feats of memory, sleight of hand, pulling rabbits out of top hats, catching bullets in his teeth – but he was a brilliant self-marketer. He was world famous. He advertised incessantly. He pioneered CSR with benefit performances. He marketed all sorts of tie-in merchandise. He appreciated the PR value of a steamy autobiography. He deliberately stoked up controversy wherever he went and sold out every show as a consequence. He persuaded celebrities like Sir Walter Scott to endorse him, and even stole Scott's nickname for good measure. He was Scotland's answer to P. T. Barnum, though many of his publicity stunts predated Barnum's. He was the greatest Brand Me marketer Scotland ever produced, second only to Thomas Lipton."

"I thought Lipton was from here. Isn't there an Ulster connection?"

"His parents were from County Tyrone, but he was born in Glasgow. He opened his first grocery store in Glasgow, though some of the early branches were in Belfast. Like Anderson, he made his name with outrageous publicity stunts. I mean huge publicity stunts. He organised enormous parades through the streets to mark new store openings. Elephants, horses, bands, the lot. He manufactured giant cheeses – we're talking *humungous* here, Ian – and filled them full of coppers. A free gift with every slice! He cut his prices to the bone and then challenged local cheesemongers, tea retailers, bacon suppliers and suchlike to match them. When these worthies complained bitterly about his ungentlemanly marketing practices, which they invariably did, they only succeeded in giving him still more publicity. He advertised on every available surface, including the pyramids of Egypt. He was one of the first to recognise the benefits of sports sponsorship. He supplied the very first World Cup football trophy. He also challenged unsuccessfully for the Americas Cup – several times, in fact – and reaped enormous PR rewards from doing so. He was a marketing genius."

"Sounds a bit like Richard Branson," the storyteller said between mouthfuls of Irish stew, heaped platters of which had arrived while Magill was bluffing his way on sustainable marketing and desperately regurgitating Ego of the Week items from the Paspi website. He was delighted to see the food, though, as he'd had nothing to eat all day.

"Branson's a pale imitation, Ian. He's a Xerox of a Xerox. Lipton's the genuine article, as is Anderson."

"Hmmm. Maybe so. But you know what people are going to say, don't you?"

"No, what?" Magill replied, rather more aggressively than he intended. The undiluted Ulster elixir was working its obstreperous magic.

"They'll say your examples of sustainable marketing are old hat. The world has changed since Lipton's time. And Anderson's."

"But marketing hasn't changed," Magill exclaimed. "The technology may be different, the context may be different, but the basic customer-oriented, attention-grabbing dimensions of marketing haven't changed. They're more important now than ever, what with so much competition, so many products, such sophisticated consumers, so much marketing going on all around! The lessons of Lipton and Anderson are as relevant as ever. More relevant, in fact, since they too were faced with countless competing products, many of which were objectively better in terms of their offerings and attributes. The markets they competed in were just as tough as today's. Tougher, in many ways."

"OK, OK, Simon. Calm down. Relax. I agree with what you're saying, but your ideas would be more marketable if you used contemporary examples, as well as Lipton and Anderson. Then you could argue that marketing's traditions are being sustained, that they still work, that they remain directly relevant to the concerns of twenty-first-century marketing managers."

Magill felt light-headed. The Irish stew was getting to him, he thought. It couldn't possibly be the Bushmills. "I see what you mean," he conceded. "Who do you suggest?"

"What about Michael O'Leary, the CEO of Ryanair? From what you've said, he sounds like the living embodiment of Thomas Lipton. Hardly a day goes by without a publicity stunt, or a controversy, or a headline-grabbing tactic of some kind. He's always baiting his competitors. He's always getting into scraps with regulators or interfering local worthies, all of whom inadvertently feed Ryanair's PR machine. His airline's low-cost business model isn't much different from the competition, but O'Leary himself keeps Ryanair at the top of people's minds."

"Yes, but O'Leary isn't customer oriented," Magill retorted curtly. "He's the opposite. He seems to despise his customers, his suppliers, his channels of distribution. He calls his customers cattle, he charges extra for wheelchairs, he refuses to give refunds even if a trip is cancelled because of bereavement, and he boasts about screwing suppliers like Boeing into the ground. That's not marketing as I understand it. It's more like customer contempt than customer-centricity. Kate Phillips would have a fit."

Dr Kane smiled sympathetically as if dealing with an innocent abroad, which in many ways he was. He explained that there was more to marketing than customer orientation, that not everything Kate Phillips said was gospel, that real-world marketing was very different from the textbooks, that Michael O'Leary might loathe his customers and make no bones about it, but he still ran the most successful airline in Europe.

There was a reason for Ryanair's success, Kane continued, and that reason was its very lack of customer orientation. O'Leary didn't pretend to be customer-centric, nor did he talk the customer-coddling claptrap that every other CEO talked. What his company did do was offer incredible value for money, the best value for money bar none, and that's what customers appreciated. *Really* appreciated.

The tough talking, ironically, was part of Ryanair's appeal. The very fact that O'Leary treated everyone like shit – customers, employees, suppliers, airport operators, airline regulators – was part of the attraction, because it was done in order to cut prices to the bone. Consumers responded to that, even as Ryanair spat in their faces.

"It's a paradox, Simon, but we live in a world of quantum brands."

"I thought you said quantum branding's bullshit."

"Oh aye, so I did." Kane smiled his defrocked cherub smile. "There's no fooling you twice." He winked at his new colleague while downing his unadulterated Bushmills. "I'm just saying that if you take a look at Ryanair, there might be an interesting angle for you. Maybe David Blaine too, for the Anderson side of things . . . "

"I'm not so sure, Ian. I'm not convinced that organisations with an anti-customer orientation can survive in the longer term. Kate Phillips's textbooks are clear on that point. Ryanair's likely to become more and more customer oriented through time, in keeping with the Wheel of Retailing theory."

"Wheel of Ryanair theory, surely?"

"Right. Right. As competition increases, or there's a down turn in the market, Ryanair'll become more conscious of customer care and eventually evolve into the kind of organisation it once undercut, like Aer Lingus or British Airways."

"We'll see, Simon, we'll see. There's one thing you ought to bear in mind, though. Customer satisfaction, orientation, centricity, focus or whatever you want to call it isn't the end, the aim, the purpose of marketing. It's a means to the end of marketing. The end of marketing is to sell stuff. Never forget that. Customer coddling is one way of achieving that end, but it isn't the only way."

"I'll bear that in mind, Ian. Thanks for the advice. It'll be a while before I get started. I have to find my feet at Hustler first. I don't even know what I'm supposed to be doing, or where exactly I'll be working. Am I part of the SOS team?"

The chubby cherub burst out laughing. The ensuing fusillade of coughing terrified the entire bar, several of whom surmised bird flu had just hit town and was claiming its first victim. When he'd sufficiently recovered, Kane croaked, "Team? What team? I'm SOS, Simon! I have some secretarial assistance, but apart from that SOS is mine, all mine."

"So you don't know where I'll be working?"

"We'll talk on the way. It's time to go. Drink up, Simon. You're about to meet your maker."

Chapter Ten

A Brown Study

"Welcome to Serendipity Associates, Professor Aherne. Or the Brady Bunch, as we like to call ourselves."

Barton Brady II was oblivious to his colleagues' sudden froideur and barely suppressed annoyance. They'd heard Barton's Brady Bunch quip on numerous occasions, and it had started to pall. Yasmin Buonarroti was particularly piqued, because she not only co-owned the company and had done more than anyone else to get it up and running, but had planted the Serendipity Associates idea in Brady's sometimes brilliant but often blinkered head. If anything, she occasionally remarked to friends, the team should be known as the Buonarroti Bunch, but it didn't quite have the same populist ring to it. It sounded too much like a management consultancy offshoot of the Mob.

She was the first to admit, what's more, that if it hadn't been for Brady's contacts, charm and cheesy grin – well nigh essential in the consultancy business – Serendipity Associates might never have got off the ground. But that was five years ago, and they'd watched a lot of PowerPoint presentations since then. Management consultancy was like the legendary shark that had to keep moving or die, and although Barton Brady was well endowed orthodontically, he was moving and shaking less and less.

Something had to be done, and Buonarroti was the person to do it. She could always quit, of course. She sometimes thought of cashing in her chips and going home to gritty, grimy Gotham. She still might. She'd had just about enough of the Strip. If it weren't for the hard-working associates she'd hired, and the fact that she was a fighter first, last and always, Yasmin Buonarroti would be leaving Las Vegas.

"We're a small group," Brady went on in his silky, Waspy way, "but beautifully formed, as you can see. May I introduce Jack Chang and Jill Eng, our creative dynamos, and that mean-looking customer at the end is Chas Rosencreutz, our commercial consigliere. Chas keeps us on the straight and narrow. Chang and Eng think us out of the box. You've already met my colleague and Serendipity Associates' tower of strength, Yasmin Buonarroti."

"Yes, yes," Emer Aherne replied. "Yasmin and I have had some interesting discussions about the Code. Very interesting. I'm pleased to meet you, Mr Chang, Miss Eng, Mr Rosencreutz. And of course it's nice to see you again, Yasmin."

"Did Yasmin mention that we're working on a product-placement deal for Dan Brown's next book, *The Solomon Key*?"

"Really? Good Lord. You kept that quiet, Yasmin." Professor Aherne forced a smile, while wondering what, exactly, these people wanted from her. She was never comfortable around consultancy types, and Barton Brady was the quintessence of consulting, with added Las Vegas.

"The deal isn't finalised yet," Buonarroti explained. "Client confidentiality. You know how it is. I'm meeting Dan in a couple of days. We're hopeful that a package'll come together. That's really all I can say at this stage."

"Oh, come on, Yasmin," Brady chivvied in a chummy, almost conspiratorial manner. "Emer's an honorary Serendipity Associate. She's a Brown Babe, too. We're here to consider her analysis of the Danster, and the least we can do is put our own cards on the table."

Aherne bristled slightly at Brady's remarks, as did Buonarroti. It wasn't that the professor disliked being called "babe" by a handsome young man. It was true, after all. Or it used to be. What she disliked was undue intimacy. She longed for the days when people treated each other with respect and weren't on instant first-name terms. Back home at Hustler, she insisted on being called Professor Aherne, much to her egalitarian colleagues' amusement. In American universities, she'd found, full professors were treated with the dignity and respect they'd earned. And she liked that. It wasn't that she was stuffy or conceited or indeed an old fogey. She got on very well with people once the ice was broken – Yasmin Buonarroti being a recent case in point. It's just that she didn't like being called Emer by someone she'd never met before: students, sales assistants and telemarketers especially. Management consultants, as well.

"You're right as always, Barton," Buonarroti said through teeth that weren't so much gritted as glued. She glanced at Jill Eng, a statuesque Nigerian American who looked as though she moonlighted for a high-kicking Vegas chorus line. Eng glanced in turn at Jack Chang, a Lilliputian Chinese American who looked like he'd been stomped on by a high-kicking Vegas chorus line. Rosencreutz sat silently at the end of the table, minding his own business. Heavy-set, jowly and vaguely threatening, he had the air of a Mob enforcer about him, a look reinforced by his wide-lapelled Valentino suit, which seemed to shimmer in the refracted sunlight.

Having been granted her colleagues' tacit approval, Buonarroti began quietly. "Our take on Dan Brown is very different from yours, Emer. SA's focus is on how best to exploit Brown's Langdon franchise.

"Like you, we quickly realised that Dan the Man is marketing minded. As an author, he affects disdain for commercial matters. They all do. It's part of the pose adopted by literary types. However, the Robert Langdon books themselves are full of references to marketing. Despite the veneer of 'eminent Harvard academic who's an authority on religious symbology,' the bottom line is the bottom line.

"The plot of *Da Vinci* hinges on the back-cover endorsements that Langdon's editor is gathering to boost sales of his new book about the eternal feminine. It's sure to be a highly controversial book, and naturally Langdon's editor is thrilled because of the sales spike that controversy usually ensures. He's also delighted by the worldwide publicity his author received during his adventure in Rome a year earlier, when he saved the Vatican from vaporisation. When discussing the activities of the Roman Catholic church, furthermore, Langdon often describes them in commercial terms: 'Constantine was a good businessman,' 'the greatest story ever sold,' the quotes from P. T. Barnum, the Illuminati's 'global publicity stunt,' the impact of the Illuminati's grisly publicity stunts on consumer demand for antimatter . . . it goes on and on."

With the briefest of pauses for effect, Buonarroti continued. "Brown may be marketing oriented, as you rightly noted in your conference presentation, Emer, but his implementation leaves a lot to be desired. There's a scandalous lack of product placement in the Langdon books. Granted, our detailed study of brand names in *Angels & Demons* and *The Da Vinci Code* reveals an eighty-eight percent increase between the first book and its sequel, which is encouraging. However, that increase is from a very low base. Only 26 brands are mentioned in *Angels & Demons*, and fewer than 50 in *Da Vinci*. This is way, way below what's possible in books of that length. A typical sex-and-shopping novel by Judith Krantz or Jackie Collins or Candace Bushnell would include around 600 to 800 brand names. A typical Stephen King would clock in at two to three hundred. Bret Easton Ellis's *American Psycho* contained more than a thousand, and it's a much shorter book than either of the Langdons.

"So the basic case we're making to Dan Brown and his people is that he needs to include more brand names, and mention them more often. The first two books miss countless product placement opportunities, which is frankly unforgivable.

"In the Gare du Nord sequence in *Da Vinci*, for example, there are people in the railway station using MP3 players, but the brand names aren't mentioned. Apple should be in there. Cellphones are in constant use in *Angels & Demons*, as are computers, yet we're not told what makes they are. Motorola and Dell must be chewing the carpet. Langdon notices the smell of Sophie Neveu's hair in *Da Vinci* and Vittoria Vetra's body in *Angels & Demons*, but no haircare products or body-spray brands are specified. P&G would kill for those promotional slots, and L'Oréal's also worth talking to. Worst of all, Brown occasionally mentions local hotels and restaurants by name when he should really be referring to Hyatt or Hilton or Holiday Inn, to say nothing of KFC and Burger King and Pizza Hut."

"Dan's a super savvy guy, no question," Barton Brady added, "but he hasn't thought this through properly. He's not making maximum marketing use of his literary real estate. And that's where we come in."

"But surely," Aherne objected, "the Ritz Hotel is cited countless times in *Da Vinci*. And isn't the lack of branding simply a reflection of the book's religious settings, where brands are largely absent?"

"Brown is getting better," Buonarroti acknowledged, "we accept that. The Ritz was a good call, though he might have negotiated a better deal with Radisson. The Mickey Mouse wristwatch was a disaster, however, since Disney doesn't need that kind of product placement; it's got more than enough promotional vehicles of its own. Just think what Swatch might have paid. Similarly, the Smart car was cute, but a Corolla would have been smarter. In *Angels & Demons*, the single most frequently cited brand is the BBC, a not-for-profit media organisation. Imagine what Sky or Fox or CNN or Bloomberg might have come up with, if only in cross-promotional airtime."

"Brown's settings leave a lot to be desired as well," Jack Chang interjected enthusiastically. "As you said, Professor Aherne, the Roman Catholic church isn't ideal from a product-placement perspective, though it's improved considerably since Benedict XVI became Holy Father."

"He's a real fashionista," Jill Eng butted in. "Prada loafers, Gucci shades, Raniero Mancinelli vestments. Benedict's a pretty cool cleric. There's a great sponsorship opportunity there for someone . . . "

"The key thing, Prof," Chang continued, "is that the church is OK, but not as rich placements-wise as some other settings. Like the 'hood. If Langdon's next adventure were to be set in the rap or hip-hop community, where bling's the thing, then we could be looking at a branding bonanza. Hollywood would be pretty awesome too, as would Vegas."

"I'd never thought of it like that before," Aherne said with surprise. "I can see how it might work, though, because research shows that when brand names get mentioned in cultural products like movies or rap music or books, it's more effective than traditional forms of advertising. It's much more believable. Almost as good as word of mouth."

"Better!" Rosencreutz cut in, without looking up from his Palm PDA. "Thirty-one point two percent better. There is no effective control over word of mouth. Cultural product placement can be managed more easily."

Aherne was taken aback by Rosencreutz's brusqueness, especially as he'd remained silent so far. She was about to inquire professorially about the statistical proof behind his confident assertions when Brady seized the moment and redirected the conversation in his emollient way.

"The crucial issue, Emer, is that Brown badly needs to increase his PPR."

"PPR?"

"Product plug ratio. He also needs to broaden his branding palette. What little placement there is in the Langdon books is concentrated on cars and jets and helicopters and guns and suchlike. There are entire product categories such as apparel, electrical equipment, household goods and health and beauty aids that remain untouched. He needs to feed and water Langdon more often as well. The guy's been starved for two entire novels and given next to nothing to drink. There are big, big branding opportunities there."

"Robert Langdon Happy Meals?" Aherne joked.

"Something like that. We've been talking to one or two blue-chip companies about *The Solomon Key* and they're going crazy for a slice of the action. Nike, Sony, BMW and McDonald's are already very interested. We're developing a range of Robert Langdon tie-in merchandise as well. You know, the usual package: action figures, computer games, trading cards, jigsaw puzzles, T shirts, key-rings, coffee mugs, fridge magnets. That sort of thing."

"An action figure of a professor?" Aherne asked incredulously. "The mind boggles. I take it there aren't too many moving parts. Let me guess, it sits silently at a desk for hours and emits a low moan from time to time. It's not exactly Robosapiens, much less Logosapiens. Goslowsapiens, more like."

"Oh, you haven't heard our killer idea," Buonarroti said gleefully, her plain pug-like face suffused with pleasure.

"Go for it, girl," Eng encouraged.

"Well, like so much of SA's work, Emer, it's more conceptual than copper-bottomed. But it's a concept with great possibilities.

Our original idea was Anti-matter Marketing, based on *Angels & Demons*. This involved a Big Bang approach to branding, with a view to vaporising the competition.

"Then we came up with something even more exciting, derived from *Da Vinci*. The Vitruvian Brand. The aim is to square the marketing circle by applying the Divine Proportion to perennial marketing problems: above- or below-the-line promotions, the balance between print and television advertising, flat rates versus commissions for salespeople, good and bad profits, known to unknown costs, the ratio of satisfied to dissatisfied customers. Then there's growth-share matrices, market-share calculations, brand-extension decisions, retail-store space allocations, product-pricepoint patterns. The possibilities are endless."

"But are all these issues explained by the divine proportion?"

"What does it matter, Emer?" Brady cut in. "Is everything explained by the balanced scorecard, or good-to-great, or even customer orientation? Of course not! The *concept* is crucial. If we demonstrate how appropriate the divine proportion is in other spheres, such as architecture and the natural world, then it's easy to transpose the concept to a management context. If we also wrap the basic idea in Dan Brown and da Vinci, then we're looking at a very, very attractive package. We could really be on to something."

"Provided Dan agrees, of course," Buonarroti cautioned.

"Of course he'll agree," Brady proclaimed. "Why wouldn't he?"

Chapter Eleven

The Kane Mutiny

"You Are Now Entering Titanic Quarter." The road sign caught Simon Magill's eye as Ian Kane's Range Rover circumnavigated a roundabout, slipped off Belfast's inner ring road and slowed below its customary 65 mph. They were coming in to land.

"Titanic Quarter?" Magill asked, slightly the worse for Bushmills. The shock of the morning's events had rendered him unusually susceptible. Drinking whiskey on an empty stomach hadn't helped, either. "Why only a quarter, Ian? Did they build a bit of the boat here, the way they do with Airbus? What section did they make? The watertight compartments?"

"Be careful what you say about the *Titanic* round here," Kane rumbled. He too was slightly the worse for wear, if well within his limit (though Kane's limit, if not quite infinite, was several orders of magnitude greater than Magill's). "RMS *Titanic* was built in Belfast, Simon. All of it. And the ship, as they say, was fine when it left here. The sinking is part of the city's folk memory, and we're big on memory, history and stuff in Northern Ireland."

Magill nodded imperceptibly. "Yes, I know. My mother's from here. My parents used to live here, many years ago. I've heard more than I ever need about Ulster's feats of memory."

"Aye, I know all about your parents, Simon. Adam Magill and Eve O'Grady," Kane said mechanically. "Lived in Eden, just outside Carrickfergus. Met when your father was attending a trainee pastor's retreat in Ballycastle, where your mother managed a dulce stall at the Old Lamas Fair. Fell in love and married, despite the opposition of Eve's parents. She renounced the Catholic faith and became a Methodist, like her husband. Adam and Eve ministered to the churchgoers of Eden, until they were chased out of Ulster by the serpents of sectarianism. A minister in a mixed marriage? They hadn't a hope. Must have been first on the hit list. Get out or be burnt out – that's what they called it back in those days."

Stunned by the potted family history, which was accurate in every detail, Magill turned to his companion. "How can you possibly know all that?" Kane calmly explained that there were no secrets in Northern Ireland; that the university checked his background before making the appointment; that everyone was checked out in Ulster, like it or not; that it was perfectly normal, nothing to worry about; and that he knew all about Simon's brother, too. Magill didn't want to be drawn on the subject of his brother's untimely death, not after the unspeakable events earlier, so he quickly changed the subject, albeit less than subtly.

"So why's this part of town called the Titanic Quarter, Ian?"

"This is the old shipyard, Simon. Harland and Wolff. It went bottom-up a couple of years ago. They're redeveloping it – apartments, hotels, museums, the usual urban revitalisation package – and they're using the *Titanic* narrative to help sell the property, basically. They're one of our biggest clients at present, believe it or not."

"SOS and the *Titanic*?" Magill said incredulously. "That's apt! A marriage made in heaven, as it were."

"Oh, you haven't heard the best bit yet," Kane wheezed. He unsheathed yet another packet of Pall Mall, and, with a well-practised one-handed manoeuvre, lit up for the umpteenth time that afternoon. He duly went through his coughing and croaking routine. He sounded like a bronchial corncrake with emphysema.

"It gets better than SOS *Titanic*?"

"The Business School is located here. We've only just moved into our new building. Well, it's an old shipyard building, rehabilitated."

Magill burst out laughing. The Bushmills had got the better of him. "Titanic Business School? I've just joined Titanic Business School? I don't believe it! The biggest new product failure in history and they've named a business school after it? Brilliant!"

88

"Hmmm. Not quite, Simon. Nobody calls it Titanic Business School." Kane exhaled heavily, exaggeratedly so. The fallen-angel smirk crept across his porky pockmarked features. "Actually, everybody calls it Titanic Business School! But not in front of the director, or any of the university's upper crust. It's officially Hustler Business School."

"HBS?"

"HBS."

"I think somebody's using that already," Magill said, wiping the tears from his eyes. And it wasn't even afternoon teatime. "Let me get this straight, Ian," he continued, his tongue loosened by Ulster's infallible truth serum. "You're the SOS guy in Titanic Business School. What does that make me?"

"Oh, you're on deckchair-rearranging duty. Unless they assign you to the band."

"Band? What band? They didn't mention music at the interview. I can manage 'Abide with Me' on the kazoo, if that helps."

"I'm not sure what's expected of you, Simon. That's the director's call. It could be cimbals, more likely drums."

"Cymbals? Drums? No triangle, then?"

A wheezy chuckle emanated from Magill's barrel chest, a barrel that was bursting at the seams and sagging at the bottom. "It's cimbals, Simon. C-I-M-B-A-L-S. It's an acronym. Stands for Cultural Industries' Marketing, Branding, Advertising and Licensing Service. It's Hustler's most profitable function, the business school's specialist area. However, I think you're more likely to be on drums. It's not up to me. You're meeting the director later today."

"Drums?"

"Dull, Routine University Management Stuff."

"Fond of acronyms at Hustler, are we?"

"You ain't seen nothing yet, young Magill. Just wait till you see our brand new building. The director's quite a character, too."

Despite the fuggy, almost oppressive atmosphere of Kane's Range Rover, Magill immediately perked up. He was looking forward to meeting Professor Emer Aherne, and said so. He'd heard that she was something else. He'd been hoping to meet her

89

at the job interview but she'd been otherwise engaged. He'd read some of her stuff and concluded that she was, well, either mad or obsessed or both. His companion put him straight. Aherne was out of the country, on sabbatical in the States, where she was working with none other than Professor Kate Phillips.

"*The* Kate Phillips? From Northwestern University? The textbook person?"

"Yes, Simon, *the* Kate Phillips. Professor O'Connell's in charge while Emer's away. You'll like him. He's on vocals, by the way."

"Vocals?"

Kane couldn't keep his face straight. "Vastly Overpaid College Administrators, Legislators and Supervisors."

"I should've guessed. There's only one thing missing. You forgot to tell me where SOS fits into this remarkable musical miscellany."

"I'm guitars."

"And guitars is ... "

"What else but Grand Unified Interdisciplinary Theory of Academic Research and Scholarship."

"Quantum theory of branding. Right?"

"Got it in one," Kane smiled. "We're here."

Hustler Business School may have looked good on an architectural drawing, but in real life it was an abomination. A massive plate-glass extension had been grafted onto a beautiful Victorian building. The graft hadn't taken, regrettably. It was supposed to represent the prow of a ship, or so the architects said, but the unsightly glass addition made the old red sandstone building look like a bloated bullfrog with an overactive thyroid.

Kane killed the engine, though it took the throbbing beast several seconds to settle. "You've got a meeting with Professor O'Connell at 4 p.m. We've just time for a cup of coffee. Make that a couple of cups," Kane added, accurately assessing his new colleague's exact state of disrepair. I'll introduce you to my assistant as well."

"What's he called?"

"He's a she, Simon. She's a woman. All woman. And remember, no slobbering on deck." The earth shook slightly beneath Magill as he leapt down from the Range Rover. Magill did likewise, though his legs almost buckled beneath him. "So, what's *she* called? What's the woman, all woman's name, Midshipman Kane?"

"May Day."

Magill was still tittering when Ian Kane cracked open a groaning panel door to reveal a high-ceilinged office with all its original Victorian features – ornate cornices, finely carved architraves, heavy wooden wainscoting, elaborate ceiling rose – impressively intact. The walls were covered with brightly coloured maps and navigation charts, as well as framed blueprints of steamship cross-sections. Two large models of the *Titanic* and its sister ship *Olympic* sailed serenely in massive glass containers moored in the middle of a time-worn wooden floor. Three equally time-worn desks nestled against the wainscoting, each guarded by a matched pair of Art Deco brass-handled filing cabinets.

The room exuded an air of expectancy, as if a rear admiral were about to appear and regale everyone with telling tales of derring-do at Agadir and analogous colonial hotspots. Only the eye-popping iMacs introduced an anachronistic note into this monument to Rudyard Kipling, Cecil Rhodes, H. Rider Haggard and the Great British Empire as was.

"You can have this one for the time being," said Kane, indicating the desk on the left, nearest the door. "SOS is over there." He pointed at the biggest and most dishevelled desk in the centre of the back wall, between two imposing sash windows complete with moulded frames, multiple panes and lambs-tongue glazing bars.

Magill was taken aback by the set-up. He'd fallen on his feet, as it were.

"And this, Simon, is my assistant, May Day."

May Day swivelled on her office chair and rose to greet the newcomer. She too was an anachronism. But what an anachronism. An anachronism to die for. May Day was a stunning Louise Brooks lookalike. A punk Louise Brooks: pixie-faced, bright-pink bob and enough metalwork on her elfin face to supply Harland and Wolff during its heyday. Why on earth, the wannabe symbologist wondered, would anyone so beautiful want to deface themselves with eyebrow rings, nose studs, lip clips and ancillary ironmongery? They didn't do her any favours, that's for sure. Not that May Day needed any favours. She was already blessed.

"Simon Magill, meet May Day. May Day, Simon Magill."

"Mayday, Mayday," Magill blurted out. "SOS Mayday, SOS Mayday."

She looked at him venomously, her emerald eyes aglow, almost incandescent. "I've heard them all before," she said curtly. "But thank you for reminding me." May Day turned away and glared at Kane. "King Billy rang. He wants to see you at half four."

Ian Kane frowned. "Four thirty? Hmmmm. I was planning to take Simon back to his hotel and get him settled in. I'll ring King Billy later. I'm sure we can sort something out."

May Day raised a sceptical eyebrow at her boss – not easy given the tonnage she was carrying – as if to say "you'll be lucky." King Billy presumably wasn't a man to be trifled with.

"King Billy?" Magill blurted out again. "King bloody Billy? What is it with all the names around here?"

With a shake of the head and a rattle of metal, May Day fixed him with a look that would melt an iceberg. "King Billy is one of SOS's most important benefactors," she snapped.

But Simon Magill wasn't at his sharpest. "King Billy? King Billy? What's next? King Kong? Captain Birds Eye? Admiral Butterfly? Commodore Computer? Cabinboy Band?"

"The cafeteria is in the annexe," May Day said in a tone of voice that would disembowel a bullock. "They do an excellent double espresso. Professor O'Connell's expecting you at 4 p.m. That's Professor Carlingford O'Connell, by the way. Don't be late. Do be presentable." She looked daggers at Kane, who'd obviously led an innocent astray. Not for the first time.

"Aye, aye, me hearties," Magill responded merrily. "Shipshape and Bristol fashion it'll be, landlubbers."

Twenty-five minutes later, after several serious caffeine infusions and a few choruses of "What shall we do with the drunken sailor?", Simon Magill had recovered his intellectual equipoise. Almost.

"Ahoy there, Cap'n Kane," the rather less than able seaman

inquired, "where's Admiral O'Connell's cabin?"

"Simon, the director's office is on the poop deck. That's the top floor. May Day will take you up. He'll do most of the talking. Just nod and smile nicely. He doesn't bite. Not on the first date, anyway."

Magill nodded. His head had an anchor attached. "Ar-har . . ."

"Gotta go. See a man about a shaggy-dog story. Catch you later."

Kane made for the door, only to look back at his new colleague mischievously. "Oh, Simon, don't forget to compliment O'Connell on the new building. He's very proud of it. It'll get you on his right side."

Chapter Twelve

The Unsinkable Brand

Situated in the bowsprit of the curtain-glass extension, Carlingford O'Connell's office was a thing of beauty. It tapered to a point and enjoyed wonderful views of both the waterfront and Belfast's verdant ring of hills. It also had an exterior walkway where the B-school commander-in-chief could keep a weather eye out for pack-ice, lifeboats and marooned strategic planners.

The interior, however, was strictly utilitarian. Thin green carpet. Ikea-like pine furniture. Little in the way of decoration, not even bookshelves. The only embellishment, apart from an enormous wall-mounted time planner, was a large brass hourglass sitting at the centre of a cheap conference table surrounded by four self-assembly Shaker-style chairs.

If ever anyone was misnamed, Professor Carlingford O'Connell was that person. He was a baptismal malapropism incarnate. Whereas his name was redolent of Celtic warriors from time immemorial – swashed buckles on the storm-tossed briny and the ongoing struggle for Irish self-determination – Professor O'Connell in person was as utilitarian as his office. He had work ethic written all over him. If not quite a human dynamo, he came across as a hyperactive sparrow. This impression was reinforced by his sharp features, frighteningly close shave, neat grey suit, neat grey hair and general aura of busyness. This was a man, Magill thought, who kept his desk clear, diary full, in-tray empty and BlackBerry bang up to date. He looked as if he was used to dividing his time into fifteen-minute blocks and charging exorbitant fees for them. A lawyer by training, Magill guessed; possibly a merchant banker or management accountant. Definitely not a marketer.

O'Connell looked up quickly. His rimless half-moon glasses caught the light. "Ah, Mr Magill. You're two minutes late. I'll be

95

with you in approximately three minutes, ten seconds. Take a seat." He motioned towards the spartan conference table. Discomfited by the distinctly chilly reception, Magill took an uncomfortable seat without demur.

Exactly three minutes, ten seconds later, the dapper director of Hustler Business School alighted on the chair opposite, inverted the hourglass and slipped into human-resources speak. Warm, fuzzy people skills weren't Carlingford O'Connell's forte, but he'd attended the requisite training courses and was conscious of his pastoral responsibilities.

"How are you, Simon? Welcome to Hustler Business School. I believe you've met my colleagues Dr Kane and Ms Day. You've also been fed and watered, I gather."

He angled his head to the side like a sparrow debating whether to swallow a worm right away or save it for later. He didn't mention the Crown Bar debacle. He didn't have to. He'd already made his views crystal clear.

Nothing, Magill surmised, gets past this guy. Or that's the impression he wants to convey. However, Pitcairn Brodie often said that the key to interpersonal prowess was recognising that everyone has a fixation, a weakness, a hotline to the child within. The social symbologist's challenge was to find the key that unlocked the incarcerated infant. Luckily, Magill already knew O'Connell's fatal weakness, thanks to Ian Kane's inside information on the acting director's inordinate pride in his new building.

"I'm very well, thank you, Professor O'Connell," Magill said smoothly. "I'm delighted to be part of the Hustler team. Dr Kane picked me up at the International Airport. Ms Day showed me to your office. Yes, I've been fed and watered. May I also say that I'm most impressed by the Business School. It's a fantastic space."

The sparrow looked as though he'd laid an ostrich egg. Sideways.

"The building's an abortion!" he squawked. "An architectural abortion! How can you think otherwise? Don't you have eyes in your head, boy?"

The sparrow had morphed into a sparrowhawk, a particularly

mean-tempered sparrowhawk with a chip on its shoulder and an aggressive recessive gene of some kind.

Silently cursing Ian Kane, who'd obviously set him up and was probably in wheezy hysterics at that very moment, Magill struggled on as best he could.

"Can you tell me what my duties are, Professor O'Connell? They weren't made clear to me at the interview and I'm keen to get started. I'm very much looking forward to the challenges ahead." Simon wasn't sure if he could keep up the pretence, though the blast of directorial hostility had done wonders for his sobriety.

O'Connell picked a piece of imaginary fluff from his immaculate sleeve. "Keen to get started, are you? I'm delighted to hear it. There's a group of clothing-industry executives in residence at the minute, on a two-day course. I'm supposed to be running a strategy session with them later this afternoon. But I have a pressing project to attend to. It's only a three-hour session. I'm sure you'll cope admirably. We'll see how that goes and talk about your duties tomorrow."

"I'd love to, Professor O'Connell," Magill bluffed. "But I don't have anything prepared."

O'Connell smiled benignly, knowing full well that his new recruit was incapacitated but also knowing full well that a baptism of fire is the proper price to pay for a belly full of firewater. He wouldn't do it again in a hurry. Not during the working week, that's for sure.

"Oh, I'm confident you'll cope, Simon. Talk to them about sustainable marketing, the stuff you presented at your interview. That went down well."

"But, but, but . . . isn't sustainable marketing somewhat theoretical for practitioners and executives?"

"Somewhat? *Somewhat*? No, not at all. Professor Aherne talks theory to executives all the time. I'm sure she's doing that in Chicago right now. I'm equally sure she'll be most impressed when she hears about your inaugural lecture. She's asked to be kept informed of your progress."

"But . . . but . . . but . . ."

The sparrow had Magill wriggling between its upper and

lower mandibles, and it wasn't going to let go. "Theory and practice are complementary, are they not? There's nothing so practical as a good theory, isn't that what scholars always say? Your theories are excellent, Simon. Or so you claimed in the interview. This is your chance to pitch them at practitioners."

There was no way out. Magill tried a last-ditch defence. "I'm supposed to check into my hotel before 8 p.m., otherwise I lose the room but still have to pay."

O'Connell airily waved the objection away. "May Day will take care of that for you. The clothing-industry session starts at 6.30."

Knowing that the newcomer was cornered, and vaguely remembering the human-resources courses he'd attended, the professor continued in a mollifying manner, "I'd be very grateful if you'd do this for me, Simon. My project is pressing and, as you can see, my time is not my own." He flicked a glance at the wall-mounted, time-management system, which was festooned with so many bright sticky labels that it looked like a Damien Hirst with chickenpox.

Magill capitulated. His time was almost up. The last few grains of sand were streaming through the upper chamber of O'Connell's quarter-hourglass, arguably the ne plus ultra of intimidating executive toys. He had one last gambit.

"I'll do my very best, Professor. Thank you for the opportunity. I'm delighted to help you out with your project. What are you working on, by the way?"

Carlingford O'Connell hesitated for a second. He glanced at his watch. He fiddled. He fidgeted. He flustered. He picked some more non-existent lint from his immaculate Jaeger jacket. He was torn between duty and desire. Desire won, for once. He reached for his hourglass and, with what was clearly a mighty effort of will, turned it over once more.

"Yesssss," Magill thought, mentally punching the air at his modest interpersonal triumph. He'd regained the ground he'd lost thanks to Ian Kane. Just wait till he got his hands on the prankster.

"I'm writing a book about the *Titanic*, Simon."

"The *Titanic*?"

"Well, not just the ship. I'm looking at the phenomenon.

Everything RMS *Titanic* stands for."

"The brand, you mean."

"Exactly!" Professor O'Connell responded eagerly, his tiny body aflutter. "The brand. That's exactly it. The *Titanic* brand extends well beyond the sinking itself. It extends to the movies, the books, the novels, the poems, the songs, the wreck, the memorabilia, the museums, the memorials, the societies, the replicas, the jewellery collections, the tourist attractions, the themed restaurants, the stage shows, the property developments, like the one we have here in Belfast. Did you know that people get married on the *Titanic*? The wedding party descends in a Russian submersible – it takes nine hours – and they exchange vows on the bridge of the shipwreck. Would you credit it?"

"Wow! That's amazing," Magill replied, feigning astonishment. He already knew about aquatic wedding ceremonies. He'd studied them on an experiential-marketing module in Stirling. They were mounted in all sorts of quirky locations: among humpback whales, in shark-proof cages, beside the Great Barrier Reef, on top of sunken Spanish galleons. But O'Connell was expecting astonishment and, as a firm believer in customer orientation, Magill gave him what he wanted.

"Sounds fascinating, professor. But why *Titanic*? I thought the whole story had been raked over from every angle. Done to death, almost." Magill's emergency caffeine infusion was starting to wear off.

"Not the business side. No one's written about the branding angle." O'Connell paused, struggling with the anal personality type's inbuilt reluctance to reveal too much. And then continued. "As you may have heard, Hustler Business School's been stuck with an . . . um . . . unfortunate nickname, on account of its location."

Magill wondered how to play this. Deny all knowledge or own up to his awareness with a sorrowful shake of the head in phoney sympathy? However, he suspected that O'Connell knew he knew about the nickname. "Titanic Business School," the new arrival said noncommittally.

"Exactly. Exactly. I was against this location . . . this building . . . in the first place. *Titanic* has the recognition factor, of course, but from a brand-positioning perspective it's horrendous. The single biggest new product calamity in history. Makes the Edsel look like a triumph. And I don't mean the TR7."

Simon smiled at what he assumed was a petrolhead joke. Another hot button to bear in mind. O'Connell was clearly wearing an anorak under his neatly pressed suit.

The commander-in-geek continued, "How can we expect to tempt executives to a business school with a nickname like Titanic Business School? Or attract MBAs? Or run short courses?"

"It certainly gives a whole new meaning to ice-breaker sessions," Magill replied in a misplaced attempt at jocularity. Even in his less than abstemious state, he could see that he'd misjudged the moment. Ever resourceful, he rushed on before the caffeine evaporated entirely.

"So, that's why you're writing a branding book, Professor O'Connell? To present a positive picture of the sinking, the disaster, the calamity?" Even the combined forces of Max Clifford and Alastair Campbell might have trouble spinning that one, Magill thought, though he sensibly said nothing.

"Exactly. Exactly." O'Connell's tiny frame look set to take off. "My book will show that there are meaningful lessons to be learned from the *Titanic*. Lessons that all managers need to know."

"What, like keeping an eye out for icebergs, Professor?"

"Yes, metaphorical icebergs, yes. Nobody knows what lies ahead in business life, Simon, or life generally. Despite the best efforts of econometricians, computer modellers, trend spotters, futurologists and cool hunters, our powers of prediction are next to nil. Then there's the whole issue of hubris. Companies and CEOs get a bit of success. It goes to their head. They think they're invincible. They think they're invulnerable. They think they're unsinkable. And then they hit an iceberg and drown. Martha Stewart, Steve Jobs, Gerald Ratner, Enron, Andersen, Coca-Cola, Brand America and that man from Barclays Bank who disparaged credit cards – Barrett, wasn't it? They can all learn from the *Titanic*. There's lots of valuable life-lessons in the story, and if my book helps promote Hustler Business School, so much the better."

"Michael Jackson."

"Sorry, Simon?"

"Michael Jackson. Michael Jackson made an album called *Invincible*. Before his fall from grace. He's another example of hubris."

"Did he, indeed? Excellent, excellent. I'll make a note of that. Thank you, Simon."

Magill didn't know which was worse: the Icarus effect of flying too close to the sun, or the begrudging buzzards who pick the bones of fallen idols. Not that he said anything. "What's your book called, Professor O'Connell? *The Unsinkable Brand*?"

"You know, I hadn't thought of that. Good suggestion! I was thinking of calling it *The Selling of the Titanic*. But *The Unsinkable Brand* has a ring to it. Excellent, excellent. Pitcairn Brodie speaks very highly of you, young man, and I can see why. How is the old rogue, by the way?"

"He was working flat out the last time I saw him."

"Pitcairn and I go back a long way. I used to work for him, you know, as a research assistant. A bit like yourself. He was a lot younger then. We all were ... "

Magill smiled politely and, with a quick glance at the hourglass, noted with relief that his time was almost up. O'Connell reached forward and inverted his executive toy once again. Simon's heart sank. He was hoping to get out of O'Connell's clutches and prepare something for the impending executive seminar. However, he'd tapped into the aquifer of O'Connell's obsession, and the gusher couldn't be stopped.

His fixation, it turned out, was the mysteries surrounding RMS *Titanic*. Magill didn't know there were any mysteries. Surely it sailed, it sank, end of story? But no, mysteries there were, as O'Connell elaborated. There was an insurance-scam conspiracy: the suggestion that *Titanic* and its sister ship, *Olympic*, switched places as part of an insurance fiddle by the White Star Line, which was almost bankrupt. *Olympic* was deliberately scuttled in *Titanic's* place, which meant that the wreck at the bottom of the Atlantic was *Olympic*, not *Titanic*.

Then there was speculation over a mysterious first-class passenger, Miss Norton, who wasn't on the official passenger list, yet was picked up by Lifeboat 6. Who was she? A stowaway? The mistress of a first-class roué like Astor or Guggenheim? A cowardly male passenger who disguised himself as a woman in order to get on a lifeboat? Part of the White Star insurance conspiracy? No one knew. She simply disappeared when the survivors were set down in Nova Scotia, and was never seen again.

Strange as the Norton story was, it was only a foretaste of the really weird stuff. The *Titanic*, according to O'Connell, had an additional deck: a secret deck that didn't appear on the blueprints, but contained an extra-secret cargo, something extremely precious that was being transported to the United States. It wasn't treasure, or armaments, or even stolen artworks. It was something much more valuable, something sacred.

Sensing Magill's scepticism, O'Connell explained that the *Titanic* was built during a period of great civil unrest in Ireland, when Home Rule was looking likely and many people in the North – especially business people – were determined to resist, by force if need be. The Ulster Covenant, a protest against the idea of Home Rule, was signed by more than half a million men and women less than four months after the sinking of the *Titanic*. When the ship was being built, what's more, it was known inside the yard as the Ark of the Covenant.

"There's reason to believe that this wasn't a nickname," O'Connell concluded conspiratorially.

"The Ark of the Covenant? On the *Titanic*? No way! Someone's having you on, Professor. Ian Kane, perhaps?"

"It's less far-fetched than it sounds, Simon. Ireland has had strong connections to the Middle East from Celtic times onward. Many Ulster Protestants genuinely believe they're God's chosen people."

"Yes, I'd heard that. But let's get real here . . . "

"Ireland was the seat of western civilisation after the Fall of Rome, and perhaps the safest place to keep the ark. Despite all the blarney about fighting Irish and a violent past, the reality is that Ireland was one of the least troubled places in Europe for hundreds and hundreds of years. Where better to secrete the Holy of Holies? However, back in 1912, when the situation finally seemed to be getting out of hand, the ark had to be moved for safe keeping. And where else would they send it but America, Ireland's home from home?"

For a human sparrow, O'Connell could smile sheepishly on occasion. "That's the conspiracy theory anyway, Simon. What do you think? Should I include it in *The Unsinkable Brand* or not?"

"Include it, professor. Include it. It's not Dan Brown, but it's definitely in the ballpark."

"Why, thank you, Simon. Thank you very much. I'm not a marketer myself, you know. Never had much time for them, to be honest. Always thought they were one step above paedophiles . . . "

"Excuse me?"

"They groom innocent children with TV ads and in-school product placement; they stuff them full of junk food and e-numbers; they're the root cause of all sorts of physical and psychological problems in later life, from obesity to shopaholism. The paedophilic comparison isn't so far-fetched, Simon."

"It's a bit much, though."

"Maybe. Maybe. Until I started work on my branding book, I thought marketers were utterly unregenerate, but I'm starting to appreciate their contribution. We must talk more, Simon. Here's my mobile number. We must talk more."

Chapter Thirteen

A Night to Remember

Simon Magill was exhausted. It had been an extremely long day. The shock of seeing Brodie's mutilated body, the narrow escape from Edinburgh's bent cops, the unforgivably boozy encounter with Ian Kane, the bizarre meeting with "Titanic" O'Connell and the three-hour off-the-cuff seminar on marketing strategy had taken their toll. He just wanted to check into his hotel, have a hot bath and sleep the sleep of the innocent.

Worn to a feeble frazzle, he struggled to open the heavy panel door of the SOS office. It creaked like something out of a *Scary Movie* spoof, which was disconcerting enough in itself, but when the door was jerked open from within, Simon jumped back with a start.

Expecting to see Ian Kane's jolly jowly features, Magill launched into a scatological payback for his colleague's earlier architectural prank. Instead, he encountered the alluring metallurgic physiognomy of May Day. "Oh, God. I'm sorry. So sorry. I thought you were Ian Kane."

She looked at him as if he was demented. Only an eighteen-carat idiot could possibly mistake her for a corpulent, cholesterol-clogged academic with one foot in the grave and the other on a skateboard. "Dr Kane's not here," she said. "He's tied up at present."

"The old rogue!" Magill quipped. It was the best he could manage. The bottom of his *bon mot* barrel was well and truly scraped, and as near to running on empty as makes no difference. "Hope his ticker can take it."

May Day smiled slightly. "Did you say ticker or pecker?" she replied, taking the bantering bait. The Irish, Pitcairn Brodie had informed him back at the Beehive, can't resist a bit of ribald repartee. Celtic catnip, he called it.

"Both, I suppose," Magill said weakly. Seizing the moment, he kept talking. "Look, Ms Day, I'm really sorry about our meeting earlier. I made a complete fool of myself. I'm mortified by my behaviour. I should never have made mock of your ... "

"Don't worry about it. Dr Kane's ... erm ... glad-handing skills are legendary. I've had to deal with much more difficult visitors than you. Compared to drunken old goats braying about the symbology of May Day, Beltane burnings, phallic maypoles and suchlike, you're charm itself, Simon."

She smiled broadly at him. Magill was smitten, her bright-pink bob and facial scaffolding notwithstanding. "Glad to hear it. No, sorry, I'm not glad you've had difficulties, I'm glad they're worse than me. No, what I really mean to say is ... I'm not surprised they hit on you ... "

"I don't recall mentioning being hit on," she laughed.

"No, sorry, what I really mean ... I don't know what I mean, Ms Day!"

"It's May, by the way. Ms Day makes me sound like an old maid."

"Apologies, May. You are so not an old maid. Sorry. Damn. Sorry."

"Forget it, Simon. Let's get you back to your hotel. It's the Malmaison, isn't it? I spoke to them earlier about your late arrival."

"That's the one," he said with relief.

"It's only five minutes away. I'll drop you off on my way home." She smiled broadly once more. Her lips. Her teeth. Her dimples...

Simon Magill felt newly invigorated. Smiles, he inferred, are the world's foremost energy resource. Oil, natural gas and nuclear reactors are as nothing to the smile of a ravishing woman. There's no time like the present, he thought. Seize the day, Simon. "May, could I take you out for a meal sometime? By way of an apology," he quickly added. "And to thank you for the lift . . . for waiting behind . . . for sorting out my hotel . . . for allowing me to share your office . . . for . . ." He was rapidly running out of reasons.

She appraised him carefully with inscrutable emerald eyes. Her bob shook slightly. May Day was completely out of Simon Magill's league. He knew it. She knew it. He knew she knew it. He was gangly, ginger and geekish, with round shoulders and a bowed back from decades hunched over computers. In later life he'd be an orthopaedic goldmine and an optometrist's horn of plenty.

She was something else again.

Simon Magill's heart sank. She's going to laugh in my face, he thought. Hardly surprising, after his idiotic performance earlier.

"Why not?" May Day said lightly. "Let's go to Nick's Warehouse. It's right around the corner. They do an excellent salmon *en croute*. I'll book us a table." She pulled a mobile phone out of the back pocket of her tight, chest-constricting Calvins. Magill's chest, that is.

"What, now? Right now?" he gasped.

May Day snapped the phone shut with a click of the clamshell. "You'd prefer another time? Sure, Simon. Another time it is." The clipped sentences belied her words.

"Now's fine. Now's fine," Magill replied, a tad too readily. He was up for it. Bath and bed could wait. "I'm starving. I've had next to nothing to eat all day."

"Let's go." May Day returned to her desk, switched off the iMac, grabbed her Chloé handbag, slipped on a sleek Chanel jacket and marched out of the former map room, leaving Magill to switch off the lights and close the creaky door behind him.

"May, May, wait a minute," he called, hurrying after her rapidly disappearing figure. "I don't have a key to lock up and my suitcase is in Ian Kane's car."

"Don't need one. And it's not," the Louise Brooks–alike answered over her shoulder, as she sped down the dark oak-panelled corridor and turned left into the soaring foyer, where three stories of vivacious Victorian atrium and 15 plate-glass metres of architectural self-indulgence interfaced uncomfortably.

"We don't lock our offices here," May Day went on. "Trust is paramount in business. That's what the director tells us. So we aren't allowed to lock up."

107

"Don't they trust us enough to decide whether to lock our offices or not?" Magill panted, after a thirty-metre dash to catch up with his colleague.

"Never trust those who talk trust," May Day said cryptically. "A wise man once said that to me."

"And you trust him?" Magill joked.

"I'd trust King Billy with my life," she said softly but forcefully.

"Ah, King Billy. Ian Kane's amigo. When do I get to meet His Majesty? Do you think King Billy knows the whereabouts of my suitcase? What's his telephone extension, 1690?"

May Day stopped dead. They were in the middle of the foyer, a few metres short of the double doors. She turned and looked him up and down, as if in preparation for a devastating put-down. "Your suitcase is in the boot of my car, Simon. Dr Kane stowed it earlier. It's unlikely you'll ever get to meet the King. Billy's the kind of person most people would rather not meet. It'll be no joke if you do run into him, believe me."

Nick's Warehouse, as its name implies, is a former bonded warehouse in Belfast's bohemian Cathedral Quarter, all exposed brick, rusty beams, angled ceilings and open-plan layout. It was quite busy for a Tuesday night, though not so busy that it felt crowded or oppressive. While waiting for their starters to arrive, May Day explained that the University of Hustler was originally called the University of Ulster, but changed its name when Larry Flynt of the eponymous magazine waved a sizeable sponsorship cheque. Finding sponsorship was the name of the game nowadays. O'Connell was apparently working on a Sinéad O'Connor Tonsorial Seminary, a Bob Geldof Diplomacy Centre, the Van Morrison chair of music-industry ethics and, his ultimate ambition, a James Cameron *True Lies* annexe devoted to aliens, terminators and undersea studies.

Having filled him in on the institutional background, May Day turned the conservation to Magill's baptism of fire with the apparel people. "What did you say to them, Simon?"

"I dazzled them with the tripping point, the subject of my marketing dissertation at Stirling."

"I'm afraid you've dazzled me too, Simon. What's the tripping point?"

"Well, a book called *The Tipping Point* came out a couple of years ago . . . "

"Did you say tipping or tripping?"

"Pecker."

May Day contorted her face with an expression that officially said *"Touché,"* but also spoke volumes to a pheromonic twenty-five-going-on-fifteen-year-old like Simon Magill. "Anyway, *The Tipping Point* was a huge bestseller and its author, Malcolm Gladwell, became the toast of the corporate world. His tipping point refers to the moment when fads, crazes, epidemics, new products and so on suddenly take off. It became a bit of a buzzword, used by everyone from marketing researchers to military planners in Iraq."

"Oh, yes, I think I've heard of it. Isn't there a rap album by that name?"

"Yes, I think there is," Magill bluffed, since he was more of a heavy-metal head, though when it came to metal heads, May Day was better equipped than most. "The tripping point is the exact opposite of the tipping point. It's the moment when good goes bad, heroes zero, booms bust, the centre cannot hold and mere anarchy is loosed upon the world."

"Neat turns of phrase, Simon. Are they your own? Apart from the bit you stole from W. B. Yeats? Were the apparel executives impressed by the tripping point?

"Yes, May, to all of the above. Almost all of the above."

"They were impressed, were they?" she said, tongue tantalisingly in cheek. "Standards are obviously slipping on our short courses. Sorry, did I say slipping? I meant tripping."

"I applied it to a bunch of formerly iconic brands that have fallen from favour: Sony, Sainsbury, Ian Schrager Hotels, General Motors, Marks and Spencer . . . "

"M&S was a good choice. I bet that went down well. Marks used to be idolised in Northern Ireland. A lot of their clothing suppliers were based here. Marks's stumble and their ruthless abandonment of the companies that had supplied them loyally for decades hit the community very hard. They're big on loyalty in this part of the world. Marks and Spencer let a lot of people down. It won't be forgotten in a hurry. People forget nothing here."

"Yes, the Marks case generated a lot of discussion. The executives were telling me that, in its desperation, M&S bought all manner of fatuous management bromides sold by fast-buck–making American consultants. And tried to apply them."

May Day raised her hand for silence. "Simon, did anyone ever tell you that you sound just like a marketing textbook?"

"All the time, though it's usually an introduction to marketing rather than an advanced-level text, unfortunately. However, when I'm really cooking, they have been known to compare me to Kate Phillips's *Marketing Management*."

"Wow! My favourite. Which edition?"

"You know it?"

"No, not really. I double as Professor Aherne's PA when she's here, which isn't often. As you probably know, she's in Chicago at the minute, working with Kate Phillips. I made the administrative arrangements for her sabbatical, so I've a pretty fair idea of Kate Phillips's stuff. For a while it was Kate this, Phillips that, *Marketing Management* the other."

"You seem to run the show at HBS," Magill said ingratiatingly. "You keep SOS on track, keep Professor O'Connell on schedule and mastermind Professor Aherne's tours of duty."

"Yeah, well, we run a tight ship at Hustler."

Magill burst out laughing. Two bottles of Chardonnay can do that to a man. "Sorry, May, it's that whole *Titanic* thing. I can't help it."

"Oh, the *Titanic* thing. Don't talk to me about the *Titanic* thing. Actually, it could've been a lot worse. Carlingford wasn't very keen on the Titanic Quarter decision. He wanted the university to acquire a completely different landmark building and refurbish it instead. But our benefactor was adamant. He threatened to withdraw his funding if the other building was chosen. The university capitulated, as it always does." May Day sipped her glass of Chardonnay and gave Simon a look that anticipated his reaction.

He played along. "What was wrong with the other building, May?"

"There was nothing wrong with it, as such. Apart from the fact that it used to be a prison."

"A *prison*?"

"Yes, honestly, a prison. There's a Victorian prison and courthouse complex close to the city centre. Carlingford's grand plan was to refurbish the prison as an executive residential block and turn the law courts into lecture theatres."

"Was he planning breakout rooms as well?"

"Possibly. There's a wonderful underground tunnel that links the, erm, residential and teaching blocks. Professor O'Connell was all for it."

"And what kind of short courses was he planning to run? Accounting for money launderers, competitive drug-dealing strategies, the ethics of white-collar crime, interrogation skills for negotiators, bomb disposal for middle managers, assault-and-battery bonding sessions, baseball bat–assisted brainstorming? Was he working on sponsorship? A Martha Stewart wing, Kenny Lay extension, Ernest Saunders seminar room, Nick Leeson lecture theatre, Robert Maxwell coffee bar, serving bread-and-water specials?"

"Well, the thinking was that because of Northern Ireland's edgy image and the perverse frisson of staying in prison, the facility would give HBS a competitive advantage in the B-school marketplace. I mean, most visitors don't come to Northern Ireland for the weather or the works of art. Many come to get a buzz from the whole conflict thing. Perhaps our most popular tourist attractions, apart from Giants Causeway and Fermanagh Lakeland, are the former trouble spots in west Belfast. The Peace Line. The loyalist murals. You can even take guided tours in police Land Rovers. If you slip a few quid to the local hoods, they'll throw petrol bombs at you. I'm told they do three-for-two special offers."

"Amazing. Amazing. Amazing," Magill said with, well, amazement. "But Professor O'Connell's masterplan didn't come to pass?"

"No, the sponsor wouldn't allow it, and we got stuck with the *Titanic* instead."

"And may God bless all who sail in her."

"That line is usually accompanied by a bottle of champagne, Simon."

"You're right, May, quite right. It's tradition, isn't it?"

"We never mess with tradition round here."

"Full steam ahead, I say."

Chapter Fourteen

The Beuys Are Back in Town

It was the seagulls that interrupted Simon Magill's full-fathom slumber. Their cacophonous cawing was just what he needed the morning after the night before. And what a night that was. After the restaurant, they went clubbing and after the clubbing they went, well, wild.

Well, OK, May Day went wild. Magill held on for all he was worth. Not that he was worth much. The stresses and strains of a long, fraught day had undoubtedly got to him. That's what he told May, and she said she believed him. Not very convincingly, but at least she said it. She also said he wasn't to worry and, truth to tell, he wasn't intending to. He was worried about something else entirely. Why on earth was May Day interested in him? She was so far out of his league that it'd take a two-day hike in seven-league boots to get within hailing distance of the delightful Irish colleen. Punk-rock division. Metalwork squad.

Perhaps she took pity on him. Perhaps she was impressed by his dance-floor impression of a legless giraffe on roller blades. Perhaps she had a thing for gangly ginger junior lecturers. Stranger things have happened. But not many.

Perhaps, he surmised in a moment of duvet-swaddled indulgence, love and hate really are as close as novel writers and movie makers make them out to be.

Perhaps it was all a delicious drunken dream. Time to wake up and, hmmmm, smells like coffee.

"Coffee, Simon?"

"Sounds good, May."

"Bacon, egg and beans, lover?"

"Sounds *very* good! Bacon, egg and beans sounds good as well."

May Day laughed lasciviously, a lovely loud melodious laugh that sounded like an orgasmic xylophone. The seagulls joined in. One of them was sitting on the cast-iron balcony of May Day's impressive apartment, which overlooked the sluggish River Lagan, across the dimpled, dappled cityscape to the rolling hills beyond. It was huge. Enormous. Certainly a herring gull. Possibly an albatross. The apartment was huge too. Palatial. If not quite fit for a king, it was worthy of minor nobility.

"Is Harry giving you a hard time?" May Day shouted over the sizzling and clattering of her skillet.

"Harry? Who's Harry?" Magill said, popping his head around the door of the small yet lavishly appointed kitchen. It was a culinary Christmas tree of hanging pots, pans, casseroles, colanders and assorted catering accoutrements. The pink-haired pixie looked decidedly out of place, though her evident dexterity indicated otherwise.

"Harry, my pet herring gull. He's pretty impressive, isn't he?"

"A herring gull? Is that what it is? I thought it was a screaming harridan trapped in the body of a flying raccoon. With rabies."

"No, lover," she said with a delicious wiggle of her skillet. "Harry's definitely a herring gull."

"You must have a very understanding landlord, that's all I can say. Most people make do with a cat, dog or python."

"I'm not most people, Simon."

"I can see that, May."

"There's no landlord either. This place is mine, all mine. Harry drops by every morning around this time."

"He's a hell of an alarm clock, that's for sure."

"He is that." May Day turned and smiled coyly. She was holding her stainless-steel spatula like an instrument of carnal correction. Magill's heart leapt, as did several other vital organs.

"Better get dressed, lover. This'll be ready in a couple of minutes."

Magill gazed down at his freckled, fuzzy nakedness. Not exactly a sight for sore eyes, especially at 8 a.m., especially in an open-plan kitchen where spitting frying-pans foregather.

"Sausage, Simon?"

"Chipolata, May."

The xylophone's erogenous tone started up again, fortissimo this time. "You said it, lover. Not me."

Magill wandered back through the pristine apartment, wondering how May Day could possibly afford a penthouse with river view. Housing is comparatively cheap in Belfast, they'd told him at the interview. But not *that* cheap, surely. Presumably they paid top dollar for PAs at Titanic Business School. Pity they didn't do likewise with junior lecturers.

His pile of discarded clothing looked strangely appropriate in May Day's minimalist modernist living room. It was as if a Joseph Beuys installation had joined the Barcelona chairs, Chronopak clock, biomorphic coffee table and Mark Rothko reproductions. A brand new B&O Beosound system stood sentinel in the corner, beside the picture window and sun-speckled balcony.

Magill dressed in yesterday's clammy clothes, half wishing he'd repaired to his hotel room instead. But when May Day reappeared bearing a brimming plate of sizzling comestibles, his rampant appetite suppressed all heretical thoughts.

As Simon tucked in, his paramour slipped onto the balcony and began feeding bacon strips to Harry by hand. She held out her arm like a falconer and the massive grey-plumaged, yellow-beaked bird alighted on her wrist to wolf down the bacon rinds. May Day placed one strip in her mouth and leant towards the gourmet gull. Harry plucked the bacon from her lips and made a strange clucking, chuckling sound.

"Gross," Magill called from behind the Tesi dining table, a steel and glass barricade that was sufficient, he hoped, to keep all but the most rabid flying raccoons at bay.

"Oh, I don't know," May Day said, as she swept back into her spectacular apartment. "Herring gulls may seem gross to you – and in many respects they are – but to me they're a perfect metaphor for capitalism, business, marketing, the whole corporate shooting match. They're cruel. They're ruthless. They're noisy. They're belligerent bullies. They scavenge in packs. They devour anything, even their own kind. They can cope in just about any

115

environment. They change their coats according to the prevailing weather ... "

Magill was taken aback by the unanticipated lesson in ornithology. May Day's degree, he'd discovered the previous night, was in European history, with an emphasis on the Age of Revolutions. She never mentioned natural history. Still, her culinary skills more than made up for her scientific shortcomings. Not that he'd ever confess to such Cro-Magnon masculinist attitudes.

"They're ubiquitous, what's more, or used to be. The number of breeding pairs is falling rapidly because herring gulls are so omnivorous that they're picking up all sorts of diseases from rubbish tips and fertilised farmers' fields. If that's not a metaphor for the current state of capitalism, I don't know what is."

"Any chance of more coffee, May?"

"You know where the kitchen is, lover. I'm off for a shower."

Fifteen minutes later, when May Day reappeared freshly scrubbed, freshly scented and freshly wrapped in fluffy towels, Simon Magill's thoughts turned again to breeding pairs, but not of the herring-gull variety. A Beuys revival was on the cards.

"What time are we supposed to be at work?" he inquired suggestively. For a sensitive soul, Simon sometimes lacked subtlety.

"It's my day off, lover," she said with a hint of a glint of a smile. "You're allowed a late start because of yesterday's inaugural lecture. We have to get you to your hotel, though, and you're supposed to be meeting the acting director again later this morning." Her hint of a glint of a smile was accompanied by an almost imperceptible flutter of the eyelashes. There'd be a hurricane in Hong Kong later if chaos theory was to be believed, though Magill was hoping for a tempest in the meantime.

"So we've got some time to kill?" Magill interrupted eagerly.

May Day checked the top tuck of her towel and said "How much time do you need, lover?"

"A couple of hours."

May Day rolled her eyes and pouted.

"An hour?"

Raised eyebrow.

"Thirty minutes?"

Quick glance at the fingernails.

"Fifteen?"

"Chance'd be a fine thing."

"Surely I'm entitled to at least ten, if only to preserve my reputation."

"I pegged you for a 3.411-minute man."

"It's 3.141, May. Don't exaggerate."

In the end, it took four. An all-comers record. Magill felt magnificent. But only for a moment.

"What's up, lover?" May Day murmured. Propped up on a pillow, with bolster behind, she pulled out a packet of Silk Cut Lights.

"Oh, I was just thinking . . . "

She lit up, exhaled forcefully and said, "Don't tell me. You're wondering whether I sleep with everyone on the first date." Dragging deeply on her cigarette, she went on. "Well, I do and I don't. It all depends. If I want a man, I have him. The days of demure damsels, who wait to be asked while preserving their dignity are long gone, lover. Get over it."

"No, no, it's not that," Magill stuttered, suddenly embarrassed by his unreconstructed outlook. "I was wondering why someone as beautiful as you would bother with someone like me."

May Day bowed her head and turned away. Her bob fell forward, covering her perfect pixie pulchritude. "I'm a pretty good judge of character," she said gently. "I've met some nasty pieces of work. You're one of the good guys, Simon. I can tell."

"Yeah, but I'm ginger and freckled. Even my father calls me a geek."

She chuckled, nuzzled into his neck and kissed him lightly on the cheek. "Freckles are cool, lover. Way cool. Didn't anyone ever tell you that?"

"No," he sighed.

"The ginger hair'll have to go, though."

"You're right, May. You're quite right. It's about time I reverted to my natural pink."

She laughed lightly, like wind chimes in a stiff breeze. "I like a man with a sense of humour. I like a man who's sensitive, vulnerable, kind. There's not too many like you, Simon. Not around here, anyhow."

"This building, you mean?"

"Apartment, lover, apartment. There's a real man on the ground floor. Hot, hot, hot. Phew, wot a scorcher."

Magill smirked despite himself. Her emerald eyes were shining. He felt his throat tighten. The laryngitis of lurve. He needed someone to talk to. He desperately wanted to unburden himself. He hardly knew her, but knew her nonetheless. He took a deep breath and, with no advance warning, blurted out the whole Brodie business.

He told her everything. The website work, the Orange Order report, the Beehive imbroglio, the killing of Pitcairn, the corrupt cops, the Order of Solomon, the threatening message on the professor's inert body. He spared her nothing, not even the compasses buried in Brodie's raddled face.

May Day stared at him, stunned. She was completely lost for words. "I'm completely lost for words," she said.

Simon Magill put his head in his hands and rocked back and forth, emitting a low moan. "The whole thing's crazy. It's like something out of Umberto Eco."

"Umberto Eco? The Italian symbologist? What's he got to do with it?"

"*Foucault's Pendulum*, the book. The one where a spoof secret society calls a real one into existence and it kills the spoofers."

"This isn't a book, Simon."

"I know this isn't a book, May. Books usually make sense. This is madness."

"You said it, lover." She smiled wanly.

Magill didn't know where to look. "Sorry, May. Sorry for getting you involved in this. You hardly know me, after all. I should've kept it to myself. It just keeps reminding me of Eco's novel where . . ."

"Forget about Eco!" she snapped. "It's Buonarroti in any event."

118

He stared at her, bemused. "You've lost me, May. Who or what's Buonarroti?"

She sat down beside him, stroked his head gently, kissed him tenderly on the cheek, and explained that Filippo Buonarroti was a nineteenth-century Italian anarchist, a professional revolutionary who invented all sorts of secret societies. The authorities not only believed that the societies existed but concluded that a conspiratorial cabal was plotting to overthrow governments throughout Europe. The more the existence of the cabal was denied, the more widespread it was assumed to be. That was where Eco got the idea for *Foucault's Pendulum*. He based the book on Buonarroti without acknowledging the source."

"You studied this in your degree?"

"Yeah, we did, sort of," she said evasively. "Secret societies played a key part in the Age of Revolutions, and Filippo Buonarroti was a prime mover."

"Is there something you're not telling me, May?"

"Buonarroti was a leading Freemason, Simon. And a member of an Italian branch of the Illuminati."

"As in Dan Brown's *Angels & Demons*?"

"The very same." A heavy sigh of defeat shuddered though May Day's elfin frame. "You're up against the paramilitary wing of the Freemasons, Simon. You're a dead man walking."

"Any chance of a last request? It'll only take 3.14159 minutes."

She laughed. But the xylophone and wind chimes were back in storage. Even Harry the herring gull took off.

119

Chapter Fifteen

The Ascent of Dan

Emer Aherne was confused. She wasn't often confused, but American mores struck her as exceedingly strange on occasion. She had no idea what Serendipity Associates wanted. They must want something, she assumed, because business in America is nothing if not bottom-line–oriented. She liked that. She liked the focus, the drive, the sheer energy of the States. She admired the directness, the show-me-the-money mentality, the lack of the shilly-shallying and endless beating-about-the-Bushmills that prevailed back in Ireland.

So why were Serendipity Associates playing games? What did she have to offer them that they hadn't worked out for themselves? They seemed to have all the Dan Brown bases covered. Surely she had nothing to contribute?

Not that she minded too much. Serendipity Associates' approach had let Aherne add an extra day to her Vegas vacation. She'd never been to Las Vegas before, and she was unlikely to return any time soon. There was still so much she hadn't seen, and the extra day allowed her to cruise the canals of Venice, explore the catacombs of Ancient Egypt, browse the brand-bedecked bazaars of Ancient Rome, stroll along the leaf-carpeted paths of Central Park and watch neo-medieval knights joust amateurishly in King Arthur's tournament. True, the fulfillment of her childhood desire to follow the Yellow Brick Road was stymied when she discovered that the Wizard of Oz theme had long been abandoned by the MGM Grand. But the Elvis impersonators more than made up for it.

Las Vegas, Aherne concluded, was an inferno by day and infernal by night. Much as she enjoyed the experience, while wondering what the nuns who made her childhood such a misery would have thought of the sinfulness on shameless display, the professor was starting to get restless. Chicago was calling her, as was her office at Northwestern, as was her latest research project on that marketing man extraordinaire, the Wizard of Oz himself, L. Frank Baum. The yellow brick road back to Baum's Yellow Brick Road was awaiting her.

Still, she was happy to hear Serendipity Associates out. It was the least she could do since they were picking up her tab, to which she'd added a helicopter ride over the Grand Canyon and nearby Hoover Dam. She'd especially enjoyed her discussions with Yasmin Buonarroti, who had impressed her greatly. As a leisurely evening meal in Delmonico's revealed, they had many things in common. However, she'd be on her way first thing tomorrow, and she could feign politeness in the meantime. SA's angle on Dan Brown had been a real eye-opener too.

"I take it product placement is Serendipity Associates' main area of interest?" she asked Barton Brady. "What other placement deals have you worked on besides Brown?"

"Oh, product placement is just a sideline for us, though we're looking at a range of tie-in merchandise for Michel Houellebecq. It's quite a challenge. Chas is taking the lead on that one. It's his baby. "

Rosencreutz said nothing, his heavy eyes fixed on his endlessly fascinating Palm PDA.

"Our main business," Brady went on briskly, "is ideas. In essence, we're an R&D facility for management fads, a hotshop for hot concepts like the Vitruvian Brand. We also offer an acronyms foundry facility."

The Irishwoman looked a bit bemused, not to say completely baffled. "Forgive my ignorance, Barton," she said, "but an acronym foundry facility? What's that when it's at home?"

Brady responded with a blank stare that even his years of schmoozing couldn't disguise. He was frankly amazed that Aherne had never heard of AFFs. Clearly, Irish professors were much, much further behind the curve than he thought. Ever the glad-hander, however, he patiently informed his guest that acronyms were very big business. Every organization WIS (worth its salt) needs TLA (three-letter acronyms) to MAB (make a buck) in today's FMW (fast-moving world), though they're VSL (very short-lived), NTP (not that profitable) and TBH (to be honest) a WOT (waste of time).

"WIN," Aherne smiled.

"Pardon?"

"Well I never."

Brady didn't get the joke, or if he did, he didn't like it very much. Acronyms were a serious matter. He stalked over to the full-length plate-glass window of his company's beautifully appointed conference room, and gazed towards Fremont Street, the original commercial focus of Las Vegas, and a kind of anti-Strip where the city's hard-core gaming was concentrated.

"Acronyms," he huffed, "make the business world go round. CEOs can't live without them. They're the crack-cocaine of corporate life. And we're the principal pushers. That's why we set up the Acronyms, Acrostics, Anagrams, Ambigrams and Analogous Alliterative Affectations Agency. A8, for short."

"Ah, I see," Emer Aherne said cautiously, "I see. I see where I fit in. You've set your eye on CODE, my modest Dan Brown acronym. You liked my marketing code construct. Is that what this is about?"

"No, no, not at all," Brady syrupped. "I think we've used CODE before. Trademarked it, in fact." He tore himself away from the fascinations of Fremont Street, turned to face the room, forced a tiny smile and raised an eyebrow at Rosencreutz.

"Creative Organisation Development Experiences," Rosencreutz announced in a gruff Noo Joisy accent. His heavy features suggested second-generation Germanic stock and inordinate fondness for his adopted city's culinary specialty: all-you-can-eat buffets. He sat immobile, protuberant eyes fixed on his petite Excel-equipped hand-held. "Two-day training programme. Sold to 36 companies, including Apple, DreamWorks, Oracle and GM. Total revenue to date, $2.5 million."

Brady took his seat at the oval rosewood table, spread his immaculately manicured hands across its gleaming top, and gave the guest a couple of generous gigawatts. "We've worked out the CODE, Professor Aherne. But your conference paper was so

123

fascinating and so full of ideas that I want my top team to hear it for themselves. If you don't mind."

The conference room's Sony projector and Vaio laptop were cleared for take-off. Brady pressed a button beneath the table. The louvre blinds closed automatically, the drapes slid together across the polished parquet floor, and a giant screen descended from a concealed recess in the ceiling. Silence descended too.

Professor Aherne went through her well-rehearsed routine. She'd delivered the *Da Vinci Code* presentation on four previous occasions: at the American Marketing Association conference two days earlier, at Northwestern University two weeks beforehand, and twice on the academic conference circuit, at Wharton and Columbia. She planned to do it a few more times before her sabbatical was over, but she acted as if this were the first performance, and her life depended on it. Which in a strange way it did.

Twenty-two minutes later, Aherne's razzle-dazzle presentation rose to its resounding climax:

> However, a code without a well-trained operator is useless, and Dan Brown is a very well-trained, very astute operator. He is what I call an "authorpreneur," a writer with an exceptionally strong sense of what the market wants. Charles Dickens, Mark Twain, L. Frank Baum, Edgar Rice Burroughs, Norman Mailer and, of late, J. K. Rowling all qualify as authorpreneurs.
>
> Dan Brown is an authorpreneur and a half.
>
> He has discovered, dare I say it, the Holy Grail of modern marketing, the commercial chalice that contains the secret of business success, the conceptual vessel that enables him to stand out from a crowd of nearly identical and, in certain respects, superior products. Brown has discovered that marketing aspires to the condition of literature. Just as great books suspend readers' disbelief, so too great brands suspend consumers' disbelief. Today's marketing-savvy consumers disbelieve everything marketers say, and the key to superior performance is making them willingly suspend that disbelief. That's what great books do. That's what great brands do.
>
> Dan Brown suspends our disbelief and then some. His books are not only about the Holy Grail, but in a world where consumption has replaced religion as the predominant ideology, they are the Holy Grail.

124

Ten hands clapped in appreciative unison as the drapes pulled back, the screen withdrew and the conference room flooded with fierce Las Vegas light.

"What, no CRAP this time, Emer?" Brady joked.

Chang and Eng stared at each other askance, wondering what was going down. Rosencreutz returned to his PDA, though even he had applauded the visitor loudly in an uncharacteristic burst of enthusiasm.

"No CRAP, Barton. That wasn't one of mine. I'm strictly a CODE girl. The crap came from someone in the audience, though I fully endorse the sentiments expressed. Don't tell me Serendipity Associates is interested in CRAP. Please don't tell me Chauvinist, Reactionary, Androcentric and Patriarchal is one of yours." She could tease too when necessary.

"CRAP's one of our bestsellers, Professor Aherne. You can't have too much CRAP in management consultancy. Right, Chas?"

Without so much as a upward glance from his handheld, SA's lugubrious consigliere said, in a monotone that made Stephen Hawking sound expressive, "Corporate Revitalisation Advice Programme. Sold to Hilfiger, Boeing, McDonald's. ImClone, Enron, Tyco, Martha Stewart, Marks and Spencer and more. Five million dollars and counting."

Brady smiled broadly and fiddled with the cuffs of his bespoke Turnbull & Asser. The Cartier cufflinks twinkled. "As I said, Emer, you can't have too much CRAP in management consultancy. You should try it some time. Cut yourself a slice of CRAP, Professor Aherne."

Aherne felt a little disconcerted as it started to dawn on her how much money she could be making in the real world if she put her mind to it. "Forgive me, Barton," she said regretfully, "but I'm still not quite sure why you've brought me here. It's awfully nice to meet you, every one of you, and it's fascinating to hear how you're developing the Dan Brown brand. However, if you've got Dan tied up and if you've got CODE covered and if you're . . . pardon my French . . . full of CRAP, why do you need me? I don't think I've got anything for you."

"Why, guys?" Brady said smoothly, looking directly at Chang and Eng, the disparate twosome at the creative heart of Serendipity Associates.

"Authorpreneur!" Eng exclaimed.

"Authorpreneur!" Chang repeated.

"Authorpreneur," Yasmin Buonarroti cut in, "would make a wonderful addition to our suite of corporate offerings. It could be a real goldmine." She glanced at her colleagues, and sensing their approval, continued. "It could, if we're lucky, be on a par with Step Away From the CSR, Talk to the Hand Brands, Dude, Where's My CRM?, No-Shit Money-Shot Killer Apps, and possibly, just possibly, Attila the Hun Reengineering."

Brady nodded sagely and added, "Personally, I reckon it might be right up there with Genghis Khan Globalisation, maybe even Vlad the Impaler Downsizing."

Aherne didn't quite know what they were talking about. Step Away From the CSR and Dude, Where's My CRM? were new to her, though she also knew that the world of management consultancy was nothing if not wacky, quirky, fad-driven. "I can't imagine the market for authorpreneurship programmes would be very big. Surely there's no way SA could make much money out of it?" she said. "We're not talking CRAP here, let alone CODE."

Brady stood up and strolled over to the window again. He checked out the panoramic view he'd seen thousands of times before, although his pose was primarily designed to impress the middle-aged yet well-preserved Irish visitor.

"Oh no, Emer," he said. "You're quite wrong. Everyone's a writer. Everyone's got a novel in them. Any fool can write a novel. But it takes real genius to sell them. SA sells the selling. That's what we do. The market's huge. Authorpreneur's like the Klondike for Serendipity Associates. Once we wrap the idea up in a pretty package, it'll make us an absolute fortune. Trust me."

Having captured Professor Aherne's attention with the promise of untold riches, Barton Brady used all his charisma to close the sale. He sat down in the empty seat beside her, looked her directly in the eye and said emphatically, "But it's not authorpreneur we're really interested in."

"It's the suffix!" chimed Chang and Eng simultaneously.

"The suffix is the goldmine!" Chang laughed.

"A bonanza!" Eng added.

Invigorated, the two creatives started rattling off -preneur possibilities, each trying to outdo the other.

"Bankerpreneur, doctorpreneur, preacherpreneur," Eng cried.

"Butcherpreneur, bakerpreneur, lawyerpreneur," Chang chipped in.

"Actorpreneur, composerpreneur, curatorpreneur."

"Professorpreneur, rapperpreneur, gangsterpreneur."

"Gangstarapperpreneur."

"Gamblerpreneur."

"Pusherpreneur."

"Hookerpreneur."

"Enough. Enough, guys. Enough!" said Brady, laughing and looking at Aherne. See what you're getting yourself into, Professor?"

She laughed and answered in kind. "Brady Bunch, you say, Barton? Crazy Gang, if you ask me!"

"Get out while the going's good, Emer," Buonarroti joked.

Chapter Sixteen

Babbling Brooks

Like many postcoital conversations, Simon Magill and May Day's pillow-talk soon descended to the ins and outs of the Marquis de Sade. Not the libidinous behaviours of libertine legend, nor the erotomane's sadly overshadowed philosophical system, but rather the famous sadist's dalliance with Freemasonry. May Day was finding it difficult to accept Magill's woeful ignorance of matters masonic. His innocence in the ways of the underworld almost defied belief.

Appalled by her lover's apparent lack of common sense, she pulled on a Ralph Lauren dressing gown, perched on an Alvar Aalto chair beside the bedroom's picture window, and, staring out across the steepled cityscape, lit up another Silk Cut Light. Exhaling, she said one thing was for certain: the Freemasons were behind Brodie's murder. It had all the hallmarks of a masonic hit. The compasses, the pocketful of masonry, the lank hank of rope – called a cable tow, apparently – the Roberto Calvi connection, the incision on Brodie's dead body, even the names of the policemen pointed to the Masons. Cowan and Sinclair were masonic surnames, it seemed.

The assassination, she admitted, might have been made to look like the work of the Brotherhood, a crude attempt to impugn the craft, but as UK police forces are known to be riddled with Masons as well as the Brotherhood's sister organisations, the likelihood was that the Edinburgh police force was involved.

"You think the Order of Solomon is a masonic offshoot of some kind, May? An assassination squad?"

"I've never heard of the Order of Solomon, Simon, though I do know that King Solomon's Temple is an important part of the Freemasons' back story. The connection was concocted in the mid-

129

eighteenth century, though some Masons claim that the craft's roots go back to the twelfth century and the Knights Templar."

May Day dragged hard on her Silk Cut and, seemingly fascinated by something on the ceiling, exhaled wearily. "The full name of the Knights Templar is the Order of the Poor Knights of Christ and the Temple of Solomon."

"Snappy brand name," Magill said grimly. "But what I can't understand is why the Freemasons would want to kill Brodie and threaten me. The Orange Order I can understand, especially in light of that report, but why wait thirty years to do the dirty deed?"

"Wake up, Simon," May Day barked with disbelief. "Pitcairn Brodie *must* have been a Freemason. He held his farewell party in the Beehive, for goodness sake. How much more of a symbological statement do you need?"

"Come again?"

"The beehive is a prominent masonic symbol. It represents the Brotherhood's ideal of working together diligently as a group, for each other, on behalf of indoctrinated insiders and against interfering outsiders. In the eighteenth century, masonic lodges were called 'hives' and the meetings were known as 'swarms.' If the Beehive was one of Robbie Burns' favourite watering-holes, as you say, that fits in perfectly. Burns was one of the foremost Freemasons of his time. The Scottish Rite is central to the Brotherhood's entire belief system. Scotland has long been a masonic hotbed. That's one of the reasons the Orange Order's so well-established there. The Orange Order's lodge structure is lifted straight from Freemasonry, as are its rituals, secret signs, initiation ceremonies and degree structure. The Royal Black Preceptory also traces its origins back to the Knights Templar, as the name of its topmost degree indicates. It's called Red Cross, Simon. Red Cross. The Knights Templar are the fabled knights of the rosy cross and Ulster's so-called Blackmen are its avatars."

Magill shook his head with astonishment. "So, you're saying the Order of Solomon is part of the Orange Order and the Orange Order is the military wing of the Freemasons?"

"Musical wing, more like. An extremist strain, admittedly. Orangemen are the mujahideen of Freemasonry. As for the Orange

Order of Solomon, I've never heard of it. Sorry."

"But why would they wait thirty-odd years to take their revenge? It doesn't make sense."

"Something must have triggered the assassination, Simon."

"Paspi. It can only be Paspi. I mean, Jesus, they carved it on his head, which is one hell of a message-board. How on earth did they find out about Paspi? What was posted on it that required such extreme prejudice?"

"Well, finding out about it can't have been a problem," she said with irritation, and not a little exasperation. "You of all people should know that. Once something's posted on the web, the world and his wife can get access to it. Or in this case, the world and his widow's son."

"Widow's son? I don't understand. Brodie's widowed mother died years ago. His ex-wife remarried and lives in Perth. His boys are in Australia, as far as I know."

" 'Is there no help for the widow's son?'" May Day whispered, as if fearful she'd be overheard. "It's a masonic cry for assistance, Simon, the Brotherhood's equivalent of SOS. Did you ever hear Professor Brodie say anything about widow's sons?"

"Not to my knowledge."

"Did your website ever feature anyone with masonic connections?"

"I don't know," Magill said curtly. "People don't usually boast about their connections to Freemasonry."

"Well, if Brodie was a Freemason, it's a fair bet many Freemasons featured on the site. They always promote their own kind. Can you remember any of them?"

Magill rubbed his temples, trying to recall inflated Egos of the Week and the innumerable Paspi postings on prominent self-publicists. He ran through a list of those he could remember – Buffalo Bill, W. C. Fields, Florenz Ziegfeld, Henry Ford, Benjamin Franklin, General Douglas MacArthur, General Tom Thumb – and it was clear from May Day's expression that they were all famous Freemasons, as were Cagliostro, Casanova, Oscar Wilde, Jacob Astor, George M. Cohan, Cecil B. de Mille, Chuck Hilton, André Citroën, William Lever and Jack Cohen of Tesco, as indeed were

Robbie Burns, Adam Smith and Sir Walter Scott.

"Surely to God you knew that Walter Scott was Scotland's big Chief Freemason, Simon? Everybody knows that. It looks as though you were running a website dedicated to famous Freemasons. And you'd no idea? Jesus, Simon. Haven't you read Dan Brown?"

"Of course I have! I've read all his books. But they're fiction, thrillers, a bit of innocent fun. They make sense, what's more. This is completely crazy, May. This is real."

"The Masonic Brotherhood *is* real, Simon. All too real. And they're not crazy. Ruthless, yes. But crazy? Categorically not."

Simon Magill's world was imploding by the minute. What little sense of stability he'd retained after yesterday's awful events was evaporating rapidly. "I had no idea, May. I didn't think. It's too far-fetched. I knew nothing about Paspi's masonic links. You'll be telling me Sir Thomas Lipton was a Freemason next."

Staggered, May Day stared at him. Her pink bob shook sorrowfully from side to side. "Sir Thomas Lipton? The Lipton's tea person? The Ulsterman? The guy who represented the Ulster Yacht Club in its Americas Cup challenges?"

"That's the one," Magill said, with a bravado he didn't feel.

"Oh yes, Simon, he was a heavy-duty Freemason. I'm pretty sure he was in the Orange Order too. I thought that was common knowledge. It is round here. What's he got to do with any of this? I take it he was posted on the website as well?"

"Yes, he was. And I'm planning to do a PhD on him."

"So you're doing a doctorate on someone and you don't even know about his connections to the Craft? God help us."

"Well, I do at least know that he was from Scotland, not Northern Ireland."

"Whatever, Simon. It's the same difference. They're not called Ulster-Scots for nothing."

"What does it matter, anyway?" Magill retorted. "Lipton's masonic links aren't relevant to marketing."

May Day stubbed out her cigarette viciously. "Not relevant? Is your head cut? The business world runs on secret handshakes, insider deals, smoke-filled rooms, old-boy networks. The Fortune

500 is a back-scratching brotherhood, or as near as makes no difference. Management consultants are mafiosi by another name. Haven't you heard of the Kotler Nostra? I meet and greet them every day, Simon. They ebb and flow through Titanic Business School. I'm no marketing expert, but even I can see that there's not much difference between Masons and marketers."

Infuriated, Magill couldn't keep the irritation out of his voice. "At least marketing hasn't killed anyone."

"Oh, you think these heavily promoted cigarettes aren't going to kill me? You think the incessantly marketed junk food Ian Kane shovels into his face isn't going to kill him? You think the environmental resources being squandered by consumer society won't be the death of us all? The Freemasons aren't as far from the free-gift givers as you seem to think, Simon."

"Get a grip, May," Magill snapped.

"No, you get a grip! Let me ask you a question. What is marketing *really* about?"

"Customer satisfaction, care, delight, relationships . . . "

"Talk sense. It's about selling stuff. That's the height of it."

"There's much more to it than that, May. You just don't understand. You haven't paid enough attention to Kate Phillips. On my marketing course . . . "

"Sorry, Mr Big-Shot Marketer, you're right. There is more to marketing than selling stuff. It's also about money and power. Money and power, Simon. You can wrap marketing up in whatever you like – customer coddling, service quality, long-term relationships, the exchange paradigm – but it all boils down to money and power. And when it comes to money and power, the Freemasons are the undisputed heavyweight champions of power plays and money matters. Wake up, Simon. You're sleepwalking your way to an early grave."

Magill took a deep breath. "The thing I don't get, May, is how you know all this stuff. How come you're an expert on the secret life of Freemasons? How come you know more about Sir Thomas Lipton than I do?"

"This may come as a surprise to you, Simon," she snarled, "but marketing academics aren't the only source of knowledge in the world. They like to think they are, but most marketing scholars don't know shit from Shinola, or Shinola from semolina, for that matter. That's what marketing practitioners tell me, anyway, and I interact with them every day. Why do you think they never read your books or your articles, or take the managerial implications of your research on board? Academia is completely out of touch. Nobody reads your stuff. Nobody's interested in what you have to say."

"I didn't mean it like that, May. With no PhD and one day on the job, I hardly qualify as a marketing scholar. I'm just curious that you're so well informed about Freemasonry. That's all. Are *you* a Mason, May?"

"No women members, lover," she said, drumming her fingers on the pack of Silk Cut, as if wondering whether to have another or not. "Freemasonry is the last bastion of male chauvinism. It's boys with toys territory. Aprons, mallets, ropes, regalia, secret hand-shakes, extra-secret codewords, rolled-up trousers, bare chests . . . it's cross-dressing boys with toys. Half-naked cross-dressing boys with toys."

"Pretty dangerous toys, if you ask me," Magill replied. "May, you still haven't told me why you're so knowledgeable about cross-dressing toyboys."

"I told you earlier, Simon. I studied it as part of my degree course. Ian Kane's also heavily into that stuff. He's a secret-society spotter, a conspiracy theory collector. He goes on about the Rosicrucians all the time. I share an office with him, remember. I have to listen to it day in, day out."

She extracted another Silk Cut and, with a what-the-hell shrug, lit up. She stared at the bedroom ceiling. "Plus there's a family connection."

The penny dropped.

"A family connection? Of course, a family connection. Now I get it. That's just great, May. You're connected to the people who are killing the Paspi. Was *this* all part of the set-up?"

"All what?" she said, with an icy intonation that, if not quite at absolute zero, was well below freezing.

"All this. Last night. Us."

"Bastard! How dare you suggest that? What do you take me for?" She stalked across the room, eyes blazing, grabbed Magill by the hair, pulled his head back with all her strength and hit him hard on the left cheek. "Get out of here!" she shouted. Right now!"

Magill rubbed his face slowly. Christ, it was sore. "Yes, maybe I should do that, May." He dressed hurriedly and pulled on his coat, before turning back to face her. She was standing by the picture window staring into the distance, but sensed his hesitancy.

"Don't waste your breath, Simon. You've said enough. Your suitcase is in the back bedroom. It's five minutes' walk from here to your hotel. Head along the river walk and cross Queen's Bridge. The Malmaison's on your right, opposite the police station. You've got a 10 o'clock meeting with Professor O'Connell."

"Let me guess, O'Connell's an Orangeman too."

"Hardly. He's descended from Daniel O'Connell, the great nineteenth-century liberator of Ireland. He's about as far from Orangeism as is possible in this place."

"At least that's something."

"Daniel O'Connell was a prominent Freemason, though. Orangeism and Freemasonry aren't synonymous, Simon."

"Great. That's just great." He slammed the door behind him.

Chapter Seventeen

Kane and Babel

Ian Kane was firmly ensconced in the Hustler Business School refectory when Simon Magill joined him, showered 'n' shaved 'n' spit 'n' polished, but feeling somewhat rough after his night to remember. He'd been hit by an iceberg, and though he hadn't quite gone down with the ship, May Day's chipolatas had left his innards in a mutinous state.

The same couldn't be said of Dr Kane, who was tucking into a gargantuan gourmandean greasefest. He obviously had some kind of barter arrangement with the Northern Ireland agri-food industry. He supplied telling tales and succulent stories in return for the sector's entire output, plus top-up supplies from the Irish Republic and further afield.

Magill sat down, sipped on an extra-strength shiver-me-timbers espresso, and peered briefly through the sheet-glass prow, where dark rain-bearing clouds were gathering behind Black Mountain. "Bastard!" he said to his chomping companion. "Thanks for the inside information on O'Connell's architectural preferences. You might have told me he was a jailhouse rocker at heart."

Kane almost exploded with laughter. It was lucky he didn't, since his mouth was full to bursting. However, his tiny swinish eyes did a jovial Irish jig. *Riverdance*, almost. He chewed vigorously, dewlap chorus line wobbling with exertion. After much exaggerated mastication, accompanied by a facial-expression performance of the I'm-keen-to-talk-but-not-with-my-mouth-full variety, he grunted merrily, "Happy to be of assistance, Simon. Don't hesitate to call SOS if you need any further organisational orientation."

The prankster unleashed his trademark pig-in-shit smile. Pig shitting gold bullion briquettes, more like. "I hear you had quite a night last night," he said, evidently anticipating a massive spill of beans from the new kid on the B-school block.

Much as he liked his chunky-going-on-corpulent companion, Magill wasn't inclined to confess all. Or even a little. Not when his new-found friend might be a leading member of the funny-handshake, rolled-up-trouser brigade.

"Yes, Ian, your colleague May Day took good care of me."

"I bet she did. Lifted and laid?"

"Lifted," Magill said firmly. "She gave me a lift to my hotel. It was very decent of her to wait for so long."

"I hear Nick's Warehouse does a fine salmon *en croute*, with Moët & Chandon to go."

Wondering how on earth Kane had found out where and what they'd eaten, Magill replied noncommittally, "Bet you've truffled there once or twice."

"I've truffled everywhere, Simon. And more than once or twice. I'm the truffle-hound of Hustler, don't you know. Can't you tell by my svelte figure? You don't get a body like this by stinting on the foie gras, crème caramel or apple sauce."

"Apple orchards, if you ask me. Herds of cattle, fields of grain, lorryloads of Guinness . . . "

Wiping the grease from his rubicund chins, Kane accepted the admonition with grace while complaining bogus-bitterly, "You sound like my doctor, Simon."

"Is he still talking to you?"

"She is. But she's getting testy."

"I bet she is."

"Tests for this. Tests for that. Tests for the other," Kane chortled contentedly. "Tests for every ailment known to man. And some that aren't . . . "

Magill could sense where the conversation was going and he tried to head it off at the pass, so to speak. "Enough already, Dr Kane!"

"I still haven't told you about my colonic irrigation experiences, Simon."

"I'd prefer to defer that one, thanks all the same."

138

A moment's silence descended as the budding bosom-buddies processed their budding bosom-buddiness. It was time, Magill thought, to address the question that had been bothering him since May Day's outburst. But he was uncertain how best to raise the subject. "I hear you're a Freemason, Ian," was perhaps a bit too direct, bearing in mind what Masons were capable of.

"Talking of doctors, Dr Kane, I was wondering about your background. Where did you do your PhD? Here at Hustler? Is it in storytelling? Are you a lapsed literary theorist? A reengineered historian? Or do you have a doctorate in business narratology? Is there such a thing?"

Kane smiled mischievously. He looked like a cheeky nine-year-old wearing blubbery body armour over a fat-suit prosthesis on top of a Michelin Man costume. "Questions, questions, questions," he pseudo-sighed. "Be still, my beating heart." He clutched his chest dramatically. "It is still beating, isn't it?"

"Nineteen to the dozen, I suspect."

Kane suddenly turned serious and adopted a grave expression. "MIT," he said. "My PhD's from MIT."

"Holy shit! MIT?"

"Yes, Simon," Dr Kane said modestly, "MIT. But I don't like to talk about it."

"Why ever not? Academia's no place for humility. MIT? I'd never have guessed."

With an affronted expression, Kane retorted tartly, "What? Don't I look like an MIT-ite?"

"No, no, it's not that," Magill stuttered apologetically. "Not that at all. It's in quantum theory, presumably?"

Mollified, Kane went on, "Glad to hear it, Simon. Because I reckon I've got Midlothian Institute of Theosophy written all over me."

"Midlothian Institute of Theosophy?" Magill let out a howl of laughter that turned heads in the rapidly filling cafeteria. An early-morning crowd was gathering, mainly apparel-industry executives on the last day of their strategic planning course. Several had waved to Magill, who'd waved back amiably. They looked as though they'd been studying late into the night. Studying menus

139

in local restaurants, studying price lists in neighbourhood bars and studying lap dancers in nearby nightclubs. Their clotted voices echoed across the airy atrium, which was splendidly Victorian at one end and B&Q greenhouse at the other. A lattice of steel staircases criss-crossed in front of the curtain-glass proscenium. Ascending and descending figures were silhouetted against the rain-bearing sky beyond, as Hustler Business School got into gear for the day.

"MIT," Kane confirmed with due solemnity. "As far as the university's concerned, I've got a doctorate from MIT. That's what I put on my CV. That's what got me the job. It's not my fault if they don't check qualifications properly."

"Midlothian Institute of Theosophy?" Magill chuckled, sipping his espresso. "I've never heard of it. And I thought I knew most of the institutions of higher education in Scotland."

"Oh, it's not an institution." Kane's porcine features lit up. "It's an online degree factory. You choose your subject and pay your fee, and they send you a fancy diploma. You can even buy robes and mortar boards and stuff. Bespoke. You choose your own design and colour schemes. With or without ermine trim. You couldn't beat it, Simon."

"Beats the hell out of a 100,000-word thesis, that's for sure. Are they still in operation? Not that I'd dream of following your scholarly strategy, Dr Kane. What's their phone number again?"

Kane put down his knife and fork. "Simon," he said semi-seriously, "I'm a storyteller. I sold a story to the university. They bought it. I practise what I preach. They haven't complained. SOS's clients get value for money, I've suspended disbelief, and that's what storytelling's all about."

"But what happens when the university suspends its suspension of disbelief? Does it suspend you?"

"Then I sell them another story, Simon. One set in Shit Creek Canoe Club. The day the paddle delivery lorry didn't get through."

"A thriller, then," Magill laughed. "What's MIT's number again, Ian? Do they have a website? Just out of curiosity, you understand."

"They shut up shop, sadly. Theosophy's out of fashion. These days it's all Kabbala, scientology, magick, Wicca, Zen. Anything esoteric, basically. Theosophy's too mainstream. Madonna and Tom Cruise have a lot to answer for."

"Dan Brown too," Magill added, seizing his chance to steer the conversation in the direction he wanted. "His books have really opened the floodgates on all that offbeat, conspiracy-theory, who-shot-JFK, Elvis-is-living-in-sin-with-Bigfoot kind of thing."

Ian Kane looked shocked, stunned almost. "Elvis and Bigfoot are an item? Damn! I should've guessed. 'I want to be your teddy bear' is a dead giveaway, come to think of it."

"Unfortunately, his feet are too big for blue suede shoes," Magill continued, sensing an Elvis-quip contest in the offing.

But Ian Kane demurred, uncharacteristically refusing to rise any further to this King-sized bantering opportunity. Instead, he glanced around the restaurant, fiddled nervously with his knife and fork, and with the stricken look of a heavy smoker in a smoke-free restaurant, muttered malignly, "Dan Brown's a chancer. His books are bullshit. He knows nothing about conspiracy theory. He's not even a good storyteller."

"Don't diss the Danster, dude," Magill replied lightly. "Forty million copies sold says you're wrong."

"The Danster, as you call him," Kane hissed, "is drawing attention to things that shouldn't be attended to."

"What things?"

Kane hesitated, shook his head, reluctant to say more. "I need a smoke, Simon. Let's go outside. You could do with some fresh air before you meet the director."

"Ten o'clock, isn't it?"

"Yes, but not in his office. He's at the Ulster Folk and Transport Museum today. You can take a train from Central Station. He's working on his . . . um . . . current project."

"*Titanic*, you mean?"

"He told you, did he?" Kane asked, a smidgen of surprise in his resonant voice.

"Yes. Amazing stuff about the conspiracy theories. I never knew. Bet you did, though."

Kane remained silent as he wheezed across the echoing atrium and pushed through the double glass doors where the cafeteria spilled onto the riverside patio during the sunny summer months. It was empty today, apart from a furtive picket-line of smokers on either side of the entrance. He led the way to a nautically themed fountain, a full-size funnel spouting gouts of icy water. Magill could taste the salt on his chilled lips. A cold wind was blowing in from Belfast Lough, indicative of a storm brewing.

Cannonball Kane perched inelegantly on the Mourne granite ledge of the striking water feature, upwind of the eruptions. *"Titanic* had a dummy funnel, Simon. Only three of them worked. The fourth was a fake. The conspiracy theories are bullshit. O'Connell's wasting his time. He's out of his depth."

"That's never stopped conspiracy nuts, Ian. I bet Dan Brown's working on a *Titanic* conspiracy novel as we speak."

"No, he's not," Kane growled. "He's writing a book about the Freemasons. It's set in Washington DC. *The Solomon Key*, I think it's called."

"Really?" Magill replied. "How do you know that? Let me guess. You're Dan Brown's storytelling consultant. Dan Brown's a pseudonym of yours. You're the Danster!"

Kane smiled briefly. "Close, but no cigar, Simon. We're twins, actually. Separated at birth. He was raised in the lap of American luxury, I was raised by feral Irish wolfhounds in the miasmic mires of County Antrim."

"Not identical twins, I take it."

"Nah, he's not as pretty as me." Chuckling, Kane sucked heavily on his cigarette, which he'd managed to light after three windswept attempts. "I read about his book on craft.com, a Freemason website. I'm quite interested in the Brotherhood. The Freemasons, that is." He glanced at Magill, sizing him up. "Purely theoretically. I'm not a Mason myself. Wouldn't want to be. It's the storytelling aspect that intrigues me. The mystery, the history, the myth, the fact that so many crazy cryptic stories seem to attach themselves to the Craft."

Magill felt a sudden urge to tell his own masonic story, a story that was nothing if not crazy, cryptic, mysterious. But he hesitated.

Something about Kane's demeanour suggested that the time wasn't right for revelations. Ian had enough on his well-piled plate, by the look of it. His normally open face was a mask of inscrutability. He was staring into the fountain in silence. For a perennially jovial individual, he looked like the happy bunny waiting for the results of its myxomatosis test.

"What's up, Dr Kane?" Magill inquired in his best bedside manner. "Cat got your tongue sandwiches, fritters, risotto, ragout, stew . . . ?"

Kane looked wryly at Hustler's latest recruit. His eyes had lost their usual sparkle. "Murder, Simon," he murmured.

"Pardon?"

"Death," he said dully.

"Excuse me?"

"Slaughter of the innocent," he whispered.

Magill stared at his new colleague, flabbergasted by the turn the conversation had suddenly taken.

"Come with me, Simon," Kane sighed. "I want to show you something. I'm going to tell you a secret. It won't take long."

Chapter Eighteen

Buy One, Get One Freemason

Less than five minutes after its high-speed departure from the Hustler Business School car park, Ian Kane's Range Rover pulled into a grimy multi-storey on the edge of central Belfast. The mismatched pair, like a latter-day Laurel and Hardy, made their stately waddling way down several narrow alleys and across a couple of inner arterial roads still sclerotic with rush-hour traffic to a quirky pedestrianised square surrounded by four-storey buildings, mainly Victorian or Edwardian interspersed with unhappy postwar intrusions.

"Let's grab another coffee," Kane said, with a weak-kneed wheeze. "Then I'm going to test your powers of observation."

A sizeable Starbucks occupied one corner of the square, its green logo glaring malevolently at every other coffee shop in the vicinity. Five minutes later, the elephantine man and his elongated companion were sipping espressos at an outside table, watching crowds of office workers scurry past, eyes fixed straight ahead, iPods in place.

"This is Arthur Square, Simon, or Cornmarket as it's known locally. It was the original commercial core of the seventeenth-century city. Belfast Castle was just behind us, where Bhs is now. The docks and wharves lay beyond the buildings opposite. The Custom House sat on that corner over there, to your left. That's where public executions were held. It's a branch of Dunnes Stores now."

"A fate worse than death in itself, Dr Kane."

Ian Kane nodded, acknowledging his colleague's feeble witticism, and continued his urban history lesson. "As the city grew, the main shopping district moved due north – to North Street, surprise, surprise – and this area became the entertainment hub. Theatres, playhouses, pubs and restaurants mainly, mixed with all manner of food stores, coffee houses and suchlike. Your pal Thomas Lipton had a shop right across the street, and where we're sitting was the city's main theatre, the Empire. John Henry Anderson played here in the 1840s, Simon. I checked on line last night. General Tom Thumb and P. T. Barnum also passed through town about then, as did Franz Liszt, as did Paganini a few years earlier, as did Sarah Bernhardt a bit later on. Even Charlie Chaplin played here as a child, before he went on to fame and fortune in the States. It's quite a historic spot when you think about it."

Magill made suitably appreciative noises while wondering when his tour guide was going to get to the point.

"What do you see?" Kane asked, a cryptic smile flickering at the corners of his mouth.

In the mottled raincloud-replete light, Ian Kane looked terrible. His pasty, flaky complexion was reminiscent of a packet of pork scratchings made from a leprous sow with eczema. "I see an overweight man who should be taking better care of himself."

"I don't mean me!" Kane wheezed. "And I do take care of myself, by the way. What could be better than a Starbucks and a smoke?" Reaching into the pocket of his brown leather jacket, he pulled out a half-empty packet of his favourite indulgence (after food, drink and more food, naturally). "Look around, Simon. Tell me what you see."

The square was undeniably attractive, if badly let down by chain clothing stores, xtra-cheap shoe shops, garish mobile phone emporia and an unimaginative pedestrianisation scheme that was further besmirched by congealed lumps of coagulated chewing gum. "I spy with my little eye," Magill recited in a childish sing-song voice, "something beginning with F."

"FCUK," Kane answered with alacrity. His mood seemed much lighter than that on display in the galley of Titanic Business School.

"Got it in one, amigo. Your turn."

The increasingly happy bunny thought for a moment. "I spy with my little eye something beginning with P."

"Payless Shoes."

Kane shook his head.

"Phone shop."

Ditto.

Every "p" Magill could think of, from pastries, Pepsi and Perrier to people, Pall Mall and pedestrianisation, met with the same response. Eventually he gave up, with an exaggerated sigh of defeat.

"How many streets run into this square, Simon?"

Magill did a quick calculation. "Five, I reckon."

"So what shape is the square?"

"Hmmm, that's a tough one, professor. Let me think. No, no, don't tell me. It wouldn't happen to be *square*, would it?"

Kane shook his head again.

"Rectangular? Rhomboid? Trapezoid? Actually, now that I look at it, it's sort of star-shaped."

"It's a pentacle, Simon. A pentacle."

"Very good. But could you choose something a bit easier next time we play I-spy?" Magill finished his espresso, thinking he'd need to head off to see O'Connell some time soon. He couldn't afford to be late again. Kane's killings would have to wait until later.

"You see that building opposite?" Kane rumbled, indicating an angular five-storey edifice with arched windows at one corner of the urban pentacle. It was studded with stucco bas reliefs, some of which looked frighteningly familiar to the ginger man. "See the compasses and set-squares, Simon? That building used to be the grand headquarters of Belfast's masonic lodges. It was built in the mid-nineteenth century, right here in the commercial core of the city, at the very time when this place was replete with theatres, food shops and Thomas Lipton's razzamatazz, and your Great Wizard of the North was doing tricks on this very spot. To me, this place epitomises the link between marketing and Freemasonry. It's the marketing side of Freemasonry that interests me, Simon."

"Marketing? What marketing? Do they sell T-shirts, key rings, coffee mugs?"

"Oh yeah," Kane wheezed ironically, "buy one, get one Free-mason . . . get your half-mast trousers here . . . sorry, sir, we seem to have run out of masonic apron and oven-glove gift sets . . . however our all-seeing-eye fridge magnets are all the rage . . . Scottish Rite shortbread's this year's bestseller . . . along with compass and set-square knick-knacks in genuine plastic . . . every home should have one."

"Do they do them in stainless steel?"

"Brass, glass, platinum, plutonium, you name it, Simon, we deliver. Don't ask for credit because a refusal often ends in death."

"I take it, then, than you're not really interested in masonic merchandising."

"No, it's more metaphorical, more symbological. It seems to me that they're both knee-deep in symbols. Dividers, set-squares, beehives, pyramids, pentacles, all-seeing-eyes on one side, and boxes, arrows, flowcharts, bullet points, pie-diagrams, circles-within-circles on the other. Marketers are pretty fond of pyramids too. Or Kate Phillips is, at least. The woman's constructed more pyramids that Rameses the Great."

"That's true. That's so true, Ian."

"They both have secret languages, rituals and ways of behaving that not only exclude outsiders but are fully understood only by the initiated, by insiders. They also make a similar distinction between theoretical and practical aspects of the craft. The Freemasons call it speculative and operative. Marketers call it academicians and practitioners."

It was an interesting theory, and he could see now where May Day had got her marketing ideas. But Simon Magill was still at a loss. "I'm not sure where you're going with this, Ian. Was a marketer murdered here by the Masons? Is that why you brought me here? Or was it a metaphorical killing of some kind?"

"Oh yes, the murders. I almost forgot."

Magill stared at his chubby companion, aghast. "Yes, that kind of thing can slip your mind quite easily."

Chastened, Kane settled his chubby features in a suitably serious mien. "A marketing man was murdered on this very spot in March 2003. His name was Ian Kane."

"I'm sorry to hear that. It's quite a coincidence, though. Is Ian Kane a common name round here?"

"Not really. The murder victim was me. I died a horrible death on this spot, as did my unborn child."

Kane could only have been taking the piss, as was his wont. Does this guy ever treat anything seriously? Magill wondered. "Well, you're not looking too bad, considering. I thought you were on the road to an early grave, but I see you're there already. Way to go, bro."

"I died in Arthur Square, Simon, when I bought *The Da Vinci Code* from the Easons bookshop that used to be over there." He indicated a building across the street from the Freemason's former HQ. The Danster, Magill couldn't help thinking, has been accused of many things, most unfairly, but this surely takes the biscuit.

Before he could say anything, however, Ian Kane launched into a detailed explanation of the death he'd died three years earlier at the hands of Robert Langdon. He had been writing a marketing textbook – a textbook unlike any other. It was a marketing textbook about the importance of storytelling, but it wasn't content to champion the art of storytelling. It demonstrated the art of storytelling. It talked the talk and walked the walk. It was a textbook written as a thriller, the first-ever management thriller: a thriller about secret marketing societies, a thriller that had its roots in historical reality.

When Kane commenced his plot summary, Magill couldn't really see the *Da Vinci Code* connection, but as the abortive narrative unfolded, he began to appreciate the unfortunate overlap. The historical point of departure was an eccentric nineteenth-century Presbyterian minister, John Carey, who lived just outside Belfast. He was ordained in 1832 and posted to a tiny country church in County Tyrone. Before long, he was accused of embezzling church funds, obtaining money by means of forged documents and espousing an anti-Christian conspiracy plot of some kind. When Carey was duly dismissed from the ministry, his replacement was shot and seriously wounded by persons unknown. On a Sunday night. In the middle of his sermon. Fingers were immediately pointed at Carey, who had an alibi, albeit an alibi who was not only unreliable but owed the accused substantial sums of money. The good Reverend Carey was tried for murder, a capital offence, but influential strings were pulled and he was unexpectedly acquitted. For eight years after his scandalous trial, John Carey disappeared from view. Rumour had it that he travelled to the United States. However, when he returned in 1843, he was an extremely wealthy man. No one knew where the cash came from, but many believed that blackmail was involved, as were the Freemasons, and that the church had contributed hush money to Carey's slush fund.

The deceitful preacher settled in Toome, County Antrim, where he made even more money from usury, property speculation and construction-industry scams at the height of the Irish famine. He built himself a fairy-tale cottage, lived in alleged sin with his housekeeper, Miss Kate Stafford, invented an elaborate lineage for himself that included just about every noble family from Richard the Lionheart to Anne Boleyn, and as if that weren't enough he constructed a quasi-masonic edifice – the so-called Temple of Liberty, Learning and Select Amusement – which was donated to the local community for lectures, meetings and similar pastimes. It contained a 2,000-seat auditorium, a library with 5,000 books, an enormous pipe organ and a 50-candle chandelier. Beside it he built an Irish round tower. Secret documents were buried beneath, so they said. The tower itself was blown over in high winds, so they also said, and the temple itself was mysteriously burnt down in 1911, when Ulster was in the throes of a constitutional crisis.

Having set out his raw material, Kane briefly summarised his storyline. It centred on John Carey's post-trial trip to the United States, where he fell in with distant relative Mathew Carey, a prominent Philadelphia bookseller, went on the road with Mason Locke Weems, a bible salesman of unparalleled marketing ability, uncovered the legendary Beale treasure, which turned out to be the secret of Jesus's bloodline, and eventually returned to Belfast in the company of P. T. Barnum. The book climaxed in a chase sequence round Arthur Square and a fist fight with Tom Thumb on the roof of the masonic building.

"Well, Ian," Magill replied when Kane finally finished his breathless exposition, "I can definitely see the parallels with Rennes-le-Chateau and the Priory of Sion. I can also see how the telling of your tale might upset certain people in the church. But if anything, Ian, your story is even stranger than *The Da Vinci Code*. It's a historical novel, what's more. Why don't you publish it anyway? Surely it's sufficiently different from Dan Brown? And anyway, it's a marketing textbook, isn't it?"

Kane heaved a sigh. "It's too late, Simon. The market has been flooded with Brown-lite books. Beige books. Lots of people have published marketing stories and novelisations of marketing problems."

"But they're all fairy stories or management parables. No one has ever written a thriller. Publish it anyway, Ian. Change your name to Danielle Brown or Danni Brown. Call your book *The Marketing Key* and get it out there before the next Robert Langdon."

"Nah, the moment has passed. I'm happy with what I've got. I don't need the hassle from religious fundamentalists, much less the Freemasons. I'm going to let it drop. Dan's already used the Danielle Brown pseudonym, in any event. He wrote a joke book about male-pattern baldness . . . "

Listening to the excuses, Magill couldn't help thinking that Kane sounded just like the entrepreneurial small firms he'd studied in Stirling. They get a great idea, take it so far, but when an opportunity for enormous expansion arises, opt for the easy life instead. He was about to tell his storytelling colleague off when a sparkle in Kane's eye gave him pause.

"This is bullshit, isn't it, Ian? It's the quantum theory of branding all over again."

"Am I so predictable, Simon?" Kane bellowed, slapping his elephantine thighs with hippopotomane pleasure, though his tricksterish disavowals seemed less convincing on this occasion.

"You bastard, Kane! You really had me going that time."

"Talking of going, Simon, Professor O'Connell doesn't like people to be late, and you're already behind schedule." Kane was a juddering mass of jubilation.

"Bastard!"

"Don't forget to sing the praises of the museum. He's a trustee. Takes great pride in the collection, so he does."

"Bastard!"

"Come on, young Magill. I'll drop you off at the station."

Chapter Nineteen

The Folks on the Hill

The Ulster Folk and Transport Museum is bipolar. Tripolar, in fact. Just like politics in Northern Ireland. It consists of three contrasting components that are nominally part of the same structure but want nothing to do with one another. On top of the pile is the folk bit, a monument to rural life at the turn of the nineteenth century. This comprises the usual array of impossibly perfect weavers' cottages, practically spotless spade mills, carefully reconstructed places of worship, and happily manure-free farmyards worked by well-nourished farmhands in acrylic costumes, who rustle up inedible dishes from days of yore and exchange scripted platitudes with passing paying customers. The good old days never had it so good.

The lower half of the hilly site is occupied by the transport section. Three interlinked aircraft hangar–ish structures contain a cornucopia of trains, planes and automobiles, as well as discordant displays of domestic doodahs that stick out like pedicures on polar bears. It's a veritable nerds' nirvana, though the compendious collection of motorbikes and roadsters pulls in sufficient leather-clad, crash helmet–cradling, midlife-stricken road warriors to give a much-needed rebellious edge to the otherwise sterile atmosphere. On most days, however, the parabolic halls echo to the sound of silence. Nothing moves. Time stands still. Destination's nowhere. "All aboard" is inconceivable.

The third building, small and somewhat dilapidated, is situated at the very bottom of the steep slope, almost on the shoreline. Comparatively few people know it's there, and fewer still take the trouble to trek all the way down, largely on account of the precipitous climb back up and the fact that they're already exhausted from the circuitous hike around the upper reaches of the site. Yet the run-down building is devoted to a star exhibit, one of the few objects that Ulster is world-famous for: RMS *Titanic*. Memorabilia, mock-ups, blueprints, scale models, monochrome photographs and a slice of the surprisingly thin, rivet-rich hull remind visitors of Harland and Wolff's greatest hit. A small back room is reserved for serious scholars, though the maritime archives are kept in the main museum building at the top of the hill.

They don't believe in making things easy for people at the Ulster Folk and Transport Museum. The buildings are all but signpost free, on the basis of an entirely plausible yet customer-unfriendly argument that the original cottages and farmsteads weren't covered in unsightly signs or information boards of any kind. So most visitors leave the museum even more confused than when they arrived, cardiovascular compensations notwithstanding.

The museum, in short, is Northern Ireland in microcosm, both physically and experientially. Politically too, the rural Republican activism, the urban Loyalist stasis and the tiny, universally ignored Alliance party at the bottom of the pile are all present and correct, in prim 'n' proper proportion.

But Simon Magill didn't know that. He followed the crowd, all two of them, to the spartan visitors' centre, where he dug deep for the entrance fee and, map in hand, made his way round the rural reaches of the folk park. Here an obsolete Orange hall, there a vintage village street, over there a prehistoric primary school. He asked an attendant for directions to the *Titanic* exhibit, but received a prepackaged peroration on the production of poteen for his trouble. He eventually wound up at Cultra Manor, the Edwardian manor house that dominated the Anglo-Irish demesne before it was gifted to the Ulster people in perpetuity. Grey slated and grim faced, it's now occupied by the museum's administrative headquarters and a teashop, the most popular stop for most consumers of indigenous culture and associated artefacts.

Magill joined the lengthy queue and looked warily at the authentic butter-and-brown-sauce sandwiches, as consumed no doubt by generations of deprived inner-city backstreet kids with rickets. Cup-and-saucer castanets in hand, he managed to find an empty table in the corner of the surprisingly busy, steam-filled cafe. He sipped on his cracked cup of extra-sweet tea, as quaffed for aeons by burly working men in oily overalls, and sighed with exhausted rambler's gratitude.

Two gregarious Americans, clearly communing in the land of their forefathers, sat at the table next to him. One was a big-boned soccer mom called Beth, the other a Bud-bellied, plaid-shirted Midwesterner who introduced himself as Chuck. After expressing their mystification at the anti-customer orientation of the museum and providing a potted summary of their ancestral Irish connections, Chuck 'n' Beth gave him directions to the *Titanic* exhibit, which they'd visited earlier.

"There's not much to see. It takes ten minutes, tops. They charge extra for it also. Go on the guided tour of the shipyard instead."

"Thanks, Chuck, but I'm meeting someone there."

"It was empty when we passed through. Quiet as the grave. You think there'd be sound effects or something. People screaming, foghorns blaring, band playing as the big boat goes down."

"I can only assume they don't want to be accused of sensationalism or cashing in on death and desperation," Magill replied, wondering why he felt it necessary to defend suboptimal marketing.

"You think they'd lose their scruples after 100 years. We commercialised 9/11 within weeks. Northern Ireland could be the Disneyland of death and destruction, if only they'd put their minds to it."

"This place needs a dose of American marketing knowhow," chimed Chuck's better half, who looked as though she was missing Wal-Mart already while refusing to sweat the small stuff in her chicken soup of the soul. "Don't they teach marketing in this part of the world?" she grinned.

"I've no idea," Magill lied. "But I know someone who thinks like you do and I'm late for our meeting. I've got to dash. Sorry."

"Give your buddy our best wishes. If you're ever passing through Kalamazoo, don't forget to call."

"Have a nice one," Chuck's husky helpmate added.

"In this weather, Beth?" Magill replied, motioning towards the rapidly descending stair-rods outside, which were lancing noisily against the cafe's picture windows.

The amiable Midwesterners smiled involuntarily, thrown by Simon's departure from the standard scripted pleasantries. Pleasantries, however, were few and far between during Magill's dash for his destination. Downhill it might have been, but he was drenched by the time he docked outside *Titanic's* memorial anchorage. He looked less like the proverbial drowned rat than a ginger tomcat who's been caught in a car wash. He squelched through the foyer. The payment booth was empty, the souvenir shop abandoned. So he dripped around the free exhibit leaving trails of water behind him. If anyone complained, Magill decided, he'd claim he was doing an impersonation of a melting iceberg. Or a performance-art tribute to *Titanic's* lost souls. He hadn't quite decided.

But no one complained, because no one was there. He called out "Anyone there?" but anyone who was there failed to respond. All was silent, except for the thunder of rain on the jerry-built building's flat roof. It sounded like the passing shower of lambeg drums on the twelfth of July. *O'Connell probably can't hear me over the percussive racket,* Magill thought, as he struggled to extract a mobile phone from the side pocket of his sodden chinos.

He punched in O'Connell's number and heard a ring-tone reaction somewhere beyond a partition at the rear of the exhibition hall. The professor didn't respond, despite the distinctive strains of "Nearer, my God, to Thee." Magill ducked behind a wafer-thin sliver from the stricken ship's hull and discovered a doorway. A narrow corridor lay beyond, with study carrels on either side, all empty. As the drumming on the roof suddenly ceased, the phone rang more loudly. It was coming from a larger room at the end of the corridor. Magill knocked. No reply. He eased the thin door open. The windowless room was empty, apart from three filing cabinets, a large metal cupboard and a decrepit desk pushed up against the end wall. The professor's phone was still ringing.

In the cupboard.

Magill wrenched open the metal doors with an almighty rattle. Carlingford O'Connell fell towards him like a bungee jumper plunging head-first off the Forth Bridge. Magill leapt aside as the professor's body crashed onto the shiny vinyl floor. The back of his skull had been staved in. Black blood had congealed around the crown of his head and lumpy pink goo oozed out from the crevices, hissing on account of the sudden fall. Even Magill could tell that O'Connell had been beaten by a heavy blunt instrument. Repeatedly.

A sharp metallic click shattered the silence behind him. Magill whirled round, expecting to be faced with a pistol-toting assassin or a thug with a club. But he was mistaken. The door had clicked shut automatically, revealing a paper-strewn desk behind. It was blood-spattered as well. The off-white walls were covered too. Either the professor had put up a hell of a struggle, or he'd been bludgeoned out of sheer brutality. An oxbow of blood meandered across the floor, bits of brain matter were attached to the pinboard, globules of God only knows what dangled from a brightly lit anglepoise lamp, basting and bubbling in the heat.

Magill groaned. Waves of nausea swept over him. But there was no way he was going to hang around for the police or any other investigative authorities. He was making for the door when something caught his eye on the deceased professor's desk. It was a wooden hammer, a heavily carved, almost decorative flat-faced hammer with brass fittings and an elongated claw. It looked more like an ornament than a murder weapon, though it was obviously fit for purpose. Indeed, it lay on a piece of paper, almost as if it were on display. In a museum.

There was something written on the paper in bright red ink. Except that it wasn't bright red ink. It was blood. Magill stared at it in horror, trying to comprehend what kind of person would fill a fountain pen with the victim's blood and leave a farewell message for stricken friends and family.

Steadying himself, Magill examined the killer's handiwork. Unlike the cryptic inscription on Brodie, this one was crystal clear, though the words meant nothing to him:

A SHIP ILL KEPT

Outraged *Titanic* buffs? Disgruntled Hustler University employees? Offended museum curators opposed to the director's Brand *Titanic* project? A brutal bigot infuriated by Daniel O'Connell's descendent consorting with symbols of Protestant Ascendancy? Another Order of Solomon episode?

Magill didn't wait to find out. He ran down the corridor, his waterlogged trainers squelching on the vinyl floor. He sprinted though the empty *Titanic* exhibition and depopulated foyer and sped up the hill as steel skewers of rain descended viciously once more.

A train was pulling into the citybound platform. He jumped on board, flopped down onto an instantly sodden seat, and forced a feeble smile at the only other passenger in the carriage, a wizened old man wearing a flat cap and insouciantly sucking on an untipped cigarette, despite the prominently displayed "No Smoking" signs.

"Desperate weather, son."

"Terrible."

"You'll catch your death if you're not careful."

Magill acknowledged the avuncular advice with a wan smile. You don't know the half of it, he thought, while wondering what to do next. Go to the police? Not a chance. Ian Kane? He doesn't take things seriously, and would assume it's a reciprocal spoof. May Day? She might be the best bet. If she'd let him darken her door. If she'd deign to talk to him. He'd just have to beg for forgiveness and unburden himself. Again.

He got off at Central Station, scythed his way swiftly though the swirling lunchtime crowds and crossed the Albert Bridge, scanning the newly built apartment blocks for May Day's palatial penthouse. A huge herring gull on the balcony gave the game away. He leant on the intercom, talked his way past the cranky concierge – a has-been boxer at a guess – and deposited a puddle on the floor of the polished lift as it ascended rapidly to the top floor.

May Day's door was ajar.

It can't be! Not another one. Not May Day as well . . .

Chapter Twenty

The Fremont Street Experience

"What do you think, guys?"

Barton Brady II looked round the gleaming rosewood table. His colleagues were gleaming too. With success. The Aherne meeting had gone well. She seemed amenable, if slightly standoffish. She'd connected with Yasmin big time. She'd fallen under SA's infallible spell, like so many before her. A new vista of money-making possibilities lay before them. Serendipity Associates had lucked out yet again. A chance encounter – in the Paris Hotel and Casino of all places – looked set to deliver serious dollars. Aherne's association with Kellogg School of Management, the peerless Kate Phillips in particular, couldn't harm their future prospects either.

"A reasonable day's work," rumbled Rosencreutz in his usual lugubrious manner. "Fair to middling." Everyone knew that meant he was extremely pleased, excited almost. He was already calculating the cash flow and revelling in the thought of a new Excel file on his precious Palm TX.

" -Preneur's a gem," Chang chimed.

"The suffix we're been searching for," Eng added with enthusiasm. "I mean, consider the extra levels we can build on the base model . . . entrepreneur . . . superpreneur . . . hyperpreneur . . . überpreneur . . ."

"And then there's innerpreneur . . . outerpreneur . . . under-preneur . . . overpreneur . . . learnerpreneur . . . pseudopreneur . . ." Chang continued.

Brady smiled one of his trademark smiles. It was time for the ritual of conquest, the company chant that Brady's Bunch rehearsed every time a deal was done or a strategic decision made. Ordinarily, they'd wait for Yasmin, who was driving Aherne out to

161

McCarran for her early flight to O'Hare. But she wouldn't object to them enjoying their moment of triumph.

"O Serendipity Associates," Brady chanted towards his co-workers in an incongruous East Coast–accented cadence.

"O Serendipitous One," they sang in response, each trying to outdo the others, Rosencreutz included.

"Does it have legs, Serendipity Associates?"

"Yes, it has legs, O Serendipitous One."

"How many legs, Serendipity Associates?"

"It's a centipede, O Serendipitous One."

"*How* many legs, Serendipity Associates?"

"It's a millipede, O Serendipitous One."

"*How* many goddamn legs, Serendipity Associates?"

"It's a goddamn gazillipede!" they shouted as one.

The Serendipity Associates' chant wasn't in the same league as the legendary IBM company song, let alone the Confederacy's rebel yell. But it helped bond the Bunch and thereby ensure the commitment they'd need when it came to the hard graft of developing the suffix and bringing it to market. The room was still echoing to the sound of goddamn gazillipede when Yasmin Buonarroti slipped in.

"Missed the company chant, did I? Oh, what a pity." She rolled her eyes at Jill Eng, who replied with a shrug that said boys-will-be-boys-best-humour-them. Or something to that effect.

"Sorry, Yasmin, we got carried away," Brady responded lightheartedly.

Buonarroti reciprocated. "I've always been meaning to ask, O Serendipitous One, what is a gazillipede anyway?"

"It's a cross between a gazelle and a millipede," Brady announced mock-officiously. "It doesn't look very pretty . . . "

"But you should see the sucker jump!" shrieked Chang and Eng in unison.

"Did Emer get her flight?" Brady inquired. "She's happy with this, us, the team?"

"Sure. She made it. And she's very happy with this, us, the team. I'm not happy though. I think there's a better prospect than -preneur. Authorpreneur's OK, but Emer's presentation included something else besides CODE, CRAP and aspiring to the condition of literature. Something that's right up your street, Barton."

"Oh yes? What's that?" the company's main man said quizzically, since he thought he had all the consultancy angles covered.

Buonarroti smiled but remained mute, seemingly determined to maximise anticipation round the table, extend everyone's agony for as long as possible and generally tease the teasers. "Well, Barton, you know the way you're looking for a knock-'em-dead blockbuster concept, something that'll get you – us – back into the management-consultancy majors?"

"Yes, I know, I know, but we've got our hands full with -preneur. The other ideas can wait. We've already decided, Yazza. We've chanted our assent."

"OK, whatever you say, Bart." He hated being called Bart almost as much as she hated Yazza. But, as Bart often pointed out, a bit of interpersonal antagonism never hurt anyone in the creative industries.

"Tell us, Yasmin," Chang and Eng cried as one. "Oh, go on, tell us!"

For a snake-oil seller supreme and teaserpreneur first class, Barton Brady couldn't take too much of his own medicine. "Please tell us," he conceded. "If it's better than -preneur, it must be something extra special."

"The Holy Grail," Buonarroti responded. "Emer mentioned the Holy Grail of marketing. The grail is a great metaphor for corporate life, customer care, team building, product development, marketing strategy, leadership . . . whatever. The quest is a primal narrative. Searching for something better, perfect, superlative, imperishable is what America was built on. That's what my grandparents were searching for when they left Italy, that's what my parents aspired to in the belly of the Bronx, that's what you and I were aiming for, Barton, when we set up Serendipity Associates."

Despite his expensively acquired education and silver-tongued acumen, Brady was taken aback by Buonarroti's uncharacteristic eloquence. "John Winthrop couldn't have put it better," he said quietly, almost humbly. "'We must consider that we shall be a city upon a hill. The eyes of all people are upon us.'"

Yasmin Buonarroti smiled at her colleagues. "Every single management consultant is searching for a grail of one kind or another: the secret of success, the key to the kingdom, the one-word answer that'll make them a million, sell the books, shape the short courses and get them on the cover of *Fortune*, *Forbes* or *Fast Company*."

The room settled down as the implications sank in. The roseate rays of the rising sun slanted into SA's conference facility. A new day had dawned. The future of Serendipity Associates looked exceptionally bright.

Jack Chang was first to speak. "We could really go to town on this, guys. King Arthur, Queen Guinevere, Sir Lancelot, the Knights of the Round Table, jousting tournaments, heraldic shields, Excalibur, Merlin, Sir Galahad, the Siege Perilous, the Fisher King, the Rosy Cross. Just think of the executive training programmes we could wrap around that lot. If the SOBs will walk through fire or tackle army assault courses, they'll definitely be game for some sword-in-the-stone action, siege-engine maintenance or trebuchet target practice."

"Better yet," Jill Eng added, "there's the whole esoteric secret-society conspiracy-theory angle. The Rosicrucians. The Cathars. The Knights Templar. The Illuminati. The Freemasons. They're all in it together. Aren't they? Dan Brown opened up that particular spigot, and look what happened to him."

"Laughed all the way to the Vatican Bank," Chang interjected.

"Bought the freakin' Vatican Bank," Eng chorused.

Buonarroti studied Brady carefully. "What do *you* think, Barton?"

The main man looked dumbstruck, as if he'd seen Liberace in a compromising position with Elton John. "You're a genius, Yasmin," he acknowledged. "It's the best idea we've ever had. Bar none. But we have to keep this in-house. It's not for sale."

Brady had visions of his name in lights alongside Tom Peters, Jim Collins and the one and only Kate Phillips. The backstage boy was back in the limelight of his imagination. The fulfillment of his personal quest trembled before him like a management-consultancy mirage. He couldn't believe his luck.

Buonarroti scented assent. "Oh, it gets even better, Barton."

"No, Yasmin, it couldn't get any better. This is unbeatable," Brady said, while dreaming dreams of overdue consultancy celebrity.

"Barton, we can make an acronym out of GRAIL, an acronym that says everything there is to say about the contemporary marketing condition and encapsulates everything SA's been arguing for the past five years."

"Impossible," Brady replied.

"Well," Buonarroti began, "L stands for Luck. That's one of ours. The concept that started the ball rolling. Remember, Barton?"

He sighed wistfully.

"R must be Retro," Chang continued, "Just look at the yestermania all around us, not least in Las Vegas."

"That's one of ours too," Eng added. "What about A?"

"I was thinking of Amplification," Buonarroti replied, "the whole buzz, viral, guerilla marketing thing that we haven't really exploited to date."

"Ambiguity's better," Brady said firmly, having committed himself to the acronym like it was one of his own. "It's more postmodern. Today's world is becoming ever more inexplicable. Branding is increasingly based on ambivalence, equivocation, paradox, uncertainty."

"Postmodernism's a hard sell," Buonarroti cautioned. "It didn't do very well last time, Barton. Postmodernism is history, anyway. Let it lie. I vote A for Amplification."

Eng nodded vigorously.

"I agree with Yasmin," Chang concurred. "We're in a post-postmodern era. Amplification works for us. We can take viruses to places they haven't been before."

"I'll take your word for it, Jack," Brady conceded with a grin. "Amplification it is then. But what about Indeterminacy for I? That works, doesn't it?"

"No," Jill Eng insisted. "Irony's what it should be. No question. Irony's in nowadays. Sprite, IBM, Diesel, 7UP, Bud, Carlsberg,

Carl's Junior, Mullet shampoo, Comme des Garçons. They're all into it. I mean, the whole Holy Grail, knights-in-armour thing is inherently tongue in cheek, isn't it? It's too kitsch not to be. It's gotta be irony, guys."

Buonarroti looked skeptically at Eng. "I had Inclusion in mind myself. These days, corporations are bending over backward to bring customers on board by including them in their decision-making processes. Think of P&G's website, think company-coordinated brand communities, think of Levi's bespoke blue-jeans system and Nike's design-your-own-sneakers software, think of the whole 'prosumer' movement. Inclusion works."

"Yes, it does," Eng acknowledged. "However, it's not really in tune with SA's beliefs about teasing and tantalising consumers. It's too touchy-feely for us, Yasmin. Irony's closer to our brand DNA."

The company's co-founder capitulated. "You're right, Jill. Absolutely right. Irony's better." Buonarroti looked around the table, absorbing the consensus. "That only leaves G. It's the first letter and it's got to be bold. It's got to set out our conceptual stall. I was thinking of G-spot, though that'll never sell in the Midwest. Vegas'd love it, though. What about Gusto – the whole energy, enthusiasm, effervescent, never-say-die side of things?"

"Glamour might be better," Brady suggested. "Entertainment economy and all that. The importance of celebrity, charisma, razzamatazz. No?"

"Genome? Gimmick? Google? Goblet?" Chang machine-gunned. "Goblet could be good, especially in light of the basic grail metaphor. I'm sure we could do something cool with goblets."

"Gambol, Gamble, Gallantry, Gregariousness, Gratitude. They all work," Eng went on, equally rapidly. "But what about Generosity or, even better, Gratuity? I'm thinking of the whole free-gift, something-for-nothing, no-extra-cost-or-hidden-charges aspect."

"Why not Gift, then?" Brady volunteered. "Given the importance of gift-giving to marketing ... "

"Give's better yet." Eng interrupted. "Gyrate? Grace? Goad? Galvanise? Grandeur? Grin? Glad? Goal? Glow? G-spot? *Why not* G-spot? Think of the reaction, the outrage, the publicity!"

166

"Let's put G on hold for the time being, folks," Buonarroti said diplomatically. "Are we agreed that it's go for GRAIL?"

Chas Rosencreutz suddenly piped up. He'd sat silently throughout the whole warp-speed discussion. But as the resident bean counter and purse-strings holder, his was the voice that really mattered. "It's a very bad idea. We're treading on dangerous territory. The secret-society angle is potentially disastrous. Remember what happened with Shibboleth Associates?"

Chang and Eng exchanged worried looks. They recalled the death threats they'd received in the days when the company's luck management paradigm was unravelling and Serendipity Associates changed its name to Shibboleth Associates. Unbeknown to them, however, "shibboleth" was one of Freemasonry's secret words of recognition. They didn't know for certain who'd made the death threats, though the sibilant similarities to Joe Pesci in *GoodFellas* gave them a fair idea. They didn't wait to find out. The name was changed back next day.

How the Freemasons' protection service found out about the name change when SA's intra-office *omertà* was in place they never discovered. Nor did they try to. "Maybe GRAIL's not such a good idea," Chang and Eng said simultaneously. "Let's stick with -preneur. -Preneur's plenty to be getting along with."

"GRAIL's a gold mine," Barton Brady said forcefully. "It's a millipedalooza. We're going for GRAIL."

"It's too close to mob territory for comfort," Rosencreutz cautioned.

"The masonic mob can kiss my buff butt."

"Our buff butt," Buonarroti reiterated. The co-owners concurred. The die was cast. The decision was made. The decision was final. Fatal.

Chapter Twenty-One

Full Force Gale

Shaking uncontrollably, Simon Magill stood outside the open door of May Day's penthouse apartment. He took a deep breath, fearing the worst. Trembling from a lethal combination of cold and concern, he pushed the door wide open and called out in a voice oscillating with anxiety, "May? May? Are you there?"

The spartan apartment was as silent as the grave of a Trappist monk.

Magill took another deep breath, girded his shivering loins and squeaked slowly down the hall, his waterlogged trainers leaving a trail of tyretracks on the polished lime floorboards. There was no one in the kitchen, bathroom, bedrooms, both guest and main. The en suite was empty too, though May Day's ample selection of unguents, aromatic oils and make-up mirrors bespoke her absent presence.

The pristine lounge was deserted. A monument to Muji-chic, it looked like a photo-spread in *House Beautiful*. Or *Wallpaper**, rather, in keeping with its ascetic aesthetic. Only the billowing curtains hinted at occupancy. The sliding doors to the balcony had cracked open and a cold wind whistled through the fissure, turning the curtains into rain-streaked spinnakers on a Tornado-class catamaran.

Magill pulled the sliding doors apart, hoping to see May Day and Harry the Herring Gull in silent communion. The herring gull was alone, however He reached out to stroke the brute in lieu of the apartment's Louise Brooks–alike, but it sashayed away down the wrought-iron balustrade. Sizing up the situation, Harry cocked his head at his rival for May Day's affections, screeched several anti-capitalist obscenities, unfurled his enormous wingspan with a sharp crack and, after a couple of warm-up flaps, beat a raucous, cawcous retreat.

The increasingly anxious intruder turned back into the lounge and closed the sliding doors. The deflating spinnaker wrapped itself wetly around him. He didn't see his assailant, but felt the whoosh of displaced air as a blunt instrument scythed towards his face at high speed.

He didn't know what had hit him. He didn't know anything at all, as bright lights burst in his head, darkness fell, and he followed it. Down. Down. Down . . .

* * *

Magill woke to see the smiling face of May Day hovering above him. He tried to say "I've definitely gone to heaven," but the pain in his face stopped him.

"Sorry, Simon. But you got what you deserved. You shouldn't creep about in someone's apartment like a rapist or pet molester."

Magill attempted the sardonic rejoinder "Lock up your herring gulls," only to hear his words reduced to an incoherent mumble. His lips felt like they'd had silicon implants. He could taste blood in his mouth. His nose throbbed, and both eyes watered in sympathy. Apart from that, he felt grand. He was in bed. He was naked. He was warm and cosy. He was being attended to by a smiling pink-haired pixie. What's not to like?

"Here, drink this." May Day held a tumbler to his swollen mouth. Magill tried to take a sip but, given that he'd more collagen in his lips than Hollywood's entire A-list, very little of the liquid got through. He felt rivulets of slobber slither off his chin onto the well-plumped pillows. He needed a napkin. A bottle or two of Nurofen wouldn't go amiss either. May Day tilted the tumbler again and again, slowly filling the victim with her healing brew. "This'll ease the pain. Don't try to talk, lover."

At least she's forgiven me, he thought. The things you have to do to get back in a girl's good books. Beloved by invalids and jetlag sufferers alike, the delicious illicit thrill of being in bed in the middle of the day crept over him.

The dream was thrilling too, but delicious wasn't the word that went with it. Delirious, more like.

He was driving his 2CV towards a crenellated castle on the coastline. It was the haunted hotel in Glenarm that he'd visited as a child with his mother. Huge waves were crashing against the battlements, but the lights were on, the bar was full and people were looking out of the picture windows as the gale-force waves seethed against them, spume soaring, striving mightily to shatter the glass. Pitcairn Brodie was there, bellowing merrily, blaspheming about Damn Brown. Carlingford O'Connell was checking prices at the bar, occasionally glancing anxiously at the hourglass on his wrist. In full bejewelled evening dress, May Day regally descended a monumental marble staircase arm in arm with Ian Kane, as svelte as ever, wearing a well-filled DJ with one rolled-up trouser leg. He turned to the picture window. The crashing waves had subsided, leaving a bloody message on the spume-streaked glass. KILL THE ILL KEPT SHIP.

Magill woke with a start, sweating. It was early afternoon. The sun was out again. A prismatic kaleidoscope of rivertine reflections rippled across the bare white bedroom wall. He could hear music from the lounge. Van Morrison's greatest hits. Simon could still sense his own greatest hit, though the initial physiognomic agony had faded to non-specific facial throbbing. His mouth felt disembodied somehow, as if it belonged to someone else. The dull ache was real enough, though.

Van the Man increased in intensity as the lounge door opened. May Day popped her pretty pixie head round the stripped-pine architrave. "Is the intruder awake yet? How's your aching bake?"

"Done to a turn," he blubbered. The words filled his mouth and seeped out at the sides, a rill of drool and sputum. What his lips had gained in lustre they'd lost in flexibility.

"I'd dress in black for the next few days," May Day advised.

"Mourning?" he spluttered.

"Goth," she giggled. "It's your best bet, lover. You've got a Goth thing going." She handed Magill one of her many make-up mirrors. As he caught sight of his bloody nose, split lips and rapidly blackening eyes, he could see what May Day meant. He looked like Edward Scissorhands wearing a ginger fright wig to divert attention from his botched nose job.

171

"Nosferatu-chic is back," she added unnecessarily. "Think yourself lucky I picked up a rolling pin rather than a kitchen knife. If it hadn't been for a noisy knife tray, you could've had a Sabatier in the kisser."

Magill smiled and winced simultaneously. "Thank heaven for small mercies," he slobbered.

"What are you doing here anyway, Simon? I wasn't expecting to see you again. At least, not so soon." Magill swallowed painfully. His saliva glands were working overtime, even if the rest of his face was on strike. "I was worried about you," he mumbled. "The door was open. I thought you'd . . . you'd . . . you know. I was worried, May."

"I'm glad you feel that way, Simon." She put her hands on her hips and pouted provocatively, just out of reach. Not that he had the strength to grab her, much less grapple with the minx. "My door was open because I'd nipped out for a second. To my neighbour's apartment. Her cat is feeling poorly."

"Oh."

"But not as poorly as you," she smiled beatifically.

"Happy day, May."

"But then I saw the muddy footprints on my nice clean hallway and, well, what's a girl to do? When I heard a big belligerent brute interfering with Harry on the balcony, he was definitely going down."

"Don't mess with animal rights, right?"

"Lucky you look like a panda, then."

"You sweet-talker, you."

"You're on the protected species list, lover man." May Day climbed onto the bed beside her bruised and battered intruder, who somehow managed to smile through the pain. "You're my Irish panda. My wild Irish panda. Oh panda. Oh panda. Oh Paddy O'Panda." She cocked an eyebrow.

"Aylesbury panda, actually. Closest living relative to Aylesbury duck, I'll have you know." The human body's powers of recovery are remarkable, or so they say, and Simon Magill was testament to that truism.

"Something's rustling in the undergrowth, panda"

"You could be right, my dear."

"What a big bamboo shoot you have, panda."

"All the better to beat you with, my dear."

"Beat me, panda . . . "

* * *

" . . . They say pandas mate once every ten years, May."

"Sorry to hear that, lover."

"But they keep going for six months or so, I'm told."

"A bit like Sting and Trudi?"

"Tantric pandas, dear heart. Tantric pandas."

"Sounds like a sex toy, Simon. Ann Summers' winter catalogue 2004. Let me guess, you were studying it for research purposes."

"What else, dear heart? One has to keep abreast of the latest marketing trends in the specialogue sector."

"I bet you do."

"It's a dirty job, May. And they were asking for volunteers. A marketing man's gotta do. You know how it is."

"I know exactly how it is. 3.141 times in one day. 3.141 minutes on each occasion. You're good, Simon, but you're no panda, let alone a tantric panda. But, hey, you're my panda. You really know how to remind a girl that the relationship between the circumference of a circle and its diameter is constant."

Magill tried to stifle a laugh. The pain was excruciating. "Oh, oh, oh," he moaned, desperately trying to purse his cracked lips.

"Is this mathematical dirty-talk too much for you, lover? I can recite the Fibonacci sequence if it helps, or whisper sweet zeros in your ear. You wouldn't believe what I can do with square roots, Koch curves and inverse functions. No need to worry about contraception, panda, we'll use the algorithm method."

"Oh . . . oh . . . ah . . . aaah! I submit, May. No more jokes. I can't stand the pain."

"Yes, we've had enough jokes for one day." May Day threw the covers back, pulled on her Ralph Lauren dressing gown and made for the bedroom door. "I'd offer you something to eat, but I'm down to my last sausage and I'm saving that for Harry." She stopped on her way out, turned back and stood silently beside the bed. She was silhouetted in the plate-glass window, shafts of early afternoon sunlight playing round her head like a saintly corona, though her overcast emerald eyes were anything but.

Simon Magill stared up at her perfect pert features, wondering yet again why someone so beautiful would want anything to do with a hopeless misfit like him, especially in his current unprepossessing state.

"Why are you here, Simon? Why are you really here? What brought you back to my . . . boudoir so soon? I thought our . . . um . . . tempestuous affair was over, seeing as I'd sold you down the river like some masonic Mata Hari."

As the morning's malign events washed back over him and swirled down the same mental plughole that had swallowed the unspeakable Edinburgh experiences of the previous day, Magill realised his psychic sceptic tank was full to overflowing. He felt tears prick the back of his bloodshot black eyes. "I didn't know who else to turn to, May."

"What's up, lover? You can tell me."

"A terrible thing happened this morning."

"Oh it wasn't so bad. Really. Try not to think about it too much, otherwise you'll get performance anxiety. And that would never do."

"Another terrible thing, May. A really terrible thing." Magill's battered expression spoke volumes, despite the badly bruised dust-jacket.

May Day stopped in full forget-about-it flow. "There's been another one, hasn't there? Another murder?"

Magill nodded helplessly.

Chapter Twenty-Two

Dark End of the Street

Stunned by the dreadful news, May Day let out an involuntary yelp. She stared at Simon Magill, eyes wide with shock. "Professor O'Connell?" she said with disbelief. "*Our* Professor O'Connell? But how? Why? Where? When?"

By the time Magill had recounted the revolting events of that morning, May Day's face was in her hands, shoulders heaving uncontrollably. Rocking backwards and forwards to the syncopated rhythm of sudden loss, she emitted a primal banshee wail. The laughing lascivious xylophone had long since left the building. Eventually, after much sobbing and spasmodic shuddering, May Day lifted her head and looked straight at Magill. Her beautiful elfin features were shiny with tears. "I think you should go to the police," she said resolutely. "Right away. There's a PSNI station just across the river, opposite your hotel. It's the only way to sort this madness out."

Magill sighed heavily. "May, I don't think I'll get a lot of sympathy from the police. Jesus, I may as well go straight to the local masonic lodge and cut out the middle-men. You said so yourself. From what I've heard of the PSNI, they'll probably try to pin several paramilitary crimes on me while they're at it, and maybe throw in the Northern Bank raid for good measure."

"Talk sense, Simon," May Day snapped, her composure collapsing like a calving iceberg.

"For God's sake, May!" he snapped back at her. "It was you who told me the police were the uniformed branch of the Freemasons!"

Livid, May Day grabbed Magill's battered face with both hands and shook it vigorously. The pain was excruciating. Her eyes were blazing, her demeanour disfigured by throbbing emotion. "Masons? More Masons? You're obsessed with Freemasons, Simon.

Get a grip of yourself. Get some help. Go to the police."

Magill pushed her hands away gently but firmly. "There was a hammer, May," he said with resignation. "An ornamental hammer. O'Connell was beaten to death by a hammer. It looked like a masonic object of some kind. The Order of Solomon. I don't know."

"It's called a maul," she said flatly, her pumped-up emotions plummeting like a punctured hot-air balloon. "In masonic symbology, mauls stand for order, control and the spiritual development of initiates from rough stone ashlars to finished blocks of masonry. They're also an emblem of the Lodge Master and a reminder of the murder of Hiram Abiff, the Brotherhood's supposed founding father, as well as a means of disciplining those who fall below the Craft's expected standards of conduct. Mauls are symbols of both self-improvement and death for the Brotherhood's enemies, both without and within. They're similar to Thor's hammer in certain respects. The maul sends a very clear message, perhaps the clearest in masonic lore."

Struggling to cope with a combined sense of surprise and inevitability, Magill tilted his battered head back and gazed fixedly at the ceiling. "There was a message, May," he said to the roof. "A written message. A message written in O'Connell's blood."

May Day reached out to him. He jerked his head away, anticipating another attempt to shake sense into him. But she stroked his bruised cheek tenderly and ran her fingers through his matted hair. "The same message as before, Simon? Kill the Popri? Wasn't that it?"

"Paspi, May. Not that the wording matters."

"So was it the same?" she asked, struggling to stifle a shudder.

"No," Magill replied with equanimity. "No. It was a different message this time. 'A ship ill kept.'"

She stared at him blankly. "'A ship ill kept'? What does that mean? Something to do with the *Titanic*?"

He shrugged. "I don't know. It's possible, I suppose. O'Connell told me a whole raft of *Titanic* conspiracy theories. Some of them involved the Orange Order, and, as we agreed earlier, the Orange Order may be involved in Pitcairn's killing. Perhaps it's the Orange Order of Solomon again. I can't say for sure. All I can say is that he's been brutally murdered, just like Brodie. The message is different, but it's the same people, whoever they are. I am sure of that."

"Did you see anyone, Simon? Did anyone see you?"

"No, no, I didn't see anyone. I think I missed them by a couple of minutes. O'Connell's body was still warm when I found him. His skull was hissing, for Christ's sake. There was blood and gore everywhere. But there was no one around. Not a sinner."

"Oh, sweet Jesus. Oh, sweet Jesus," she moaned.

Brimming with blame and self-loathing, Simon Magill couldn't hold back. He told her that it was all his fault, that he was bad luck, born unlucky, that his whole family was cursed. His parents were run out of Northern Ireland back in the early days of the Troubles. His big brother, Peter, joined the army in order to do his bit for queen and country, only to be butchered in West Belfast. As May Day's eyes filled again, he informed her – in a voice bitter with remembered pain – that Peter didn't exactly go out in a blaze of glory. He was off duty. He met some babe in a bar. It turned out to be a honey trap, a set-up. He was found on waste ground nearby, his throat slit and dick sticking out. Of his mouth. They'd cut his dick off, stuffed it down his throat Mafia-style, and hacked away at his corpse. They reckoned his killers were fans of *The Godfather*.

Naturally Simon's father was devastated, destroyed; mortified as much as anything. Think of the shame. The son of a Methodist minister getting murdered in Belfast like that. He withdrew into himself thereafter. There was nothing his second son could do to get through to him. He even studied theology to impress the old git, but he'd ceased to care. Still didn't.

Simon's mother was destroyed too. Clinical depression, ECT, more depression, more ECT, Alzheimer's eventually. She didn't recognise him nowadays, though the strange thing was that she was still a whiz at number games, brainteasers, puzzles. But only mathematical ones like kakuro or Sudoku.

"She's a Sudoku star, May. Believe it or not. Doesn't remember her own son, mind you. So I recite the digits of pi whenever I visit her. It's our only form of communication."

"I know how you feel," May Day sobbed. "My father was shot dead by the British army on his way to work one morning. It was so sudden, so unexpected. I'd had an argument with him before he

177

left that day. I still haven't forgiven myself. We were completely apolitical before that. But afterwards . . . "

Magill was fighting back the tears too. "Shit City," he spat out. "That's what my big brother called Belfast. Another shit night in Shit City. The land of shits and scrubbers. That's what he used to say."

"And the shit fountain keeps spouting," she sighed.

"What are we going to do, May?"

"I don't know, Simon. I need to think. She got up quickly, tied her dressing gown tightly and strode resolutely from the room. A few moments later, Van Morrison started up again. He couldn't make out the track. Like all Morrison's songs, it involved moving on up along the ancient avenue to the higher ground where the back street jelly roll is in the garden wet with rain on golden autumn days like this when the healing has begun, begun, begun, begun, begun, begun, begun . . .

Magill struggled out of bed. His clothes had disappeared. Wrapped in a duvet, he looked like a lanky snowman with coal for eyes, carrot on top and a battered beetroot where the nose should be. Thus equipped, he went in search of May Day for the second time that afternoon. The sliding doors onto the balustraded balcony were open once more. She was staring out over the churning flotsam-infested river, swollen with rainwater. A lone sculler struggled against the current, his sleek craft slicing through the murky torrent.

A line from F. Scott Fitzgerald, Magill's favourite author, sprang to mind: "So we beat on, boats against the current, borne back ceaselessly into the past." The past is past, however. This is about the future. The future is all that matters. Simon Magill steeled himself. No more running. No more fear. No more tears. No more cowering in cardboard boxes. He resolved to see this through to the bitter end. Whatever it took. Even if he died in the process. Fortune favours the brave.

"I've got a rolling pin, May, and I'm not afraid to use it. Step away from the seagull. Anything you wear may be taken down and used in evidence."

May Day looked over her shoulder and smiled feebly at the officious snowman. She was shivering as he enfolded her in his

178

designer duvet overcoat.

"You were supposed to be going back to Edinburgh tomorrow, to get the rest of your things."

"Supposed to be . . . "

"Can you manage without them?"

"Sure."

"You'll have to, Simon. You need help. Proper help. Serious help. I know someone who might . . . who *will* . . . help you." She shivered despite the burgeoning body heat.

"A family connection?"

"Depends what you mean by family. He's connected. Well connected. All the connections you'll ever need."

"If he's connected, put me in contact with him."

"It's just that . . . " May Day held him tightly. He could feel her heart pounding as she searched out his battered face and planted a ferocious kiss on his broken lips.

For once, Magill remained indifferent to the searing pain. "It's just that . . . what? If he *can* help and *will* help, May, I'm up for it. Whatever it takes. I'll be fine. This is no time to get choosy."

Snuggling even tighter, she cleared her throat. "It's just that he's connected to things most people aren't connected to, Simon, and don't want to be connected to or know too much about."

"May, I'm already connected to things that I shouldn't be connected to and don't want to be connected to, things that I'd really rather not know about. He might be the very person that'll get me – us – through this nightmare."

"But there are things around here . . . this part of the world . . . very serious things . . . that most of us prefer to avoid if we can help it."

"Is he a policeman?"

"Oh God, no! The police'll do anything he tells them, though."

"Sounds good to me. Is he a Freemason, by any chance?"

"Not to my knowledge, Simon. I'm sure he's got influence among the Brotherhood, though. He knows everything, everyone, every angle, near enough. He probably knows more secret handshakes than the Duke of Kent."

"Does he know about O'Connell, Brodie, the bloodstained messages, the rest of this madness? If so, I'll take the risk."

May Day looked up at him, mute.

"He's a terrorist, isn't he?"

"We don't use words like that any more."

Despite the direness of their situation, Magill couldn't restrain a sigh of would-you-credit-it exasperation, "Don't tell me terrorism has had a politically correct makeover. What are they called these days? Armalite executives, Semtex operatives, kneecap comptrollers, community workers? But, you know what, I really don't care what the terminology is or what dirty business they're into. Make the call."

With a shrug of you-asked-for-it resignation, May disentangled herself from Simon's swaddling clothes. She paused, kissed her fingers and placed them gently against his bruised lips. Then slipped back inside.

Magill could hear her lift the phone in the lounge and hit speed-dial. He clutched the wrought-iron balcony and gazed down at the jostling jetsam in the river below. He tried to close his ears to shut out what was happening in the room behind him. The sculler rounded a bend ahead and disappeared from view.

Simon's thoughts turned to the peerless Pitcairn Brodie, whose affable roar he'd often heard echo across New College courtyard. It seemed like a lifetime ago. In reality, it was less than two days. He fondly recalled the old rogue's reaction to the news of his Hustler job. He remembered his drunken warnings about Northern Ireland. Most of all, he recollected the vow he'd taken in Brodie's memory, the vow he'd signally failed to live up to. He wasn't going to fail again. No matter what.

A pink-haired pixie was standing beside him, looking more beautiful than ever. "He's coming to pick you up."

"Who?"

"King Billy."

"Jesus!"

"Jesus wasn't available, Simon. King Billy's always on call. He'll be here in fifteen minutes. Says to stay out of sight till he arrives. Your clothes are almost dry."

"Can I borrow a toothbrush?" Magill said, with a forced grin.

"It's a Magnum you'll be needing."

180

Chapter Twenty-Three

Fine Place, Rough People

Exactly fifteen minutes later, a harsh buzzing noise interrupted Magill's sorely needed coffee break. He set down his Muji mug and started pulling on his distressed reefer jacket as May Day made for the apartment's intercom.

"Taxi for Magill." The accent was simultaneously sibilant and harsh, almost indecipherable. Evidently overdue for a service, the intercom cackled and clicked with interference.

Magill frowned at May Day as if to ask, "A taxi?"

She shrugged her shoulders and struggled to smile. "This is it. Time to go. Ring me later, lover?"

He squeezed his squeeze tightly, patting her back once or twice for reassurance. With a final backward glance as she stood surrounded by the doorframe as if posing for a Jack Vettriano portrait, Simon slipped into the empty lift. A taxi was idling outside. Incongruously, it was an old-fashioned London cab – big, black, boxy, battleship-shape, and making more noise than a tumble drier filled with spanners. Enormous coils of exhaust fumes wrapped themselves round the throbbing ironclad like a deleted scene from a cheap 'n' nasty horror movie, which was somehow appropriate. The stench of diesel was overpowering.

A wizened little man sat behind the wheel. Purple of nose and hollow of cheek, he sported a flat cap and a singularly surly expression. He had the face of a badly cracked mug-shot.

"King Billy?"

The old man glanced at Magill with disdain and not a little loathing. His jaw clicked ominously as he struggled to formulate a reply. "Do I look like King Billy, you ginger fucker?" Click. His jaw ricocheted once more; an audible punctuation mark. He was evidently in the middle of a bad-denture day.

Understandably irritated by the taxi driver's lack of customer orientation, and emboldened by his determination to see things through no matter what, Magill answered the offensive oaf in his finest Home Counties accent. "I'm terribly sorry, but I have absolutely no idea what King Billy looks like. I've never been introduced to the fellow. If it helps, however, you remind me of the little Irishman in the *Benny Hill Show*, the stooge he slapped around incessantly. May I have your autograph?"

The look on the old man's face was priceless. He grinned broadly, almost malevolently, only for his loose top plate to disengage with an unattractive rattle. Click. "You don't know King Billy?" Click. "You'll know him soon enough, Gingerbap." Click. "Get in the back." Click. "Keep your head down." Click.

Magill did as he was bid. The leather banquette had been slashed, the floor was stained, cigarette butts and chewing gum were scattered like popcorn confetti, and a faint aroma of decay, or was it putrefaction, permeated the appalling vehicle. A dangling fir-tree deodorant strip, or several, was sorely needed. Rear seat-belts were conspicuous by their absence.

The tumbling spanners segued into a cement mixer filled with breeze blocks as the malodorous museum-piece revved up for departure. Busy streets slid by, as did a hodgepodge of architectural styles and states of building maintenance. They were climbing steadily, occasional steep hills forcing a lower gear on the grinding dreadnaught, whose exhaust seemed determined to exceed the Kyoto protocol single-handedly.

Click. "Yer wee doll gub ye?" Click. The rising intonation implied a question. Magill hadn't the foggiest what Mr Grumpy was saying.

"Pardon?"

Click. "Yer face." Click. "She hit ye?" Click. A rattle of castanets rose from the front seat as the Fixodent-free chauffeur cackled at his own side-splitting crack.

Magill caught sight of himself in the rear-view mirror. Thick-lipped and black-eyed, with bruised nose and bright ginger hair still spiky from afternoon bed-head, he looked like a clown who'd been shot from a cannon in Chipperfield's Circus and missed the safety net. For fear of setting off the front-seat Geiger counter, he smiled by way of reply.

The cab was coasting along a sunlit arterial road lined with mini-marts, bakeries, tobacconists, fast-food emporia and awning-covered greengrocers, all busy and bustling and doing brisk business, as were plentiful pubs. Magill turned to look through the rear window and saw a rolling meadow of buildings hedged by malachite hills, pierced by half-buried headstones of office blocks and multi-storey car parks.

The taxi turned hard left into a side street that was an architectural curiosity in itself. One side comprised traditional two-up-two-down early- to mid-Victorian terraced houses. The other was made up of recently built bungalows, complete with tiny walled gardens and ornate wrought-iron gates. Every single house bar one boasted a flag of some sort, Union Jacks mainly, interspersed with saltires and Ulster's own standard, a striking red cross on white ground. On a windy day, Magill thought, the street must look like a mixture of the United Nations and a used-car forecourt. The antiquated taxi belched, backfired and clattered to a halt, the spanner spin-cycle complete.

"Do I owe you anything?"

Click. "No charge, Gingerbap." Click. "Order of Solomon." Click.

"Wha . . . *what* did you just say?" Magill gasped, astounded by the driver's glottal announcement.

Click. "No charge, sonny." Click. "Solomon's orders." Click.

"Solomon?"

Click. "King Billy Solomon, who else?" Click. "Don't ye even know who yer dealing with?" Click.

An instant hit of adrenalin surged through Magill's battered body like a double Bushmills downed in one. Fight or flight? That was the question. His first thought was the latter, but remembering his earlier vow of dedication, he fearlessly chose the former, knowing all the while he'd regret it. Order of Solomon? At last. Bring it on!

As the concrete blocks cascaded round the departing cement mixer, Magill heard a harsh metallic sound behind him, like a heavy bolt being pulled out of its sleeve. The door of the only flag-free terraced house was wide open and filled by a bullmastiff. A big, beefy, brawny bullmastiff – three parts bull to one part mastiff – with bulging biceps, barrel chest and a bloated belly that was closer to pressurised keg than six-pack. But impressive all the same.

He wore a black Adidas T shirt and tracksuit bottoms that stretched over his distended abdomen like a kettle drum. With his brilliantly burnished bald head and carefully cropped goatee, the belligerent bullmastiff looked like Vin Diesel with implants. And implants in his implants. Sinuous tattoos snaked up his muscled forearms, slithered beneath the skin-tight T shirt and reappeared at the base of his monstrous neck, which he was either breaking in for a water buffalo or had borrowed on approval from the Minotaur. His features were surprisingly effete, almost pretty – pert nose, sensuous lips, periwinkle-blue eyes – but they were lost in the glistening enormity of their physiognomic setting.

"Bout ye, mucker."

Magill didn't know what the salutation meant, but he'd heard it several times since his arrival in Belfast and assumed it was part of the local vernacular, alongside idiomatic circumlocutions like "soitis," "soaam," "yo ho," "dead on," "stickin' out," "wee buns," "shut yer bake," "catch yerself oan" and "yousens."

"Pleased to meet you, Mr Solomon," Magill replied, and bravely went for a handshake.

King Billy stretched out something that looked like a baseball glove. It enveloped Magill's extended epicene exoskeleton. "Been in the wars, mucker?" His bonny blue eyes danced with malevolent benevolence.

"I had an altercation with a rolling pin."

"Looks like you lost."

"It crept up on me."

"Never trust a rolling pin, mucker. They're not like ladles or carving knives. You always know where you are with a ladle. And a carving knife." He roared with laughter at this private joke. It sounded like castrated bison with a hernia.

"I'll remember that next time, Mr Solomon."

"It's Billy. My friends call me Billy." He paused for two beats. "My enemies don't call at all."

"Why's that, er, Billy?" Magill stuttered, uncertain about his precise acquaintance status.

"Because I tear their fuckin' throats out," Solomon replied savagely. His tiny eyes did a brief fandango. Magill wasn't sure whether he was joking. It sounded like a joke, but almost everything about his alpha-male demeanour suggested otherwise.

"Come on on on in, mucker," the benignly bellicose bullmastiff continued. "Would you like a wee cup of tea in your hand?"

"Love one, Billy."

"Sit yourself down. Buttered pancake? Gravy ring? Paris bun? Slice of Veda?"

Wondering what the local delicacies were, though suspecting they weren't integral to the South Beach Diet, Magill politely declined. "No, I'm fine, thanks all the same. Tea's OK."

He took in the knocked-through living room. Surprisingly, it was filled to capacity with over-stuffed chintzy furniture. Only a La-Z-Boy–style recliner and plasma-screen TV attested to King Billy's lowbrow predilections. The walls, however, were lined floor to ceiling with book-bloated shelves: everything from cheap paperbacks and well-thumbed reference works to gilt-trimmed collectors' items and substantial philosophical tomes, Nietzsche and Schopenhauer in particular. There were even some business and management books: Peters, Porter, Phillips and more. A cracked copy of Dan Brown's *Deception Point* lay spread-eagled on an arm of the sofa.

Five minutes later, Solomon returned with two cups of tea. In his mighty mitts, the crockery looked as though it had been stolen from a doll's house, with menaces. As hospitable hoodlums go, he looked for all the world like a kind-hearted cut-throat.

"Interesting collection of books you have. Planning on doing a doctorate?" Magill joshed.

The change was instantaneous and mercifully brief, but terrifying to behold. Solomon's affable features mutated into a mask of unbridled ferocity. Magill's condescension had not gone unnoticed.

"I've got two already, *mucker*." Never had "mucker," whatever it meant, sounded so intimidating. "I'm thinking of starting a third."

As King Billy set the fragile bone china on the glass coffee table, Magill couldn't help noticing that he had two stars badly tattooed on the back of his hands, both pinkies of which were missing. This had the fearsome effect of making his four-pronged paws appear even more powerful. "You've a double doctorate?" Magill asked, with sufficient awestruck astonishment to calm the bullmastiff's beast within. "Wow."

"Don't sound so surprised, mucker. Every ex-con in Ulster has a degree or two. There's not much to do in the Maze apart from distance-learning and dirty protests. Life inside is less about hard labour and hard men than hard reading and hard marking. There are more PhDs in the IRA than fuckin' NASA. The UVF has more letters after its name than I've whacked Sinn Feiners."

"So you're actually Dr Dr King Billy Solomon?"

"At your service, *Mr* Magill."

The stress on Magill's singular lack of scholarly standing didn't go unnoticed either. Calculating that he'd unsettled the brute and that an unsettled brute might let something slip about Brodie or O'Connell, Simon decided to pursue a policy of provocation, foolhardy though it was. "The beauty of doing a doctorate inside, I suppose, is that there's no way the external examiner'd fail it. I mean, what examiner in their right mind would deny a degree to an assassin?"

The tiny teacups rattled ominously as King Billy sat down on the sofa directly opposite Magill. "Oh, it's all above board. Open University and all that." The bullmastiff took a delicate sip from his bone-china cup. If he'd had a pinkie to spare, no doubt he'd have raised it. "We know where the fuckers live, mind you."

Still determined to needle the beast, affable though he seemed on the surface, Magill continued his antagonistic line of questioning. "What are your doctorates in, then? The electromechanics of testicular torture? The aerodynamics of concrete blocks and petrol bombs? Punishment beatings: a sociological perspective?"

Solomon leaned forwards. His massive torso overshadowed the tiny coffee table. The veins in his neck stood out like throbbing hawsers. His cyan eyes were pools of pellucid menace. So smooth and unlined was his huge face that Magill surmised it had been Botoxed repeatedly. Either that or King Billy should licence his anti-ageing secrets to Laboratoires Garnier.

"Do you really want to know what makes me tick?" Solomon demanded, like a bomb about to explode. All he needed was TNT written across his black T-shirt and a strip of fusewire dangling from the polished pate. Magill had lit the blue touch-paper of the red rag on the tip of the iceberg that broke the camel's back.

"Of course I do," Simon said with a confidence he didn't feel but was determined to impersonate. "Any friend of May Day is a friend of mine," he added bravely.

"Lovely girl, May Day," Solomon replied, relaxing. "Lovely girl. She means an awful lot to me, as does her mother." His demeanour was improving by the second. "She knows how to handle a rolling pin too," he added, with a brief smile at Magill's bruised and battered features. He did his herniatic bison thing again.

The malevolent moment had passed. It wasn't so much a case of the iceman melteth as a fizzing fusewire being extinguished with a couple of seconds to spare.

"OK. I'll tell you my story, if you can stand it, but let's hear yours first. Darling buds of May says you're in trouble. Spit it out, mucker."

Magill spat his story out, as instructed, in gobbets of ill-digested pain. It was a relief to talk about it, strangely, if only because Solomon was such an attentive audience and evidently had experience of the matters under discussion. He sat immobile as Magill unburdened himself, even when the Order of Solomon entered the equation.

He reacted on only three occasions. When Professor Brodie's name was mentioned, he smiled a smile of recognition. He asked Simon to repeat the exact wording of the murderers' messages. And at the climax of the O'Connell story, he broke the tension with a cruel joke about the professor's mobile phone being on vibrate or defibrillate or some such.

Voice cracking with catharsis, Magill brought his grisly tale up to date. "That's about it, Billy. I hear you're an expert in these things. Does it mean anything to you? You can start with the Order of Solomon."

"It means nothing to me, mucker," he announced with what sounded like authentic ignorance. "I've never heard anything like that before. And I thought I'd heard everything. The Order of Solomon is new to me too, and just so as we're clear here, *this* Solomon didn't order the hits on Brodie and O'Connell." King Billy thumped his chest by way of emphasis, looking not unlike a mountain gorilla with alopecia.

Although he was effectively back to square one, Magill was relieved to hear that Solomon wasn't personally involved in the imbroglio. He quite liked him, despite everything – not least his commendable self-control in dealing with stroppy Brits. "It has something to do with the Freemasons, doesn't it? May Day felt it was the Freemasons, or possibly the Orange Order."

King Billy dismissed the suggestion with a wave of his paw. "It's not the Freemasons. The Freemasons are transvestite Rotarians. They're harmless these days. Don't believe what you read in Dan Brown. The Masons are deep in the decline phase of their product life cycle, as is the Orange Order. Isn't *that* the term you marketers use?"

Magill frowned and stared down at his hands, disappointed by the evident incomprehension of this so-called expert and the pointless digression their conversation was taking. He couldn't keep the testiness out of his voice. "Marketing? What does marketing have to do with anything?"

"I don't know for certain. At least, not yet. I need to check a few things out first. But marketing is something that connects everything you've mentioned: Brodie's consultancy, the Paspi website, O'Connell's book, your new job. There may be other connections, probably are. Nevertheless, marketing's one of them. The golden rule, in my experience of these matters, is that everything's connected and tracing the connections is vital."

"Right."

"There's something else as well, mucker."

"What's that, Billy?"

"It concerns the biggest issue in marketing today."

"Sceptical consumers, you mean?"

Solomon shook his monstrous head.

"Product proliferation? Product parity? Communications clutter? Disruptive technologies?"

King Billy remained silent.

"Sustainability? The tripping point? Storytelling shortcomings?"

The alopecic gorilla looked at Magill quizzically, as if dealing with an ignoramus. "Fakes," he said firmly. "Fake brands, fake fashions, fake pharmaceuticals, fake places, fake services . . . bootleg Dan Brown books." He nodded towards the volume splayed on his arm-rest. "Everything's fake these days, mucker. Marketing is being destroyed by fakes. They're the zombies of business life and they're wreaking havoc."

"Fair point. But I don't see the connection to the murders of O'Connell and Brodie. Are you saying their deaths were faked?"

"No," King Billy replied, "but the apparent perpetrators of the murders may be fakes."

"Fake Freemasons, you mean? Fake Order of Solomon?"

"Or fake stories about the murders and their discovery."

"Sorry?"

"You're a fuckin' fake, Magill." Solomon reached behind a chintz cushion, whipped out a pistol, pointed it at his astonished guest and pulled the trigger.

189

Chapter Twenty-Four

Viva, Viva, Las Vegas

Dusk was his favorite time of day. Dusk in the desert was always spectacular. But dusk in Las Vegas was more spectacular still. If not the greatest show on earth, it was right up there with David Copperfield. Or Celine Dion at Caesar's Palace.

As the last vestiges of the day made way for the fluorescent fireworks of the night, Las Vegas was a place of wall-to-wall wonder, a place of perpetual promise, a place of anxious anticipation, a place of gut-wrenching expectancy. What will happen over the next few hours? Will it be fame? Will it be fortune? Will it be failure? Will it be flame-out? Is my luck in? Is it your night? Is our ship about to sail? All will be revealed. Let the party unfold. Roll the dice and be damned.

Paris, France claims to be the City of Light, though it's long been eclipsed by Nevada's neon nirvana. The Paris Hotel & Casino is a spectacular exception. Try as it might, it can't compete with the original. The view from the Eiffel Tower Bar and Restaurant, however, is one of the best-kept secrets in town. It overlooks the Bellagio and, when the world-famous fountains are performing their staggering syncopated routine, it's the best place to be in the best place to be: Las Vegas.

Barton Brady II stirred his Chivas Regal on the rocks in the restaurant-bar's air-conditioned comfort while watching the Strip's surging sweating crowds in front of the fountains as they checked their digicams and jostled for an unobtainable unobstructed view. Yesterday had been a good day. A red-letter day in his company's red-letter-littered history. But this morning's meeting had been even better.

Not much work was done afterwards, admittedly. He himself was so excited by the impending grail trail that he'd blogged about it all afternoon. But what the hell. Things were lookin' good. Aherne was on board. Another sexy suffix had been added to SA's money-spinning roster. And, best of all, GRAIL was glimmering on the horizon.

Boy, was he keen to get back on the road. He'd had more than enough behind-the-scenes activity. He was a showman at heart, and in a town full of showmen, he was determined to show that he was the showman's showman. Management consultancy was a branch of showbusiness, after all, though most shows he'd seen didn't have a particularly impressive razzle-dazzle quotient or score highly on the razzamatazz-o-meter. He'd show 'em.

Brady sipped his nectar of the Nevada liquor gods. It was almost as smooth as he was, but not quite. Yasmin could run the show at Serendipity Associates while he was strutting his stuff on the circuit. A break from each other wouldn't do either of them any harm. He'd noticed her mounting frustration and she'd noticed his restlessness, indifference, ennui.

Yasmin wasn't the most interpersonal person – quite the opposite – but what she lacked in gladhanding she more than made up for in sheer good fortune. Maybe Aherne could be persuaded to hook up in some formal capacity. Clearly, she and Yasmin had hit it off and he'd noted the avaricious look in her academic eye when Chas started talking figures yesterday. Emer had the ear of Kate Phillips, what's more, or so she said. And the imprimatur of the prodigious Professor Phillips, even at second hand, wouldn't do SA any harm.

What was it, he often wondered, with American executives and Ivy League business professors? Few of them had any management experience to speak of. The garbage they filled students' heads with on MBA programmes was fit only for the dumpster. They might be wunderkinds at calculus, but most couldn't sell a chili corndog to save their sorry asses. Their journals were utterly unreadable, even the sections entitled "Managerial implications." *Especially* the sections entitled "Managerial implications." A manager'd need to be in pretty dire straits before turning to that meretricious mumbo-jumbo. She'd be in even direr straits if she did.

Slipping off his aquamarine Zegna jacket, Brady draped it carefully across the back of his barstool. Satisfied with the angle of the dangle, he drank a deep draught of the king of malts, its rocks rattling contentedly against his orthodontic competitive advantage, and lifted a finger for another. Chainsaw Charlie, the Paris's legendary one-legged bartender, leapt into action.

There was a commotion in the crowd below. It suddenly parted like cooking oil on a hot griddle. Distant sounds of shouting and screaming could be heard, dully, through the plate-glass windows. Fist fight? Cardiac arrest? Pickpocket-induced diversion? Elvis impersonator gone postal?

The doppler wail of cop-car sirens and contrapuntal clang of accident and emergency vehicles soon added to the hubbub, as did the reassuring whump of TV-station helicopters. It must be serious when the buzzards of post-industrial society start circling overhead. Shots of mayhem on the Strip, with the Bellagio fountains in the breaking-news background, were way too good to miss. Ratings would rise by the minute so long as the incident wasn't too trivial. The higher the gore, the higher the Q score.

Chainsaw Charlie switched on the widescreen TV and zapped through the channels till the scene outside his windows snapped into view. Everyone turned to watch. Why look down on a scene of confusion when television covers it so much better? The feed from the voyeurcam was intermittent, the sound crackly. Brady knew that these effects were added in real time by the studio production team, but they provided the necessary sense of caught-live-on-camera verisimilitude that crystal-clear reception didn't. If they couldn't fake reality in Vegas, where could they fake it?

Between the calculated crackles and helicopter-blade backbeat – protooled and mixed to perfection – Brady gathered that a crack-fuelled panhandler had shot a passing conventioneer from Duluth, in town for the Hewlett-Packard retailers' rally. Unprovoked apparently. Wrong place at the wrong time. One minute savouring the sight of Bellagio's aquatic chorus line and dreaming of profitable peripherals, the next fighting for life on the Strip's scorching sidewalk, while doing his bit for local station ratings. Life may be what happens when you aren't looking, or so the old chestnut goes, but death is an accident always waiting to happen.

The serendipitous nature of business life and death never ceased to amaze Barton Brady. What amazed him even more was the belief, espoused by B-school professors in particular, that commercial life was intrinsically controllable, predictable, certain. Their models, theories and nutrition-free pie charts implied that everything could be managed. And managers bought this blarney because they wanted to believe things could be brought under control. Management consultants and savvy professors duly pandered to this belief. What was the rallying cry that made and sustained Kate Phillips's illustrious academic career? That's right, Analysis, Planning, Implementation and Control. The reality, of course, was Accident, Providence, Inexactitude and Contingency.

Consider Serendipity Associates. He went into consultancy by chance. He met Yasmin by accident. He got lucky when his aspirations to gurudom ran aground. He bumped into Chang and Eng in a bar, on the day they were downsized from Accenture. Only one of his associates joined the company by the conventional want-ad, background-check, psychological-profile route, and that was Chas Rosencreutz, SA's rock-solid sheet anchor.

Even the recent Aherne encounter was a fluke. Conferences weren't his thing, and academic conferences were the nearest thing to hell this side of a Jamie Cullum concert. Indeed, if it weren't for the Dan Brown connection and Yasmin's powers of persuasion, he wouldn't ever have gone to see the wild Irish rose or have -preneur to play with.

The Stripside sirens started up again. The unlucky computer dealer from Duluth was gurneyed-to-go and whisked away to a waiting ER. The roiling crowd was coagulating once more and the carrion-seeking choppers were flying the coop in search of fresh televisual prey, preferably mangled and mutilated.

Brady realised that his own luck would run out in the end. He and Yasmin had had a hot streak for five years now, and nothing lasts for ever. Maybe SA's days were numbered. But equally, maybe the really good times – the guru times – were about to begin. Who could tell? What the hell? Business was a crapshoot at the best of times, and a rigged roulette wheel at worst.

His cellphone rang. He checked caller ID.

"Yo, Yasmin. How's tricks?"

"Hey, Barton. Saw you on TV, bossman. Sipping your Chivas in the Eiffel Tower, staring at some sap shot on the Strip." She was in a good mood. He could tell. He was feeling pretty mellow himself.

"Some sap shot on the Strip," he echoed. "Bit of a tongue-twister, that. Caught the action on TV. Just another night in Sin City, eh?"

"Yeah, I watched you watch it. There was an aerial shot of the Eiffel Tower barflies staring at the Eiffel Tower on TV."

"Must have been another channel. I didn't see me see me."

"I guessed as much. Nobody waved or raised their glasses."

"So, what's up, partner?"

"I just had a call from Emer Aherne. As I'm off WOWing tomorrow, I thought I'd give you a heads-up before I go. I've an early start."

"WOWing? Is that a Tom Peters thing? I thought Tom was a busted flush. Didn't he confess he'd cooked the data for *In Search of Excellence?* Tom's the Milli Vanilli of management consultancy. Don't waste your time, Yasmin, we've work to do."

"It's not Peters, putz," she laughed. "Milli Vanilli dates you, by the way. The current cultural reference is Ashlee Simpson. Didn't you see her out-of-sync lipsync on *SNL?*"

"Gee, sorry I missed that," he said mock-sarcastically. "OK, so Tom's the Ashlee Simpson of solution salespersons. What is WOWing, or have I missed another crucial cultural reference?"

"Women's Oppression Workshop. Emer invited me and I'm keen to check out the babes. You never know what might turn up. We aren't Serendipity Associates for nothing."

"Go for it, Yazza. I'm all for women's oppression."

"D'oh. Tell me something I don't know, Bart," Buonarroti laughed.

"What's Aherne's message that can't wait?"

"It's about the grail quest. Apparently Kate Phillips is holding a conference at Kellogg for – get this – Marketing Illuminati. Starts Friday. I've never heard of them, but apparently they're a mystical marketing society of some kind. Sounds like an old-boy association for New-Age academicians, conspiracy geeks and defrocked Freemasons. I'm not certain, though."

"Doesn't Emer know? She's Phillips's bosom buddy, isn't she?"

"She says she doesn't know the full details, and Kate is keeping mum. Maybe Phillips is planning a new product for the consultancy circuit. It's very timely, what with the Danster 'n' all."

"Maybe you mentioned GRAIL to Aherne en route to the airport, and she's taken it back to her marketing mentor."

"I said nothing to Emer," Buonarroti barked.

"Well, how did she know to tell you about the Illuminati? Why would she mention it unless you'd told her about the GRAIL quest?"

"I didn't tell her. You told her yourself. In that blog of yours. Emer was checking to see if you'd blogged about yesterday's meeting and found the GRAIL material. She mentioned the Illuminati thing because she thought SA'd be interested. She's doing the company a favour. She's one of us, remember?"

"Sorry, partner. I am a putz. The excitement of getting back in the consultancy ring's getting the better of me. I'll give Phillips a bell tomorrow. See what's what."

"You do that, partner."

"Enjoy your workshop, Yasmin."

"I'll tell you all about it in a day or two, Barton."

"Wow! Can't wait."

"Oppressorpreneur has a ring to it, don't you think?"

"You're talking my language, Yazza."

"Don't I know it, Bart."

Brady finished his Chivas Regal, left a hefty tip and waved goodnight to Chainsaw Charlie. Immaculate as ever, he took the elevator to the faux French casino floor and, on a whim, stepped outside for a breath of fresh air. The heat was oppressive, even at 9 p.m., though that didn't deter the crowd in front of the Bellagio, where the fountains fandangoed on cue every half-hour. The HP retailer from Duluth was a distant memory. DOA, he later found out.

Just another night in Sin City.

Viva, Viva, Las Vegas.

Chapter Twenty-Five

All the Sixes, Clickety Click

The gun clicked. The chamber was empty. King Billy pulled the trigger again. Empty. Again. Empty. Again. Again. Empty. Empty. Although he was frozen with fear, Simon Magill was determined not to show it.

"Postmodern Russian roulette," Solomon said with a chuckle. "No bullets. But it still scares the shit out of you."

"I thought you weren't supposed to point guns at people unless you intend to use them," Magill replied calmly.

"Who says I don't?" Solomon smirked. "Tell me your story again, and make it the truth this time."

"It is the truth!" Magill shouted, as much from relief as anger.

Solomon smirked once more, evidently enjoying the reaction he was provoking. "Humour me, mucker," he said in a tone that didn't invite levity.

Aggrieved, Magill tried to counter with an equally authoritative intonation, but his rapidly melting vocal cords pitched his speech an octave or two above normal. If not quite Mickey Mouse on helium, it was definitely in Michael Jackson territory. As he recounted the story again, somewhat faster than before, Solomon interrupted him more frequently. Magill had the distinct feeling that King Billy's interrogation technique was well honed.

When it was over, the interrogator nodded appreciatively, having satisfied himself that Magill's story stacked up, implausible though it was. He placed his pistol on the coffee table in front of his exhausted interviewee. "It's a Glock. Take it. You'll be needing it. There are bullets in the top drawer over there." He indicated an ineptly assembled MFI MDF VFM cabinet in the corner.

Magill was appalled. "No. No thanks. I don't want it."

"It's all right. It's yours, mucker. To keep. The IRA are holding an arms-decommissioning fire sale. Everything must go. Three-for-two deals all over the shop. Buy One Glock, Get Other Firearms Free."

Magill pushed the gun away. "No thank you, Dr Dr Solomon," he said with an attempt at contempt. But Jacko was back and hitting the helium big time.

"You'll need it, mucker. I have to go out. On business. You'll be here on your own. I'm on all sorts of hit lists, though they usually shoot first round here and check identity cards later."

Somewhat chastened and not a little embarrassed, Magill answered uncomfortably, "I don't know how to use it. I've never fired a gun before."

"You got a BlackBerry?"

"No, not any more. I used to be a real Berrybugger, but I broke the disgusting habit."

"Well, if you can manage a BlackBerry, you can handle a Glock 17. It's lightweight plastic, feels like a kid's toy, but fires like a fuckin' elephant gun."

Magill shook his head firmly. "I'd rather not. I'm very clumsy. I'd only end up shooting myself."

King Billy thought for a moment. "Suit yourself. I'll call Wee Joe. He knows you already, so he'll be happy to babysit for half an hour or so."

Bemused by the bizarre turn the babyminding conversation was taking – images of tiny-tot-targeted BlackBerries with rapid-fire action started to swirl around his stream of consciousness – Magill was thrown by the name of his alleged acquaintance. "I'm afraid I don't know any Joes, Dr Dr Solomon, Wee or otherwise."

"Sure you do, mucker. He brought you here. The taxi driver. Wee Joe Monroe."

"The taxi driver's going to protect me, is he?" Magill snorted dismissively. "What with? His delinquent dentures?"

Solomon ran a massive paw over his glistening head. A tattooed lady undulated on his upper arm and a drumlin swarm rippled where his biceps used to be. He asked if his guest had ever heard of the Shankill Butchers. On account of his family background, Magill knew that they were a group of Loyalist psychopaths who preyed on innocent Catholics and sliced them up for fun. King Billy elaborated, explaining that the Shankill Butchers not only sliced, diced, taunted and tortured their victims, but beat them with wheel braces, cut their throats right through to the spine and unceremoniously dumped the bodies afterwards.

Like most people, Simon believed that the Butchers had been caught and put away for good. Wrong again. Not all of them were caught. The driver of the taxi used to transport the victims got away scot-free. The others were reluctant to rat on him since he was the most vicious of them all. "He still drives the taxi sometimes, mucker. You can see the bloodstains on the floor."

Simon Magill wasn't renowned for his goldfish impressions, but as he opened and shut his mouth in astonishment, the resemblance was uncanny. "Wee Joe's a Shankill Butcher?"

"Wee Joe's the Shankill *Master* Butcher," King Billy corrected. "Be very careful what you say to him. Whatever you do, don't make jokes about his name. When he was younger, people used to call him Marilyn. He thought they were saying Marlon and then he caught on. Jellied tongue was on offer in the butcher's thereafter."

Thank God I didn't go that far, Magill thought with relief. A grumpy pensioner with a grudge was one thing, a touchy master butcher with a tongue-severing habit was something else entirely.

"He hasn't mellowed with age either," King Billy continued. "A couple of years ago, someone told him to his face that he looked like the wee Ulsterman on the *Benny Hill Show*. They never found the body, though bits of it turned up all over West Belfast."

Magill swallowed. It was painful. His mouth was a dry as a dromedary's scrotum. "I think maybe I'll try the Glock after all. If it's just like a BlackBerry . . . "

"Nah," King Billy said with a smile, as he rose regally from the imperial sofa. Its springs genuflected with relief. "Wee Joe's the man for you, mucker. You'll be OK so long as he keeps his teeth in. If he pulls out his top plate, you're fucked."

Simon was still coming to terms with the Toothless Joe babysitting scenario when he saw Solomon saunter past the window and on up the street. His walk was almost as distinctive as his appearance, a kind of rolling strut with occasional gyroscopic juts of the head to maintain forward momentum. With mobile phone clamped to his ear, he looked like a narwhal in a karaoke bar trying to keep in tune with "Jailhouse Rock." Bet he went down a bomb during the marching season.

The hearse for hire turned up a few moments later. Relieved, Magill could see that Joe the Ripper's teeth were firmly in place. He was carrying a black leather briefcase of some kind.

"What's in the briefcase, Joe?" Magill inquired pleasantly by way of a conversational starter for ten. He immediately wished he hadn't. Wee Joe smiled a preternaturally porcelain smile, opened the case with a resounding snap of the silver hasps, and lifted the elegant lid. Inside was a glistening set of butcher's knives on a bed of black velvet: cleaver, carver, hacksaw, big boning knife, small serrated slicer and more besides. The full murderer's monty.

Click. "Like what ye see, Gingerbap?" Click.

"Very impressive, Joe."

Click. "King Billy says I've got ta take care of ye." Click. "I've been lookin' farward to takin' care of ye." Click. "Still want that autygraph?" Click.

He pulled out his carver, held it up to the light and slowly turned the glittering instrument, admiring its shimmering surface. Reaching into the carrying case again, he extracted a lengthy sharpening rod and, after a couple of probationary strokes, lapsed into contented silence as steel scraped against steel in spine-chilling rhythm.

"You do that to relax?"

Wee Joe glanced at him, the tempo of his scraping increasing fractionally. Scrape. Silence. Scrape. Silence. Click. "Aye." Click. Silence. Scrape. Silence.

"Stressful life, the butchery business?"

Scrape. Silence. Scrape. Silence. Click. "Aye." Click. Silence. Scrape. Silence.

"You work round here?"

Scrape. Silence. Scrape. Silence. Click. "Nah." Click. Silence. Scrape. Silence. Click. "I'm retired." Click. Silence. Scrape. Silence. Scrape.

Realising that repartee was futile, Magill searched through the bookshelves for something to pass the time. Squashed in the corner of the bottom shelf, beside a full set of fake *Encyclopaedia Britannicas*, he found two extremely thick, black-bound PhD theses. One was called *A Cultural History of the Performing Arts in Nineteenth-Century Belfast*. The other, incredibly, was entitled *Porter's Five Forces and the Drug-Dealing Business*.

Magill flicked though the impressively scholarly tome, fascinated to learn about the structure of an enormously profitable though illicit industry, to say nothing of its barriers to entry, supplier bargaining powers, new competitive threats and emergence of substitute recreational products from alcopops to pornographic websites. The results of a questionnaire survey of dealers, users, shippers and mules were also presented, as was an impressive culminating model of competitive advantage in the criminal industries based on Nietzsche's eternal return of the same.

While wondering what the response rates to Solomon's questionnaire were, as well as the incentives he might have used to increase them, Magill's intellectual idyll was interrupted by a fusillade of orthodontic noises-off. He feared that Wee Joe's top plate had gone walkabout and that his time had come. But no, the Steradentertainer had set down his psychotherapeutic accoutrements and was clearing his throat prior to saying something of import.

Click. "Heustabreed dogs." Click.

"Heustabreed? Sorry, who or what's heustabreed? Is it a local delicacy, some variation on hot dogs?"

"Click. "He." Click. "Usta." Click. "Breed." Click. "Dogs." Click. "King Billy usta breed dogs." Click.

"Did he, indeed? Did he show them and such? Crufts? Win any prizes?"

Click. "Bullmastiffs, sotheywere." Click.

"Figures."

Click. "One of them attacked him, soitdid." Click. "Near bit his leg aff." Click. "He strung it up in the outhouse." Click. "Piano wire." Click. "Muzzled." Click. "Took two weeks to die, soitdid."

Click.

"Jesus. What about the others?"

Click. "Put them down, sohedid." Click. "Skinned them." Click. "Billy's a dab hand with a hunting knife." Click. "Made an overcoat out of the pelts." Click. "Still wears it, sohedoes." Click. "On special occasions." Click.

"What special occasions would that be?" Magill asked, aghast.

Click. "Funerals, mainly." Click. "Parties as well." Click. "Gets good wear out of it, sohedoes." Click.

Magill's mind raced at the thought of the parties King Billy might attend in natty attackdog outerwear. Long Kesh reunion parties. Drugs Trade Association parties. Shankill Butcher barbecues. Or perhaps he organised paramilitary party plans, pyramid selling schemes for ex-cons. Like Tupperware, only with jemmies, crowbars, skeleton keys, sawn-off shotguns, safe-breaking requisites and bespoke baseball bats for kneecap comptrollers.

The reverie was interrupted by Magill's increasingly garrulous babysitter. Click. "You were afeart, weren't ye?" Click.

"Sorry, Joe, I didn't quite catch that."

Click. "Afraid." Click. "You were afeart when I dropped ye aff." Click. "I could see it in yer eyes." Click. "You were getting ready to run, weren't ye?" Click. "Think yerself lucky ye didn't." Click. "Shinner tried to run once." Click. "Billy chased him up the street, sohedid." Click. "The big man can't half move." Click. "Caught up with him at the funeral parlour." Click. "There was a service goin' on, sotherewas." Click. "Kicked the shite out of him in front of the mourners." Click. "Shot him in the face beside the coffin." Click. "Everyone clapped, sotheydid." Click.

Lost for words, Magill had no idea how to respond, other than to say, "Bet you had fun times together in the Maze."

Click. "I've never been in prison, Gingerbap." Click. "King Billy did my time for me, sohedid." Click. "I owe him my life, soado." Click. "I'd kill if he asked me to, soawould." Click.

"Has he ever asked you?"

Click. "Not recently." Click.

"Glad to hear it."

Click. "But I live in hope." Click.

"Nice."

Click. "Yer lucky he likes yer wee doll, soyeare." Click.

"Hope it stays that way."

Click. "We'll see." Click.

A rolling strut paraded past the window, the gyroscopic jut in overdrive. Wee Joe carefully replaced his honed carving knife and sharpening steel in the black velvet receptacle, clicked the hasps shut with a resounding snap and got up to leave as King Billy barrelled into the room, fleshy face flushed with excitement.

Click. "I'll be seeing you, Gingerbap." Click.

"Missing you already, Mr Monroe."

Chapter Twenty-Six

King Solomon's Mine

King Billy Solomon rolled into his elongated living room like a crown green bowling ball with the jack in its sights. A "Bout ye!" was about to burst forth, like Big Bertha at the Siege of Verdun, when he spotted his theses copulating on the floor. "Doin' a bit of light reading, mucker?"

"Just had a flick through one of them. Wee Joe wanted to talk, and I wasn't going to stop him while he had his silverware to hand."

"Wise move, mucker." Swooping like an overfed osprey, Solomon scooped up both volumes, glanced at them dismissively and carried his prey back to the corner, behind *Britannica*.

"How come you didn't publish the Porter stuff, Billy? It's very interesting research, well written too. The bits I read were far better than most of the stuff in mainstream academic journals. The subject matter alone is, er, fascinating."

Solomon threw himself down on the La-Z-Boy. "I tried. I tried. In my first flush of enthusiasm, I submitted manuscripts to all the top journals. But your august scholarly organs didn't want to know. The criminal industries are beyond the academic pale, apparently, even though they epitomise business life: intense competition, commodity products, fluctuating demand, sourcing concerns, global distribution channels, severe penalties for failure, value chains like you wouldn't believe, strategy executions to die for."

"Killer apps, too."

The behemoth burst out laughing. His Brobdingnagian belly wobbled ominously. "Sometimes you have to kill to make a killing."

"I'll take your word for it, Billy."

205

"That's the title of the article I sent to *Harvard Business Review*."

"And they rejected it? Can't think why."

"Aye, well, that was all a long time ago," he replied, with a sorrowful shake of his refulgent head, as if wishing life had turned out differently. "Other things came up. Some things went down. What goes around comes around. With interest. You know, Simon, Nietzsche was right when he talked about the eternal return of the same. Freddy was some pup. He really knew how to frighten people, academics especially. The terrorist of thought, Nietzsche was."

Magill made a mental note to steer clear of Nietzsche, while observing that King Billy presumably maintained an interest in matters academic, since he was one of Hustler Business School's biggest benefactors, according to May Day. Solomon shrugged and made it clear that his HBS connection was closer to an investment than a donation. He wasn't the benefactor type, though he lived modestly and channelled what little money he made from his business operations back into the local community. Clearly his interest in the drugs trade was more than just academic, though when Magill raised the topic, King Billy dismissed it instantly.

"The drugs business is peanut buttons, mucker. So's smuggling, kidnapping, arms dealing, bank robbery, DVD piracy, protection rackets, pre-paid punishment beatings. They're no big deal. Small potatoes."

"They're pretty big potatoes if you're being beaten or punished to order."

"Business is business. Punishment beatings are our bread and butter, mucker. A bit of light assault and battery on a Friday night and your beer money's sorted for the weekend. Couldn't beat it."

"So, if punishment beating's pin money, where's the action these days?"

The La-Z-Boy groaned in agony as the elephant seal sat up. "Come here till I show you something."

With a burst of agility that took Magill by surprise, King Billy surged out of the living room and charged upstairs. It sounded for all the world like a wildebeest's stag party. The top floor of the house was knocked through like the living room below. An impressive array of state-of-the-art computer equipment, colour printers, DVD burners and so forth occupied one end of the gloomy curtained room. Hundreds of copies of *The Da Vinci Code* DVD were piled on racks in the centre of the workspace, as were best-selling CDs, video games, Microsoft Vista software and pornographic classics like *The Sperminator, Shaving Ryan's Privates, White Men Can't Hump* and *ET – The Extra Testicle*.

"I thought you said DVD piracy was peanut buttons, Billy?"

"It is, mucker. But it's a steady earner." He opened his arms and performed a remarkably nimble pirouette. "This is also the command centre of our global spamming operation. Bootleg Viagra, mainly, and DIY penis-implant kits." He nodded in the direction of an enormous stack of sealed cardboard boxes that filled the back half of the room. "The Nigerian 419 scam is also run from here, as are our iPorn operations and online casino, rollemandweep.com. We're working on a cyber protection racket as well. Watch this space."

Despite his understandable reservations, Magill was deeply impressed. "It's very sophisticated, Billy. Don't the police give you any bother?"

"Getagrip, mucker. They're our firewall. Or they used to be. It's all changing. The whole industry's in flux. The demand's enormous and growing by leaps and bounds, but there's far too much capacity. These days it's all about cutting costs, consolidation, conglomeration, backward integration and economies of scope. The criminal industry – Crimind, we call it – has long been fragmented, small-scale, family business–based ... "

"Your idea of a family business isn't everyone's idea of a family business, Billy."

"That's true. But the ideas of Porter, Peters, Phillips and so on are having a big impact on Crimind thinking. Reengineering, downsizing, benchmarking, delayering, outsourcing, core competencies and what-not are the talk of the criminal classes these days, as are marketing and advertising."

"Above the line and below the line certainly take on a whole new meaning in the cocaine marketing business."

King Billy chortled. "Mock if you want, mucker, but there's a buncha wise guys in Las Vegas who're rewriting the classics for the Crimind market: *In Search of Malfeasance, Bad to Worse, Straight to the Gut, The One-Minute Murderer, Who Moved My Machete?, The Interrogator's Dilemma, The Ripping Point*."

"*Deep Six Sigma*'s a bestseller, no doubt. Or is it *Six-gun Sigma, Six-shooter Sigma, Six Smith and Wesson*?"

Solomon did his castrated bison impersonation and continued matter-of-factly, "Aye, well, there's also an awful lot of interest in branding. Obviously the Mafia's the Microsoft of our sector and Al-Qaeda aspires to Wal-Mart. Hamas is aiming for Hermès, ETA is our MTV, the Farc guerrillas have FCUK written all over them and Baader-Meinhof is just Burberry by another name. They expanded too quickly in the 1980s and are still paying the price."

"So where do the UVF and IRA fit into the picture?

"Oh, the UVF isn't into branding that much. We swear by Jack Welch. We see ourselves as the GE of global terrorist networks. Forget wet work. Forget blood and gore. Forget extortion and execution. Forget products full stop. Services are where it's at. Training. Consultancy. Software development. Spam delivery systems. Hitperson scheduling programmes. JIT armaments inventory control. We work behind the scenes. Our days in the front line are over. We're intermediaries these days. Impresarios, really. Top-slice the action. That's all. Our business has never been better and we've got management thinkers to thank."

"The IRA too?"

"Aye, well, they're into identity theft in a big way. They've 'disappeared' so many people over the years that their databases are bigger than Cisco Systems'. They've rigged more votes than the FT 100 has gerrymandered shareholders' meetings. I hate to say it, but IRA Inc. is best in class at PR, branding, marketing and communication. They're top-of-the-line terrorpractors, right up there with the KKK. They're the BMW of Crimind, the ultimate killing machine. And now that pickings in Ireland are slim, they're planning a big franchising push under the slogan 'IRA Inside' – Iraqi Republican Army, Iranian Republican Army, Israeli Republican Army, Indonesian Republican Army, Icelandic Republican Army. You've got to hand it to them. They're the HBS of the criminal-industrial complex."

"Hustler Business School?"

"Don't bite the hand that feeds you, mucker. You remember the Northern Bank raid a few years back?"

"Twenty-six million, wasn't it?"

"Guess how much your new business school cost?"

"I can't imagine."

"Never let it be said that the IRA has done nothing for the local community. They're Ulster's biggest export. They must be due a Queen's Award for Industry, not that they'd collect it."

"I thought the UVF and the IRA were mortal enemies. Yet here you are singing their praises and helping launder their money. May Day said you were Titanic's biggest benefactor."

"Strategic alliance, mucker. Venture capital. We learnt it all from you business-school types. We read your books in the Maze. You've only got yourselves to blame. But the bottom line is that we do it better than you. We really know how to downsize and reengineer and delayer and kill the competition. We really know how to manage relationships with customers. Our customer-complaints procedures are second to none. Nobody complains twice, take it from me. Our customer service is to die for. We don't fuck around, mucker. Look and learn."

Magill's head was reeling. He wasn't quite sure how to take this stuff. On the one hand, Solomon might be doing an Ian Kane and pulling his leg in time-honoured Ulster-trickster fashion. On the other hand, it was awfully plausible Criminality was an industry of sorts and, given the boom in business and management how-to, self-help, made-easy books, surely the criminal classes must be taking classes just like everybody else. And when you factored in the sector's manifold role models – Nick Leeson, Ernest Saunders, Robert Maxwell, Jonathan Aitken, Kenny Lay and Martha Stewart – it didn't seem so far fetched. Student recruitment on accountancy courses *increased* after Enron. Kate Moss's billings *went up* after she hit the white stuff. Winona Ryder was *asked to model* for Marc Jacobs after stealing his wares from Saks Fifth Avenue. Dan Brown's *Da Vinci Code* boosted the intake of Opus Dei, for God's sake! If that's what's happening in the mainstream, then heaven only knows what's going on in the murkier corners of capitalism.

Solomon was warming to his theme. "You look sceptical, Simon, but it's all down to simple economics, the theory of natural advantage. What natural advantages does Northern Ireland have? Like Singapore and Taiwan, we've next to none. No gas, no oil, no coal, no iron, no minerals, no diamonds in the rough, even. We've a wee bit of wind on the north coast, some good agricultural land and a couple of half-decent harbours. That's it. But we have criminal resources in abundance. When it comes to secret societies, what's more, we're world class. And always have been. The De Dannan, the White Boys, the Peep O'Day Boys, the United Irishmen, the Catholic League, the Fenian Brotherhood, the Orange Order, the UDA, the UVF, the IRA, the PIRA, the Real IRA, the Red Hand Commandos . . . the list goes on and on and on. You know Michael Porter's theory of clusters, the idea that certain places specialise in certain activities and gain competitive advantage as a consequence?"

"Silicon Valley, Wall Street, Madison Avenue, Hollywood – that kind of thing?"

"Aye, well, we're the Silicon Valley of secret societies, the Hollywood of funny handshakes, the Madison Avenue of Freemasonry, the Wall Street of whack-em-and-stack-em."

"A kind of clandestine conspiracy cluster?"

"Got it in one, mucker."

"But I always thought America was the epicentre of secret societies and conspiracy theories."

"Aye, and who do you think built the fuckin' country? The Scots-Irish. Us. Us, mucker! Ulster men and women. And we took our conspiracies with us."

Magill was half convinced, but decided to call Solomon's bluff. "Ian Kane told me that there was another natural resource in Northern Ireland, and that's storytelling. You're all yarn spinners here, he said. You're spinning me a yarn, aren't you, Billy? The very idea of Crimind is ludicrous, let alone its globalisation. Strategic alliances among secret societies is an oxymoron, if ever there was one. Conspiracy theories don't have any basis in fact, despite Dan

Brown's showboating."

"Is that so, mucker? Let me tell you something. Ian Kane's a fat fuck. Let me tell you something else. There are two types of people in Northern Ireland. Those who believe the conspiracy theories, and those who think they're being put about to make people paranoid."

"And then there are those," Magill retorted sharply, "who believe the conspiracies are being invented by expert storytellers in order to pull the wool over people's prying eyes."

Solomon shrugged. "What, you don't believe your own eyes, mucker? Who do you think killed your buddies Brodie and O'Connell? Who left you bloodstained messages? Who's setting you up, Simon? You're the one who thinks it's the Freemasons in league with the, what was it again, Order of Solomon? You're the only one who claims to have seen the bodies. Brodie's execution hasn't been on the news and O'Connell's on shore leave from Titanic Business School. I checked."

Magill sighed wearily. "I don't know, Billy. I thought you were going to tell me. I thought you were the Order of Solomon. They've obviously got rid of the bodies. It's all a smokescreen of some kind."

"Misdirection, mucker. Misdirection. That's what it's called. Misdirection's at work here. I can smell it."

"I thought misdirection was something stage magicians did. They get the audience to look one way while they perform the stunt elsewhere. That's what Anderson did, and he was the best stage magician there ever was."

"Correct!" King Billy answered enthusiastically. "I studied stage magicians as part of my thesis on the cultural history of Belfast – Robert-Houdin was much better than Anderson, by the way – and that research taught me more about business than Porter ever did. Marketing *is* magic, Simon. Always has been, always will be."

"Not too many marketers'd agree with that. Not Kate Phillips and the standard textbook writers, that's for sure."

"I know, I've read them. They're all wrong. Marketing is magic through and through. Marketing's full of hocus-pocus, abracadabras, riddle-me-rees and incomprehensible incantations, as is management-speak generally."

"Well, that's one way of looking at it."

"It's the way of looking at your situation. Misdirection's the key here. We're looking one way and the action's taking place in another."

"What direction, Dr Dr Solomon?"

"It's funny you should ask me that, mucker. Have you ever heard of P2?"

Chapter Twenty-Seven

P2, or Not P2?

Simon Magill was getting tired of Billy Solomon's grandstanding. He suspected that just as a big cat plays with its prey, the humungous hard man was trying to wind him up and work out how pliable he really was. In order to find his breaking-point, perhaps. King Billy liked breaking people, that was for sure. But Magill had broken some time ago, when O'Connell's mauled corpse came tumbling out of the museum cabinet. He broke before that when he encountered the compasses embedded in Brodie's blood-filled eye sockets. He broke before that when his mother lost her beautiful mind; his father spurned him; and his butchered brother was brought back from Belfast in a box. Far from breaking yet again, Simon Magill was finally pulling himself back together thanks to the marvellously mercurial woman in his life and his absolute determination to see this dreadful business through, come what may.

"No," he said sarcastically. "No, I don't know what P2 is. Let me guess. A boy band? A television station? An MP3 player, from Samsung maybe? A primary-school class that comes, oh, somewhere between P1 and P3?"

"Pucker up, mucker," the big man responded, ignoring Simon's tone. "This is where it gets interesting. P2 is a secret society."

Magill felt like yelling "Whoohooo!" but the grotesque thought of puckering up to King Billy, or even a *ménage à trois* with Wee Joe in tow, had rendered him speechless. There's only so much trauma a mucker can take.

The powerful Sun workstation surged into life as King Billy settled his prodigious form on a puny swivel chair, like a bag of flour balanced on an eggcup. With a surprising turn of manual dexterity, he speedclicked his way though a colourful cavalcade of conspiracy websites. While Solomon was making up his mind, Magill couldn't help wondering whether the workstation was fake as well. Presumably the brotherhood of fake makers sourced from each other in a counterfeiters' equivalent of Buy British. Fake or not, it was a pretty impressive piece of kit.

"P2," the powersurfer said, eyes fixed on the 23-inch screen, "or Propaganda Due is an Italian secret society. It was founded in the 1970s, though some trace its origins back to the *Grande Oriente d'Italia* in the late nineteenth century, and even to the Egyptian Rite of Count Cagliostro in the eighteenth. Everyone who was anyone in 1970s Italy was a member of P2, and when its activities were exposed in 1981, the scandal brought down the government of the day. Silvio Berlusconi was a member, as was Victor Emmanuel, the Prince of Naples, as were leading figures in the media, the military, the judiciary and the government. As was a banker called Roberto Calvi.

"The Mafia money launderer found hanging under Blackfriars Bridge?"

"The very same, mucker."

"You whacked him, Billy?"

The bulging bag of flour burst out laughing. "Nah, I was still at school. And Wee Joe was . . . um . . . otherwise engaged."

"So what's the connection?"

"P2 popped Pope John Paul I, who died suddenly in 1978. It was put about that Ulster Protestant extremists were behind the hit."

"Misdirection?"

"Misdirection, mucker. Marketing, moreover."

"Steady on, Billy. Marketing has its faults, but by and large it prefers to care for customers, not crate them."

"P2 was the brainchild of a marketing man called Licio Gelli. A successful textile manufacturer, he was also a racketeer, a mercenary, a blackmailer, a money launderer, a CIA agent, a KGB double-agent, and an agent for looted artworks, among others. As an arms dealer, he sold Exocet missiles to the Argentinians before the Falklands War. As a card-carrying fascist with links to Franco, Mussolini, Ceauşescu, Opus Dei, Juan Perón and more, he used his logistics expertise to ferry Nazi war criminals to South America. As a faker first class, he was behind the Priory of Sion, the famous hoax about Mary Magdalene being the wife of Jesus and giving birth to the son of the Son of God."

"*The Da Vinci Code!*" Magill gasped. "You're telling me that Licio Gelli's the man behind Dan Brown?"

"Not as far as we know, though there is a textual connection. In *Angels & Demons*, Brown mentions the hit on Pope John Paul I and blames it on the Bavarian Illuminati. In reality it was P2."

"I still don't see what this has to do with me, with Brodie, with O'Connell."

"Gelli was a Freemason."

"The poster-boy of Freemasonry, by the sound of him."

"He was expelled from the Freemasons because his organisation was tarnishing their good name. It was his expulsion that brought the whole P2 edifice down and with it the government of Arnaldo Forlani." King Billy had finally settled on a website, and sat back to let Magill look. "The full story's here on masonicinfo.com. The Freemasons are the best source of information on Gelli because of the damage he did and is still doing to them . . . "

"So P2 was a kind of fake Freemasonry?"

"Fake Freemasons set up by a marketing genius."

"A Crimind genius, I think you mean."

"Same difference, mucker. They also say that the marketing mastermind's work goes on. In America somewhere, thanks to the CIA connection. Chicago's the most likely location, on account of its Italian heritage, Mafia links and suchlike. Alongside Ulster, Chicago's the foremost cluster of clandestine criminal conspiracies in the world. Mobtown, we call it."

"You said 'they say', Billy. Who are 'they,' and how come they can't say anything more specific?"

"Don't you worry about who they are. No one knows for sure. I don't know myself, and I'm a heavy hitter, so to speak. The organisation keeps changing its name, which is common practice in my business, as you might imagine. It's been rumoured that they go under the name of P4 or 4Ps or 7Ps or something similar."

"P4? 4Ps? Chicago? I don't think so, Billy. You're getting mixed up with introductory marketing textbooks."

"Could be, mucker. It sounds a bit far-fetched. Mind you, Martha Stewart in jail sounds a bit far-fetched too, as does Michael Jackson's acquittal. Donald Rumsfeld's connections to Halliburton are pretty odd, too. They say Bill Gates is the Antichrist and Citroën's chevrons are the work of the Masons."

"Yeah, and Elvis shot JFK."

"Nah, that was Sasquatch in an Elvis outfit."

"But Oscar Wilde was Jack the Ripper, right, and aliens kidnapped Shergar?"

"Nah, I kidnapped Shergar, mucker. Blamed it on the IRA. They're still getting stick for it."

"Misdirection, Billy?"

"Misdirection. Now that *was* magic, mucker!"

"What did you do with it, Billy? It's not easy to hide an animal of that size, much less a thoroughbred."

The beefy black-packed bag of flour didn't answer immediately. He was logging off and powering down his workstation. Eventually, when the humming stopped, he turned to his battered interlocutor. "Fed it to the dogs. Kept them going for weeks."

Magill shifted uneasily. Wee Joe hadn't been bullshitting. Or had he? Simon asked about the dogs, and King Billy replied that he had to put them down in the end. Wee Joe did the needful, though it broke his heart. Solomon seemed genuinely upset. It's nice to know, Magill thought, that equine assassins have feelings too.

"Would you like me to get you a cup of tea, Billy? Or something stronger?"

King Billy led the charge downstairs, and once settled in the adipose embrace of his over-stuffed sofa, replied "Tea's fine, mucker. Nothing stronger, thanks all the same. I'm teetotal. Have been for five years. Did some crazy things in my youth when I'd had a bellyful." He patted his kettledrum affectionately. "Took a lot to fill a belly like this."

"I bet it did." Magill carried on into the tiny kitchen, which was not only neat and tidy but devoid of contents. The cupboards were bare. The fridge was bereft, not even the obligatory nugget of mouldy cheese. There was no sign of the delicacies he'd been offered earlier. Teabags, milk and sugar were the only indulgences available.

"On a diet?" Simon shouted in the general direction of the living room. "Atkins, is it? GI? Hip and thigh? South Beach?"

"West Belfast, mucker," King Billy bellowed back. "It's fish 'n' chips with everything round here, and deep-fried Chocolate Orange for afters. Couldn't beat it for Vitamin C."

Despite everything, Magill found much to admire in his hitman host. In many ways, he reminded him of a politician or CEO, that curious combination of charm and calculation, always weighing the odds while working a room. Magill couldn't make up his mind whether King Billy was a polymath, a psychopath, or both. His was a quantum personality, if there was such a thing. "You seem to be out of ingredients, Your Majesty. I thought royalty had suppliers by appointment."

"Aye, well, the medics by appointment have me on a strict diet at the minute. Had a bit of a scare a while back. I've lost three stone in the last eight weeks. I'm doing more exercise too, though I've always pumped iron . . . smashed heads . . . broken backs . . . the usual keep-fit thing."

"Tough regimen, is it?"

"Aye, it is. When I can't stand it any more, I walk up to the home bakery on the corner, take a sniff of the warm bread and dander back home again."

"Misdirecting the taste buds."

"Something like that, mucker. The only time I buy anything's when I have visitors. Tea's all I've got in the house. Make mine strong, with one sugar." There was a pregnant pause from the living room. "Fuckit, two sugars!"

"Misdirecting the medics, eh Billy?"

"Misdirection, mucker. It's all about misdirection. You know, I used to be a magician when I was younger. I had the hands for it. I could palm cards, coins, scarves, rabbits. The kids round here loved me."

"Is that where your interest in cultural history came from?"

"Partly, partly. When I was a wee boy, I used to read all about the big stars on stage, and I wanted to be one of them. Could've made it too. Had the patter 'n' all. Looked good in the monkey suit. Did a wee bit of juggling as well, started with tennis balls, worked my way up to baseball bats. Then in a club on the Falls Road one night, I crossed a local hood and lost a couple of fingers. Things were never the same again. I couldn't palm, couldn't juggle, couldn't misdirect people because they wouldn't keep their eyes off my mutilated paws. The bastard paid for it, though. He paid for it big time. Even today, I still miss the stage. It's hard to beat the old smoke and mirrors. Magic is . . . *magic*."

"Is that why you have that pentangle tattooed on your hands, to remind you of the magic circle, the conjuring, the legerdemain?"

The resting baseball-bat artiste stared sadly at the backs of his massive appendages. "They're not pentangles. Can't you count, mucker? They've six points. They're Stars of David. I'm Jewish. Tattooed them myself, one night when I was drunk. That's what happens when you put the brew in Hebrew."

Christ, Magill thought. The man's completely mad. A bipolar, baseball-bat-juggling psychotic polymath prestidigitator who's on a strict diet and suffers, no doubt, from body-image angst. "What's a nice Jewish boy doing in the Ulster Volunteer Force?"

Solomon extruded something between a laugh and a shrug. A lhug. "You've heard the old joke that people tell about the polarised communities in Ulster, 'Are you a Protestant Jew or a Catholic Jew?'"

"Yes, my mother used to repeat that one whenever she talked about her bigoted homeland."

"Well, you're looking at a Protestant Jew. There used to be a big Jewish community in Belfast. Most of them left during the Troubles. My father ran a kosher butcher's on the Antrim Road. I helped out. Wee Joe used to work for us, so he did. He used to have a knife-throwing act. It was him who got me started on the variety circuit. Kept an eye on me 'cos I was so young. Anyway, my da got killed in the Troubles. The shop was blown up by an IRA bomb. He was in it at the time, working late for the Hanukkah rush. So I joined the UVF to do my bit. An eye for an eye."

"Was that before or after the Falls Road incident?"

"They sort of overlapped. The Jewish magician was a good disguise. Got me into all sorts of places, all sorts of trouble. My kosher butchery skills came in handy too."

"Are kosher burgers big in this part of town?"

"Not as big as Black Preceptory Pudding, mucker!"

"With marching seasoning, presumably."

The bison was back and ready for action. "All this talk of food's making me hungry. I could eat the arse off a rhinoceros, piles 'n' all. I'll have to go up to the bakery for a quick sniff. I love the smell of bagels in the morning. Afternoon's good too. I'll get Wee Joe to keep an eye on you for twenty minutes."

Wee Joe was all Simon Magill needed right then. "Don't bother him, Billy. I'm sure I could handle that pistol. Unless . . . maybe I could walk up to the bakery with you as well? I'd like to clear my head after the thump it got earlier."

Solomon thought for a moment, weighing up the possibilities. "I don't want you to be seen on the main road. But we can walk up to the Shankill together. Then you turn back when the taxi arrives, OK? Wee Joe's all right, mucker, as long as he keeps his teeth in."

As they sauntered up the sun-spilt street towards the arterial road a hundred or so metres away, King Billy explained the sectarian geography of west Belfast: how the Protestant and Catholic areas abutted one another; how the religious affiliation of an area could be quickly assessed thanks to flags, murals and painted kerbstones; how he did business with his strategic alliance partners on the other side of the Peace Line, a seven-metre high wall between the Protestant Shankill and Catholic Falls; and, the thing that exercised him most of all, how the two working-class communities had an awful lot in common despite everything that'd happened during decades of strife, not least the shared privations of inner-city life.

Solomon and sidekick had almost reached the Shankill Road when a belching black taxi appeared. It was sitting near a T junction, twenty yards down a side street. "There's your ride, mucker. See you in a wee while."

As Solomon walked on, his rolling jutting strut set on full-steam ahead, Magill turned down the narrow side street, which

219

ran parallel to the main road. He was about five metres short of the taxi when it started up and chugged off in a cloud of diesel. Very funny, Joe.

He'd almost caught up when it roared off again with a clash of ancient gears and clang of tumbling spanners. Magill was not amused. If you do that again, you grumpy old git, I'm gonna get one of those knives and shove it where the sun don't shine.

Magill's hand was on the rear-door handle when Joe pulled the stunt for a third time and turned the corner into another side street, perpendicular to the Shankill Road but parallel to King Billy's. Simon had had enough. He turned to go back the way he had come.

A skinny, pasty-faced man was barring his path. He had a furled umbrella in one hand and the cable of an electric toaster, with appliance attached, in the other. He looked like a postmodern knight errant, an Ulster crusader: capeless, hapless, gormless. So ludicrous was the sight of Sir Dualit, whose nose was running with a streaming head cold, that Magill was almost lost for words. But not completely.

"I'm on my way back to my *friend* Billy Solomon's house," he said in a voice that carried the necessary don't-mess-with-me conviction.

"You're a friend of King Billy's, are ye?" The query came from another direction entirely. Magill swivelled round to see a second, much bulkier man, wearing a balaclava and brandishing a baseball bat.

"Get in the taxi, Ginger," Dualit said in an exceptionally glottal Ulster accent, wiping his nose on the sleeve of his denim jacket.

"Someone wants to have a wee word with ye," Balaclava added, resting the baseball bat on Magill's shoulder and rotating it slowly.

Chapter Twenty-Eight

Crouching Minger, Flying Drag Queen

Although he had killed innumerable terrorists, stiffed countless sleazeballs and kickboxed his way out of many a tight corner in all sorts of computer games from *Tomb Raider* to *Grand Theft Auto*, Simon Magill knew that resistance was futile. He was no match for two hoods with attitude. And baseball bats. And lean mean grilling machines. He climbed into the cab, convinced that he was about to meet the same fate as Professors Brodie and O'Connell, but hoping that he'd get a chance to make a fight of it. He'd picked up a few unarmed combat moves in his misspent youth thanks to big brother Peter, and while several years in front of computer screens had taken the edge of his tae kwon do, he was still good for a tae or two.

The opportunity didn't arise. Less than ten minutes after being picked up, Magill and his new-found friends Dualit and Balaclava were dropped off in a street indistinguishable from the one they'd left, except that all the houses were empty, boarded up, waiting for the wreckers' ball to begin. Several were burnt-out shells, ossified skeletons of fossilised stegosaurs.

Balaclava prodded his prisoner from behind while Dualit shoved open the festering front door of a dilapidated terraced house almost identical to Billy's. Magill was bundled into the bijou front parlour, which smelt of rising damp and seeping sewage. The walls were bare, as was the floor, its buckled boards broken in places, exposing inky blackness beneath. A single wooden chair, *sans* seat, was the only stick of furniture. Cosiness clearly wasn't high on the home-owner's agenda.

Magill's captors bound him tightly to the broken-bottomed chair. Dualit, the acned, adenoidal head-cold sufferer, stuffed phlegm-filled tissues into Simon's mouth and sealed the heaving cavity with strips of duct tape. Once he was secured, they left the room, pulling the parlour door tight behind them. The terraced house fell silent.

Before long – ten minutes, possibly, though it felt like forever – Magill was starting to think that either he'd been left to die of thirst and starvation, to be gnawed by rats and nibbled by stray dogs until the accidental discovery of his bloated, stinking corpse by an unsuspecting demolition crew, or else his captors were trying out some kind of down-market sensory-deprivation treatment.

He was determined not to break. Something had to be done. But his bindings were so tight that any movement was guaranteed to throw him to the floor, with arseless chair attached. Not the most dignified way to go, though if he were lucky and the floor didn't give way, he might be able to crawl outside with broken-backed backpack attached.

There was a noise from the back room. A clicking noise. Wee Joe was in the building? The clicking rose to a crescendo, then lapsed into silence. That's the teeth coming out, Magill concluded. It'll all be over soon, unless Ulster's überassassin intends to extend the agony. No matter what, he was going to be brave. Not just because he owed it to the memory of Brodie and O'Connell, or because of the solemn vow he'd taken, but because he knew that his deathbed demeanour would get back to May Day, and above anything else he wanted her to think well of him. Would that things had turned out differently, he thought with agonising regret, but he was determined to remain defiant. Wee Joe? Yo ho!

The parlour door didn't open, however. Some time later, the clicking recommenced. The psycho's psycho and his snotty sidekicks were playing games. Is this what they did in the gory glory days, Magill wondered? He tried to steel himself for the cold-steel treatment to come.

Strangely, the clicking was getting faster and faster. Far too fast, in fact, unless Wee Joe was chewing the fat with fellow beneficiaries of the Shankill Butchers' Benevolent Fund. But there was no accompanying chatter. Just a clickety-click that was getting ever louder, ever faster. Maybe Wee Joe was practising speed lip-reading with his evil twin brother, Wee Willy? Silence descended

222

once more. The door still didn't open.

It was late afternoon when the party started in earnest. Dualit and Balaclava burst in, having been fortified by several hot toddies in the interim. Legend has it that a feed of Irish whiskey gives a man the strength of ten men, and Magill's captors lent credence to the myth. Despite his streaming cold, Dualit lifted Simon and his faux-teak attachment as if he was no weight at all. Balaclava lent a hand. Together, they carried their package into a back room as dank as the front, and set it down beside a massive kitchen table.

Across the table was the most beautiful woman Simon Magill had ever seen. She must have been in her late thirties, but she was stunning, a cross between Monica Bellucci and Andrea Corr, with bright blue eyes, Pre-Raphaelite tresses and cheekbones that were sharper than Wee Joe's favourite cleaver.

Only a pair of narrow, tightly pursed lips betrayed her true purpose. Either that or she was concentrating very hard. She was absorbed in a newspaper, and apart from a quick glance at the litter-borne oaf who'd been carried into her imperious presence, remained utterly impassive. With a few flicks of her felt-tip, she completed a puzzle, exhaled loudly, and tossed the scribble-filled newspaper across the table towards Magill.

"Sudoku's a bitch," she said. Even her accent was adorable. "Give me a cryptic crossword any day." Magill could see she'd made short work of the *Guardian's* ripsnorter. She nodded at his bearers. Dualit ripped the tape from his mouth, taking half a pre-ripped lip with it, while Balaclava placed a glass of Irn-Bru in front of him. He hoped it was Irn-Bru.

Magill spat out the tissues, drank deeply and replied with reckless contempt. "My mother's a Sudoku samurai, but I'm more of a *Doom* man myself."

"You will be doomed," she smiled, "if you don't tell me who you are, why you're here and what you're getting up to with King Billy."

"Doomed just like Brodie and O'Connell?" he barked at the smirking bitch. "Tell me something. Who are you? Why am I here? What business is it of yours who I am or who I'm with? What's with the solitary confinement, the rickety-chair treatment and that godforsaken clicking? Some kind of torture you learnt in the high-security wing with the rest of the psycho viragos?"

"Questions, questions, questions," she said sweetly, "You tell me first. Who's Brodie? What has Declan O'Connell got to do with all this? The last I heard he was serving life for killing two Brits with plummy accents and arrogant manners. A bit like yourself, pretty boy."

Still talking, she reached down into a bulky tote bag on the floor and pulled out two long steel rods, which she set casually on the table. Sharply pointed at one end, they gleamed dully in the early-evening light.

"Am I going to get the Brodie treatment, then? Best get on with it. Because I'm telling you nothing, bitch."

She reached into her bag once more. And pulled out a big ball of wool. Picking up her knitting needles, she cast on with aplomb and started clicking rapidly. "Now," the Bellucci–Corr combo said cheerfully, "let's start again. Who are you? Who's Brodie? What does Brodie have to do with these . . . mmm . . . instruments of torture? I'm Ultima, incidentally. Ultima Sullivan."

Magill almost burst out laughing with relief, though his lacerated lips inhibited anything too uproarious. Before he knew it, he'd spilled the full story, from job interview to present painful predicament. Ultima made sympathetic noises from time to time, asked him to repeat certain details, actually clapped with joy when piphilology took a brief bow, and at one point told her enforcers, Minger and Drag Queen, to take themselves off. She also made a note of the murderers' messages, and for some strange reason was particularly taken with Professor O'Connell's prematurely aborted research project. So much so that Magill couldn't resist asking, "Are you a *Titanic* buff too?"

"No, but I did my doctorate on the women's movement during that period, and I can see some connections."

"Your doctorate?" Magill couldn't believe what he was hearing. "Not another one! Does everyone in this place have a doctorate?"

"Only old lags with several life sentences to serve and sad bookish bastards without a life to speak of."

"Ah, so you've been detained at Her Majesty's Pleasure. May I ask what for? Assault with a deadly knitting needle?"

"Accessory to murder," Ultima said matter-of-factly. "I was quite . . . well . . . attractive when I was younger, and did my bit as Brit-bait. Like all men, soldiers think with their . . . um . . . copulation equipment, and so I set them up for others to take care of. Some of them were nice boys, little more than youngsters, but war's war. My conscience is clear."

"And you salved your conscience with a doctorate on the women's movement?" Magill said ferociously, staggered by what he'd just heard. Was his big brother one of Sullivan's conquests?

A pained look passed briefly across her profoundly beautiful face. Magill almost felt sorry for hurting her.

"Something like that, Simon. There was a know-thine-enemy side to it too. My PhD was on the women's Orange Order. I know it's hard to believe, but Orangeism was once at the forefront of the women's rights movement. More women than men signed the Ulster Covenant of 1912. There was an emancipatory side to the 'Ulster Will Fight' era, though that's a very distant memory, unfortunately."

"And the *Titanic* was the Ark of the Covenant, the pride of patriarchal Ulster Protestantism? Is that the connection you were making?"

"No, no, it's something else entirely. The various conspiracy theories I'd never heard them before. They must be recent accretions. They're very interesting. Very interesting."

"Let me guess, Ultima, you're planning a second PhD on male chauvinism during the sinking. Wasn't it terrible that those poor oppressed women and children were forced into the lifeboats instead of drowning on equal terms with the misogynist patriarchal phallocrats?"

She flashed a faux-sultry look, the one that had driven numerous sex-mad squaddies to distraction and ultimately their doom. "Maybe I'll do that, Simon. After I finish my MBA."

"An MBA? I should've guessed. King Billy isn't the only *capo di* capitalist round here."

"Solomon's a big banana, the biggest bent banana in Belfast. He's ripping us off, we reckon. His idea of a strategic alliance is at

odds, shall we say, with ours. We're watching him very carefully."
Flicking away a lock of hair that had fallen across her face, Ultima
adopted a modest, almost demure, expression. "I, by contrast, am
just a humble dot-com operator."

Simon Magill didn't want to bond with this woman. He really
didn't. But he couldn't help himself. "E-commerce, eh? I'm a bit of
a digi-dabbler myself. What's your domain name? Do you sell
anything else besides equal-opportunity knitting needles?"

Ultima threw back her head and laughed. Magill could well
understand why Odysseus strapped himself to the mast and
stopped his shipmates' ears with honey while circumnavigating
the sirens en route to Ithaca. "We're in a period of transition at
present. Balaclava.com's not doing so well now that the peace
process has kicked in and there's no real call for balaclavas,
especially not our bespoke, hand-knitted, finest cashmere
balaclavas."

"Oh really? I'd've thought there'd be a big export market for
products like that, particularly in the Middle East."

"No, sadly. They're not big balaclava wearers over there. They
prefer their own brands of burqa, niqab, chador and suchlike."

"So the balaclava business is shrinking rapidly?"

Odysseus could have done with an iPod. "A bit like our
balaclavas when they're not hand-washed properly."

"Yeah, that blood and cordite and stuff must be a real bitch to
get out."

"Semtex is the real killer."

"You said it, sister," Magill replied tartly. His equipoise was
starting to return from its wanton wanderings. "Who'd have
thought the Northern Ireland peace process would wreck parts of
the local economy? And there was silly me thinking that peace
is a good thing. So what are you selling instead?"

"We're thinking of diversifying into angora iPod covers, Aran
laptop doilies and merino Xbox-macassars."

"Amazing. And what are you planning to call your new e-
venture? Or are you sticking with Balaclava.com now that you've
built up the brand name?"

She blushed. Odysseus' earwax melted. "Promise not to laugh,

Simon, but we're thinking of Knits Templar. What do you think?" she said coyly, as if she cared about his opinions one way or the other.

He couldn't help laughing. "Knits Templar? Now I've heard everything."

Ultima pouted provocatively. "What's wrong with Knits Templar?"

"Nothing, nothing," he replied. "It's just that it's so in tune with King Billy's conspiracy-cluster theory. The Knights Templar just had to get in on the act."

"It's Knits Templar, Simon, not Knights Templar. Though there is a connection. I've researched it. The Knights Templar were very big players in the medieval wool trade."

"Quite." He gave her his extra-special lop-sided grin, which combined with his striking hairdo and cute freckles had proved irresistible to incalculable beautiful women. Well, 3.14159 or thereabouts.

"That's quite a kisser you've got there, pretty boy."

"Thank you, Ultima."

"That black-eyed, ginger-haired thing you've got going? It's hot."

Ultima packed away the knitting, picked up her newspaper and prepared to depart. Magill's surprisingly pleasant ordeal was over. She made for the door and stopped for a second, as if weighing her options. "It's so hot, in fact, that I want to show you something, Simon. Something you'll never forget."

Chapter Twenty-Nine

Simon Magill and the Last Crusade

Belfast is a beautiful city. Or, to be more precise, it is a city in a beautiful setting. Situated at the head of Belfast Lough, an estuarine processional way, the conurbation is encircled by escarpments, the Antrim Plateau on one side, Castlereagh Hills on the other. The most striking view of the city, however, is not from its seaward approaches, nor even from the shoulders of Samson and Goliath, giant yellow cranes that stand guard over the Titanic Quarter's once mighty shipyard.

The premier panorama, rather, is reserved for tourists arriving from the International Airport, thirty kilometres north-west of the city centre. The prim fields of the County Antrim countryside steadily give way to the outposts of peripolitan crapscape– warehouses, car dealers, distribution centres, flatpackplexes – that garland each and every city in the western capitalist protectorate. All of a sudden, the humdrum airport motorway crests the encircling escarpment and plunges precipitously into the Belfast basin beneath. The conurbation spreadeagles from harbour to horizon like a starfish etherised upon a table, lagoon-like Belfast Lough to the left, black smudges of city-centre high-rise to the right. Most first-time visitors find it hard to reconcile this stunning vista of urbane urbanity with their mental image of a malevolent metropolitan warzone. When the sun is shining, a rare event admittedly, they often think they're dreaming, demented or roaring drunk.

That comes later.

The view on the way out of the city is much less prepossessing, though as most departees are recuperating from Promethean hangovers and severe arterial infarction brought about by close encounters with the hi-fat, hi-salt, hi-fatality Ulster Fry, this picturesquelessness isn't considered a problem. People just want to get home and lie down in a darkened room until their blood pressure subsides or coronary thrombosis carries them off, whichever comes first.

Simon Magill's blood pressure had fallen markedly since escaping the fetid off-Falls hovel. The circulation had returned to his lower limbs too, and although the taste of his gag would have him gagging till Doomsday, he had much to be grateful for. Not only did the scars of incarceration not bother him unduly, but he was almost beginning to enjoy himself. Seated together in the racy sports seats of Ultima's impressive company car, an Audi TT roadster with soft top retracted, the passenger and driver looked for all the world like carefree toy-boy and stunning sugar mamma respectively, albeit a sugar mamma with unorthodox taste.

Having belittled her dot-com adventures, Magill felt obliged to make amends with reciprocal tales of e-comm woe. He told her of his first attempt to make an i-fortune: Spamazon.com, a site that sold Monty Python memorabilia. Sadly, the ISP assumed it was a front for nefarious Soviet spammers and promptly shut it down. Then there was SimpleSimonSays.com, a netiquette website that unfortunately failed to impress its target market, since few consumers were prepared to take advice from a self-confessed simpleton, much less pay for it. For the life of him, however, Magill couldn't comprehend why FoesReunited.com, a site where sworn enemies and embittered divorcees got to trade eye-watering insults, didn't take off. He guessed it lacked the self-evident allure of Knits Templar, the cyber-scion of Ulster's conspiratorial cluster.

"What do you know about the Knights Templar then, Simon?" Ultima inquired as her roadster rocketed past a noisome line of trucks struggling up the outer urban incline.

"Not much," he replied truthfully, "apart from what I've read in *The Da Vinci Code*. Weren't they a group of Christian knights who protected pilgrims in the Holy Land around the time of the Crusades? After their defeat, they retreated to the south of France, where they got entangled in the Cathar heresy and were burnt at the stake for their trouble, but not before they'd hidden the Holy Grail, aka Mary Magdalene."

230

Caught in the vortex of her open-topped Audi, Sullivan's thick curly hair swirled around her head like a jet-black halo. She restrained her Helen of Troy tresses with one hand while steering erratically round a high-speed right-hand bend with the other. "Well, that's a garbled version of the garbled version in Dan Brown. The reality of the Templars was very different. They were an extremely powerful organisation, one of the first multinationals. They were exceptionally wealthy, partly on account of the lucrative wool trade, but primarily because they guaranteed safe passage to the holy shrines and received bequests of valuable property in return. They acted as a kind of clearing bank, what's more, whereby pilgrims paid in deposits in one country and made withdrawals in another . . . "

"Medieval ATMs, so to speak," Magill interrupted.

"And they charged for the service as well. They were also very marketing-savvy. Comparatively speaking, their red-cross logo was emblazoned on more surfaces than Nike's or McDonald's is nowadays: flags, armour, horses, castles, churches, stained-glass windows and especially their tabards, which were the Crusader equivalent of sponsored soccer kits. You name it, the Templars had their logo on it. They were very sharp operators, the biggest brand in Christendom."

"Ultima, you make them sound like a combination of Apple, Benetton, Chelsea, DFS, Expedia and First Direct."

"Well they were, Simon, they really were. They were immensely rich and powerful. So rich and powerful, in fact, that penniless princes had it in for them. They were set up by Philip the Fair of France and accused of heresy, sodomy, necromancy, devil worship, bestiality, pretty much every deadly sin known to man . . . "

"Or beast . . . "

"Quite. On Friday 13 October 1307, all their properties were seized by Philip the Fair in a carefully co-ordinated coup, though some of them were later transferred to the Knights Hospitaller or the Knights of Malta."

"But Philip didn't get all of them . . . "

"Correct, Simon. The Templars were forewarned and managed

231

to ship some of their most valuable possessions out of La Rochelle to a secret destination, a destination still unknown, though many believe it was somewhere in the British Isles."

"Oh yes, of course. The Rosslyn Chapel manoeuvre."

"Not quite. The Holy Grail isn't in Rosslyn."

"Sorry, I forgot," Magill backtracked. "It's in Paris, isn't it, under the glass pyramid in the Louvre? That's where Mary Magdalene is interred."

The Audi slowed down as Ultima slipped off the motorway, seemingly following signs for the International Airport some ten kilometres distant. "Again, not quite. Dan the Man misled the masses. Deliberately, I believe."

"Don't diss the Danster, dude," Magill retorted, with a momentary memory of more innocent times in the Beehive. "Why would he do that?"

"To throw people off the scent."

"Misdirection, you mean?"

"What was that, Simon? I didn't quite catch it with all the wind noise. Mis-what?"

"Misdirection," Magill repeated forcefully. "King Billy said misdirection's the secret of magic. And marketing too. Get people looking one way when the real jiggery-pokery's going on in another."

"Yes!" she cried, with an emphatic thump of the steering wheel. "Misdirection! That's exactly it. Misdirection. Desperate Dan was misdirecting the masses."

"So," Magill said eagerly, "the Holy Grail really is in Rosslyn."

Ultima turned to look at him. Astonishingly beautiful though she was, he would have preferred his wayward driver to keep her eyes firmly on the road, if only because a busy roundabout lay ahead. "Have you ever been to Rosslyn, Simon?"

"Of course. It's just outside Edinburgh. When I read *The Da Vinci Code*, I made a literary pilgrimage one afternoon. They have tours organised and everything. I was a little bit embarrassed to be part of it, to be honest, but great fun was had by all, as they say."

"Didn't you find it a bit . . . mmm . . . ostentatious? The chapel, I mean."

"Oh God, yes! As ornate as they come, and I've been in quite a few churches and chapels thanks to my father, who used to have a serious brass-rubbing habit. When I was a youngster, he dragged me to places that were so far off the beaten track the locals thought doublet and hose were the height of fashion."

"You haven't seen John Galliano's latest collection, then?"

Odysseus was back and heading for Lotophagi. "Fair enough, Ultima, Rosslyn's a bit excessive. But what's wrong with extreme decorating? It never did Laurence Llewelyn-Bowen any harm."

"Simon, the Knights Templar were a very, *very* austere organisation. They were medieval minimalists, in many ways. They were warriors. They were Spartans. They were Ryanair, only less ruthless. There's no way the Templars'd go for a gaudy Gaudí lookalike, especially not for their most precious possession. Unless, of course, they had an ulterior motive. The real reason it's gaudy, therefore . . . "

"Is to attract people's attention!" Magill interjected. "Or rather to divert people's attention. You're saying that Rosslyn's really a smokescreen in stone, a sort of camouflage chapel?"

"That's exactly it, Simon. And Dan Brown acknowledges as much in his book, though he promptly sets aside his own sworn testimony. Misdirection's the perfect word, because above almost anything else the Knights Templar were great magicians. They were outstanding warriors, but they were also *magi* in the proper sense. That is, very wise men. They were philosophers, cabalists, Gnostics. They were guardians of esoteric secrets, arcane secrets, occult secrets. Even Baigent and Leigh, the guys who sued Dan Brown for appropriating their appropriated evidence, acknowledge that the Knights Templar were great sorcerers. They learned a lot in the Middle East. Truly, they were masters of misdirection."

"So masterful, Ultima, that millions of people are still searching for the Holy Grail. Searching without much success, it has to be said."

Having negotiated the roundabout successfully, the Audi TT slowed down, pulled over and stopped. Ultima engaged the handbrake as if she was seducing a lovelorn lance-corporal, looked directly at her awestruck passenger and cooed, "Until now, Simon. Until now."

Chapter Thirty

I Wish I Was in Templepatrick

"Yeah, right. Pull the other one, Ultima." Having sat at the feet of Ian Kane, Ulster's master prankster, Simon Magill wasn't going to be taken in again, no matter how alluring the trickstresse. "I may be a geek, but I'm not gormless."

"Take a look at that signpost, geek."

Magill looked ahead. He'd been so preoccupied with his driver's discourse on the Knights Templar that he hadn't paid any attention to their whereabouts. They were parked at the edge of an unremarkable Irish village. Houses, hotels and churches were scattered along one side of a straggling main street. The other, unusually for Ireland, consisted of a high roughstone wall – certainly a couple of hundred years old, possibly more – with tall trees behind, beech and sycamore mainly. Immediately in front of them stood an elaborate signpost, far too elaborate for the modest village it announced. The signpost said "Welcome to Templepatrick."

"Templepatrick?" Magill stared at the signpost, his credulity rising by the second. "The Templars were here? Saint Patrick was a Templar? No way! You'll be telling me he married Mary Magdalene next and that Gerry Adams is their direct descendant, the Son of God or some such."

Heavy traffic whizzed past, heading for the airport, honking and spitting diesel fumes. Ultima tried to speak – it sounded like "Gerry's no angel, take it from me" – but her words were drowned out.

She started the Audi, drove two hundred yards down the main road and turned right through a sizeable gap in the ancient wall. It was a footpath-free side road, lined with mature trees. Rolling parkland could be glimpsed between the overarching branches.

With nary a glance in her rear-view mirror, much less a flick of an indicator, she pulled over under an autumnal canopy where profound silence reigned, even though they were less than a fifty metres from a busy road.

"To answer your questions in turn, Simon. Yes, the name Templepatrick has significance. Yes, the Knights Templar were based here. Saint Patrick died six hundred years before the Knights Templar were established, and although he does mention a pulchritudinous hottie he came across at the slave market, he definitely didn't marry Mary Magdalene. Unless he was heavily into necrophilia."

"The things the Catholic priesthood get up to, Ultima. It never ceases to amaze me."

She smiled a thin smile. "This really will amaze you. Most people round here associate the name Templepatrick with Saint Patrick, who was brought up in these parts and established a ministry in the area. But the Temple also refers to a Knights Templar preceptory that was established here in the twelfth century, seven hundred years after Saint Patrick did his ethnic-cleansing thing with the Irish snake population."

"And this was where he jumped the bones of Mary Magdalene?"

Sullivan ignored Magill's sophomoric remarks. "The preceptory was very low key, so low key in fact that it isn't listed on standard inventories of British and Irish Templar properties. It was acquired by the Knights Hospitaller in their post-purge landgrab, and the original owners have been forgotten down the years."

"Not like Rosslyn."

"Stop interrupting, Simon. This is where it gets interesting. As I mentioned earlier, and as you know from Dan Brown, some prominent Templars escaped Philip the Fair's swoop. They sailed from La Rochelle with unspecified treasure on board. We know they made for Scotland, where they established a renegade colony, lent their support to Robert the Bruce and prepared the ground for Scottish Freemasonry, which long predates the English version of the Craft. We also know they stopped off in Ireland on the way.

Robert the Bruce's kingdom, remember, included both Scotland and the northern half of Ireland. Dalriada, they called it. Baigent and Leigh, Dan Brown's nemeses, traced the most likely routes from La Rochelle and concluded that the Templar treasure-fleet undoubtedly docked in Ireland. This is all well established. The Templar influence is still evident today, most obviously in the Black Preceptories and the Ulster flag, a red cross on white ground. It's even apparent in little things like the Ulster bap and champ."

"Well, I've seen the flag and heard of the Black Institution's connection to the Crusaders, but bap? Champ? What the hell are baps and champs, Ultima?"

"Baps are floury rolls, but the name refers to Baphomet, the satanic beast that heretic Templars worshipped, according to Philip the Fair. Champ is the acme of local cuisine, Ulster's signature dish alongside the infamous Fry. It's a delicious mixture of mashed potatoes, buttermilk and scallions. The name derives from *tcham*, a white, copper-studded substance that Masons in the ancient world used to spread on the apex of obelisks and statuary. It was a kind of skim-plaster finish, of great symbolic significance. A bowl of champ is a gustatory echo of Ulster's primordial connection to the ancient Middle East."

"Christ, you never know what you're eating nowadays."

"Laugh if you like, Simon, but this is documented fact. Indeed, when local people eat champ, they unfailingly mould it into a pyramid-shaped structure topped by a golden knob of butter. How symbolic is that?"

Magill digested the culinary nugget as Sullivan continued, her erogenous voice becoming more and more animated. "What we still don't know for certain is where exactly in Ireland the Templar fleet dropped anchor. Generations of grail hunters have searched high and low for the Irish connection. They've investigated all the known Templar sites and scouted out places with Temple in their name, without success. But they overlooked the most obvious one of all, partly because it isn't listed on the standard Templar inventories, partly because of the Saint Patrick connection . . . "

"Misdirection!"

"Any more interruptions, pretty boy, and I'll ring Minger and

Drag Queen." She settled herself again and continued the local-history lesson. "Partly because Templepatrick is inland and grail hunters tend to concentrate on sites near the coast. They forget, however, that Templepatrick was a real crossroads in its day, a stopover on the main overland route between Donegal and east Antrim. It has been a crossroads since the dawn of time, in fact. In Celtic times it was on the main road from Tara, the capital, to Dunseverick, Ireland's oldest hillfort, on the north Antrim coast. There are dozens of ancient burial mounds, standing stones, tumuli, cairns, raths and so on in this area. There's even an Irish round tower a couple of miles from here. And you know what they say about Irish round towers."

"I *do* know this! Pitcairn Brodie mentioned it to me once. That's where the monks hid their illuminated manuscripts and their monastery's holy objects during the Viking raids. That's why the entrances are well above ground level. They could be accessed only by rope ladders, and when the Vikings appeared on the horizon, the monks climbed in, pulled up the ladders and waited for the raiding parties to leave. The Vikings suffered terribly from seasonal affective disorder on account of those dark Scandinavian winters, so they soon got bored and left."

"Well, that's one theory, Simon. Round towers also concentrate telluric currents – what you English call ley lines. They are a source of tremendous spiritual energy that we've known about ever since Ancient Egypt. All round towers are precisely aligned astronomically, and even though they're made from sandstone or limestone, they invariably possess uncanny paramagnetic powers. Irish round towers acted, in effect, as a sort of enormous geospiritual generator. That's where the intellectual energy for the great flowering of early Irish civilisation came from. The monks were living, working and worshipping in a giant cerebral forcefield that has generated the growth and flowering of civilisation throughout the ages, from Ancient Egypt on."

Simon Magill was lost for words. Bereft doesn't begin to describe it. "Jesus!" was the most he could manage and even that was a stretch.

"Jesus has nothing to do with it. Templepatrick lies on the main telluric channel in this part of the world. It's a kind of spiritual conduit, a place of exceptional power, one of the most powerful in the British Isles, second only to that concentrated on the Glastonbury area, which has long been associated with King Arthur, the Holy Grail, Camelot, Avalon and suchlike."

Magill shook his head with disbelief. The pain heretofore associated with sudden movements had virtually disappeared. "But why isn't this place crawling with grail hunters, Ultima?"

"It's not common knowledge."

"But with a place name like Templepatrick, surely someone must have made the connection at some time or other?"

"HIPS."

"Come again?"

"H.I.P.S. Hidden in plain sight. Templepatrick's a classic case of hidden in plain sight, the notion that the best place to hide something important is in a place so obvious nobody sees it. The dollar bill is the classic example, as are the hidden messages in Leonardo's *Last Supper*, the symbolism of the Great Seal of the United States, the masonic iconography in Walt Disney movies. Your hero Dan Brown discusses HIPS at length in *The Da Vinci Code*. Except in the classic trickster-tricked tradition, he too was fooled. He fell for the Rosslyn bluff, even though he was aware of its status as an architectural imposture. The boy still bought it. He also bought the Mary Magdalene hornswoggle."

"The Danster was misdirected?"

"Yes, Simon, he was. The misleader was misled, though in fairness Dan wasn't the only one to be duped. The Knights Templar were pretty adept magicians, don't forget. There's nothing intrinsically wrong with falling for things, you know. We all need things to believe in, despite what narrow-minded utilitarians and neo-Benthamites maintain. The success of Dan Brown's books is testament to humankind's need for something to believe in, even if it's hocus-pocus, stuff and nonsense or conspiracy-theory claptrap. Most people are searching for meaning. Some find it in organised religion, others in New-Age belief systems, others in shopping, consumption, cosmetic surgery, designer brands. They don't teach any of this on my MBA course, but marketers like you, Simon, are filling a void, a void that was once filled by the Holy Grail. Marketing is intrinsically utopian, it seems to me, the buying and selling of tiny utopias like clean hair, fresh breath, happy families, idyllic holidays and defeating the depredations of age, infirmity and cellulite. Cellulite especially. Marketing men misdirect consumers to a better world, an impossible world, a world that people want to believe in and belong to."

"I'm not certain Kate Phillips sees it like that, Ultima. But I know what you mean. The Holy Grail is a necessarily chimerical quest for illusory meaning, just like Roman Catholicism and Manolo Blahniks."

Sullivan waved her hands in disagreement. "No, Simon. No. Did I say that? Did I say that the grail was a chimera or an illusion? No, I did not. There *really was* a Holy Grail and it was neither illusory nor invisible, nor a bloodline for that matter, despite Dan Brown's misdirected claims to the contrary. The grail *really* existed and it was secreted in the Templar's Templepatrick preceptory, a couple of hundred metres from here."

Chapter Thirty-One

The Man Nobody Knows

Barton Brady II was in a bind. It was 8 a.m. – 9 a.m. Central Standard Time – and a burst of phone calls hadn't done the trick. Phillips's administrative assistant at Northwestern had systematically stonewalled him. The professor was on vacation. The professor was an emeritus, and came in only from time to time. The professor's schedule wasn't her responsibility, though she was certain a conference wasn't on it. Not until the AMA winter conclave in St Petersburg, FLA, where Professor Phillips was the keynote speaker.

How come, he asked, she was familiar with Professor Phillips's winter conference plans, but not her daily schedule? The administrative assistant mumbled something about university forward-planning systems. She was bullshitting. He told her so. She put the phone down sufficiently firmly to let Brady know the conversation was over. He suspected she wanted to slam it down, but the university's customer-care standards – and service-quality monitoring software, doubtless – wouldn't let her.

Next up was Emer Aherne, Serendipity Associates' honorary associate. However, *her* administrative assistant said Aherne was working at home all week, dammit. The assistant refused to divulge the visiting prof's home number, and a check with the local telephone company drew a blank. He might as well have sent a message by carrier pigeon or Native American smoke signal for all the luck he was having.

Brady felt his frustration rising. He knew what was happening. The unavailability of Phillips and Aherne made them all the more desirable. The more they resisted his blandishments, even though they didn't know they were resisting his blandishments, the more he had to get hold of them. He'd struggled with insatiable yearnings for years. In his youth, it had been fast-acting drugs and even faster-acting women. In adulthood, it had been gambling, drinking, drugs and sexual deviancy, as well as the car, the clothes, the house, the hot tub, the whole nine yards of bells and whistles, kit and caboodle. In his career, it had been promotion, a corner office, a company of his own and acclaim from his peers in the business community. Goddammit, he was gonna get on the cover of goddamn *Fortune* if it goddamn killed him.

Knowing what was happening wasn't, of course, the same as coping with it. His addictive personality, the default condition of gotta-try-it, gotta-buy-it, gotta-gotta-gotta-gotta-get-it consumer society, had landed him in all sorts of trouble with parents, teachers, colleagues and, on occasion, the cops. It had also landed him in diverse rehab clinics, countless therapists' couches and mind & body bookstores beyond number. There wasn't a New-Age treatment he hadn't tried. He even got addicted to addiction treatments. There was always another wacky panacea promising a cure, an answer, an opportunity to throw good bucks after bad.

He pinged an email to Phillips and got an out-of-office reply. Jesus H. Christ, he hated those things. Are academics *ever* in their offices? And why are automated replies so vague? Where the hell are the SOBs when they're not in the office? Lying on a beach? Lounging around the university library? Undergoing life-threatening surgery? Sipping cappuccino down the corridor? Sitting in the office deliberately ignoring their customers while surfing same-sex porn sites? Not enough information, guys!

OK, Emer, you're up. Inevitably, she wasn't listed on NWU's online listing, the fate of visiting professors worldwide. He worked out what her email address might be, given the format of her colleagues'. There's only one thing more irritating than out-of-office replies, and that's the non-deliverable-message insult. It was the cyber equivalent of the finger, instantaneously flipped to fanny-picking fools who clog the internet with ill-considered messages and contribute to World Wide Web warming, a virtual environmental catastrophe in the making.

Brady tried to relax and breathe deeply as he had been taught, at breathtaking expense. He exhaled slowly, determined to keep the pangs of unrequited desire at bay. He knew how to handle this. He'd turned it into a management money-spinner, after all. His marke*tease* paradigm was predicated on that very premise. Make consumers desperate to get their hands on your hard-to-get brand. Tease them. Tantalise them. Make life deliciously difficult for them. It worked, what's more. It worked for Beanie Babies. It worked for the Ford T-Bird. It worked for the iPod Nano and the Xbox 360. It worked for Hermès, whose limited edition Birkin bag had driven fashion victims wild worldwide. It worked for Harry Potter, in the early days at least, when there weren't enough books to go round and kids were going crazy to get their grubby hands on them.

Unfortunately, it worked on him as well. He could feel the inner urge building to bursting point. Deliciously difficult didn't begin to describe it. He needed to take his mind off Phillips. Who gave a damn about her conference? She couldn't have come up with anything as good as GRAIL. What had she ever done, anyway? OK, she was marketing's foremost guru, the author of the much-imitated-but-never-bettered student textbooks. But did she have anything to back it up? Did she have any beef in her buns, as it were? Her eminence, he reckoned, was largely a result of her longevity, the fact that she got a head start in the early 1960s, back in the days of the Ford and Carnegie reports, when new blood was badly needed in US B-schools. She lucked out. She was in the right place at the right time. He knew all about serendipity. It applied in academia as much as any other domain.

He checked out her home page. The usual scholarly hokum. They're all the same. Bullet-pointed boilerplate, that's what they are:

- Published in this journal, that journal, the *Journal of Obscurity*, the *International Review of Irrelevance*, the *Horseshit, Bullshit and Uttershit Quarterly* (incorporating *Apeshit Annaler* and *Deepshit Gazette*). Ho-hum.

- Long lists of imposing names: names attached to endowed chairs, names attached to illustrious awards, names attached to grant-awarding bodies. Who are these freakin' people?

- Inventories of blue-chip companies – Mars, Merck, Motorola, Merrill Lynch and many more – they claim to have done consultancy work for. A courtesy call from the PR department counts as consulting, presumably.

- Catalogues of books published, all with minor variations on the same title. *Marketing Management* this. *Strategic Marketing* that. *Principles of Marketing* the other. Same contents too, no doubt.

Lord almighty, don't these people have any imagination? Imagination deficit disorder is a serious condition. Don't their employers know this? Jesus H. Christ, the real world would eat them alive.

Brady felt the gnawing subside. The derangement of desire was drifting away into the air-conditioned ether of his luxurious McDonald Highlands home. Another triumph for the therapists' art. As he scrolled to the bottom of Phillips's home page, something caught his attention. Her books had apparently sold more copies than all competing textbooks combined. They had been translated into twenty-five different languages and were bestsellers in all of them. Special editions, written in conjunction with local nonentities, had been published in Europe, Australasia, Canada and countless other countries. It's hard to quarrel with certified sales figures, assuming they're properly calculated and not an invention of publishers' inventive publicists.

Worse was to come. Phillips had appeared on the cover of *Fortune*. And *Forbes*. And *Business Week*. And *Fast Company*, for Chrissakes. She had contributed the definition of marketing to *Encarta, Encyclopedia Britannica* and no doubt *Wiki-freakin'-pedia*. She had a goddamn postage stamp issued in her honour in Papua New Guinea, or some such hellhole. She was ranked fourth in the Leading Thought Leaders' List, after Peter Drucker, Bill Gates and Jack Welch. Jesus Christ, she's even ahead of Jesus Christ! She was the only marketing academic, alongside Ted Levitt, to feature regularly in *Good Business Guru* guides. When she ran her bespoke executive coaching workshops, Tom Peters was the warm-up act, with Stephen Covey as understudy.

Brady pulled a slim volume from the bookshelf behind his Brobdingnagian desk. *Milestones in Management Thought.* A fairly short journey, by the look of it. Little more than a day trip. Phillips was there, however. In the Pullman car, goddammit.

Apart from the introductory textbooks, the bitch had made her name by broadening the marketing concept and applying it to every conceivable sphere of activity: churches, charities, colleges, cities, countries, cultural activities. She'd come up with all sorts of snappy marketing notions – metamarketing, megamarketing, syncromarketing, turbomarketing, societal marketing, lateral marketing, Neanderthal marketing et al. – that'd been featured in innumerable top-notch executive-oriented journals like *Harvard Business Review, California Business Review, Columbia Journal of World Business, Business 2.0* and, inevitably, *The Marketer.*

Not only was there more to this woman than he thought, but she'd been doing for decades what he'd been doing since setting up Serendipity Associates, in ignorance of her achievements. He thought he'd been breaking the mould when all he'd done was reinvent the wheel. Naturally, no one had noticed. His clients hadn't, anyhow. The half-life of corporate concepts was vanishingly short, six months max, and getting shorter by the season. No one called them crazes these days, or even fads, much less trends. They were more like mini-fads, micro-fads, fadettes. A brief blip on the corporate radar was the most that could be hoped for. They were cast aside faster than Kleenex in a frat house.

It was demarketing, however, that really threw him. Demarketing, Phillips had demonstrated more than thirty years ago, aimed to dissuade customers rather than attract them, as for example when stocks were scarce or running out fast. Ironically, though, the very act of demarketing served to increase demand, which led to further rounds of demarketing and ever-increasing demand. Demarket your way to marketing success, in short. Holy shit, it was marke*tease* by another name. A better name. The 'ho had beaten him to the punch. More than a generation ago, goddammit.

Well, she wasn't going to do it with GRAIL. He was gonna get into this Illuminati gig if he had to sacrifice a 'nad. Both of them. Fuckit.

Chapter Thirty-Two

Show Me the Malory

Simon Magill was caught up in the moment. If not quite forgotten, the scalding tribulations of the past two days were bubbling on the back burner. Boiling, rather. The Holy Grail did that to people. Regardless of whether King Arthur was a mythical figure or not; irrespective of the timeless tales of Camelot, Lancelot and the fabled Fisher King; notwithstanding the hold the legend had over generation after generation of creative writers and artists, from Chrétien de Troyes and Sir Thomas Malory to Richard Wagner and Steven Spielberg; and despite the interminable debate over what, precisely, the Holy Grail is or was – a chalice, a container, a book, a precious metal, a symbolic narrative, a fountain of youth, a receptacle for the philosopher's stone, an alchemic transition from base metal to gold, a euphemism for the descendants of Mary Magdalene – it still fired the imagination, stimulated the senses, stirred the blood.

Magill's included. His face was flushed, his freckles aflame. With his windblown ginger hair, an inevitable tonsorial side-effect of gadding about in a convertible, he was the spitting image of an embarrassed Belisha beacon.

"What are we waiting for, Ms Sullivan? Hit it!"

Ultima slipped the Audi TT into gear and set off down the deserted access road. On one side the overhanging trees cast dark shadows across the twisting, turning track. On the other, rolling parkland undulated towards Six Mile Water, a verdant river valley. They came to a halt at a tiny T-junction. A modest wooden signpost pointed left to Castle Upton and right to Templeton graveyard.

"Castle or graveyard?" Magill asked eagerly.

"Hold your horses, Simon. Let me show you something." The Audi turned left. Its wheels crunched loudly on a loosely gravelled driveway, which veered slowly to the right. With high hedges and trees on either side, the effect was akin to an arboreal burrow, a beguiling pine- and laurel-lined tunnel. Magill was beginning to feel the way Sir Gawain must have felt as he approached the haunt of the Green Knight.

The curving avenue of greenery stopped suddenly. Castle Upton lay before them. It was a large, ivy-girt manor house, not much larger than a McMansion. Magill couldn't hide his disappointment. "That doesn't look like a Crusaders' castle to me," he said like a frustrated Ikea customer whose handyman husband had failed to follow the assembly instructions properly.

"No, it's not. Castle Upton was built in 1610 on the site of the Templar preceptory, and remodelled on countless occasions since. If you look carefully, however, you can still see echoes of the original. The two round towers are the oldest part of the building. They are similar to those on many Templar buildings, such as Tamar in Portugal, Monzón in Aragón, Garway in Herefordshire and, Dan Brown's favourite, Temple Church in London. The original building had battlements, as well as fairytale cones on top of the towers, similar to Templar strongholds like Carcassonne. Even today, the entrance is reminiscent of a Norman barbican. Note the Knights Templar cross above the front door and the flared crosses all along the frontage. This is the real deal, Simon."

Magill hadn't noticed the crosses. They were everywhere, even on an adjacent stable block, which Ultima informed him had been constructed in the 1780s by Robert Adam, Scotland's most famous architect and a prominent Freemason.

"The rooms inside are covered in Templar crosses too," Ultima added.

"Too many crosses, perhaps. Misdirection, possibly?"

"Precisely, Simon. Rosslyn rides again. The few grail hunters who have rummaged round here have concentrated on the castle and its supposedly haunted cellars. But there's nothing there. I checked."

"So where did they hide it, if not in the castle?"

"Templeton graveyard, of course," she smiled triumphantly. Magill made for the Audi, about to leap back in. Ultima stopped him with a raised hand. "Let's walk, Simon. It's only a couple of minutes away."

Eager beaver first, last and always, Magill set off like a lilty. Visitors to Ireland often assume that a lilty's akin to a leprechaun, and certainly the word carries connotations of sprites, brownies and little people generally. But a lilty is in fact a turn of speed – a velocity, no less – that's unique to Ireland, somewhere between two-men-and-a-wee-lad and shit-off-a-shovel. It's the pace that's used to get where you're going when you shouldn't be starting from here.

"Slow down, Simon. Slow down. There's no rush. Temple-patrick has been a place of pilgrimage since the dawn of time. Enjoy the moment."

She was right. As they walked back down the bough-black bower and the last rays of autumnal sunshine glittered off Six Mile Water in the river valley beneath, Magill could feel the telluric currents throbbing underfoot as they had done since time immemorial. Unless it was a heavily laden lorry on the airport road nearby. Immured behind the walls of Castle Upton, however, he liked to think it was the former.

An old entranceway with high stone gateposts stood at the bottom of the path. A patch of rough ground lay beyond. Again, Magill felt a pang of disappointment. It's never like this in Steven Spielberg movies, he thought, let alone Dan Brown novels.

"Close your eyes, Simon."

He did as he was bid. Ultima held his hand and led him a few steps forward. The ground was rocky and uneven. He stumbled a couple of times and would have fallen if not for her surprisingly strong grip, indicative of long hours in the fitness suite or decades assembling and disassembling automatic weapons. Lock and load.

They stopped. She turned him ninety degrees to the right. "Open your eyes."

Magill gasped at the sight before him. It really was like the movies. A Tim Burton movie, to be precise. Gothic doesn't begin to describe it. A dark line of compact, closely packed cypress trees led up to a walled graveyard, complete with ornate iron gate, elaborately carved archway and obligatory set of three broken steps in front of the creepy crepuscular entrance. God's paintbrush added the finishing flourishes. Everything was edged in red and gold, courtesy of the setting sun.

Ultima strode purposefully down the path. Magill lagged behind, drinking in the scene as instructed. "It'll be dark soon," she said over her shoulder. "No time to dally, Simon. You don't want to be stranded in an ancient graveyard after dark."

"As long as it's not a Native American burial mound, we'll be OK," he joked.

Ultima Sullivan laughed lightly as she made her way down cypress alley. It sounded like the call of a distant curlew in the forbidden forests of faerie fantasy. If a big bad wolf showed up, Red Riding Magill wouldn't have been taken aback, though seven dwarves might have thrown him.

Snow White's sexier big sister motioned for the frog prince to join her. "Indian burial mounds have nothing on Knights Templar cemeteries. Just wait till you see the mausoleum, Simon."

Magill started after his companion and caught up just as she mounted the time-grooved steps to the elaborate gateway. The graveyard was approximately forty metres by forty, with five-metre walls on all four sides. A sward of slanted headstones, weathered statuary, eroded cherubim, broken funerary urns, and mossy ledgers at crazy angles occupied every inch of space, or so it seemed. Thick swags of ivy hung from the perimeter walls, gravemarkers and almost every conceivable surface. Mature yew and holly trees were scattered hither and yon. And slap bang in the middle stood a magnificent granite mausoleum, brooding malevolently in the empurpled twilight beneath a carnelian sky.

"Quite something, isn't it?" Ultima whispered. Speaking aloud would have seemed inappropriate, disrespectful almost. The silence of the headstones called for compliance with an unwritten code of conduct. "The graveyard dates from the fourteenth century, around the time of the Templars' fall from grace, though the mausoleum was added in 1789 by Robert Adam. It's the final resting place of Arthur Upton and some of his sons. No daughters, naturally. Note the ashlar frontage and Knights Templar cross on the fanlight over the entrance."

Magill couldn't miss it.

The intrepid questors picked their way though a maze of Celtic crosses, sandstone sarcophagi, angel-topped marble stelae and well-tended family plots fringed with railings or kerbstones. The mausoleum was open. Ignoring the eerie atmosphere that accompanies semi-darkness in any graveyard anywhere, they went in. It was about four metres square and completely bare, apart from graven memorials to the Upton family, brave soldiers by and large, who served with distinction in Britain's colonial campaigns of yesteryear, yestercentury, yesterslaughter. The austerity was almost noble in its stiff-upper-lipped restraint.

"Is this where we should start digging?"

"You can if you like, Simon, but you won't find the grail. You'll only find St Patrick's well, which is directly below us."

"If it's not beneath us, Ultima, where is it?"

"The grail's not here."

"Not here?"

"It's gone."

Chapter Thirty-Three

O Brotherhood, Where Art Thou?

Raised expectations, dashed hopes and the stress and strain of yet another nightmarish day were starting to get to Simon Magill. The spring tides of adrenalised excitement that surged through his battered body like the Severn bore, only to ebb equally quickly, were playing havoc with his normally ebullient personality. Not only was he having more mood swings than a bipolar bull moose on Ritalin, but he was finding it hard to keep the testiness out of his voice. "It's gone, is it? More misdirection, maybe? It's buried somewhere else in the graveyard, right? Somewhere less obvious?"

"Yes and no," she said enigmatically.

"Which is it? Yes or no? Don't tease me, Ultima. Please. I've had a very trying day." Magill's meditative moment of telluric wonder had passed. He could sense that the solution to the mystery of Brodie's brutal murder, the mystery of O'Connell's mauled corpse, the mystery of the killers' sick messages, the mystery of the secretive Order of Solomon, was near at hand, if not quite within his grasp.

"That's what the squaddies used to say," she responded in a cadence that carried undertones of needless loss, mourning almost.

"Sorry?"

"Back when I was Britbait. That's what they used to say. Don't play games, Mary. Stop teasing, Sally. Little did they know what was in store for them."

"I see. What's in store for me, Ultima?"

"Well, it isn't the Holy Grail, Simon. Because it's disappeared. It went some time ago, long before you or I were born."

"Where did it go?"

"I don't know. I'm working on it."

Magill had had enough. "Ultima, why did you bring me here, if the grail's gone?" he said crossly.

"Because you might have helped me find it, Simon. Or track it down, at least."

"Me? What do I know about it? You'd be better off with Steven Spielberg. Or re-reading Dan Brown."

Ultima walked right up to Magill, within inches of his face, and placed both hands on his shoulders. Her angelic voice echoed off the bare-walled, high-ceilinged mausoleum. "Dan's not here right now, and anyway he doesn't have the information you have. I don't think you know anything about it, though. In fact, I'm certain you don't. But you said something this evening that could be a clue to the grail's whereabouts."

"SimpleSimonSays, eh, Ultima? I knew that website's time would come," he said wryly. In the gloom, Magill could see a glimmer of pearly phosphorescence as Ultima's eyes sparkled, despite the encircling darkness. If her face didn't quite lynch a thousand Brits, it must have done a lot of damage to the Royal Marines.

Punching him playfully, she responded "FoesReunited might be a better bet. I'm actually referring to *Titanic*, Simon. The conspiracy theories Carlingford O'Connell was working on. The stuff about the ship carrying secret treasure of some kind, an exceptionally precious object."

"OK, let me get this clear. You're saying they transported the Holy Grail in the Ark of the Covenant on the *Titanic*."

"You're getting warm, Simon."

"Sorry, I almost forgot. It was wrapped in the Turin Shroud at the time."

Ultima laughed. "And they said Dan Brown was crazy."

Relieved that the anticipation was almost over and some kind of explanation was imminent, Magill joined in. "Anyone would go crazy with his royalties. Have you ever thought of writing a novel, Ultima? Because this is a real humdinger. *Foucault's Pendulum* territory. *Illuminatus* trilogy. *The Crying of Lot 49*.

"Oh, there's a lot more to come, Simon."

"Don't tell me Rasputin was in on it too? Goddamn Russkies!"

"Not to my knowledge, though W. B. Yeats and Maude Gonne were definitely in the frame with their Hermetic Order of the Golden Dawn. Gonne was the most beautiful woman of her day, and a feminist to boot. Even Saint Patrick would have been tempted."

"You're teasing again. I may not be getting warm, Ultima, but I'm definitely getting hot under the collar."

"OK, Simon, OK. This is what we know. First, the Holy Grail was buried here, and removed at some stage. Second, the *Titanic* was transporting something important, but we don't know what. It could have been the ark, since there's a well-known theory that the Ark of the Covenant and the Holy Grail are one and the same. Robert de Boron said as much in the thirteenth century, and he was writing less than twenty years after *Perceval*, Chrétien de Troyes' inaugural grail romance. Whatever it was, Simon, it had to be transported from its hiding place in Ulster when civil war seemed imminent. The obvious place to take it was the home of the brave and the land of the Freemason. Not every American was or is a Freemason, but the contemporary Knights Templar are headquartered there."

"King Billy said it was the Northern Irish who built America."

"He's right. They did. Northern Irish Freemasons above all. Much as I abhor Ulster Protestants, it can't be denied that they carved America out of the wilderness, long before we Catholic Irish turned up in the mid-nineteenth century. Sixteen American presidents had Ulster antecedents, from James Monroe, Andrew Jackson, James Polk, James Buchanan, and Andrew Johnson right down to William McKinley, Theodore Roosevelt and Harry S. Truman. All of them were prominent Freemasons. Six of the signatories of the Declaration of Independence were of Scots-Irish stock, as was the Secretary of Congress at the time, as was the guy who printed the document. Davy Crockett, Kit Carson, Stonewall Jackson, Sam Houston, Ulysses S. Grant . . . the list goes on and on. All of them were from here, or hereabouts. They knew how to fight, I'll give them that. The Freemason-infested Scots-Irish made America what it is, Simon . . . "

"A bigoted bully that's arrogant, truculent, intolerant, belligerent and convinced it's something extra-special, the promised land of the chosen people."

"Correct."

"So, when the U. S. of A. is throwing its weight about, it's actually getting in touch with its inner Orangeman?"

"Correct."

"And that's why they sent the grail to America, because they knew the obdurate arseholes there would never surrender or give an inch?"

"Correct."

"But the key point, Ultima, is that America was by far the safest place to take the Holy Grail?"

"Correct."

"Only it went down with the *Titanic*."

"Perhaps. I don't know for sure. I only made the connection this afternoon when you were talking about Professor O'Connell."

"Retrieving it could be a problem, mind you. Maybe James Cameron can help?"

"He's Scots-Irish as well, Simon."

"I can see it now: *Titanic – The Return*, with the strapline, 'It Ain't Over Till It's Overboard . . . Over and Out . . . Over and Above the Abyss.'"

"Maybe we don't need to raise the *Titanic*. Because there's something else you said: the name of the mysterious female passenger who turned up safe and well but wasn't on the official register."

"Norton, wasn't it? Miss Norton."

"That's the one."

"What's the connection?"

"Castle Upton used to be called Castle Norton. The Nortons were here long before the Uptons. It was the Nortons who acquired the site of the old Templar preceptory, and they were the first to build on it. If anyone discovered the Holy Grail, it was the Nortons."

"The mysterious Ms Norton was a courier?"

"Perhaps, Simon."

"And she survived the sinking?"

They looked at each other in wonder and said in unison, "Eat your heart out, Cameron!"

A crescent moon greeted the light-hearted twosome as they escaped the austere mausoleum. Abetted by the collateral glow of the neighbouring Hilton hotel complex, it provided sufficient light for them to pick their way though the bumpy, buckled graveyard. In the darkness, the cemetery looked as though it had been hit by an earthquake. Steeply angled monumental slabs lay in anything but peaceful repose. An alabaster Celtic cross emitted an eerie luminescence. Otherworldly shadows were cast by clumps of sculptures. In the absence of proper pathways, they had to traverse a badly fitted corpse-filled carpet that was in need of what monumental make-over artistes call "lift and level."

"I'm not sure you're any better off," Magill observed. "There must be thousands of Nortons in America. And if our mystery woman was a courier, as you suspect, then anyone could have it. Heaven only knows who she passed the parcel to, if anyone. The *Titanic* sank a hundred years ago, near enough. The grail could be anywhere. All you know for sure is that it was here once upon a time. And that it's unlikely to be at the bottom of the Atlantic Ocean."

Ultima paused and held out her left hand, motioning for Magill to take it once more. "That's true, Simon, but it's another little piece of the puzzle. When you get enough pieces, things can fall into place very quickly. Crosswords are like that. Sudoku too."

Magill slipped his hand into hers, fingers intertwined. Far from being expensively maintained, Ultima's thin fingers were unpleasantly calloused – a side-effect of her serious knitting habit, he surmised. The IRA godmother held him tightly while rummaging in her bulky shoulder bag with her spare hand. "You've been very helpful to me, Simon. Very helpful. But . . . but . . . but . . . "

Having found what she was looking for, Ultima pulled a black-barrelled object out of her bag and aimed it straight at him.

Chapter Thirty-Four

Simon Magill and the Temple of Doom

They say that blood runs cold in moments of primal fear. Simon Magill's circulation didn't quite run cold, but it definitely dropped a degree or two. Ultima had got what she wanted, and for all her allure she was still an assassin at heart. He was expendable, just like all the others she'd exploited down the years, his brother possibly included. Magill regretted not hanging on to King Billy's proffered pistol; he regretted that the mysteries of the past few days would never be solved; he regretted that he had failed to live up to the standards of his mentor, Pitcairn Brodie; he regretted that he'd never see May Day's pretty pink bob again, or make love to Van Morrison. His music, that is.

Unlike his brutally murdered big brother, however, Simon Magill was determined to die with dignity. He heard a sharp click. There was a sudden flash of light and his eyeballs began to burn.

"Nice torch, Ultima."

" . . . but there's another part of the puzzle I still haven't shown you, Simon."

"Where are we off to now?" Magill sighed with relief. "A dripping crypt? An underground passage? A haunted mansion?"

"No, Simon. We're standing right beside it. Don't you want to see where the Holy Grail was buried?"

"I thought you said it was in the mausoleum."

"No, I didn't. You jumped to that conclusion, pretty boy, when I told you digging was pointless because the grail had gone. The grail has gone. Long gone. But even when it was here, it wasn't buried beneath the mausoleum. Too obvious."

Magill curled his lower lip, which wasn't easy. "Of course. Way too obvious. It's not like the Templars to do anything obvious.

Misdirection's their middle name, hocus-pocus their modus operandi."

"They were businessmen first and foremost, Simon, with an eye for the main chance. Like all savvy businessmen, they used magic and misdirection as a means to that end. They misdirected competitors who'd steal their markets. They misdirected suppliers who'd try to rip them off. They misdirected key constituents, such as greedy kings and princes who wanted a slice of the Templar action. They misdirected consumers, who were told what they wanted to hear rather than the truth, the whole truth and nothing but the truth. Consumers can't handle the truth, Simon, at least not from an unreliable source like marketers. Even if marketers were to tell the absolute truth, as Marks and Spencer tried to do with those disastrous TV ads featuring big naked ladies shouting 'I'm normal,' consumers aren't inclined to believe it because of its inherently tainted source. A little misdirection goes a long, long way in business."

"It doesn't say that in the textbooks."

"Maybe the textbooks are misdirecting you too, Simon. Have you ever considered that possibility?"

The sharp shaft of torchlight skimmed over assorted off-kilter memorials to long-forgotten fighting men and warrior mothers who died in childbirth. It shone on the grave of Josias Welsh, the grandson of John Knox and a charismatic preacher in his own right, who turned Templepatrick into a celebrated hotbed of religious dissent. It cast strange gothic shapes on the smooth surrounding wall, like an 18-certificate shadow play. The light came to rest on a nondescript piece of crazy paving in the lee of the mausoleum's west wall. "Not much to look at," she said, with an indicative nod of the head. "But wait till you see this."

They were staring down at a flat limestone slab, a severely weathered ledger. The lettering on its pockmarked face was illegible, near enough, and rendered even more so by verdigris-like lichen on the surface.

"What am I supposed to be looking at?"

"Turn it over and you'll see."

"You can't be serious, Ultima. You're asking me to desecrate a grave. My father'd have a fit."

"Simon, you were pretty keen to dig up the floor of the mausoleum when you thought the Holy Grail was there, and you didn't even have a shovel. This grave has been desecrated many times before now, not least by those who interred the grail. But if you're not interested, let's go. I'll take you back to Billy's."

Magill smuggled his fingertips under an overgrown edge of the eroded ledger and lifted. He huffed and puffed impressively, but it was glued to the ground.

"Put your back into it, pretty boy."

He tried again, managed to get some movement and lifted the slippery slab about six inches, only to discover that its weight had inexplicably increased exponentially. The ledger fell with a resounding thump that vibrated somewhere under their feet, albeit well above the bowels of the earth. The diaphragm, or thereabouts.

Ultima sighed a sigh that spoke volumes. "Weakling! You spend too much time in front of a computer screen and not enough in the gym. Here, let me try." She shouldered him aside and squatted beside the slab like a champion weightlifter doing the clean and jerk.

Simon Magill might not have been a man's man, unless a man's man is defined as someone who can recite pi to a thousand decimal places. As a firm believer in the eternal feminine, furthermore, he had never regarded women as anything other than a superior species. But there was something about Ultima Sullivan's dismissive remark that touched a primordial androcratic nerve – the eternal masculine, if you will – and he was determined to try again. He placed a hand on his gym-toned companion's shoulder and squeezed. "Third time lucky."

She stood up and stepped back, smiling sceptically. Magill eased his *Tomb Raider*–toned fingers under the slab, summoned the aid of the Neanderthal within, and lifted the ledger as if it were a piece of polystyrene. The pitted slab crashed to the ground with a thump that vibrated all the way to the planet's pancreas and points south. Even in the torchlight, he could see that the grass beneath the ledger's penultimate resting place was flattened, matted, bleached.

"Don't look there, Simon. Misdirection, remember. Check out the back of the slab."

The verso of the flat stone was covered in strange symbols, evidently carved by a master monumental Mason at some time in the distant past. Magill had never seen anything like it, or them, before. Vaguely reminiscent of sans-serif Hebrew, if there is such a thing, the chiselled symbols comprised a complex congeries of right angles and dots.

"What is it, Ultima? Ogham?"

"Don't be daft. Ogham's fifteen hundred years old and consists of incised vertical lines. The Celts were long gone when this gravestone was dressed and lettered. Time-wise it's closer to Loxian than Ogham."

"Loxian? What's Loxian?"

"A brand-new ancient language invented by Enya's lyricist for her latest CD of New-Age ditties."

"So it was carved in the last couple of years? That doesn't make sense."

"You should listen to people a bit more carefully, Simon. I said it was closer to Loxian than Ogham. And so it is. The incisions were made about a hundred years ago, maybe more."

"How do you know that?"

"Simple. I got an IRA forensic team to check it out. They used a dating technique called thermoluminescence."

Even with his recent exposure to the mores of Northern Ireland, the local behaviour never ceased to amaze Simon Magill. "The IRA has forensic teams? Thermoluminescence labs and the like?"

"No, of course not. We have an . . . mmm . . . arrangement with the PSNI. A strategic alliance, of sorts. We scratch the palms of their hands, they check scratches for us."

"Fair enough, Ultima. You win. What do the symbols mean?"

"I don't know for certain. I do know that the inscription "is a hundred years or so old. I *also* know that it's a secret code used by Freemasons. It's called the pigpen cipher. Each of the shapes stands for a letter of the alphabet."

"What does it say?"

"That's the problem, Simon. I know it's in code, but I can't crack it."

"Crossword puzzles and Sudoku no good to you, then?"

"The real problem is what cryptologists call substitution, where one letter is replaced by another: A becomes D, B becomes K, C becomes Z, and so on. In this case, the symbol that stands for one letter is replaced by the symbol for another. It's probably a pigpen version of the Caesar shift cipher, where the Roman emperor replaced each letter in his secret message with the one three places further down the alphabet. In this particular case, of course, it's the meaning of the symbols that's transposed. Technically, it's called a symbolic transposition cipher. But regardless of the technicalities, unless we know what the symbolic key is, the code's impossible to break."

"Hmmm," Magill muttered. "I bet my mother could've cracked it in her heyday."

"Oh, cracking Caesar ciphers isn't a problem, Simon. Far from it. Even if the letters of the cipher alphabet are randomly substituted, as opposed to using a straightforward transpositional shift in one or other direction, they're still fairly easy to crack. Notwithstanding the four trillion trillion possible combinations, we can use the known frequency of letters in the English language to help us. E is the most common letter in English, followed by T, A, O, I and so on. Simply count the frequency of the letters or symbols in the coded message and you're well on the way."

"So you have a good idea of what these symbols stand for?"

Ultima pointed to a symbol like a V doing an impersonation of algebra's "less than" sign. "I initially thought that it was either E or T, since it's the most frequent. Actually, I strongly suspected that it was T because of the local context. Templars, Templepatrick, Templeton or, as we uncovered today, Titanic. Unfortunately the resulting message was gibberish, as it is if I use E, or A, or every conceivable variation, both shift cipher and randomised. Then I thought perhaps the message wasn't in English. I've tried Old English, Gaelic, Latin, French, Ulster-Scots, believe it or not, and even Hisperica Famina, which was a cryptic symbolic system used by religious orders around the time of Saint Patrick. But without success, I'm afraid. I've reached a dead end."

"I presume reversing it didn't work either?"

"Reversing it?"

"Well, Ultima, the message is on the reverse of the slab. And if the Templars' descendants were great misdirecting magicians, as you say, then it could be that smoke and mirrors are at work. Mirrors especially. The symbols on the slab may be mirror writing. By the look of them, the actual symbols wouldn't change when reversed, but their meaning would. Have you tried that yet?"

A look crossed Ultima's face that wasn't so much astonishment as "out of the mouths of babes and buffoons." "No, Simon, I didn't try that. It never occurred to me. Technically, I suppose, it's a symbolic transposition cipher, with reflection . . . hmmm . . . that's very interesting . . . "

Magill smiled triumphantly. The physiognomic pain was as nothing to someone powered by the inner Neanderthal, the eternal masculine and, not least, the telluric currents of Templepatrick. "You should spend more time in front of a computer screen and less time pumping iron, Ultima. A gamer would have got that right away."

"*Touché*," she said, with a phosphorescent smile.

"We're quits," he replied. "Shall I make a note of the symbols? We can work on them where the light's better. Would you happen to have a mirror and a pen in your bag of surprises?"

"Yes, I've got a mirror but the pen's a lethal weapon in disguise. Fires tranquiliser darts. Got me out of a few sticky situations when I was a volunteer, I can tell you."

"You're joking, right?"

"The name's Ultima, Ultima Sullivan," she laughed. "Licensed to knit."

"Let me guess," Magill quickly countered. "*Thunderball of Wool, Merino Royale, On Her Majesty's Stitching Service, You Only Purl*

264

Twice, The Man With the Crocheted Gun . . . "

"Funny you should mention that, Simon, because Balaclava. com's thinking of developing a line of Aran armalite covers, raglan RPG protectors, two-ply petrol-bomb coasters. What do you reckon?"

"Where are the venture capitalists when you need them?"

Ultima clicked off her torch. The crescent moon, aided and abetted by the Hilton Hotel's collateral illumination, cast a silvery pall over the ancient graveyard. "No need for a pen, Simon. I have the message written down already. What do you think I've been working on for the past couple of years?"

"I guessed that, but I just want to get out of this graveyard before the headless Templar horseman turns up with repossession in mind."

"I know the perfect place."

Chapter Thirty-Five

The Odyssey

Irish culture is literary rather than visual. Compared to its verbal arabesques, its architectural epics are few in number and often provided by outsiders. Most Irish buildings are banal or boxy at best, and a blight on the landscape at worst. Town planning is an Irish oxymoron. There are so many cowboy developers in Belfast that it's twinned with Deadwood, Dodge City and Tombstone. Or ought to be.

Belfast's Odyssey Centre typifies Ulster's architectural blindspot. Hunkered at the edge of the Titanic Quarter, within spitting distance of Hustler Business School, it looks like a squashed armadillo. For the houseproud executives of the local tourist authority, it is nothing less than a "signature project", a stirring symbol of the rundown town's remarkable renaissance. But the signature is illegible and the symbolism misbegotten. It is the architectural equivalent of roadkill.

The Odyssey's interior isn't much better. Far from being a fountain of fun, filled to overflowing with cheerful pubs, exciting eateries, throbbing nightclubs, stimulating cinemas, amusements as far as the eye can see and ass-kickin' concerts by head-bangin' rock bands, the Odyssey arena is a vast, freezing barn with the aesthetics of a North Korean nuclear reactor. Undergoing meltdown. Luckily, the city's inhabitants are blessed with a collective masochistic streak and, after many years of casual violence, they're happy to have somewhere to go to relax, even if it looks like a Ukrainian tractor factory designed by Tracey Emin.

Nestling in a corner of this cornucopian silage container is the Titanic Bar & Grill, a theme restaurant based on Belfast's biggest celebrity calamity after George Best, Alex Higgins and John De Lorean. Poignant photos of the ill-fated liner line the walls, reproduction memorabilia fill plaintive display cabinets, and the provender on offer replicates the first-class bill of fare on that fateful April night. It's a little-known fact that Astor, Guggenheim, Straus and co. were tucking into burgers, fries and buffalo wings before heading for the lifeboats with a carry-out raspberry milkshake. Sadly, such nuggets of information often slip though the colander of history or are ignored by past-times panhandlers.

As theme restaurants go, the Titanic Bar & Grill is unlikely to go global, since its basic premise is rather less appealing than Planet Hollywood, Hard Rock Café or even TGIF, though the latter on a busy night makes the North Atlantic look inviting. However, for Simon Magill at least, the Titanic Bar & Grill represented a substantial step up from the evening's earlier necrofest.

They took a table in the corner, under a massive mug shot of Captain Smith – the source of inspiration, surely, for the incomparable Captain Birds Eye – and set to work on the pigpen cipher. Or, rather, one version of the Freemasons' signature cipher, which confusingly comes in American pigpen and British pigpen.

British pigpen cipher

American pigpen cipher

At least the Titanic's service was shipshape and Bristol fashion. A nautically embellished waiter heaved to, hailed the starving survivors and handed them the drinks list that accompanied the liner's final repast. Resisting the temptation to ask for extra ice, or even inquire when last orders were called – by the cut of the waiter's jib he'd heard every *Titanic* jibe imaginable, many times over – Magill ordered a Diet Pepsi, as did Ultima. That ship was definitely ahead of its time, he thought.

Ultima pulled a pocket compact out of her capacious tote bag, slipped on a pair of designer reading glasses, which only added to her infinite variety, and set to work on the cipher. "There is," she said, while painstakingly transposing the symbols, some of which remained unchanged, "a fly in the ointment."

"Don't you mean fly in the soup, Ultima? As in 'Waiter, waiter, there's a lifeboat in my soup!' 'Think yourself lucky, sir, because there aren't enough for everyone.'"

She ignored Magill's tasteless remark. "No, I mean a fly in the pickle jar you've got yourself into. The date of the ledger inscription was 120 years ago, plus or minus ten. In other words, it predates *Titanic* by at least twenty years. A decade I could understand, because a ship of that scale takes a long time to plan and build. But twenty's a stretch. Even allowing a bit of leeway, it still comes out around 1900, twelve years before the sinking . . . "

"There is the Morgan Robertson episode," Magill suggested. "O'Connell told me about it."

"And that is?"

"A book. A novel written in 1898, ten years before the *Titanic* was built. It told the story of the construction of a great ocean liner, the SS *Titan*, a ship with water-tight bulkheads. On its maiden voyage to New York, it hit an iceberg and sank, with enormous loss of life."

"Now that's what I call eerie."

"The idea of the *Titanic* was in the air before *Titanic* was built, Ultima. It was predestined, almost. Not inevitable, but maybe the Freemasons behind the ledger were in touch with something, the telluric currents you were talking about. When I was studying marketing in Stirling, one of the lecturers claimed that artists and

269

writers were ahead of the curve. They could sense emerging social trends much better than market researchers equipped with their tick-box questionnaires. Marketers, he said, would be better off reading novels than reading Kate Phillips. I thought he was mad at the time, but in light of the ledger I'm not so sure."

"Or our forensic team could've got it wrong."

"There is that," he smiled.

"Well, we'll soon find out. Fingers crossed." Having transcribed the transposed symbol sequence, she set about the translation using the British pigpen notation. Magill, meantime, caught the waiter's eye, ordered two First-Class Burgers and Steerage Shakes, with White Star Line side-salad to share. By the time the order was taken, the translation was complete:

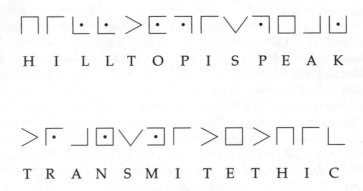

They were no better off than before. Neither Ultima nor Magill could make sense of the cryptic message, though it did carry connotations of the United States, as the shining city on the hill, and the transmission of something important. Perhaps Dan Brown was right, or almost right. Perhaps the Holy Grail wasn't a physical object but a state of mind, an attitude, a work ethic?

Baffled, they tried several other possibilities: the American notation, the E shift, the T shift and even reversing the letter sequence – a possible double-double bluff by the Templars – but the transpositions made even less sense than "Hilltop I Speak Transmit Ethic."

Ultima's enchanting face had settled into pursed-lipped repose, the look Magill had first encountered a few hours earlier off the Falls Road. She exuded an air of nonplussed irritation that didn't lift when the waiter arrived with their immemorial repast. "If he says 'Enjoy!' I'll scream," she stage-whispered to her bright-haired, black-eyed, broken-faced companion.

"This should go down easily, sir, madam."

"Arrrrggggh," Magill retorted in the bantering Belfast manner. "Do you tell everyone that joke?"

"Not everyone, sir. We usually say 'Enjoy!' but you . . . er . . . look different."

"You don't like my black eyes? This look's all the rage in London, let me tell you."

"What part of London's that, sir? The panda house in Regent's Park Zoo? The Natural History Museum, marsupials annex? The recovery room of a Harley Street plastic surgeon?"

Magill glanced at his name tag. "You get a lot of tips, do you, Able Seaman Thomas McStravick?"

"Only from people who look different. Not everyone wants servility. Sometimes you have to mix it up a bit. People remember you that way, I find." Emboldened, Able Seaman McStravick motioned towards the symbol-strewn sheet of paper. "Is that a new kind of Sudoku? The grid looks a wee bit different from the others I've seen."

"Yes, Thomas, it's Sudoku for the innumerate."

"That's different."

"It certainly is. Thanks, Thomas."

They tucked in disconsolately. In an attempt to distract his frustrated confederate, Magill inquired about her unusual Christian name. He'd assumed it was a derivative of "ultimate" – a diminutive that was singularly apt given her singularly striking appearance – but the reality was even more remarkable. It was derived from Ultima Thule, an enchanted island in Norse

271

mythology, akin to the Blessed Isles of Irish legend or the Hesperides of Greek myth. Ultima Thule was apparently a utopian idyll, a Scandinavian Shangri-La, endlessly searched for by generations of intrepid explorers. It also inspired a Nazi secret society, an occult organisation founded by Rudolf von Sebottendorff, who was not only a rabid Freemason but a mentor of Adolf Hitler. The organisation maintained that the earth was hollow and sought to demonstrate that the Aryan race came from the lost land of Atlantis.

"Incredible," Magill replied when Ultima's nomenclatural lecture had finished. "You're named after a secret society. That just about takes the ship's biscuit."

"You did ask, Simon."

"I did."

"A conspiracy for a conspiracy. You gave me *Titan*, I gave you Thule. Tit-for-tat chilling, we call it round here."

"Right. Right. Your parents have vivid imaginations, Ultima, that's all I can say."

"My mother does. I'm not sure about my father. He ran out on us. Left my mother pregnant at sixteen. Disappeared off to Scotland. We never heard from him again. My mother remarried. A good hard-working man, who was shot dead by the Brits."

"Jesus, I'm sorry to hear that."

"Yes, well, we all have our horror stories. Some are more horrible than others." She smiled a sad smile. "Anyway, that's the story of my name, Simon, since you asked."

"It's different, I'll give you that," he said echoing their waiter's affably insolent remark.

Magill looked around for Able Seaman McStravick. He was keen to try champ, the legendary local delicacy that the ancient Irish smeared on top of round towers. When he turned back, Ultima was staring at him with energised exuberance. Her eyes sparkled like champagne bubbles at a boat-naming ceremony (whereas Magill's looked like they'd been hit by a bottle that's bounced off the hull). After nibbling absent-mindedly on an elongated White Star French Fry, she waved the stump excitedly, like a strict schoolmarm threatening a recalcitrant pupil. "That's it!" she exclaimed. "Think differently. We need to think differently. We need to look differently at the transcript."

"You think it could be in Latin, Loxian or, what was it, Hisperica Famina?"

"Well, possibly, but it's more likely to be a simple case of substitution rather than transposition. That's the most basic distinction made by cryptographers."

"Sorry?"

"Minimal slog. Smiling loam. Million mags. Liminal smog."

"Excuse me?"

"Sing I'm a moll."

"Never heard of it, Ultima. I know 'I'm a Believer,' 'I'm a Man,' 'I'm a Fool for Your Love,' 'I'm a Lumberjack and I'm OK,' but 'I'm a Moll' is new to me. The Corrs, is it? Sinéad O'Connor?"

"They're anagrams of your name, Simon Magill. It's an anagram, an anagram!" She scribbled frantically on a Titanic Bar & Grill napkin like two men and a wee lad shovelling lilty shit. "I've got it!" She held out a scrap of tissue paper. "That's the bottom part of the message, Simon."

"I don't believe it. No way. It can't be!"

Chapter Thirty-Six

Barton Brady's Big Mistake

Brady's frustration was increasing by the minute. He rang Professor Phillips again. The suspicious administrative assistant cut him off as soon as she recognised the caller. He pinged another email. Still outta the goddamn office. Browsing in Barnes & Noble, no doubt.

Aherne also unavailable.

Irritation.

Frustration.

Action stations.

He called United, booked a seat on the lunchtime shuttle to O'Hare, and arranged a rental with Hertz on his way to the airport. He tipped the Yellow Cab driver $10 on a $15 fare, even though he'd no luggage to unload. *A la* E. M. Foster, a few greenbacks properly distributed help keep minions' memories alive. He had morphed from needy greedy to gladhandin' goodguy in no time at all. Mr Jekyll was in hyding again, as he invariably was, except on therapists' well-padded couches and very well-padded bills.

Be that as it may, Barton Brady II – alumnus of the Slick Willy Clinton school of pump 'em, hump 'em, dump 'em – was now in session. He strolled confidently, proprietorially, through McCarran's polished palm-peppered halls, the finest product of America's dream factory. Unlike the poor saps feeding the last of their holiday dollars into the terminal's slot machines, he had broken his gambling habit. But not his smooth-talking one.

He always traveled coach. He always got an upgrade. Brady liked the check-in challenge, and, as a first-class finagler, never failed to finagle First Class. As on this occasion. He called his SA PA from the first-class departure lounge, where he sipped a half double-decaf half caf with a twist of lemon, and chewed absent-mindedly on a lo-cal, no-nut, sans-salt, sugar-free, yeast-reduced, additives-extracted, char-grilled complimentary cinnebun with added Jell-O extract, and told her to cancel all appointments till he returned. His diary was empty anyway. Officially, he was out of the office on brainstorming business, the grail trail. But she needed to know on the off-chance that something on-message might come in when he was out of town.

Less than an hour after leaving home, Brady was strapped into his seat-cum-kingsize-cum-barcalounger and interfacing prior to take off with fellow members of the first-class cabin cabal. Mutual acquaintances were noted. Business cards were exchanged. PDAs locked, docked and stocked each other with back-scratching bytes. Deals'd be done in the fullness of time.

Three hours and two hi-balls later, Brady was striding through the nave of Terminal 1, O'Hare's clerestoried aeronautical cathedral, cerise Versace suit uncreased, two-tone Gucci loafers gleaming and limited-edition Girard-Perregaux set to 3.15 p.m. CST. His Cadillac Escalade was ready and waiting. Not for him the troglodytic car rental desks in the lowest circle of airport hell. Car rental companies were arguably the leading exponents of marke*tease* – boy, those guys really knew how to torment their customers – but Brady knew how to avoid the taste of his own marketing medicine.

It was 4.30 p.m. when Barton Brady II slipped through the prestigious portals of Kellogg School of Management, a cereal-box-style monument to Modernism situated at the heart of Northwestern University's striking lakeside campus. He took the elevator to the marketing department on the third floor. Phillips's office occupied a corner, naturally enough. The door was firmly closed. An administrative assistant remained on duty in the open-plan sentry box outside. It was the assistant he'd spoken to earlier, Cicily Joyner.

"I'm here to see Professor Phillips," Brady said in his most ingratiating manner, with just enough of his orthodontic hi-beams to make it happen. Cicily didn't recognise the voice, since it had been smothered in several layers of mellifluous Barton Brady-grade maple syrup since its earlier anxious incarnation.

"Do you have an appointment?" she asked, sucking in the suit, the smile, the simper, the smarm, the shtick, the shit-on-a-stick.

"No, but Kate and I go way back," he replied, with a fractionally raised eyebrow. It implied a degree of intimacy with the seventy-year-old professor that, if not quite biblical, was certainly certifiable. "I thought I'd call in to see her as I'm in the area." He flashed the hi-beams again. "I have something . . . um . . . urgent to impart, and it's a one-on-one issue. But if she's not available, that's OK. Tell her I called. Have a nice one, Cicily." He turned to leave.

The professor's affable African-American secretary had seen and heard it all. A constant stream of supplicants called at Kate Phillips's door. And she had strict instructions to see them off. It wasn't that Professor Phillips was aloof or unfriendly – quite the opposite – it was simply that the more time she spent blessing the pilgrims, the less time she had to write new books, update old editions and spread the good word. Hence, getting rid of casual callers was an important part of Cicily's job description. It had to be done politely, of course, since they were all potential book buyers or, in the case of educators, a crucial component of the student textbook purchasing process. Antagonising the customer is not the smartest of strategies, unless you're CEO of Ryanair or Oracle, or in the business of demarketing visitors to the marketing department, as Cicily ultimately was.

To be sure, the recipients of this deliberate demarketing strategy reacted in very different ways. Some tried to sweet-talk their way round the immovable object. Others went into an embarrassing begging-bowl routine. Yet others got testy, which immediately settled their hash, and yet others played the do-you-know-who-I-am? card. Few, however, had the gumption to try reverse psychology, Brady's trademark tease-the-teaser twist.

"Let me just check, Mr . . . ?"

"Brady," he said in his best Yale drawl, a demotic adaptation of the aristocratic accent that rendered it both intimate and intimidating. "Barton Brady II."

"I think she's gone for the day, Barton. But if you'd like to take a seat in the wailing room – sorry, the waiting room – I'll see what

I can do."

Things are going to plan, Brady thought as he settled himself in the anteroom, which was situated sufficiently far from the prof's office to allow her to slip off surreptitiously if her gentlemen callers were too insistent and would be satisfied only with the sight of an empty office. Another deliberate attempt at demarketing adorned the waiting-room walls. A mural of the great and good of the Kellogg marketing department looked down on him. At the very top of the cartoon, Saint Phillips sat on a cloud disbursing scholarly benedictions to the lesser luminaries beneath. Most visitors, Brady correctly concluded, would so be browbeaten by the empyrean depiction – which forced them to reflect on their own unexalted place in the marketing firmament – that they'd make for the exit without further ado. But Brady was made of sterner stuff. He rather liked the Edenic mural. Except that Kate Phillips was sitting on *his* cloud.

Cicily popped her ever-amiable head around the door. It was clear from the look on her face that the professor hadn't fallen for the teasing trick. Demarketing demarketers is difficult, especially in the absence of pleasing packaging, gift-wrapped and gleaming. "Professor Phillips is about to leave for a meeting in Chicago. She won't be back today, I'm afraid. She's got a fundraiser this evening and her schedule is solid all day tomorrow. And the day after that."

Brady's mellifluous mask slipped momentarily. "A conference, perhaps? Something to do with Marketing Illuminati, possibly?"

Cicily had a strange look on her well-nourished face, as if she were trying to place the speaker but couldn't connect the rude SOB earlier with the SSB in front of her, sonofabitch having segued into silky-smooth bastard.

"No, no. No conferences, Barton. Departmental committee meetings tomorrow. Job talk on Saturday, which is unusual but the only day everyone can manage. She says she'll be able to fit you in on Monday. Does that suit you?" Cicily asked solicitously, knowing full well it didn't.

Magill responded with an unstoppable rhetorical combination of sweet talk, begging bowl, testy tincture and do-you-know-who-

I-am?, accompanied by a demarketing overlay. "Sure thing, Cicily, though I *so* wanted to see her again. I'll try not to take my frustration out on the PAs in our place, Serendipity Associates, the leading management consultancy west of the Rockies. Guess I better go and kick some butt," he smiled.

Fearful of the wrath of Kate, Cicily stood firm. "Monday is the best I can do for you, Barton. Don't be too hard on them."

"Does she have five minutes now? You said she was about to leave for a meeting in Chicago. I'll walk her to her car." Barton was confident Phillips's Chicago meeting was BS, and even more confident that with his unsurpassable interpersonal skills, he'd soon finesse his way into the Illuminati confab. If Cicily had said Phillips has already gone to Chicago, he'd have been beaten. However, she'd left the door open a fraction, and that was all a fast-talking, sales-pitching, silent-running SSB like Barton Brady required. There wasn't anyone anywhere who could resist his smarmy charms when he chose to turn them on, and Kate Phillips was going to get the sweeter-than-sweet-talk treatment with added aspartame.

"Let me just check, Barton." He knew she'd be in trouble. He felt for her. The wrath of a cornered academic is terrible to see. Some sociologists are so sociopathic they'd chew off their own limbs rather than socialise. Indeed, many autocastrate in preference to communing with capitalists, even capitalists disbursing consultancy funds. Sorry, Cicily, but needs must.

Naturally, Brady screened out the deliberately raised voices in the corner office. Phillips was obviously pretending to bawl out her incompetent administrative assistant in a transparent attempt to bounce the unwanted visitor into an embarrassed retreat. However, he knew it for what it was, the last-ditch death throes of a determined demarketer. He too could decode demarketing. Cicily returned with a resigned expression that said it all. He was in. The prof would be putty in his hands.

"Professor Phillips will see you now, Mr Brady."

Chapter Thirty-Seven

Anagramalama

Ultima Sullivan passed the notated napkin to her consort. If they noticed anything at all, most diners in the Titanic Bar & Grill would have considered it an innocent gustatory gesture, devoid of meaning or content. But for Simon Magill it was a momentous moment. His world, already shaken by the grotesque events of the past two days, was about to collapse like a line of first-class deckchairs on the eponymous supership as it foundered in the frigid waters of the North Atlantic.

He felt a shiver down his spine as he took the proffered scrap of paper. Time stood still, though not so still that he overlooked the greasy stains his chip-dipped fingers were leaving on the liner-logoed napkin. It said RMS Titanic. The hand-written message also said "The RMS Titanic."

"Transmit Ethic is an anagram of 'The RMS Titanic,'" she said with the self-satisfaction of a successful puzzle solver. He'd seen the look innumerable times on his wonderful mother's face.

Magill was shaken but not surprised. It merely confirmed their suspicions, their expectations, their conspiracy theories. "What does the rest of it say, Ultima?"

"Give me a second, Simon." A few moments later, the crossword supremo looked up. Her stunningly beautiful face was scarred with bewilderment. "I don't believe it myself," she announced in a tone that, if not quite gob-smacked, was certainly within spitting distance.

Just as laughter is contagious, so too is surprise. "Wh . . . wha . . . what is it, Ultima?"

"Simon," she said quickly, "remind me of the warning messages left by the killers of Professors Brodie and O'Connell. O'Connell's was 'A Ship Still Kept,' wasn't it? What was Brodie's again?"

"'Kill the Paspi.' O'Connell's was 'A Ship Ill Kept.' 'Ill,' not 'Still,' Ultima."

She jotted the grisly expressions on another napkin. "That's the exact spelling?"

"I think so. I'm pretty sure, though I never actually got to see Brodie's, and I wasn't taking notes at O'Connell's. I hope you're not stringing me along again, Ultima, like you did with the grail. It's getting beyond a joke. These are serious matters, deep waters."

She smiled a wan smile and looked at Magill with an expression best described as regretful pity. "Simon, the top part of the Templar message is . . . Kate Phillips. The O'Connell message is an anagram of Kate Phillips. The Brodie message is . . . "

"Kate Phillips?"

She nodded and passed the paper over. The entire ledger message read "Kate Phillips The RMS Titanic."

Magill wasn't quite struck dumb, but his natural eloquence had taken a severe beating. "It can't be," he gasped. "It can't be. Not *the* Kate Phillips."

"Well," Ultima replied calmly. "The only Kate Phillips I know . . . "

". . . is the world-famous marketing guru based in Chicago," Magill cut in. "Surely it can't be."

She evaluated his statement for a second. "Simon, you said King Billy made a Chicago connection. You said King Billy thought it was marketing-related. You said . . . "

"But *Titanic* sank almost a hundred years ago! Are you saying that Kate Phillips was on board when *Titanic* foundered and sank? She's in her late sixties at the most, seventy max."

"Weeellll," Dr Sullivan's inner pedant pronounced, "if the Holy Grail is the fountain of youth, as some suggest, then it's not impossible. It's improbable," she went on professorially, "but not impossible. There may be a simpler explanation, however. Perhaps her parents or grandparents were on board. It's not unusual for children to be named after grandparents, particularly ones who've gone through a traumatic experience. There's an easy way to find out."

She called Thomas McStravick over and, intimating that it

282

might be worth his while tip-wise, asked him to bring *Titanic's* passenger list, a leather-bound copy of which sat resplendent in one of the restaurant's many display cabinets.

Thomas paused for a second, since removing memorabilia was against the rules, but fearful that his forthcoming tip might be compromised, or even go the way of the ill-fated liner, he relented with much extra-special-favour semaphore. "Luckily, the manager's off duty tonight," he said. "Please be quick or all our customers will be wanting mementos with their milkshakes."

After briefly running her calloused fingers round the White Star logo embossed on the exterior of the beautiful commemorative binder, Ultima flicked though the passenger list. It was arranged alphabetically, by class, by crew, by survivor, with biographical details where available. "There she is. There she is! Miss Kate Phillips, no less. She was travelling second class and, yes, survived the sinking."

Ultima read on, her eyes widening with astonishment. "My, my, my," she muttered. "Unbelievable!"

"What is it? What is it?"

"Just wait till you hear this, Simon. Miss Kate Phillips was travelling under an assumed name. She was eloping with a married man – a businessman, a confectionery magnate, the Jelly Bean King – who'd deserted his wife and family to run off with his mistress, who was pregnant at the time of the crossing. He drowned. She survived, moved to the Midwest and disappeared from the record."

"Let me see."

Ultima handed the leather-bound inventory to her fellow passenger and he read the Kate Phillips story with equal amazement, possibly more.

"OK," he said, handing the book back to Thomas, who was hovering anxiously. "Let's step back for a second. What exactly have we got here? A boat with the grail. A coded message on a Templar tomb. A passenger with an alias on the *Titanic*. A possible descendant of Kate Phillips, *Titanic* survivor, at the centre of a Chicago-based Freemasonic cabal of marketing assassins, who leave calling-cards in the form of blood-stained anagrams."

"And a true Brit stuck in the middle of it all," she added helpfully. "Whatever *it* is. Whatever they're called. P4, wasn't it, Simon? The Order of Solomon, you say?"

"It's madness, Ultima. Beyond bizarre. Beyond Dan Brown's most fevered imaginings. Professor Brodie's death was bad enough, but the culprit being the world's leading marketing scholar beggars belief. Unless it was someone trying to implicate Professor Phillips. Misdirection, possibly."

"It's one hell of a deception, that's for sure," Ultima replied. "Did Phillips have any dealings with Brodie? Did she feature on the website, for example?"

Magill assented with a tiny nod. "Yes, she was on the website. I posted her bio myself. He may have had other dealings with her. I don't know for certain. Brodie did a lot of clandestine marketing consultancy work. He didn't talk about it much."

"It's fair to infer, then, that Phillips is a Freemason of some kind, since the website was a front for the Brotherhood. Isn't that what you found, Simon?"

"But there aren't any female Freemasons, Ultima. Masonic lodges are women-free zones. That's why it's called the Brotherhood, isn't it?"

"No, no," the pedantic paramilitary retorted, "that's not strictly true. Like the Orange Order, certain early offshoots of Freemasonry were proto-feminist. Count Cagliostro's Egyptian Rite was very strong on women's rights, for example. You can't rule out masonic involvement on gender grounds alone. Quite the opposite, in fact."

Magill took a deep breath and set his face with determination. "So where do we go from here, Ultima?"

She set down her knife and fork, thought for a second or two, and looked Magill straight in the eye. "I think you have to go to Chicago, Simon. That's where the trail of clues leads. You have to have it out with Kate Phillips, even if only to find out if she's the right Kate Phillips."

"And track down the Holy Grail while I'm at it, I suppose."

Ultima put on her reading glasses, paused for effect and said vivaciously, "Go forth, brave knight. Let thy heart be true. Keep an eye out for evil spirits. Or Jim Beam, at least."

"Why don't you come with me, fair Lady Balaclava?"

"I'd love to, Simon, but as a convicted terrorist I'm barred from the United States. They won't give me a visa. I've applied many times without success. Unlike my fellow convict, brother Gerry Adams, I'm still taboo." She picked up her cutlery and started attacking the First-Class Burger with a ferocity that would do justice to Wee Joe Monroe. "Maybe my kid sister will go with you."

"Yes, I could do with a minder," Magill retorted with a snort.

"Make sure she brings her knitting needles. She may have trouble getting them through airport security, mind you. Perhaps she could bring one of those pens with the poison darts instead."

"She's not an IRA operative, Simon. She's very nice. You'll like her." Ultima took a sip of her Steerage Shake, set the tall glass on the cramped wooden table and slowly revolved it several times, while smiling conspiratorially.

Ordinarily, Simon Magill would have wondered what was going on or questioned what he was getting into. But he was so shell-shocked by the series of recent revelations that his national default setting – impeccably mannered Englishman abroad – took over. "Yes, yes, I'm sure your sister's very nice, Ultima. I'm sure I'll like her immensely."

"That's good to know, Simon, because she likes you. That's what she told me, last time we spoke."

"Pardon?"

"You know her, Simon. You know her intimately, I've been told." Ultima laughed a lascivious laugh that was, well, reminiscent of a xylophone he'd heard not so long ago. "Don't look so surprised, pretty boy. A little birdie told me. A big birdie, actually. A herring gull, to be exact."

"Wha . . ."

Chapter Thirty-Eight

Hurry, While Shocks Last

Ultima Sullivan's dark eyes were dancing with delight. Despite his abashed amazement, Simon Magill couldn't help but be delighted too. "May Day's my sister. My stepsister, to be precise. That's my apartment she's living in. Well, one of them, anyway. We move about a bit in my line of business, as you can imagine. Obviously, the apartment's in her name and she likes to think of it as her own. But that's OK. We're very close."

Magill nodded appreciatively as a modicum of enlightenment dawned. "I was wondering how she could afford it on a business-school salary. I didn't realise it was bought with blood money."

"Forgive me, pretty boy, but when I heard a Brit with army connections was dating my sister, I decided to keep an eye on your coming and goings. When I discovered you were swanning around the Shankill Road, bosom buddies with King Billy Solomon, I just had to find out what was going on. I had to hear it from the horse's mouth, so to speak, without dissimulation."

Magill was staggered. "But how on earth did you catch on so quickly? I only met May Day yesterday."

"Simon, we monitor everything that's happening. We have to. Our lives depend on it. The Laganside apartment is under constant surveillance. It took all of five minutes to run a check on you, panda . . . my panda . . . my tantric panda."

Trying and failing to hide his embarrassment behind a strawberry Steerage Shake, Magill smiled sheepishly, fearing further intimate revelations in the middle of a far from empty restaurant. If she brought up his pi performance statistics, he'd abandon ship without further ado. However, the conversation took a completely different turn, though not a happy one.

"I'm sorry about your brother, Simon."

He had to ask. "Was he one of yours?"

"No, no, he wasn't," Ultima said softly.

Magill was sure she was lying. He could easily smash the glass in his hand and exact fearsome revenge on the alluring assassin. But what was the point in settling old scores with further rounds of violence? It wouldn't bring his brother back, or return his mother to mental health. His father used to preach forgiveness, after all, even if his practice left a lot to be desired. "I'm sorry about your stepfather, Ultima."

They ate in silence.

"There's something I still don't understand."

"What's that, Simon?"

"May Day said King Billy was family. He's a convicted Protestant paramilitary, affiliated with the Shankill Butchers. He told me himself. How can he possibly be part of your family?"

Ultima smiled enigmatically. "I don't think May was referring to family in the blood relation sense. More like the Cosa Nostra sense. You don't listen properly, Simon. You need to be careful about that. It could get you into trouble."

"More trouble, you mean."

"Correct. King Billy is a businessman, Simon. He's part of the Ulster Crimind family. He has no loyalties or unbreakable commitments, other than to the almighty dollar, and gets none in return. Except from his psychotic minder, Wee Joe Monroe. Religion doesn't come into it as far as he's concerned. People like King Billy are only interested in the marketing opportunities that ancient hatreds provide: the Ulster-flag concession, the rebuilding-trade rackets, the guided tours of former trouble spots for American tourists with more dollars than sense. Our side does exactly the same. Republicans control the west Belfast market segment. Loyalists control the east and the north."

"Who controls the south, Ultima?"

"Rotarians, Simon. The Rotarians. They're the most ruthless of the lot, though their violence isn't physical."

"There's another thing. If King Billy is a loose cannon with a psychopathic sidekick, why didn't May Day send me to you instead of Solomon?"

"Because I didn't know who you were. Well, I knew your name, rank and serial number, as it were, but I didn't know who you *really* were and what your agenda was. May Day wanted me to help you – she rang – but it was safer to channel you through Solomon. Except I didn't expect the pair of you to hit it off."

"How do you know we hit it off?"

"The top floor of Billy's house is bugged, Simon. Industrial espionage goes on even in Crimind. We monitor him constantly and we know he shows his set-up only to people he trusts. He's killed people for snooping. Butchered them. The man's a maniac, believe me."

"I don't know what to believe any more, Ultima. I don't know that I ever did."

"That's why you need to confront Kate Phillips and clear the air once and for all."

"I could send her an email."

"'Dear Professor Phillips. Sorry to bother you, but a mentor of mine has been brutally murdered and I found a message from your good self incised on his skull. Do you happen to know anything about it? Another colleague of mine has been hammered to a pulp and again your calling card was found beside the body. Oh, and by the way, do you happen to know the whereabouts of the Holy Grail or have it in your possession? Look forward to hearing from you. Ciao.'"

Magill sighed heavily and slurped his Steerage Shake noisily.

"Best face up to her, Simon."

"And how am I going to do that. Jump on the next flight?"

"Why don't you ring May Day? She might be able to help. As I understand it, she has a colleague in Northwestern, working with Kate Phillips."

"Of course. Emer Aherne. I'd completely forgotten. But I've never even met her."

"You're a colleague, aren't you? And May works for her. It's your best bet, Simon."

Ultima dipped into her bag of tricks and pulled out a BlackBerry. She made a "forgive me" face while firing up her handheld. "I'm a complete BerryBitch. Never leave home without it."

289

"Yeah, it does everything except fire poison darts."

"They're working on it, though. Mine has a sharp spike that comes in very handy during interrogations."

"Or if you want to remove stones from horses' hooves."

"That too, Simon. The terrorist special edition. It's a joint venture with the Swiss Army Knife people. Could be big this Christmas. Order now. Hurry while stocks last."

Ultima looked away, her eyes focused on the middle distance, as she spoke rapidly to her stepsister. They exchanged pleasantries for a minute or so, Ultima joking that she'd run into May's boyfriend and he'd taken her out on a date. But the siren's demeanour soon turned serious. Her answers became clipped and curt.

Magill tried to catch Ultima's eye, signalling that he wanted to speak to May. His dinner date waved her hand impatiently, concentrating on what her sister was saying. Magill could hear the concern in May Day's voice despite the tinny reproduction. Ultima, by contrast, looked energised, at the top of her game, as if making rapid executive decisions in times of organisational crisis.

Five minutes later, she cut off her BlackBerry, turned to Magill and snapped, "Eat up. We're leaving. We've got to get you out of here." She caught the waiter's eye and motioned for the bill. Able-bodied Seaman McStravick jumped to attention, sensing that his big tip was imminent.

"Ultima, what on earth's going on?"

"Give me a minute, Simon," she said sharply. While Magill settled the tip-topped bill, she rebooted her hand-held, thumbing the buttons with dexterity. The kind of dexterity that could come only from years in a prison cell with nothing but knitting needles for company. She glanced at Magill from time to time with the appraising eye of an expert. He tried to talk to her, but it was evident he had become a bit-part player in a bigger game that he didn't understand or control. A even bigger game, rather, that he didn't understand or control.

"That's it. You're booked." She set the BlackBerry down and exhaled with relief. "You have your passport with you, I take it?"

"No, of course not. Why would I carry my passport with me?

It's in my suitcase. At the Malmaison."

"Mary, Mother of God." Ultima picked up her BlackBerry again, got back on the line to her stepsister and, despite Magill's increasingly impolite attempts to grab the instrument in order to exchange a couple of sweet nothings with his sweetheart, if only to assure her that he wasn't two-timing her with big sis, she continued to ignore him. After rattling off crisp instructions even more rapidly than before, she finally flicked her BlackBerry off and stowed it in the hold of her bag. "OK, let's go." She rose from her seat.

Simon Magill sat where he was, an aggrieved expression on his badly swollen, black-and-blue face. He looked like a particularly grumpy panda, tantric or otherwise.

"No," he announced. "I'm not going anywhere until you tell me what's going on. Why won't you let me speak to your sister? Why all the cloak-and-dagger stuff? Are you trying to impress me with your hey-I'm-a-big-time-terrorist performance?"

"You want to be impressed, Simon?" she replied icily. "You *really* want to be impressed?" she inquired with venom. "I'll impress you, Simon."

With a you-asked-for-it expression, Ultima sat down. She took a moment to compose herself, then lent over the table. Her cerulean eyes glittered like an iceberg in the North Atlantic.

"King Billy is dead," she whispered. "He's been shot. Outside a home bakery on the Shankill Road. Impressed now, Simon?"

Chapter Thirty-Nine

Song of Solomon

They say the passengers on the *Titanic* were disorientated by the unspeakable events of 14 April 1912 even as the foundering unfolded. The alarm bells and calls to muster stations were disregarded by some and dismissed as impossible by others. Many went back to their cabins for a little lie-down long after the first lifeboats had launched. Harry Elkins Widener, whose heartbroken mother endowed the eponymous memorial library at Harvard, spurned a proffered lifeboat seat and returned to his suite. The twenty-seven-year-old had forgotten the book he'd been reading. By the time he got back on deck, his ticket to safety had already departed, half empty. Legend has it that he smoked a last cigar with Isidor Straus and John Jacob Astor, resplendent in their dinner jackets as the unsinkable ship went down.

Simon Magill was beginning to know how the passengers felt. He found it hard to take the killing of King Billy on board. It seemed inconceivable, yet somehow inevitable. When Ultima informed him that Solomon had a blueberry bagel in his mouth at the time of the slaying, Magill's absurd first thought was that the victim had reneged on his diet. Much more fearsome thoughts were to follow.

"Do they know who did it?" he asked in a stunned voice. "The Mafia? Al-Qaeda? P4? Surely not the Order of Solomon?"

With a sympathetic look on her fraught features, Ultima reached across the tiny table and placed her calloused hands over his. "No one knows for certain. But Wee Joe Monroe thinks it's you. Apparently he spotted you getting into a Republican taxi this afternoon. He thinks you set Solomon up. He's coming to get you, Simon. His cab's sitting outside May Day's apartment. He's been there for the past couple of hours."

She stood up and walked quickly out of the restaurant. Magill followed. The Odyssey was fairly quiet, as it was on most Wednesday nights, but its vast concourse was threatening, intimidating, almost malign. They made for the car park, Ultima scoping out any dangers ahead.

Rightly concerned about his girlfriend's welfare, Magill spoke anxiously, urgently. "Wee Joe hasn't threatened May or anything, has he?"

"No, he knows better than that. May's not in danger. *You* are, Simon. We have to get you out of here before he tracks you down. Mickey and Dragobert are dead already. He got to them. Ripped apart on the Falls Road, they were. In broad daylight. Blood and body parts everywhere."

"Who are Mickey and Dragobert?"

"Minger and Drag Queen, the volunteers who picked you up this afternoon. Mickey McGuire and Dragobert Quinn. I recruited and trained them myself. And now they're lying disembowelled on a slab. It's my fault. I should never have asked them to go. Mary, Mother of God."

Magill found it hard to feel sympathy for Dualit and Balaclava, though he did the best he could in the circumstances. Ultima looked as though she was about to burst into tears. "Don't blame yourself. Wee Joe killed them, not you."

"Yes," she replied savagely, as she slipped behind the wheel of her Audi, after checking it systematically for booby traps. "But it's still my fault. I'm to blame. Christ, I've had enough of this dirty business."

However, the dirty business hadn't had enough of her. It might have been a fairly quiet night at the Odyssey, but it was a busy night at the car-park exit. A long line of traffic had built up, jostling to get out. The Nazi crash barrier was practising its salute, though it was a painfully slow learner.

As they sat waiting their turn, Ultima filled Magill in on the arrangements she'd made, courtesy of her BlackBerry. His flight to Chicago, ex Belfast City via Heathrow, had been booked for first thing next day. A hotel had been arranged for that night, which she was about to take him to. She'd then return to Malmaison, gather up his belongings and drop them off with the bell captain. May Day had been in touch with Professor Aherne and she'd meet him on arrival at O'Hare. All Magill had to do was sit tight and get himself to City Airport.

"I take it May isn't coming with me."

"No, Simon. You're on your own. It's much less risky. Don't worry, though, she'll be waiting for you on your return."

"With the Holy Grail, Ultima."

"Don't come back with your two arms the one length," she warned, with a wan smile.

"I'll be happy to come back with my two arms intact."

"If you don't get out of here before Wee Joe catches up with you, absent arms will be the least of your problems."

Immediately behind them in the exit snake sat a baleful black taxi. It belched, backfired and broke wind, as flatulent cabs are wont to do. Convertibles are particularly susceptible to foul fumes, and Magill was gagging on the diarrhoeic diesel. Ultima looked increasingly anxious too, but not on account of the noxious emissions. She kept flicking her eyes to the rear-view, and locked the doors automatically.

"Do you know how to handle yourself, Simon?"

"I do, but I believe in self-restraint. I cold shower regularly and avoid carnal thoughts." The shocking news of Solomon's slaying and its serious personal implications were getting to Magill. "I'm thinking of buying a penile cilice, Ultima. For emergency use only. What do you reckon?"

"You don't need a cilice, Simon, you need to see sense. I meant do you know how to use a weapon?"

"Just like a BlackBerry, isn't it?"

"There's a Glock in the glove compartment. I think the taxi behind us is hostile."

"All taxis are hostile in my experience, Ultima. And not just to the passengers. Other road users don't stand a chance."

They finally escaped the fascist crash barrier and sped off under the complex tangle of feeder roads for the Holywood dual carriageway. The taxi had caught them by the lights. Ultima gunned the Audi along the access road and entered the flow of traffic at nearly NASCAR pace. The taxi was still on their tail. Ultima accelerated faster and faster, weaving in and out of the lanes on the lumpy, bumpy surface. The taxi somehow kept up.

Ultima was determined to stay in front, for good paramilitary reasons presumably, to the point of jumping traffic lights and cutting in front of the turbocharged cab. The ride in the Audi was uncomfortable enough, what with Ultima's insufficiently advanced driving skills, but in the taxi it must have been like the space shuttle during a particularly challenging re-entry.

"OK, Simon, our turning's just ahead. As soon as we take a left, I'll pull over. You jump out and take cover. If the taxi stops behind me, whack the driver. Don't forget the safety catch."

He nodded. I can do this, he thought. I can do this for Brodie. I can do this for my brother, I can do this for the people Wee Joe butchered. Just think BlackBerry . . .

The Audi turned hard left into a steeply angled, hedge-lined street that fell away rapidly towards the nearby lough shore. Magill leapt out, cocked his Glock and ran back towards the junction. Only to see the taxi sail past at high speed, the driver gesticulating rudely at the parked Audi.

"False alarm," Ultima said to her pistol-packing companion when he rejoined her moments later. "Bloody taxis! Think they own the road. The drivers are terrible in this place, Simon."

"Tell me about it."

"Love to, pretty boy, but there's no time. Your accommodation's just round the corner."

With its jealously guarded five-star status, the Culloden Hotel is as good as it gets in Northern Ireland. Overlooking Belfast's "gold coast" and a few hundred metres from the Ulster Folk and Transport Museum, the Culloden is the former episcopal palace of the bishops of Down, albeit extended, upgraded and fitted out to the highest hotelier standards. Built of imposing grey granite, midst heavily wooded grounds, it is the abode of passing rock stars, visiting football teams, now-you-see-them celebrities and, for one night at least, a marketing academic on the run. Whatever strings Ultima pulled, they worked like a polished Polish puppet show. Magill was ushered into a room on the first floor where he sprawled on the bed, exhausted, elated and feeling slightly seasick thanks to a combination of Steerage Shake and storm-tossed voyage.

There was a knock at the door. My stuff, Magill thought. That was quick. Fumbling for a tip, he eased open the stout wooden door, and was knocked backwards as its weight sent him flying. It had been kicked open, and Magill caught the full force of the impact. Before he had time to get up, someone was on top of him, holding him down, pressing his face into the carpet. A huge carving knife appeared in front of his nose. Out of the corner of his eye, Magill could just make out a familiar bald head. It was Wee Joe Monroe. He was grinning maniacally, his toothless face alight. Even without his dentures, the smile took years off him. He was revelling in it, reliving his glory days of mass dismemberment. "Told ye I'd take care of ye, Gingerbap."

As the shimmering steel pressed against his throat, Magill's life flashed in front of him. He'd always assumed that only happened in potboilers and B-movies, but as his dead brother, demented mother and disappointed father passed silently before his eyes, he knew that the old saw was no saw after all. Only the cackle of a butcher going about his business with ruthless efficiency broke the deadly silence of the autonomic diorama. He wondered how his father would take the news. With indifference, most likely. He wondered what May Day would do. Shed a tear and move on, no doubt. Well, he wasn't going to lose her so easily! With a sudden twist, learned many years ago on the martial arts mat with big brother, he flung Wee Joe off.

And woke up with a start. He'd fallen asleep fully clothed. The telephone was ringing insistently. He desperately needed a drink of water. "What . . . what . . . who is it?" he croaked.

"Simon, it's May. I have to be quick. They may be eavesdropping. I just want to tell you to be careful in Chicago and that I'll see you soon."

"I love you, May Day."

"You're stressed, Simon. We'll talk when you get home. A taxi will pick you up first thing. It's booked for 6.35 a.m. Don't get in unless the driver says 'Ultima sent me.'"

"May, why didn't you tell me about Ultima?"

"I did, Simon. I mentioned my paramilitary family but you weren't listening. Gotta go, lover."

"Love you, May."

"Turn on your TV. *News 24*."

"Love you."

"You too, lover."

Magill set the phone down, wondering if he was wise to wear his heart on his sleeve. Why not, he thought. If Wee Joe gets his hands on me, I'll be wearing more than my heart on my sleeve.

He poured himself a complimentary Bushmills, a triple, and switched on the television, flicking through the channels for the local news. There it was. A long-range shot of King Billy covered in a sheet, bag of bagels beside the body. The street had been closed to traffic, yellow scene-of-crime tape fluttering in the breeze like bunting during the summer marching season. The self-satisfied reporter was doing a piece to camera. He couldn't believe his luck: he was getting to say those priceless words "The king is dead," though sensibly he didn't add the corollary, "Long live the king." A pre-recorded insert showed a bar on the Falls Road where two further victims, Mickey "Minger" McGuire and Dragobert "Drag Queen" Quinn had had their throats cut. The PSNI, according to the smug reporter, were working on an organised-crime angle. The brutal slaying of Professor Carlingford O'Connell and the mysterious disappearance of Professor Pitcairn Brodie, a Scot with strong Ulster connections, were also believed to be linked to Solomon's killing. A shot of Hustler Business School filled the screen, and even with a no-publicity blanket over his head – it was more like a horse blanket, actually – the unmistakable figure of Dr Ian Kane could be seen wheezing his way out of the great glass goitre towards a waiting police car.

"A known associate of Solomon," the voice-over continued, "was arrested on suspicion of money laundering. He was later released without charge."

Magill was about to pick up the phone and call Kane when there was a knock at the door. "Just a minute," he shouted. He grabbed the bottle of Bushmills by the neck. Determined to give the caller a hangover he'd never forget, Magill slipped the chain into its sleeve and gently opened the door a fraction while keeping his bottle arm aloft, ready for action should the coming shove prove too much for the paltry security device.

It was a Culloden porter carrying Magill's bedraggled suitcase. The look on his face spoke volumes. And it wasn't *Great Expectations*. It was the kind of look that had to be stared down with folding money. Magill duly obliged.

There was no point in unpacking, as he'd only have to repack in a couple of hours. He stripped off his odorous clothing, took a much-needed hot shower and, fearing recurring dreams of Wee Joe doing his knife-throwing act, swallowed a couple of Bushmills-shaped sleeping tables.

Less than twelve hours later, he was on United 949 en route for Chicago O'Hare. No one stopped him at check-in or passport control, despite his bleary, black-eyed law-breaker look. The police dragnet on Hustler hadn't got to B-school bottom-feeders like him. Thus far they'd netted only big fish akin to Ian Kane – and fish don't come much bigger than the great white tale-teller.

"Chicken or fish, sir?" the United attendant inquired.

"Chicken, please."

Chapter Forty

Here's Looking at You, Kate

Why do movie stars seem smaller in real life? Partly it's because many are indeed altitudinally challenged, as are many musicians, artists, thespians, politicians and fashionistas (catwalk supermodels excepted). Partly it's because the cinema screen distorts our natural sense of scale: actors not only appear much larger than they are but the viewing angle from the stalls forces us to look up at them. Nevertheless, the principal reason for celebrities' itsy-bitsy-osity is the inevitable mismatch between expectation and consummation, anticipation and attainment, image and reality. The superhuman images on screen or in glossy magazines can't possibly be matched by reality. Thus our excessively heightened expectations remain frustratingly unfulfilled when we encounter celebrities in the flesh.

The same is true of world-famous shopping streets or holiday resorts or, for that matter, iconic brands, which unfailingly fail to live up to consumers' anticipatory yearnings. Pumped up by promotional puff and PR palaver, consumers often feel a tinge of dissonant disappointment when they finally get to stroll down that celebrated shopping street, or stay in that exclusive holiday resort, or acquire that iconic brand they'd heard so much about.

Management gurus suffer from a similar problem inasmuch as their aura, their reputation, their legendary status is difficult to live up to let alone sustain over the long term, as is executives' inordinate confidence in their purported transformational capabilities.

Professor Kate Phillips suffered particularly badly from the expectation/consummation mismatch. Her reputation as the guru of gurus, the seer of seers, the superstar of marketing superstars didn't usually survive an interpersonal encounter. It wasn't that she was nondescript or anything other than perfectly normal. It's simply that she wasn't as physically prepossessing as her stellar reputation implied.

She was pleasant, petite and well preserved, as Barton Brady immediately noted when he was ushered into her office. But he was still disappointed with the immaculately attired, carefully coiffed, lightly perfumed and remarkably wrinkle-free individual he'd been introduced to. Only the intelligent grey eyes, which twinkled with good humour and tolerance for the infinite foibles of humankind, indicated that Brady was dealing with someone special, someone whose IQ was well ahead of his on the bell curve. By several standard deviations.

That said, Brady wasn't intimidated by Phillips's superstar reputation. Quite the opposite. He had little time for academics as a rule, though he appreciated that they occasionally came up with workable ideas or meaningful metaphors, which could be turned into significant revenue streams by supersmooth smarmerpreneurs like himself. With a PowerPointastic slideshow, a sprinkle of stardust, a coating of razzamatazz and the obligatory overlay of just-do-it exhortation, even the most unpromising academic concepts could be transformed into marketable corporate commodities. The majority of marketing scholars were abysmal at marketing themselves, and their EQs, if not quite in the lowest quartile, were some way south of the median. Brady knew only too well that just as politics is showbiz for ugly people, so too academia is showbiz for smart people. But most academicians didn't know that. Not so smart after all.

On two counts, then, Barton Brady underestimated Kate Phillips. Her physical inability to live up to her billing, coupled with the taint of academese, counted against her in his book. She was completely unostentatious, what's more: no watch, no rings, no pins or brooches, no costume jewellery of any kind, apart from an old blue locket on an old gold chain. Her office too was unremarkable. Far from being a reflection of Phillips's world renown, with deep carpets, immense desk, gargantuan chair, distinguished awards scattered here and there, plus a light dusting of tastefully chosen artworks, it looked like a workshop. An intellectual factory, in effect. Piles of papers, mounds of books and tottering towers of computer printout were stacked higgledy-piggledy on every available surface, vinyl-covered floor included. The chairs were cheap, the filing cabinets were battered, and peeling posters dangled drunkenly from the plain white walls, which were trellised with dangerously overloaded institutional bookshelves. If it hadn't been for the picture windows overlooking a pleasant tree-fringed park, and the sheer size of the corner office, no one would have guessed the marketers' marketer lurked there.

Even so, Brady was much too EQ-literate to let on. He greeted Professor Phillips joyously, as if she'd just escaped from a hostage-taking situation in Baghdad, even though their only previous meeting was between the pages of *Business Week*, where Phillips's latest achievements were being praised in one section while SA was advertising its wares in another. For the first time since meeting Yasmin, furthermore, Brady felt he was dealing with someone who could see past the performance, through the bedazzling bonhomie and beyond the brand-name-bedecked body to the superficial, egotistical flimflam man beneath. Or perhaps she was unable to disguise it as well as the air-kissers, ass-lickers and honey-drippers that Brady dealt with on a daily basis.

Her handshake was less limpet than limpid, insubstantial to the point of invisibility, and her modest, almost apologetic demeanour did little to hush Brady's gush. He'd disgorged his contacts, achievements, company's annual billings and more before she had a chance to inform him that she'd only five minutes to spare before her important meeting downtown.

"OK, Professor Phillips, I'll cut to the chase." Brady flashed a halogen grin and continued. "I've come up with a new idea, a radical concept that'll take the marketing consultancy world by storm, a concept that'll rock the socks off Jim Collins and have Tom Peters begging for mercy."

"People would pay good money to see that, I'm sure," Phillips replied politely.

"It'll turn McKinsey into yesterday's men, Boston Consulting into the distempered dogs they are and, as for Bain's so-called compass, it can swivel on this."

"Really."

"I've had an article accepted for *Harvard Business Review*," he lied. The distinguished academician struggled to convey the impression of being deeply impressed. "You wouldn't believe the boot-licking and palm-crossing I had to do to get that." Brady rubbed his forefinger and thumb together and raised a conspiratorial eyebrow as if to say, "You catch my drift, Prof?"

"I don't doubt your powers of persuasion, Mr Brady."

"My friends call me Barton."

"So how may I help you, Mr Brady?" the august academic answered circumspectly.

At this point, most ordinary people would have taken the hint. But Barton Brady was better than that. He wasn't offended in the least. Like most smooth operators, he had the hide of a rhinoceros wearing reinforced-concrete body armour. Insults that would stop lesser mortals in their tracks ricocheted harmlessly off his impenetrable ego.

"Well, Professor, I fear my idea overlaps one of yours. I'm working on a Holy Grail metaphor. Marketers are knights errant. Consumers are damsels in distress . . . "

"Gender-neutral damsels and knights, I take it."

"There's no shortage of errants in dresses where I come from, Prof."

Rictus grin doesn't begin to describe the look on the septuagenarian's face. Rictus grimace is closer. But Brady continued unawares. "We're on a utopian quest for the marketing grail. We're searching for the secret of eternal corporate youth, the philosopher's stone of management practice. When all is said and done, marketers sell utopian visions of better tomorrows; we turn ugly ducklings into swans; we populate the world with jolly green giants and honey monsters on one hand, and slay the dragons of bad breath, fungal infection and zits on the other. GRAIL is an acronym that captures the spirit of our turbulent marketing times. It stands for Glamour, Retrospection, Amplification, Irony and Luck. We're working on the G-spot, though"

"Interesting."

"The key point, Kate, is that the pursuit of marketing

orientation is a noble quest, an unending quest, a . . ."

Phillips cut him off. "And the Holy Grail of marketing is G.R.A.I.L.?"

She's taken the bait, Brady thought; start reeling her in. He amped up the orthodontic candle-power. "Precisely, Professor! And the idea's infinitely extendable. There's the round table thing, the sword in the stone thing, the secret society thing, the conspiracy theory thing. It's a conceptual cornucopia."

"I see."

Brady paused so that Phillips could say something positive or react with enthusiasm. But as she seemed deep in thought, he did what all successful salespeople do – keep talking.

"Here's the kicker, Kate. I gather you're running a conference. For Marketing Illuminati. It's good. Very good. But not as good as the Holy Grail. Since Dan Brown dissed the Illuminati in *Angels & Demons*, the shine has been taken off illuminations. Here's what I suggest . . . "

She smiled impatiently at the pitchman, waiting for the inevitable low-ball offer.

"What say you and I come to a mutually satisfactory agreement, a licensing deal of some kind, even though there's nothing legally to prevent me pushing ahead on my own. But I'm an up-front, plain-dealing, honest-as-the-day-is-long kinda consultant, and if we can cut a deal, we can help each other. With your reputation and my resources, we'll clean up on the circuit. Drop the Illuminati shtick, Professor Phillips, and come join SA's grail quest. What do you say, Prof? Do we have a deal?"

The renowned academician picked up her briefcase and slipped on the Sears herringbone jacket that had been hanging on the back of her black plastic chair. Only a noticeable tightening around the eyes and slight involuntary spasm in her left cheek betrayed her true feelings. Her response, nonetheless, was professorial in the extreme.

"I'm deeply flattered by your offer, Mr Brady. And I'm enormously impressed by your imaginative conceptualisation. I'm sure Tom Peters will be whimpering as you anticipate, and both Bain and Boston will have much to chew on, shall we say. However,

I have no knowledge of Marketing Illuminati. I have never heard of any such organisation, and conspiracy theory isn't really the sort of idea I'd associate myself with. I'm a marketing scientist, not an alien abductee. I'm deeply sorry. I regret that you've come here on a wild-goose chase, if I may say so. I understand from your emails that you flew in from Las Vegas earlier this afternoon especially to see me. I wish I could be more helpful, more hospitable. But I'm late for a meeting, I have a fundraiser this evening, and my diary's full for the next few days. Sincere apologies."

Barton Brady nodded slowly, as if he were carefully considering the professor's remarks. But as an experienced management consultant, he'd been bullshitted more times than Colonel Saunders shat chicken nuggets. Better yet, he'd bullshitted right-back-at-you more often that he'd had chargrilled cinnebuns in airport departure lounges. "I feared you might say that, Professor Phillips. The only thing is, I was reading an article about you on the plane. It was an appreciation of your academic contributions down the years by a guy called Stephen Brown."

"I've never heard of him, Mr Brady. Any relation to Dan?"

"Not to my knowledge. But this is what he had to say about your work." Brady pulled a Xeroxed article from his gilt-edged Vuitton briefcase and prepared to earbash the senior citizen with its contents.

"I really have to go, Mr Brady. I'm already running late."

Brady reached an arm out to bar the professor's way as she made to walk round him. "This'll only take a second, Kate."

Astonished by his impertinence, the superstar scholar glared at him. But only for a moment. Her calm carapace was back in place almost instantaneously.

"Professor Kate Phillips," Brady read with relish, "is particularly partial to the paranormal . . . She mentions magic, mysticism, mythology, soothsaying, foretelling, rebirthing, pyramidology, alchemy, time travel and good-luck charms. She refers to all sorts of otherworldly figures including trolls, leprechauns, giants, ghosts, ogres, aliens and missing links . . . She also exhibits a conspiracy-culture-immersed interest in brain washing, mind control, subliminal messages and secret societies that is the twentieth-century equivalent of the nineteenth century's fascination with the occult, the esoteric and the unknown."

"Complete nonsense, Mr Brady. Now, if you'll excuse me ... "

Summoning up his best Las Vegas grin, Brady replied, "Don't you recognize yourself, Prof? The guy did a detailed content analysis of your published articles and it seems to me that the deal I'm proposing is right up your street. Spaceship. Mothership. Whatever. That alien abduction's a real boner, I gather."

"You've been misinformed, Brady," Professor Phillips said snippily.

In the circumstances, Barton Brady had no alternative but to play his ace. "Emer Aherne says you've got an Illuminati gig coming up. What do you say to that, Prof?"

Phillips drew herself up to her full height, which couldn't have been more than 5' 2" or 5' 3" at a pinch. "Professor Aherne is a visitor in this department. She is unaware of our processes, our procedures, our corporate culture. She must have misheard, or misinterpreted, or simply misunderstood. I can assure you, Mr Brady, there's no Marketing Illuminati and there is no meeting organised. The only meeting I'm aware of is the meeting I'm already late for. I really must go."

She brushed past Brady, stomped to the door of her office, jerked it wide open and gazed back at the visitor. It wasn't a love-struck look.

"Thank you for calling, Mr Brady. I wish you well with your grail quest."

For all his faults, Barton Brady II knew a lost cause when he saw one. "If you change your mind, Kate, give me a call."

"I'll do that, Mr Brady."

"Here are my contact details." He pressed a beautifully embossed, best-money-can-buy business card into Professor Phillips's reluctant palm and left.

The door slammed behind him.

Chapter Forty-One

Oak Park 'n' Ride

Most people would have departed the department with what little dignity they had left. Being ejected from a university office is embarrassing at the best of times, but when a world-famous guru is doing the asking, it's the academic equivalent of a well-aimed boot up the butt while being savaged by German Shepherds.

But Brady was made of sterner stuff. As the door closed behind him, he stopped, stooped and pretended to tie the non-existent shoelace of his Gucci loafers, while listening to the activity within. He heard Professor Phillips pick up her phone and, after a lengthy pause indicative of connecting to voicemail, say abruptly, "Emer, we need to talk. Can you drop by later? I'll be heading home around 5.30."

The downtown meeting wasn't so urgent after all, Brady thought to himself. Perhaps the evening fundraiser was about raising something else as well. Raising the consciousness of fellow marketing illuminati, maybe? There was only one way to find out.

Brady said his fond farewells to the friendly yet formidable Cicily Joyner, giving her sufficient interpersonal strokes to ensure she'd remember his name next time. He ambled down the polished corridor, took the sluggish elevator to the Kellogg mezzanine, and checked out the foodcourt-filled atrium, the only busy, buzzing focal point in an otherwise sterile building. Five minutes later, he was sitting in his rental, sipping a to-go latte and patiently waiting for the swami of swamis to appear. Fortunately, the faculty parking lot had a single exit, and as Kellogg's golden goose warranted a specially reserved space – one of the very few – there was no way Phillips could escape unnoticed.

At 5.35 p.m. precisely, a slightly built figure, well wrapped up against the mid-October chill, emerged from a side door. The

Windy City's winter wasn't too far off, and thanks to its position on the very lip of Lake Michigan, Northwestern's spatial situation was more windswept than most. What it gained on the swings of central Chicago's skyline, wonderful views of which could be seen from the campus, it lost on the roundabouts of its lakeside setting. Off-and onshore breezes, full- and fuller-force gales and curious microclimatic snowstorms that smothered the campus but left inland uncovered were near enough the norm.

Not long after the pocket-sized professor appeared, an extra-large Lexus exited the parking facility and, with Brady's Caddy in distant tow, slowly picked its way through the rush-hour traffic, along Emerson Street, up Golf Road, across Lavergne Avenue, down Church Street to the Edens Expressway, heading south. It was 6.45 when Phillips turned off the Eisenhower Expressway for Oak Park, one of the metropolitan area's most prestigious suburbs, six miles west of downtown.

The marketing textbook business had evidently been good to Professor Phillips. Very good. Only the most stellar university professors could possibly afford to live in upscale districts like Oak Park. Mature tree-lined streets, imposing detached houses – many more than a hundred years old – and front yards that the Chicago Bears could use for pre-season training are ordinarily out of the league of all but litigators, legislators, movie stars, celebrity CEOs and movers and shakers in the criminal-industrial complex.

Famously described by famous local resident Ernest Hemingway as a place of "wide lawns and narrow minds," Oak Park's principal claim to fame is not merely well-known local worthies like Papa H, Bob Newhart, Kathy Griffin or even Dan Castellaneta, the much-loved voice of Homer Simpson. Its renown, rather, rests on manifold marketing maestros. Over the years, Oak Park has been the breeding ground of multifarious marketing magi. It is situated on the commercial equivalent of telluric currents. Frito-Lay lines, so to speak.

Ray Kroc, the presiding genius behind one of the greatest marketing achievements of the twentieth century, hailed from Oak Park, though the organisation he built doesn't bear his name. It was Kroc, however, who spotted the potential in a two-bit burger stand run by two unambitious brothers, Dick and Mac McDonald. Kroc was a milkshake-maker salesman at the time, and it was the McDonald's order for eight machines – no one needed so many milkshake-making machines, not even in California! – that intrigued Kroc sufficiently to prompt him to take a trip to San Bernadino, where he saw the set-up that changed his life. And the world. The first Kroc-stocked McDonald's opened just down the road from Oak Park, in Des Plaines, and countless thousands followed in its beefsteak wake.

Brilliant as Ray Kroc was, he was a mere amateur compared to Edgar Rice Burroughs, another of Oak Park's outstanding marketing citizens. If ever anyone epitomised the premise behind "authorpreneur," it was Edgar Rice Burroughs. Seventy years before Harry Potter movies, merchandise and memorabilia were colonising the world's shopping malls and cineplexes, Burroughs' fictional creation, Tarzan, was doing the same. And more besides. Apart from the movies and tie-in merchandise, which Burroughs developed against the advice of professional marketing experts who feared he'd dilute the Tarzan brand, Oak Park's premier authorpreneur organised hugely successful Tarzan Clubs along the lines of the Boy Scouts and Girl Guides. Brand communities weren't Burroughs' only invention. He extended his semi-simian brand to real communities, in the form of themed property developments. He purchased and parcelled out a prime piece of Los Angeles real estate, which is still known by the unforgettable name of Tarzana.

The mart-smarts of the ape man notwithstanding, Oak Park's foremost finagler was Frank Lloyd Wright, the world-famous architect and self-publicist extra-extraordinary. True, he owed much of his larger-than-life persona to the incomparable Elbert Hubbard – a gilded-age hybrid of Peter Drucker, Richard Branson and Andy Warhol – but Oak Park's finest finally surpassed his brand-me mentor. Lloyd Wright not only commenced his career in Oak Park, where his first studio still stands, but he built several bootleg houses in the suburb while he was working for Louis Sullivan, who forbade "homers" of any kind. It was in Oak Park, furthermore, that Frank Lloyd Wright perfected his Prairie House

311

style, which revolutionised domestic architecture at the start of the twentieth century, and it was here that he forged America's most strikingly original architectural idiom, an idiom that is instantly recognised – and much imitated – even by those who know little, and care less, about the architect's ignoble art. Nowadays, Lloyd Wright is mainly associated with Madison, Wisconsin, where he established a proto-utopian community centred on the ancient Celtic legend of Taliesin, but it was in Oak Park that the builder of Unity Temple, Fallingwater and the Guggenheim Museum found his voice and made his mark.

Living in a Lloyd Wright house is a mark of distinction at the best of times. But living in one of his signature buildings in Oak Park, a designated historical district, not only sets its owner way above the common herd but indicates that he or she has more specie than savvy, since Lloyd Wright houses are in need of incessant TLC. Many believe they are abysmally built. Most are happy to cover the repairs in return for the prestige of residing in a landmark property.

Professor Kate Phillips had specie as well as savvy, and when Barton Brady saw her Lexus stop in front of the Cheney House on North East Avenue, even he was impressed. He pulled over under a gloriously autumnal overhanging oak, thirty yards from her front yard and with a clear sight of the house. He settled down to wait. If she was going to a fundraiser, she'd be back out and on the road in less than an hour. As he suspected, however, there was no sign of vehicular departure.

There was an arrival, though. At 7.45 p.m., a Ford SUV with tinted windows cruised down North East Avenue and turned into Phillips's showhouse. Two people got out, one of whom he recognised. They rang the doorbell, and Phillips answered. The professor had showered and changed into comfort clothing. After exchanging cordial greetings, she ushered the arrivals inside. A few moments later, light sprang from a room at the rear of the house, illuminating a line of trees along the back fence.

Time to eavesdrop, thought Brady. He eased out of the rental, closed the door softly and took up position behind the rumpled trunk of a full-grown oak. Although it wasn't quite dark, and although Phillips's abode adhered to the wide lawns if not the narrow minds of Hemingway's Oak Park put-down, the garden was sufficiently overgrown to provide ample cover for someone whose experience of espionage was confined to *Mission Impossible* movies and taking in the Strip from the Eiffel Tower Bar and Restaurant.

Brady was no architectural connoisseur, let alone a purist, but on reaching the edge of the rear patio he suspected that the hot tub wasn't part of Lloyd Wright's original design. The rising steam and towel-prepped loungers suggested that the professor's party was preparing to repair to the rear and take in some mid-October air. But the ground floor was in darkness, the doors were locked and the drapes were pulled tight. The first-floor living area, by contrast, was brightly lit, and Brady could just make out three figures sitting around the kitchen table: Phillips, Aherne and a tall, thin man with bright ginger hair who looked as though he had been badly beaten up. Black eyes, split lips, big yellowing bruise on his left cheekbone and a glowing nose that begged for Band-Aids – Jack Nicholson *Chinatown*–style – indicated that, whoever he was, he'd been roughed up recently. Illuminati or not, his proboscis was sufficiently luminous to light up the kitchen unassisted.

Unable to hear what they were saying, Brady got as close as he could by standing on a trashcan. He could see Phillips hold court. Though the voices were still indistinct, the distinguished academician's evident loquaciousness stood in marked contrast to the monosyllabic answers he'd received a few hours previously. The battered redhead then started talking. Half man, half punchbag went on and on for what seemed like forever. It was obviously something of great import, because he was getting more and more agitated. But Phillips retained her zen-like calm throughout, absorbing what her visitor was saying.

Brady was so caught up in the kitchen confidential conversation that he didn't hear the early-autumn leaves rustling behind him, or if he did, he ignored them. However, he couldn't ignore the metallic click of the cocked Colt .38 pressed into his butt. Nor did he ignore the words of the person holding it. "Step away from the trashcan. Put your hands in the air. No sudden moves, Barton."

The shock of his capture was one thing, and the shock of a loaded weapon shoved up his ass was another. But the shock of being called by his Christian name was something else again. Even that, however, paled into insignificance beside the shock of vocal recognition. He knew the voice of his assailant. He'd worked with her for years.

"Yasmin? Yasmin? What are you doing here?"

"I was waiting for you, Barton. I knew you'd show up sooner or later. Come and join the party. There's a surprise waiting for you."

"What's with the gun, for Christ's sake? We're partners, remember?"

Brady was standing by this stage, facing away from his erstwhile colleague, arms embarrassingly aloft. Courtesy of his peripheral vision, he could see the kitchen klatch staring down at them. Only the ginger man looked surprised.

Prodding him in the back with her handgun, Buonarroti answered evenly. "No, we were never partners, Barton. You grabbed the glory, I did the work. I built the business up by the sweat of my brow and you swanned around with your airhead smirk, taking all the credit."

"Management consultancy's all about smirking and schmoozing. You know that, Yazza. I'm the front man, you're the behind-the-scenes wizard. We have an agreement."

She nudged him round the side of the low-roofed residence, under the enormous overhanging eaves towards the mahogany front door.

"Well, the agreement's about to change. Schmoozing has its place, Brady, but arrogance, egomania, self-glorification and condescending androcentrism don't. All you've ever cared about is getting your fuckin' face on the cover of *Fortune*."

"*Forbes* would do, Yazza. *Business Week*, maybe. I'm not choosy. And what's with the androcentrism?"

"Don't call me Yazza, you sonofabitch. That's androcentric for a start. The Brady Bunch is bust, Barton. Got it?"

There was activity behind the front door. Brady could hear it being unbolted, double mortice locks he reckoned, and the security

314

systems being immobilised.

"We can sort this out, Yasmin. Put the gun away. I'm parked down the street. Let's walk away before things get out of hand."

"It's too late, Brady. This is where your GRAIL trail ends. Welcome to Castle Corbenic."

The heavy door swung open and Emer Aherne smiled a smile of happy recognition. "Nice to see you again, Barton. Rooting around in the garbage cans, were we? Not for the first time, I bet."

"You Irish bitch! What have you done to Yasmin? Filling her head with well-woman bullshit? You'll pay for this."

"*Céad míle fáilte* to you too, Barton."

"Stuff it up your bony Irish ass."

"Tell that to the professor, partner. We're waiting for you in the kitchen. And don't try anything funny."

She held up her hand and wiggled a Smith and Wesson as one would a stick of sugar candy.

"Actually, do try something funny, Barton. I've been dying to pull this trigger. I haven't shot anyone for, oh, at least five years. I vowed I'd never do it again. But I'll make a special exception in your case."

Chapter Forty-Two

Kitchen Confidential

"How was your flight?"

The speaker was tall, thin, middle aged – early fifties, perhaps – with closely cropped brown hair and sharp features. She had an air of anxiety and impatience that diminished her otherwise impressive presence. In her youth, she must have been quite attractive, but the severe look and shapeless outfit didn't do her any favours. Sackcloth chic may yet have its moment on the catwalks du monde, but it wasn't turning heads in O'Hare's international arrivals hall.

"Pretty smooth," Magill replied. "Immigration was the only problem, as you might expect. I told the officer I'd had cosmetic surgery. She said I should ask for a refund. The in-flight movie was terrible as well. Apart from that, everything was fine. Thanks for waiting."

Professor Aherne was privately grateful for Magill's battered physiognomy. If it hadn't been for the black eyes and bruising, she'd never have recognised the Hustler colleague she hadn't yet met. She'd been told what to expect, and as a means of readily identifying someone in the busiest airport in the world, it beat the hell out of a copy of *The Times* and a carnation in the button-hole, especially when your eyesight's not what it was and wearing glasses is something vestigial vanity won't allow. The two-hour wait while her guest cleared immigration wasn't what she had anticipated, but homeland security was a law unto itself and equally unpredictable.

"Oh yes? What kind of horrible Hollywood mush did they inflict on you?"

"*The Da Vinci Code*. Have you seen it yet? Tom Hanks is Robert Langdon. Talk about miscast. He was hopeless. Forrest Gumps he

317

can handle. Action men are way, way beyond his range. And as for his haircut, it was the mullet that time forgot. Either that or a squashed jackdaw perched on his pate."

Enjoying her Hustler colleague's candour, which reminded her momentarily of home, Aherne suggested he keep his voice down, especially in the Midwest, where the locals don't take kindly to criticism of all-American icons, much less attacks on descendants of Abe Lincoln like Tom Hanks. Unabashed, Magill proceeded to give her a blow-by-blow account of the movie, interjecting cutting comments on its misrepresentation of the source material. It was a full five minutes before Aherne could drop her Dan Brown research into the conversation.

"Sorry, I didn't realise you're a fan."

"I'm not," Aherne answered truthfully. "I thought the book was unspeakably bad. I'm interested in the marketing aspects, that's all. They illustrate my ideas on Celtic marketing."

Magill was tempted to take her to task for disparaging a literary giant but common courtesy commanded he inquire about Celtic marketing instead. He'd read some of her stuff prior to his Hustler interview on the assumption she'd be on the panel, and he reckoned the woman was demented. But recent events had tempered his attitude. Asking about Celtic marketing also allowed him to delay discussion of the real reason for his visit. He needed to gather his jumbled jet-lagged thoughts, so a few courteous enquiries wouldn't do any harm.

As they made their way out of the crowded terminal across a vast prairie-sized parking lot, Aherne waxed lyrical on her world view.

"Academic marketing is characterised by what I call the Anglo-Saxon approach or mindset, Simon. It's been preoccupied with order, rigour, rectitude and control. It's been obsessed with model building, hypothesis testing, and an unending search for law-like generalisations. Marketing academics berate practitioners for not doing it properly, for not being sufficiently objective or scientific. They seem to think that if only recalcitrant practitioners would shape up and do what the models, the theories, the textbooks tell them, then everything in the marketing garden would be rosy."

318

"You don't buy that?" Magill asked, knowing full well from her foaming-at- the-mouth publications that she loathed Anglo-Saxon marketing with a vengeance. Naturally there was no British–Irish resentment at work. Yeah, right.

"Buy it? Never! My aim is to usurp it. But I realised long ago that critique is insufficient, as are mockery, disparagement and so on. It's not enough to refute Anglo-Saxon marketing, Simon. It has to be replaced, otherwise people stick with what they know. Unless they're given an alternative, they'll continue to read the same old textbooks, subscribe to the same old theories and absorb the same old claptrap that marketing educators have been peddling for the past fifty years."

"And that's where the Celtic marketing concept fits in, Professor Aherne?"

"Got it in one, Simon. It's Emer, incidentally. Celtic marketing embraces magic, mystery, imagination, storytelling, spirituality, the sublime. It rejects the objective, dispassionate detachment of the established marketing paradigm and replaces it with subjectivity, involvement, passion. Celts look to art rather than science, to paganism instead of pragmatism, to the poetic not the prosaic. Celtic marketing asks academics to commit to commitment and consign carceral calculation to the conceptual trashcan. All the great brands nowadays embody passion, commitment imagination. Apple Computers is a classic case in point. It's Celtic to the core. We academics need to reconfigure our thinking instead of continuing to assume that we know best or that we have the technology or that if it weren't for myopic managers everything would be fine. I suppose I'm saying that the marketing academy needs to abandon its dictatorial patriarchal mindset and adopt a listening, feminine outlook."

She doesn't lack passion, that's for sure, Magill thought. No wonder most people think she's mad. "Ah, the eternal feminine. Isn't that Dan Brown's line?"

"It is," Aherne said.

The curtness of Aherne's reply surprised Magill. It implied end of conversation, even though they'd only just reached Aherne's car, a monstrous Ford SUV. Celts weren't too worried about the environment, evidently.

"The thing I can't grasp, Emer, is why you and Professor Phillips are working together. Surely she's the embodiment of the traditional Anglo-Saxon mindset you deplore. She started it, didn't she? It was her textbook I studied as an undergraduate. Isn't she, like, the Antichrist of Celtic marketing?"

"Mmmmm. It's complicated, Simon. I'll explain when we get on the expressway." She glanced at Magill's battered suitcase. "Is that all your luggage?"

Magill nodded, made some crack about travelling light and, after erroneously making for the driver's side – as visitors from the sinistral British Isles are prone to do – clambered into the front passenger seat of the behemoth. There was someone in the back seat: a much younger woman with a plain face, sallow complexion, pugilistic mien and no-nonsense demeanour.

"This is Yasmin, Simon, a close friend of mine. Yasmin Buonarroti, Simon Magill; Simon Magill, Yasmin Buonarroti." They greeted each other in accents that weren't so much poles as planets apart, Jeremy Irons on one side, "Iron" Mike Tyson on the other.

When the initial manoeuvring was over and Aherne had made it onto the expressway – with only two wrong turns – she reverted to her favourite topic of conversation: herself. "Yes, Simon. It does seem like a strange mix. Some people think Kate and I are polar opposites . . . "

No, thought Magill, some people think Phillips is the mother of all marketing gurus. Most people don't think about you at all, Professor Aherne, and those who do think you're barking.

". . . but she's much more open-minded than the textbooks suggest. By their very nature textbooks are dogmatic and dictatorial. Kate's not like that at all . . . "

You could've fooled me, Magill surmised silently to himself. Phillips, surely, stamped her trademark approach on every domain imaginable. She was a scholarly sausage machine. If any academic was demonstrably dogmatic, it was Kellogg's top dog. Bitch rather.

". . . and anyway, I'm not working *with* her."

"Oh, I was told you're doing some research together. Writing a textbook. Ian Kane mentioned it."

"Not together," Aherne interrupted. "In opposition. We make our case on alternate pages. She argues for the Phillips paradigm on the rectos and I do the same with Celtic marketing on the versos. It's a kind of dialectical argument."

"But won't the very fact that you're between the same covers, sharing the billing on the jacket, undermine the distinction? Your Celtic marketing concept will simply be absorbed into Phillips's mainstream marketing concept. It'll be the kiss of death for Celtic marketing, won't it?"

As soon as the words escaped his battered lips, Magill knew he'd broached the topic he'd been studiously avoiding. And so it proved.

"I hear you know a lot about the kiss of death, Simon. Care to tell me about it? Care to tell me why you're here and what we can do for you? I'm happy to help a colleague but the story I got from my secretary at Hustler was, well, lunatic."

Magill hesitated. Staring at the glass and concrete Tetriscape of central Chicago looming larger than life to their left, he was understandably reluctant to recount his undeniably unorthodox story.

"It's OK, Simon. I have no secrets from Yasmin. She may be able to help. Tell all."

As the traffic sped by on both sides – Saturns, Chevys, Hummer H2s and every heap of scrap under the sun – Magill told his preposterous tale of murder, mayhem and marketing. The *Titanic*, the Holy Grail, the death of King Billy and all the rest spilled out as the interstate traffic thinned. Aherne took an off-ramp, circumnavigated a clover-leaf and pulled up at the first set of stop lights they'd encountered since his arrival. The confessions continued to pour out.

"Let me get this clear, Simon. Someone has been killing your colleagues – *my* colleagues – and leaving bloodstained messages from Kate Phillips, a Kate Phillips who's got assassins at her beck and call, survived the sinking of *Titanic* and is holding onto the Holy Grail for the Knights Templar."

"Yeah, that's just about it, Emer."

321

"And they said Dan Brown was crazy."

"Dan Brown *is* crazy," Magill retorted. "For allowing Tom Hanks to be cast as Robert Langdon . . ."

Aherne laughed. Her SUV swung into a beautiful tree-lined area. Quivering gently in the evening breeze, the autumnal leaves were shimmering shards of gold. The front gardens were immaculate, even as cascades of arboreal cast-offs rained incessantly on the emerald shag-pile carpets. Aherne turned into the drive of a red-brick low-slung building with enormous overhanging eaves. It looked a bit like a fire station that had failed to rise in the oven.

"Well, Simon, your concerns will soon be answered. This is Professor Phillips's place. She's expecting us."

Magill heaved the Ford door open and looked down. "Do I rappel the rest of the way or are they sending up a rescue team? I'm getting nosebleeds at this height."

Yasmin slapped him boisterously on the back. "Looks like you've had a bunch of nosebleeds already, buddy." She threw his bag at him. "Catch you later."

"Aren't you coming with us?" Magill asked.

"Nah, I've gotta wait here for someone."

The front door opened and a tiny grey-haired woman stepped out. "Welcome to Chicago, Simon." She offered a limp hand and, after exchanging pleasantries about the rapidly darkening street, the garden, the weather, the hard winter ahead, she led the party through the house, pointing out its salient features. Magill had never been in a Frank Lloyd Wright house before. He couldn't understand what all the fuss was about, first-floor living space apart. Dark, gloomy and forbidding was his overwhelming impression. The only exception was the commodious kitchen, which had swapped the austerity of Lloyd Wright's design for twenty-first-century comforts.

They spread themselves around the kitchen table, a Lloyd Wright original. It reminded him a little of Brodie's Hubbard cupboard. When the coffee drinking, cookie crunching and general Phillips-dominated chit-chat had subsided – she told them ghostly tales of the house's former inhabitant, Mamah Cheney, who had a scandalous affair with the celebrity architect only to be gruesomely murdered in 1914 – Simon ran through his story once again. It was an expurgated version on this occasion, largely because Magill, strangely, found himself flushing with embarrassment as he told his tale of killers, corpses and cryptic messages to a demure old lady – a demure old lady who happened to be implicated in the assassinations.

When he had finished, a profound silence descended on the room. Only the thrumming of the refrigerator and avian interruptions from the trees in the back yard disturbed the oppressive calm.

"What, precisely, do you want to know?" Professor Phillips asked briskly, as if it were a post-presentation Q&A.

Magill had so many questions he didn't know where to begin. "The Holy Grail," he blurted out. "The *Titanic* . . . "

She looked at him sympathetically, like a sex therapist coping with the aftermath of a DIY penile implant. "Yes, it's true. The Holy Grail was entrusted to my grandmother by a stranger on *Titanic*. She was only nineteen at the time. She was eloping with her lover, the Jelly Bean King, and pregnant with my father. She didn't believe the grail story of course – who would? – though she was also informed that it had to be held in trust for her granddaughter, Kate Phillips. Who wouldn't accept the gift under such circumstances? However, I've always believed it was the power of the object itself that persuaded her to accept it. The grail chooses its recipients, Simon, it isn't chosen by them."

"So the Holy Grail really does exist. It isn't a bloodline or a manuscript."

"Yes, it does. No, it's not. Do you want to see it? It's here in this very room. Hidden in plain sight."

Magill looked round. Coffee cups. Cookie jars. Pots and pans. Painted wooden cupboards. Old-fashioned range. Massive Welsh dresser. "Well, I assume it's not the microwave oven."

"That's the Ark of the Covenant," Aherne quipped.

"I'll show it to you," Phillips laughed. An inscrutable smile played at the corners of her mouth. She was about to speak when a disturbance outside distracted her. Voices were raised, one bellowing like a *T. rex* trapped in a tar pit.

"Ah," the professor said. "Our company is complete."

Chapter Forty-Three

Heart of the Ocean

"Come and join us, Lancelot. You wouldn't want to miss out on the grail unveiling, especially as you're part of the plot. Take a seat."

For once, Brady was dumbstruck. He didn't know whether to laugh at the crazy old bitch or denounce her for stealing his idea, just as he'd suspected. "I don't know what's going down here, Phillips, but you'd better have a good excuse. I don't take kindly to having pistols pushed up my ass. The cops'll hear about this."

Chuckling to herself, as if amused by the brass neck of the buffoon, Phillips calmly replied, "They will after I shoot you, Brady. I'm quite within my rights. You were trespassing on my property, a national monument, and trying to steal stuff from the trash prior to peeping in on an old lady you harangued at the university earlier and whom you followed home. Stalker! Now sit down like a good boy, and speak when you're spoken to."

Optionless, Brady wrenched a Lloyd Wright chair from under the kitchen table and planted himself down like a moody pre-teen. "The rich bitch got you by the balls too, buckaroo?" he snarled at Magill. "And not only the balls by the look of you, buddy. Touch this face, Phillips, and my attorney will sue your ass from here to Vegas."

Phillips's *sang froid* snapped. "Gag him, Yasmin. If he says a word, garrotte the garrulous fool." When Brady was trussed, she turned back to Magill. In an icily calm and frighteningly professional manner, the petite septuagenarian inquired, "Now where was I, Simon?"

Understandably disturbed by the interruption and sudden appearance of automatic weapons, Magill sought to return the conversation to less threatening concerns. "You said the grail was in this room, Professor. And you were about to show it to me."

"Ah yes, here it is." Placing her hands behind her neck, Phillips unclasped an antique locket and, after letting the chain cascade into the palm of her left hand, offered the artifact to her astonished visitor.

Magill hesitated before reaching out to take it. "I thought it was a cup or chalice of some kind."

"There are many theories about its physical form," she responded softly, as if distracted by dreams of ancient days and ways, "largely on account of its intermittent appearances. The grail materialises only from time to time. It was clearly described thus in the Arthurian romances from de Troyes onward, but most people mistakenly believe it's a religious relic like any other. Many, as you say, think it's a vessel of some kind, others assume it's precious metal, hence the connection to *prima materia*, the philosopher's stone, the secret of eternal youth, the transmutation of base metal into gold. But as you can see, it's actually a combination of all of these. The grail is a receptacle made out of semi-precious stone with a gold inlay."

The locket was undeniably beautiful. A masterwork of lapis lazuli, the bright blue stone much prized by the pharaohs of Ancient Egypt, it was perfectly circular with a tiny Templar cross etched on the front in gold filigree.

"Your grandmother was wearing this on the *Titanic*?"

"Yes," the professor sighed, her grey eyes distant, distracted. "My grandmother, Kate Phillips, was wearing it when she was picked up by Lifeboat 6. Legend has it that she was given the locket by her lover as a parting gift, before he perished on that terrible night. James Cameron incorporated the legend into his blockbuster movie. The reality was less dramatic, though much stranger than Cameron's imaginings. My grandmother wore the locket every day for the next fifty years, when she passed it on to me. I was entrusted with it on my twenty-fifth birthday. I'd just got my doctorate and was about to take up a position as an associate professor. My professional achievements are entirely due to this precious gift. It has given me eternal life. In an intellectual sense, of course."

Magill was sitting directly opposite Brady and could see him roll his eyes. He too thought the story, if not actually on board RMS *CrazyLady*, was definitely walking up the gangplank. In light of recent events, however, he'd become increasingly sceptical about his scepticism. Some still remained, nevertheless. "You say the grail chooses its recipients – and Dan Brown makes the same point – but everyone knows objects don't have minds of their own. It makes for a nice story, but the reality's very different."

"On the contrary, Simon, almost every belief system in the world, Western scientism excepted, maintains that physical objects are animate, often sensate – sacred and precious objects especially. Even in the West, many New-Age theologies, such as Lovelock's Gaia hypothesis, assume that the world is a living, breathing organism. Ever since Karl Marx's seminal analysis of commodity fetishism, where he describes a wooden table dancing of its own accord, astute marketing analysts have understood that objects have minds of their own. Consumers believe it too. Talk to fashion victims about buying shoes and you'll hear countless tales of Jimmy Choos calling out to them. Candy demands to be eaten. Chocolate bars button-hole passers-by. Everyone knows this. I call it extrasensory consumption. Indeed, if garden variety candy bars can persuade reluctant consumers to do their bidding, just think what the Holy Grail is capable of."

"It's strange, though, that the Holy Grail should seek out a marketing educator, a business-school professor. I thought it was supposed to be a *sacred* object, a precious thing uncontaminated by crass commercial considerations."

Phillips sighed heavily, as if plagued by a student with severe learning difficulties. She looked at him patiently.

"To the contrary, Simon. There's nothing more apt. The grail is all about marketing. It always has been; it always will be. Joseph of Arimathea, who caught the blood of Jesus in the sangreal, was a very wealthy merchant. The Crusades were as much about money and trade as Jesus and Mary. The Knights Templar were the biggest bankers in Christendom. The holy relic business was a medieval marketing scam. Thomas Malory, the writer of the definitive version of the grail legend, was a commercial traveller who was jailed for con artistry. The monks of Glastonbury Abbey 'discovered' the graves of Arthur and Guinevere in the twelfth century and used them to attract pilgrims to, and generate more wealth for, their institution. It was place marketing, pure and simple. The modern marketing concept was invented by traveling Bible salesmen such as Mason Locke Weems, who barnstormed the southern States in the early eighteenth century. The grail has always been about making money, as the post–Dan Brown takings in Rosslyn Chapel, Saint-Sulpice and even Rennes-le-Chateau in the Pyrenees bear witness. It was never San Greal, Simon, it's always been Sale Greal. Jesus himself was a tradesman."

"So you're saying that despite all the religious and spiritual connotations, the Holy Grail is basically about marketing, about making money, about moving the merchandise? You're saying it contains not the secret of eternal life but the secret of marketing success?"

"Precisely," Phillips affirmed with emphasis. "What is marketing, Simon, if not a means of turning functionally identical products into precious objects, branded objects, singular objects of consumer desire? Marketing is the post-industrial transmutation of base metal into gold."

Still puzzled, Magill looked querulously at the Sale Greal. "I can't work out what the secret is, Professor. It looks like a beautiful old locket to me. Nothing more."

"You have to open it, Simon. The grail's a receptacle, remember. It holds the secret. It isn't the secret itself. Never confuse the contents with the container. There's a little catch on the side." She was smiling at Magill, appraising him with her intelligent eyes. "There's a price to pay for secret knowledge, however. Perhaps you should quit while you're ahead. It's often best not to know these things."

The urge to look inside was almost overwhelming, but caution won out. "What's the price, professor?"

"Oh, you don't discover that until you've looked inside," she replied enigmatically. "It's not a supermarket where all the prices are clearly marked. This is an unbreakable bargain you enter into. Or not, as the case may be."

Suspecting a trick, Magill was reaching out to return the grail when Brady suddenly intervened. "I'llkk. Paykk. Thekk. Pricekk. Youkk. Bitchkk!" he shouted through his facial restraint.

He seized the locket, flicked it open and looked inside for what seemed like a long time. "Ikk. Thoughtkk. Askk. Muchkk." He snapped it shut and threw the precious artifact on the table as if it were a discarded Coke can.

In the manner of a cheap smoke-and-mirrors conjuring trick, the beautiful blue locket burst open on impact. It looked exactly like an old-fashioned fob watch, spinning round and round on the polished surface, chain circling in sympathy. Its contents were revealed for all to see. It was empty.

Chapter Forty-Four

Gimme Gimme Gimme a Brand After Midnight

Another cheap trick, Magill thought, as a sharp pang of despair pierced his shattered body. All this has been for nothing. But the despair he felt was trivial compared to what lay in store. Professor Phillips gazed at him with an air of resignation. She'd been waiting for her postmodern Perceval to pose the prescribed question and he hadn't.

"The grail is there, Simon. The secret of marketing success is right in front of you if only you have eyes to see it."

Deeply dejected, he shook his head. Waves of weariness swept over him. The enormous strains of the past few days were proving overwhelming. His adrenalin reserves were exhausted; his vows had been in vain. But he wasn't yet ready to quit.

"It's a locket. Lockets are symbols of love. Marketers who love their customers will succeed. Surely it's not as simple as 'love conquers all'?"

Phillips laughed. Aherne and Buonarroti joined in.

"Love the customer? Customer orientation? You're mistaking the container for the contents again. Customer orientation is fatal. Customer-centricity is the *cause* of marketing's present ills: product proliferation, communications clutter, cynical consumers, anti-capitalist protests, wanton waste, environmental degradation, our sybaritic society, the focus-group think of politicians who've bought into the customer-focused worldview. If ever anything exemplified the trouble that customer orientation gets marketers into, it's Blair's Britain and Bush's America."

"Forgive me, Professor Phillips," Magill retorted caustically. "Forgive me for parroting the mantra of customer orientation.

How could I be so foolish? I must have read it somewhere. Somewhere like *your* books, the books every marketing student devours avidly, absorbs religiously and eventually acts on. Are you saying that all the books you've written are wrong, that everything you stand for is mistaken?"

Sitting impassively at her Lloyd Wright kitchen table, Phillips responded to Magill's ironic invective with imperturbable indifference. "Not mistaken, Simon. Misinformation. Misdirection. Misorientation. Think about it. If ninety-nine percent of the world's marketers accept what the textbooks tell them, then the remaining one percent is in a highly advantageous position. No? Knowing the secret's no guarantee of success, of course, since it's necessary to act on the information. But if ninety-nine percent of the competition is chasing the chimera of customer orientation, then that makes *our* long-term success so much more certain. They zig, we zag."

Magill curled his lip. He felt his temper rising. "So it all boils down to zigga-zagga? I don't believe you. You're misdirecting me again. Marketing managers are sharp. They're not sheep. No one would fall for anything as puerile as that."

Sensing the rising tension, the great marketing guru placed the palm of one outstretched hand onto the fingertips of the other and called time out. She suggested drinks. While Aherne and Buonarroti bustled about pulling snacks from various cupboards and hidey holes, Phillips led the way into the cavernous lounge. It was simultaneously arty, understated and eminently livable, a testament to the tastemaker who'd furnished the showhome. Although a large brick fireplace occupied pride of place, the room's most distinctive features were its half-timbered pitched roof and beautiful stained-glass windows, which were further complemented by bountiful bijou bibelots. Warhols dotted the walls. Lalique uplighters cast a welcoming glow. Comfortable Eames chairs and elaborately patterned Persian carpets punctuated the parquet. There's money in misdirection, Magill thought, as he settled into an enveloping armchair and sipped a calming Bushmills.

"You were saying," Phillips observed from the comfortable sofa opposite, "that it's impossible to fool all of the marketers all of the time. I'm afraid you're wrong, young man. Like all ideologies, good or bad, the customer-oriented marketing concept is imperceptibly absorbed into the corporate body like slow-release pharmaceuticals. It soon becomes the norm: accepted, unquestioned, constantly reproducing itself. Just like communism, Christianity, Islam, science, Nazism and more. If something as hideous as anti-Semitism can become a societal norm, as it did in inter-war Germany, it's easy to see how customer orientation can become omnipresent in consumer society, both unchallenged and unchallengeable."

Despite his scepticism, Magill couldn't help agreeing with the professor's argument. He recalled his own symbological reflections in central Edinburgh when struck by the ubiquity of consumer fashions and fads. Most consumers were followers, not leaders. Most consumers, he once read – though he thought the idea crazy at the time – don't really know what they want, apart from more of the same. They are unable to think out of the box. Hence when marketers espouse customer orientation, they end up producing more and more of the same and offering less and less variety. The upshot is a poor choice of bad apples. While consumers could never be described as sheep, unless they were particularly capricious sheep, they tended to forage in flocks and possessed a herd mentality.

"Indeed," Phillips continued, expanding on her theme as scholars are wont to do, "the belief in customer orientation is so engrained nowadays that when companies fail or marketing strategies implode, the organisations blame themselves for being insufficiently customer oriented. If only they'd been more customer centric they would have succeeded. An entire industry of commentators perpetuates the myth, moreover. Ask yourself: are there any management gurus or CEOs who *don't* chant the mantra of customer orientation? Criticising the consumer is as unacceptable in executive suites as the N-word is in American society as a whole. The few who do disparage customers, like Ryanair's O'Leary or Oracle's Ellison, are laughed off as the exceptions who prove the rule. Customer centricity is ingrained and ineradicable. The basic premise of customer veneration is never *ever* challenged. And that being the case, I and my fellow members of the . . . um . . . brotherhood are able to maintain our edge over the competition."

"P4," Magill said flatly. "Or is it the Order of Solomon?"

"P4," Phillips replied. "It's P4. I've never heard of the Order of Solomon, Simon. Perhaps that's what P2 is calling itself nowadays. I hope so. I'm sure you're familiar with the Italian pass-off that's caused us a lot of trouble down the years."

Raising his half-empty whiskey glass in a mock "cheers" salute, Magill responded to Phillips's organisational problems with a distinct lack of sympathy. "I understood P4 was the bastard child of P2. My mistake, obviously."

"Not so," she replied, refusing to rise to Magill's needling. "Fakes are the bane of brands. P2 is a fake P4. Our organisation is much, much older. Almost as old as the Holy Grail itself. Naturally, our august institution has changed a lot since the early days, but only because society around it has changed. Just as Western society has substituted the ideology of consumption for the ideology of religion, and just as society has evolved from a low-tech agrarian ethos to a high-tech information ethos, so too our organisation has adapted to changing circumstances. That's why we talk about the Sale Greal rather than the Holy Grail. Make no mistake, however, the basic principles remain unchanged. Our watchwords are the same. The 4Ps are inviolate."

Taken aback by his antagonist's dramatic counterstrike, Magill could only gasp. "The 4Ps? You're joking, right? The 4Ps you published in all your books? The 4Ps you practically invented? Product, Place, Price, Promotion?"

The septuagenarian smiled coyly. "Just my little joke. Forgive me, Simon. The proper 4Ps are something else entirely. They're an encapsulation of the mantra we go by: Principal Principle Protracted Protected. It's a reminder of our basic belief system – our ancient belief system – that must be adhered to in perpetuity and never revealed to outsiders on pain of death. It's the key to our marketing code of practice. It's the principle contained in the locket. It's the secret of the Holy Marketing Grail, the Sale Greal."

"But the locket is empty."

"No it isn't, my postmodern Perceval. The secret is there but you can't see it. You were given an opportunity to ask the right question but you didn't. Regrettably."

Magill sat silently, sipping his drink. "May I ask a question now?"

Phillips finished her Bushmills, the ice rattling loudly in the silent room. "You've had your chance. But go ahead."

"Did you or your P4 henchpersons kill Pitcairn Brodie, Carlingford O'Connell and King Billy Solomon?"

The professor poured herself another Bushmills and offered the bottle to Magill. He refused her implied truce. "Yes, Simon, Brodie was killed on the orders of P4. He was betraying our secrets on his website, and the price of betrayal is death. O'Connell was on the point of betraying us in his book. He had to pay too. King Billy I know nothing about. I've heard of him, of course. He takes care of certain things for our organisation. Housekeeping matters, mainly. He subcontracts, I gather. Or used to."

"Brodie and O'Connell were P4 members, I take it, not unfortunates who stumbled on your secrets and paid the price?"

"They were," Phillips affirmed calmly. "An organisation like P4 has to be policed. The brethren know this. We call them brethren, by the way, not Illuminati." She flicked a glance at Barton Brady and went on. "All brethren swear an oath of loyalty. As they advance through the organisation from the P1 level to the P4 level, they are initiated into our secrets and take on additional responsibilities. They also have to recommit themselves to the cause with further oaths of fidelity. Betrayal is a capital offence."

"But why would Brodie and O'Connell want to betray you?"

"I don't know for certain. Betrayals are rare, but they tend to be triggered when ambitious brethren are blackballed by those in the level above them. Both Brodie and O'Connell were blackballed by their betters: Brodie by P3 and O'Connell by P2. Many are turned down. It's inevitable, given the hierarchical structure of our organisation. P1 is 40,000 strong, P2 has 4,000 initiates, P3 contains 400 outstanding marketing citizens, and there are just 40 P4s. Our brethren can do the math. Since the commercial advantages of membership outweigh the disadvantages, most initiates accept the decisions of their peers."

"But Brodie and O'Connell didn't," Magill interrupted. "They betrayed the organisation and paid the price. It's a very high price, professor. Exorbitant, I'd say."

Phillips topped up her visitor's glass unbidden. "They were bad men anyway, Mr Magill. They deserved to die. Brodie's report on the Orange Order's branding strategy led to the establishment of Tara, a Protestant paramilitary society committed to reclaiming Ulster's Celtic heritage. But Tara spawned Kincora, a paedophile prostitution racket centred on an East Belfast orphanage that scandalised Irish society back in the late 1970s. There are consequences to our marketing actions, Simon, and we must accept responsibility for them."

"But why O'Connell? He hadn't even published his *Titanic* book. And why the bloodthirsty anagrams? Why couldn't you have punished their betrayal some other way?"

Enthused for once, Phillips's air of professional calm evaporated instantly. Her grey eyes lit up. Maybe it was the Bushmills. Or maybe the conversation had finally taken the turn she was waiting for. "O'Connell was Brodie's assistant on the Tara report. He bore responsibility too. He *intended* to reveal our secrets in his book. That was sufficient. His death served a useful purpose, as did the anagrams. We don't normally use them when disciplining brethren."

"So why did you use them this time?"

"Because we wanted to get *you* here. Because we need you. Because we have big plans for you. For both of you."

Chapter Forty-Five

Down and Out in Oak Park, Ill.

To say Simon Magill was stricken hardly begins to describe his stricken state. He stared into the distance as he tried and failed to absorb the professor's shocking statement. It was as if his synapses had gone on strike in a kind of neuro go-slow. Not that he was concerned for his personal safety. He was long past caring. What shook him was the fact that the unspeakable events in Edinburgh and Belfast had been nothing more than an elaborate conjuring trick, a grisly exercise in personal misdirection designed to deliver him to an architectural showhouse in Chicago.

"Are you saying," he looked sharply at Phillips, "that May Day set me up?"

"Aided and abetted by her stepsister," Emer Aherne answered from the depths of her Eames armchair.

Magill struggled to compose himself. "But ... I ... but ... I love May ... and she loves me."

"Did she tell you that?" Aherne asked matter-of-factly.

"No ... yes ... yes, she did, sort of. Why would she want to trick me?"

"Because her mother asked her to." Aherne replied. "Because I arranged it with May and my stepdaughter, Ultima."

As another interpersonal shockwave swept over him, Magill could do little more than whimper, "But why? What have I ever done to you?"

"It's not me. It's P4," Aherne answered, without a trace of emotion. "Try not to take it personally," she added, though Magill wasn't exactly comforted by his colleague's business-is-business attitude.

"I'll try not to, you fucking gorgon," he snarled. "Anyway, why me, what have I ever done to you or P4?" Out of the corner of his eye he could see Buonarroti fiddling with her pistol, while looking questioningly at Phillips. The professor shook her head imperceptibly.

Aherne stood up and sauntered over to her Hustler colleague, casually spinning the Smith and Wesson on her forefinger like an Irish Annie Oakley. "If you wish," she replied coldly, leaning over his chair threateningly, "I can provide a long list of reasons why you're here. You assisted Brodie with his website. You're an accessory to betrayal. You assisted O'Connell with his brand book. You're an accessory to additional betrayal. Ignorance of the law is no defence, as everyone knows. You also made a presentation at Hustler in which you intimated that you were getting too close to P4 for comfort."

"What?" Magill snapped back, refusing to be intimidated by the rootin' tootin' Celtic cowgirl. "You mean the tripping point? The lecture on Marks and Spencer I gave to apparel executives? You're killing me for *that*?"

Sagacious as ever, Professor Phillips intervened, smoothly assuming the role of good cop to Aherne's bad. "No, Simon, not the tripping point presentation. We're thinking more of your presentation at the Hustler job interview, your State of the Marketing Union address."

Magill was gobsmacked. "How do you know any of this? You weren't there, nor was Clint here, nor was Noo Yoik there, nor was May Day."

Phillips stayed Aherne's increasingly itchy trigger finger and reminded Magill that there were twelve people on his interview panel, that she had connections, that nothing went on in marketing that P4 didn't get to hear about. The organisation's tentacles stretched to every corner of the world, and their Chamber of Commerce contacts channelled all the information they ever needed to know. They had 80,000 ears to the ground, not to mention ample Crimind contacts to hit, pop, whack or mutilate anyone P4 considered subversive, overinquisitive or dangerous.

As Magill's anger abated and the fact of May Day's deceit sank in, the confusing events of the past three days kept being projected onto the home-cinema system of his memory, though the movie didn't make much sense. He could understand why Ultima Sullivan had led him up the garden path. He wasn't the first Brit she'd tricked, the duplicitous Jezebel. But May Day's double dealing was hard to take.

He motioned for more Bushmills, and with an air of regret if not resignation said, "But why bring me here? Why not just kill me in Ulster? Why go through all the grotesque anagrammatic rigmarole? A bit excessive, isn't it?"

"Simple Simon," Phillips answered, "we need you for our reconsecration ceremony. It takes place tomorrow at noon. We had to get you here intact, undamaged, virginal. We couldn't kidnap or drug you, obviously, what with airport security the way it is these days. We didn't have the time to ship you in the hold of a cargo vessel. The only way to get you here was to scatter clues, set an intriguing trail for you to follow. We knew of your fondness for Dan Brown's books, so we concocted a little conspiracy theory. All we had to do was nudge you in the right direction, help you on your way.

"You came to us, Simon. Under your own volition. We didn't twist your arm. If it's any comfort to you, we were going to take out Brodie and O'Connell in any event. That's what led us to you. You just happened to be in the right place at the right time from our perspective. Wrong place, wrong time for you, of course. It isn't personal. It's appropriate in a way, since so many things in business life are serendipitous. Both good and bad. Some people have made careers out of that very fact." She motioned towards Brady.

Phillips's words weren't much comfort, to put it mildly, nor was her attempt to console him with the news that his co-captor, Barton Brady, was much easier to snare. A single phone call from Yasmin, an automated out-of-office email and a routine brush-off by Phillips's administrative assistant were sufficient to send him on a fool's errand to Chicago. A noncommittal interview with Professor Phillips took care of the rest and brought him panting to Oak Park. Brady sat silently in his chair during this ruthless summary of his shortcomings. Magill hoped he was hatching a plan. He looked like the all-action, go-getting, plan-hatching type. A fool he might be – Magill couldn't talk – but he seemed like someone with get up and go. Their best bet, Magill concluded, was to keep Phillips talking. Like King Billy, she might let something slip.

After finishing off her drink, Professor Phillips spoke to Aherne and Buonarroti. "Time to lock up our charges, ladies. They've a busy day ahead of them tomorrow, and you need your rest before the ceremony."

"Surely we're entitled to know something about this so-called ceremony of yours? The least you can do is tell us what's going to happen," Magill said, hoping that this sneaky appeal to Phillips's professionalism would get her started again. He soon wished he hadn't asked.

"You are going to die a gruesome death. You will be sacrificed . . . executed . . . killed in keeping with the votive traditions of our organisation."

After pausing for effect, the professor went on, "I can't pretend your death will be instantaneous. It won't. Nor shall I insult you by implying that it will hurt me more than it will hurt you. It won't. You will suffer terribly before the ceremony is over."

Phillips recounted the complex history of the organisation and its leaders in an incantatory tone, a voice that mesmerised even as it informed. She explained that P4 was founded by Count Cagliostro, a superlative eighteenth-century marketing man who possessed prodigious magical powers, clairvoyance and reincarnation included. He based elements of his creation on Templar and Arthurian legend and established cycles of organisational reincarnation and rules governing the line of succession.

The essential point, as far as Magill could make out, was that Cagliostro set up a masonic-style organization loosely affiliated to the Bavarian Illuminati. More pertinently, it permitted Jews, women, people of colour, subservient groups and, not least, the trading classes to participate, dominate and ultimately use their membership for commercial advantage. The professor also itemised in tedious detail the lives and achievements of the ten leaders, or phillippissimi, of the organisation since Cagliostro's time: Filippo Buonarroti, Niccolo Paganini, Jean

340

Robert-Houdin, P. T. Barnum, Mark Twain, Frank Lloyd Wright, Charlie Chaplin, Salvador Dalì, Calvin Klein and current incumbent, Michael Jackson.

"Michael Jackson?"

"Michael is a marketing genius. Or was, rather. He's been a disappointment to us and to himself. He feels he's let P4 down and has asked to be relieved of his responsibilities. I've tried to explain that this is a normal part of the P4 lifecycle. Like many natural phenomena, our organisation is subject to cycles of change. Animal, vegetable and socio-economic cycles wax and wane, as do product, brand and retail life cycles in marketing and commercial life generally. But Michael blames himself for marketing's recent troubles. He's standing down and won't be dissuaded. End times are always traumatic and turbulent organisationally, though our phillippissimus doesn't see it like that, sadly. His abrupt resignation has caused problems, not least organising the reconsecration ceremony at short notice. However, tomorrow's investiture will propitiate the marketing gods. The ceremony requires two votive offerings. Your lives are being sacrificed to the gods of marketing. Marketing, as you astutely observed in your Hustler job talk – *too* astutely observed – eats its young. It is only through death that our organisation remains alive. It is thanks to you that marketing can be made sustainable once more. Sustenance is all. The gods must be sustained. Satisfied. You must be sacrificed. It is a great honour, a noble cause. Yes, your death will be gruesome. But it will also be glorious. You are dying so that marketing may live. Always remember: pain is fleeting, glory eternal."

Having sat silently thorough Phillips's lunatic history lesson, Barton Brady suddenly snorted. If ever a snort spoke volumes, it was Barton Brady's snort. It was the "Oh yeah?" "Whatever" "Bullshit!' of snorts, with a touch of "Talk to the hand" thrown in.

"Ah, Mr Brady," Phillips said coldly. "Nobility is wasted on you. Sacrifice is not something you're familiar with. You have been pampered and cosseted from birth. You have had a glittering and gilded career. You have everything that androcentric society can bestow, even a modicum of professional accomplishment. You now have an opportunity to be famous. Really famous. Your moment has come. You are going to die tomorrow, Mr Brady, along with Mr Magill. You have gazed on the grail. You have handled the grail. You have manhandled the grail. Both of you must die. You would have to die even if tomorrow's ceremony were cancelled."

Magill interrupted Phillips's flow. "If that's the case, Professor, how come Emer and Yasmin aren't part of your barbaric ceremony? How come you are still alive? Didn't you ever mishandle the grail in your youth, before you were appraised of its secrets? Ignorance of the law is no defence, remember."

Phillips turned to Magill, staring deep into what felt like his soul, her grey eyes penetrating, almost painful. "Emer and Yasmin didn't handle the locket as you and Brady did. They *are* part of tomorrow's ceremony. Thanks to Professor Aherne's recent discovery, we are able to induct a direct descendant of our organisation's first elected phillipissimus, Filippo Buonarroti. As a result, Emer and Yasmin are honorary members of the altar party; a great privilege."

"What about you, Professor?" Magill snapped with a boldness that in his current situation qualified as either incredible foolhardiness or outstanding bravery, or both. "How come *you're* still alive?"

The grey eyes bored into him. "Alive, dead, why do marketing educators constantly resort to such crude dichotomies? So many things in this world – in marketing – are neither *either* nor *or*. Either/or thinking is the bane of our field. Why not both/and? Why not embrace both *both* and *and*?"

Despite his muzzle, Brady snorted eloquently once more. Magill seized the moment, hoping that something of import was about to be revealed, something that might help them avoid their grisly fate.

"Do you expect us to believe you're both alive and dead? Do you really think we'll fall for horseshit like that? Pull the other one, it's got a Dracula DVD on it. Whoops, sorry, I forgot, the grail quest, the philosopher's stone, the secret of eternal youth. Intellectual eternity not enough for you? I hate to put this to you, Prof, but if you really want to look younger, I'd recommend cosmetic surgery."

For a second, Magill thought he'd pushed Phillips over the edge. She retorted in kind, "You look as though you've had a procedure or two yourself, Simon. Ineptly performed at that."

But she quickly recovered her zen-like composure. She stood up and started clearing away the empty whiskey glasses. "It's time we drew this illuminating conversation to a close. But before we call it a night, let me do my professorial thing and test you on the little lecture you've just heard. Did you notice anything that connects all the phillippissimi?"

"I couldn't care less, Professor," Magill snarled. "Unless the right answer gets me . . . us . . . off the hook."

"We don't use a hook, Simon. The ceremony's much more gruesome that that, rest assured. The answer, young man, is that they're all involved in the cultural industries. The cultural industries have always been unresponsive to customer-oriented approaches. They've always been a hold-out. Ironically, though, they always held the secret of marketing success, though no one thought to look. The assumption has always been that the arts are a marketing backwater – that if only they'd become more customer oriented they'd be so much more successful. I've even written a book along those lines. My best-ever piece of misdirection, if I may be so immodest."

Magill interrupted her flow once more. He'd had enough of her attempts at exculpation.

"That may well be the case, Professor Phillips, but if you look at that group of people – Paganini, Twain, Chaplin – the thing that connects them is fame, yes, fortune, yes, but *failure* as well, abject failure, the failure that comes from being part of your crazy, murdering, self-perpetuating fellowship. I bet Michael Jackson rues the day he fell into your clutches and participated in your lunatic schemes. No wonder the poor guy went bananas."

"Yes, it's a shame about Michael. He wasn't up to the task. Madonna would have done a better job. But the brethren's vote is final. Dan will do a much better job. He's the perfect man to lead us into the next great cycle."

"Dan? Dan who?"

"Dan Brown, of course. I thought you'd appreciate the symbology, gentlemen. You, Magill, a big fan of the best marketing man around. And you, Brady, the person who's hoping to expand the market for Dan Brown merchandise. Just think, you will be dying for Dan. What better way to go? Except that the fictional deaths in *Angels & Demons* and *The Da Vinci Code* are nothing compared to what you'll experience tomorrow."

Chapter Forty-Six

Whack First, Yack Later

The cellar door slammed behind them. Brady lay in a crumpled heap at the bottom of the wooden stairs thanks to a final friendly shove by his pistol-packing partner, Yasmin Buonarroti. His immaculate Brooks Brothers shirt was torn in several places. Ordinarily, the super-sartorial Serendipity Associate would be deeply upset by such unconscionable brand abuse. But once Simon Magill had helped him to his feet – no broken bones, orthodontics intact – and carefully removed the gag that had restrained him all evening, Barton Brady was full of beans.

He prowled the cellar like a lion auditioning for Siegfried & Roy. He checked the slit windows. Too narrow to slip through. He tested the cellar door. Too stout to shift. He shouted for help at the top of his voice. Too much for his former colleague. The door was unexpectedly yanked open. Although Magill couldn't quite make out what was happening, he heard the muffled report of a silenced weapon.

Brady was hurled back at high speed as if he'd been hit by a pump-action ray-gun. He tumbled down the stairs like a trainee stunt man, while trying to cope with what must have been excruciating pain. As he rolled about on the bare concrete floor, Magill could see two tiny darts impaled in his upper torso.

"How do you like my new toy, Barton?" Buonarroti called from the top of the stairs. "Painful, isn't it? If I hear another squeak out of you – either of you – I'll increase the voltage next time. This is a Taser Turbo, guys, and it goes all the way up to eleven. It's the equivalent of a hand-held electric chair, and I'm dying to try the 'fry 'em' setting. Keep the noise down and get a good night's rest. You've a big day tomorrow."

With a mighty effort, Magill picked Brady up for the second time, only to see him crumple again with a twisted ankle. "At least it's not broken," the amateur paramedic said after assessing the damage. "However, it'll be painful for a couple of days. If you live that long."

"Oh, I'll live, buckaroo," the patient grimaced, failing to stifle a groan. He struggled to rise, shoving his co-captive aside. "I'm gonna get outta this place."

"Well, you won't be running outta here, *buckaroo*," Magill retorted. "Unless you can hop like a kangaroo, buckaroo. But, hey, see if I care. I can run faster than you, buckaroo, and while you're bounding down Oak Park's main drag, dodging Taser Turbo darts, I'll be half way to O'Hare."

"You don't like the buckaroo, buddy?" Brady said, sinking back to the floor, smiling his smile of smiles and extending a pampered hand. "*We're* gonna live, buddy. We're gonna get out of this place."

Returning the smile, albeit with a painful wince – where's the lip balm when you need it? – Magill pumped the proffered hand and said, "I'm not too keen on buddy either, but I'll live with it if you can keep us alive and get us out of here. What did you make of Phillips's story?"

"It sounded like buckaroo shit to me," Brady replied, settling uncomfortably against an empty packing case. Unlike many American cellars, which function as barrels beneath the downpipe of domestic detritus, Phillips's basement was eerily empty. "All that phillippissimi crap and BS about reincarnation, it's straight outta Aleister Crowley. He was a bullshitter too. A brilliant self-marketer, but a first-class bullshitter. I know bullshit when I see it – management consultancy is Bullshit Central – and that was 24-carat bullshit."

Magill nodded. Never in his wildest dreams did he imagine he'd be discussing Aleister Crowley in a cellar in Oak Park, Illinois. "Admirer of the Great Beast, are you?"

"Nah," Brady replied with a childlike grin. "I was a big Led Zeppelin fan when I was a teenager. Loved all that rock 'n' runes stuff. Zep were heavily into Crowley and I got into him too. For a while. Much later on, I realised that Peter Grant, Led Zep's manager, was the key to the whole thing, the power behind the throne, the person who made it happen. He became my marketing role model, only with extra servings of charm. Grant didn't do charm. It's my specialty. My curse. What's your curse, Simon?"

Egomaniac though the man patently was, Magill felt himself warming to Barton Brady. His renunciation of charm was, well, charming in a way. Simon ran through his story once more. With all the rehearsal, it was turning into a mini masterpiece of compression and synthesis.

"Holy moly!" Brady whistled when his bedraggled companion had finished. "Holy rollin' moly." He shook his head with amazement, the corners of his mouth turned down. The look on his face hovered between credulity and cynicism. "If you'd told me that a week ago, Simon, I'd've laughed in your face. But I've thought a lot about the grail in the past few days and I'm tempted to believe you. However, it still sounds like something out of Dan Brown shitlit."

"Don't diss the Danster, dude," Magill said automatically.

"Oh, you're worried about the locum phillippissimus who's planning to slit our throats tomorrow? Sorry I hurt your feelings, buddy."

Simon Magill had never met Dan Brown. He had no reason to defend him, especially given his current dire straits. He knew nothing about the man, but sensed from his books that Dan was fundamentally decent, not the kind of person who'd slit someone's throat. Except in a fictional sense. He could see that the Danster might want to join a secret society for research purposes, especially if it was similar to the Freemasons. Brown's forthcoming book was about the Freemasons, and there was no way he'd be allowed access to a conventional lodge, not after his treatment of Opus Dei in *Da Vinci*. But Magill, perhaps naively, refused to buy into Brady's Big Bad Brown scenario.

"Do you really think that a man who subscribes to the idea of the sacred feminine, a man who's so in touch with his feminine side that he's been accused of sexual self-harassment, a man who's created some of the most feisty fictional female characters this side of Lara Croft and V. I. Warshawski. Do you really think a man like that'd be involved in something so heinous?"

Brady said nothing. He slowly removed a shoe and sock and massaged his swollen ankle. Wincing with pain, he looked up at his fellow cellar dweller.

"There's something else going on here," he said with deliberation. "I can feel it, Simon. A hidden agenda. Misdirection. Isn't that the word Phillips used? There's something we aren't seeing, something we've overlooked."

"Something the . . . um . . . babes upstairs aren't telling us?"

"Babes, babes, babes," Brady reiterated. "Where have I heard that before?"

"You live in Las Vegas, Barton, and you're wondering where you've heard 'babes' before?"

Brady grinned. "I'm not thinking of showgirls, Simon. I'm thinking girls, women, the feminine, the eternal feminine. That's it. That's it! Of course!" He raised his hand, high-five style. Magill fived it on trust. "The list of phillippissimi. Did you notice anything about it? No women. Not one. Not a single freakin' one."

"Phillips said something about Madonna, though."

"Yeah, that she was passed over in favour of Jackson. She also said something disparaging about 'androcentric' society when she was running through my alleged shortcomings, right after you were goading her into an indiscretion. I assume that's what you were trying to do, Simon, and I think you succeeded."

"Maybe, Barton," Magill replied, "though I don't see any connection or pattern."

Brady was getting excited. The effervescent enthusiasm that had captivated Madison Avenue and won countless clients for SA in the early days before cynicism and ennui took root was now in magnificent evidence.

"There's more, Simon. There's more. When Aherne made her presentation on Dan Brown . . ." Sensing Magill's confusion, he elaborated, " . . . to Serendipity Associates, in Vegas, she didn't hide her opposition to Brown's supposed sexism. When Aherne hooked up with Yazza, they were going to some sort of, I don't know, feminist consciousness-raising seminar. Yazza mentioned meeting up with the babes. I thought it was a lesbian thing with Aherne. Not that I cared. I was happy for her."

The enthusiasm faded as quickly as it had appeared. Brady's effervescence dissipated as the reality of his situation hit home. "I . . . I . . . I can't believe she'd do this to me. There's nothing we couldn't have talked through. I admire her more than anyone. She's creative, she's gutsy, she's incredibly lucky, she's everything a management consultant should be, bar sweet-natured smooth-talker. Jesus H. Christ, what's going on here?"

"I'm not sure, Barton," Magill confessed, desperate to rekindle his partner's creative fire. "However, if anyone can crack it, you can. I read your 'Fortune Favors the Brand' article in *HBR*. It was one of the most innovative papers that journal's ever published."

The charmerpreneur smiled briefly and replied with what seemed like genuine modesty, "Ancient history, Simon. But thanks anyway."

"You're definitely on the right lines, Barton. The feminine angle is compatible with the grail legend. I read a book about the Holy Grail on my flight from Ireland, a cultural history of the concept, and the female angle appears again and again and again. Apart from the Mary Magdalene thing, the Arthurian version is full of powerful women: Guinevere, Morgan Le Fay, the bearers of the grail in the Fisher King's castle. Avalon was a matriarchal society, for heaven's sake!"

"I didn't know that."

Magill's own enthusiasm was rising, and, although he was nowhere near as charismatic as Barton Brady on song, it wasn't bad for a skinny ginger guy with black eyes and broken lips. "The grail may have been rediscovered by the Knights Templar, an organisation of warrior monks, but its secrets passed down through the Cathars, whose priests were female, as well as the Troubadours, like Chrétien de Troyes, who venerated the sacred feminine above all else. It's curious, is it not, that a secret society claiming ownership of the Holy Grail should have so few females in positions of leadership, Phillips excepted? And she's undead and maybe not even a woman, if her claim to be Cagliostro's reincarnation is correct. It's strange too that she should live in the house of a notorious philanderer who treated women like chattels, Mamah Cheney especially."

"Yes," Brady cautioned, "But Phillips also made that remark about androcentrism and claimed that Cagliostro was way ahead of his time because women were included in the organisation. Maybe the reincarnated count is appalled by the way his organisation turned out and is determined to wreak havoc."

"Sounds crazy, Barton, but them everything about this is crazy. All we know for certain is that we've got an organisation going through a traumatic transition, a secret society predicated on the eternal feminine but with its glass ceiling intact, and a collective that's about to appoint a new leader whose feminist credentials are suspect."

"Maybe it's much, much simpler, Simon. Maybe it's just a marketing issue. The other thing that connects all the phillippissimi is marketing. Maybe, in classic Michael Porter fashion, the society's facing new competitors or substitutes. For all we know, there could be a new kid on the conspiracy-theory block. Perhaps it's a takeover attempt. A hostile takeover attempt."

Magill thought back to his discussions with the late King Billy. Solomon might have been misdirecting too, just like May Day and Ultima Sullivan, but the stuff he said about Crimind rang true. Criminality is big business, and businesses of that size have all sorts of management issues to deal with. The restructuring, the delayering, the brand building, the core competencies, the strategic alliances, the globalisation of competition that King Billy mentioned suddenly starting making a lot of sense. "A takeover you reckon, Barton?" he echoed.

"Taking out, more like," Brady asserted. "If they're anything like the Las Vegas families, these people whack first, yack later."

"Even feminised families?"

"The mob isn't big on equal opportunities, from what I can gather, bud . . . Simon."

"Buddy's OK, Barton. I guess we'll find out soon enough. Let's stay alert and seize the moment if and when it comes."

"Yeah, let's," Brady answered. "However, I suspect the babes have something else up their sleeves. Suicide bombing, possibly.

Yasmin's a Muslim. Her family's from North Africa. They faced a lot of discrimination in the early days. They still do. Emer Aherne's connected to the IRA in some capacity, and we all know what they're capable of. Phillips is undead anyway, or so she says. Maybe we're looking at marketing apocalypse, the self-immolation of a degenerate organisation."

"Or maybe they'll just slit our throats and be done with it, Barton. There's no point worrying about suicide bombers in little black dresses by Chanel, or in Pringle twinsets and pearls."

Brady looked at Magill unswervingly, all chutzpah, smarm and egomania set aside. "I say we make a run for it, Simon. They'll get me but you might escape. It's worth a shot."

"We're in this together, Barton. All for one, one for all."

Magill raised his hand for another high five. The prisoners slapped palms. The do or die were cast.

Chapter Forty-Seven

The Wild Bunch

Impending death is the father of steadfast relationships – extreme speed-dating, so to speak – and in the few hours before dawn Simon Magill and Barton Brady became brothers in arms. If not quite Butch and Sundance, much less Riggs and Murtagh (let alone Lancelot and Galahad), they enjoyed the kind of comradeship First World War infantrymen must have felt before going over the top. An odder couple was almost impossible to imagine: gangly ginger Englishman with broken face, black eyes, split lips *et al.*, and sleek 'n' smooth, primped 'n' pampered, brandname-bandoleered Las Vegan. But they talked the night away, recalling first loves, last loves and love-to-loves in between. Brady did most of the talking.

Lloyd Wright's mullioned slit windows gradually lightened and a desultory dawn chorus kicked in. They could hear movement in the kitchen upstairs. The scent of freshly brewed coffee percolated down to the perma-pair-bonded prisoners.

"Do you think the condemned men will be given a hearty breakfast?"

"I very much doubt it," Brady replied in a weary talked-out monotone.

"How long before they come for us, you reckon?"

"Hard to tell, bud. In the movies, the ceremony usually takes place at midnight in a dripping crypt, with candles and altars and pentangles and chanting Greek chorus and the goddamn goat of Mendes. Gratuitous sex too."

"I don't think this'll be like the movies, somehow."

Magill was right. Far from waiting till midnight, or even dusk on All Hallows' Eve, the captors came for their captives around mid-morning. There was no final repast for the condemned men, only a cup of lukewarm coffee. Less mess during the disembowelling, they were affably informed. The ceremonial venue, they were also told, would be as uncryptlike as could be imagined, an anonymous conference room on the NWU campus. Less conspicuous, apparently. Less hassle, less fuss, less likely to be interrupted. Altogether more businesslike, more in keeping with P4's basic premise.

"I just don't know, Simon," Brady announced as they were bound and bundled into Aherne's SUV. "There's just no romance in human sacrifice these days."

"What we lack in Las Vegas razzamatazz," Phillips volunteered before setting off separately in her Lexus, "we compensate with barbarity."

"The function room faces east," Aherne snapped. "The ceremony is scheduled for vespers, Jerusalem time, Templar time, and it's taking place on Black Friday. Is that enough romance for you, smiler?"

Magill weighed in, determined to defend his newfound friend and goad his captors into a potentially life-saving indiscretion or misjudgment. "Halloween's too commercialised, is it? The most magical day of the year – Samhain bonfires, Baphomet rising, telluric currents at full voltage, pentagrams a gogo – destroyed by dreadful marketing types? Tell me, Emer, do you buy your costumes from Harry Potter apparel suppliers, or are they made to measure?"

With the butt of her Smith and Wesson, Aherne hit Magill full in the face. "It's the six hundred and ninety-ninth anniversary of the Templar treachery, if you must know. Now shut it, shit-for-brains."

The pain was excruciating but inconsequential. Magill tried again. "Is that with or without the ten days added by the switch from Julian to Gregorian calendars?" Aherne buttpunched him once more. On the nose this time.

"What's our cover story, Emer?" Buonarroti asked as she settled into the driver's seat beside Brady, in front of Magill.

"Harry Potter, as it happens." Aherne shouted from the rear, where she could keep a wary eye on both captives. "The room is booked for a private meeting of PASPI, the Potter Appreciation

Society for Patriarchal Illuminati."

Magill and Brady exchanged knowing glances as their captors laughed at what they assumed was a private joke. "Hey, Simon," Brady called. "You're finally gonna meet the Danster. Do you think the wussy Harry Potter look will suit him? He's more of a chinos, rollneck, sports coat kinda guy – a man's man, wouldn't you say?"

"It's your turn for gag duty," Buonarroti shouted to Aherne over the growl of the Ford in low gear, and the Irishwoman was more than happy to oblige. She needn't have bothered with the duct tape, however, for all the time the journey took. Post rush hour, they had a pretty clear run, and less than 45 minutes after leaving Cheney House, Buonarroti was swinging onto Sheridan and turning left along Campus Drive to the Norris University Center.

The SUV pulled up at a side entrance of the neo-brutalist building. Brady and Magill were spirited into a waiting elevator that ferried them swiftly to the second floor. No one saw them arrive, and doubtless their exit would be equally efficiently managed. They were deposited in a cramped anteroom and trussed together with a silken rope that tied Magill's hands behind him and Brady's in front. Strung tightly together in such a fashion, it was impossible to escape, or even face each other without considerable effort. Buonarroti ripped off their shirts, exposing Brady's bronzed torso and Magill's pale and interesting counterpart. She double-checked the storeroom, which contained nothing but plastic chairs stacked floor to ceiling, and locked the door as she left.

Aside from occasional be-brave glances and gritty nods of the we're-gonna-get-out-of-this-mess variety, the hogtied twosome could do nothing but wait. They could hear a crowd gathering in the convention room behind them, their voices a low buzz of excitement and expectancy. The sickly smell of incense wafted under the door and an anticipatory stomp began. It might or might not have been part of the ceremony, but the boom, boom, boom of the crashing feet sounded frighteningly similar to the tomtom beat of countless cowboy and Indian movies Magill had seen as a child.

Be brave, he said to himself. Die with dignity. Don't die like

Peter. Die with your head up, not your pants down. He struggled to keep May Day out of his thoughts but found he couldn't. It was far too late for tears of regret or rage, though. Because the stomping suddenly stopped. Silence reigned for several seconds, then a lone voice ululated. It was bewildering yet beguiling. God knows what the unsuspecting student body enjoying early lunch in the food court three floors below would have made of it had the otherworldly sounds carried that far. But they didn't.

The double doors of the storeroom swung open. Aherne and Buonarroti stood at the entrance wearing diaphanous silver surplices with heavy brocade at collar, cuffs, waist and hem. Dazzling multi-strand necklaces of gold braid, emeralds and amethysts coiled around their throats like kaleidoscopic serpents. Aherne wore an elaborate tiara of beaten gold, sapphire and jasper presumably indicative of her higher standing in the P4 hierarchy, and carried a ruby-pointed silver spear in one hand and a smoking brass censer in the other.

Emer Aherne, seneschal for the day, led the way. Magill and Brady followed, trying to maintain a modicum of dignity despite the silken belay that bound them together as they ascended the ceremonial Matterhorn. From the opposite side of the capacious convention room, the double doors of another antechamber opened. A beaten gold bier, carried at shoulder height by two elaborately coiffed, scarlet-soutane-wearing female adepts, emerged slowly from its sacristy to the audience's evident appreciation. The respective parties walked towards each other and merged at the central passageway. The grail procession was complete, bier bearers in front, votive party behind.

All seated, but turning round excitedly, the assembled marketing multitude was a couple of hundred strong – P3 and above was Magill's guess – and dressed in a similar way to Aherne and Buonarroti, who brought up the rear of the procession. Magill glared fearlessly around him as he walked, recognising many faces from the front covers of *Forbes*, *Fortune*, *Fast Company* and *Entertainment Weekly*. No one returned his fierce, black-eyed gaze.

Heavy drapes lined one side of the auditorium, pulled tight to shut out the light. A dais dominated the eastern end of the room, though in the candlelit semi-darkness Magill found it difficult to identify the individuals on stage. As he got closer, he could see the elaborate set: a massive altar draped in heavy linen corporal embossed with red Templar logos. At either end of the altar, two huge menorah-style candlesticks stood sentinel.

A figure in ceremonial shimmering purple silk chasuble with black and silver cincture stood behind the corporal, arms crossed over her chest. It was Phillips. Behind her, three more figures stood at ease holding magnificent golden halberds. Immediately beyond them the rear wall was covered with Knights Templar symbols: crosses, shields, flags and oversized Freemasonoid insignia. Despite himself, Magill couldn't help but admire the stage set, presumably the work of the Crimind services company that had assembled the P4 roadshow and would doubtless disassemble it in double-quick time. Debord's "society of the spectacle" was everywhere, so it seemed, though with such a showbizzy membership nothing less than totally over the top would have sufficed. A dank crypt it might not have been, but the Louis Ballroom had the right atmosphere for a secret-society meeting. On Broadway.

The stomping and singing resumed, slowly at first, then rising to a crescendo as the altar party reached the dais. It was only then that Magill recognised the three halberd-holding, headdress-wearing, silver amice-sheathed figures behind Phillips: the past, present and future phillippissimi, Calvin Klein, Michael Jackson and Dan Brown. CK looked a little uncomfortable, since the outfit wasn't really his style. Jackson's disfigured face was lit up with childish glee, as befitted an inhabitant of Neverland. Dan Brown stared stoically ahead with a somewhat self-conscious air. His eyes betrayed a mixture of fascination and fear. His demeanour screamed "I'm a celebrity novelist, get me out of here." But not just yet.

The bier bearers reached the dais and set the redemptive reliquary before Phillips. After a muezzin-like incantation, she opened the ravishing receptacle and removed an intricately carved chalice, placing it reverentially on the altar. She reached into the container again and with a flourish pulled out a golden gladius,

357

the short stabbing sword with heavy hilt that was the staple weapon of gladiators and Roman legionnaires. She raised it in the air, turned to Dan Brown, bowed deeply, and then set the ceremonial sword on the altar next to the chalice. Was this, Magill wondered, the treasure the Knights Templar found beneath Solomon's temple in the twelfth century, or simply an elaborate piece of stagecraft? The Englishman had been misdirected so many times that he'd lost any sense of where fact ended and fiction began.

With a cue-like glance at Aherne, Phillips unclasped her lapis lazuli locket and placed it carefully in the sacred vessel. As the procession took the final few steps onto the stage, the shallow chalice began to glow, throwing Phillips's expressionless face into grotesque relief. Brady was obviously having trouble with his ankle. Magill could feel the rope tense behind him. He paused to give his partner some necessary respite. Sensing that the human train had stopped, Aherne half-turned and glared at her dilatory Hustler colleague. Simon stepped forward quickly, only to slip on the top step.

As he plunged forward, Magill heard a collective gasp from the audience and a grunt from Brady as their connecting rope jerked unexpectedly. The collective gasp quickly turned to shouting, screaming and assorted noises off. With his arms tied behind him, Magill found it difficult to struggle to his feet. As he looked up, he saw Aherne staring down at him maniacally. Blood was pouring from her nostrils and the corners of her mouth. Further gouts of blood were spouting from her neck, which had lost its elaborate jewellery and gained a razor-sharp dagger – a dagger that went in one side and out the other like a grisly parody of Frankenstein's monster's bolts. Behind Phillips, Magill could see the phillippissimi being hurried off the dais by concerned members of the brotherhood. Showman first, last and always, Michael Jackson moonwalked his way to safety.

The room was in uproar. Only Phillips remained calm amid the mayhem, taking everything in while keeping a watchful eye on the intended sacrificial victims. So intense was her stare that Simon Magill didn't immediately notice the blood on his shoulders and back.

"Am I hit, Barton?" he cried, spinning round to his companion. Brady was on his knees. A dagger was impaled in his chest, almost to the hilt. His torso was covered in blood, and what little life he had left was rapidly ebbing away. "Barton! Barton!" Magill shouted. He tried to clasp his comrade-in-arms, determined to assist in some small way, but his hands were tied and it was much too late. Brady smiled a trademark Brady smile and fell forward. Dead.

Simon wept. All the pain he'd felt in the past three days finally came to a head. He couldn't do anything to staunch the tears. Nor did he want to. Amid the pain – pain for Brady, pain for Brodie, pain for May Day, pain for his mother, father, brother – he experienced a strange sense of relief, release, repose. He didn't know how long he had been kneeling there, weeping for a friend he couldn't touch in death or caress in sorrow. But when he finally looked up, Phillips was looking down at him.

"Come with me," she commanded, slicing his silken cord with the gladius.

He cradled Brady in his aching arms. "Why should I, you bitch? Piss off and leave us alone." He dared her – defied her – to kill him then and there.

"Dan's in danger," she replied.

"What?"

"Buonarroti's taken Dan Brown. Kidnapped him. He's in great danger. Come with me. Now!"

Magill felt like a scuba diver breaking through to the surface. The sudden gasp of air. Reality bites. He followed her mutely to the wings of the stage. There on the carpeted floor, pinned down by several extravagantly attired Hogwarts alumni, sprawled Wee Joe Monroe, thrashing, struggling and swearing like a drunken sailor who's lost his wooden leg. Magill paused beside the psychotic knife-thrower.

The butcher glared up at him and hissed in his toothless lisp, "I missed ye, ye fucker. Missed ye twice, ye bastard. Get ye next time, Gingerbap."

"I don't think so, Joe." Magill kicked him in the mouth. As hard as he was able. And slipped out of a side exit behind Phillips.

Chapter Forty-Eight

United We Stand

"I don't know why I'm doing this," Simon Magill spat at his driver as the speeding Lexus hurtled west along Dempster Street.

The professor jumped a stop light and swung hard right onto the Edens Expressway before formulating a reply. "You're doing it because you care, because you're an admirer of Dan Brown, and because you want to understand the events you're involved in. There's a lot you don't know, Simon."

"I don't think I want to. Not after Barton." Magill took a deep breath and exhaled slowly, trying to collect his thoughts. "Dan Brown can take care of himself."

Eyes fixed firmly on the fizzing traffic flow ahead, Kate Phillips reached across and patted him kindly on the right knee. "Look on the bright side. At least you're still alive."

"Yes, but will I stay that way?" he retorted.

"Well, provided we don't have an accident on the way to the airport, and you don't catch your death from that bare chest of yours, you'll be alive for a while yet."

"Airport? Why the airport? Where are we going?"

The diminutive professor glanced left and right as she sped through the speed limit en route to the sound barrier. "We're going to the airport because that's where Yasmin's taken Dan. The only place they'll be heading is back to Las Vegas. We've got to get there before she does what I think she's going to do."

Phillips motioned towards a carrier bag on the back seat. "There's a Northwestern T-shirt in there. It's a gift for my nephew's eleven-year-old son. You can borrow it if it fits. We have to hurry. All the Las Vegas flights leave around three on Friday afternoons. We've less than an hour to get there."

"Surely security'll stop them. If Buonarroti's threatening Brown with a gun or a knife, there's no way she'll get them through the X-ray machines. All he has to do is shout for assistance. They'll never get to Las Vegas, not dressed like that, they won't."

"You'd be surprised Simon. They're dressed quite modestly compared to most Americans on vacation. Especially in Vegas."

That's true, Magill thought. He'd seen more clashing colour combinations in the past two days than he'd witnessed during two years of Pitcairn Brodie. The only thing more ostentatious than Americans' vacationwear was their sportswear. Items affiliated with college football teams were especially unspeakable, none more so than Northwestern's. He pulled on the bright purple Wildcats T-shirt, which only just reached his navel. And they say Chicago's a conservative city.

"What about airport security, though?" he continued. "They'll never get through."

"Oh, I suspect Dan doesn't know what's planned for him. Yasmin was working on some Robert Langdon merchandising deal. They had a meeting arranged anyway, I understand. I'm sure Yasmin has spun some plausible yarn about spiriting him to safety. Only he's not safe with Ms Buonarroti."

As they picked their way through O'Hare's aeronautical obstacle course – ticketing, check-in, security, departure lounge, boarding by seat row only – Phillips set Magill right on the whys and wherefores of the past three days. The late lamented Barton Brady was correct: there had been a feminist plot. P4's failure to appoint female phillippissimi had long been a sore point, among younger brethren in particular. Madonna had been snubbed in favour of Michael Jackson. Calvin Klein was preferred to Donna Karan. Charlie Chaplin was elected when Mae West was in her pomp. It had been like this ever since Jenny Lind was passed over for P. T. Barnum.

The election of Dan Brown was the last straw for many female brethren, especially in light of his pre-*Code* chauvinism and the alternative candidate, J. K. Rowling. Had the election been held in 2000, when Harry Potter mania was at its peak, Rowling's reputation as a marketer of genius might have carried the day. But the subsequent troubles of Michael Jackson, coupled with the irresistible rise of Dan Brown – clearly a secret-society aficionado – persuaded many conservative P4 members that it was no time to take a chance. So they voted for a safe pair of patriarchal hands.

Inevitably, the more extreme members of the organisation rebelled and threatened secession. An anti-Brown faction called BABES – Bitches Against Brown's Egregious Sexism – set out to subvert the succession. BABES was led by ambitious Irish firebrand Emer Aherne, who later adopted and indoctrinated a new recruit, Yasmin Buonarroti. Not only was Buonarroti descended from one of the earliest members of the organisation, when it was still comparatively matriarchal, but she also had access to Dan Brown, who embodied everything Emer abhorred.

Despite her concerns, Professor Phillips surreptitiously supported BABES, if only as a means of reforming an increasingly moribund organisation. Marketing's mid-life crisis was evident to many outside commentators; insiders suspected that senescence was imminent. Something had to be done.

But Phillips knew something that BABES didn't, namely that Dan Brown was a reluctant phillippisimus. He didn't really want the job in the first place. But because he'd been elected unanimously – by acclamation, not application, something unprecedented within P4 – Dan wanted a way out with honour. So Phillips came up with a plan that would give the reformist rebels what they wanted, and what she herself desired, while allowing Brown to step aside without alienating P4's conservative rank and file. It involved human sacrifice, or rather the impression of human sacrifice. Dan, she knew, would resign rather than perform his official sacrificial duties, and a new election would have to be called, thereby opening the door for J. K. Rowling.

But why, Magill inquired, was it necessary to go to such lengths, to actually *kill* Brodie and O'Connell, for something as trivial as an intra-organisational act of misdirection? Phillips reminded him that marketing was anything but trivial, and sometimes you have to kill to make a killing. The principal difficulty, she explained, was that the only P4 ceremony requiring human sacrifice was reconsecration when a serving phillippissimus stood down early.

For her plan to work, the incumbent had to resign, but Michael

Jackson steadfastly refused to do so. He loved the pomp and pageantry of P4. He considered himself the king of PoP (point of purchase), and the rightful heir of P. T. Barnum. There was no way he'd ruin his hard-earned reputation as a marketing maestro. Therefore, two known paedophiles within the organisation were eliminated in order to concentrate Michael's mind. Although he had been completely exonerated on charges of child abuse, even the king of PoP could see that stepping aside might be in his own best interest. Dan could then resign at the reconsecration ceremony, as was his right. With J. K. Rowling at the tiller, P4 would be set fair for the foreseeable future. Phillips was sure of that.

She was also sure that, as a descendant of the organisation's first elected phillippissimus and the latest lover of the late Emer Aherne, Yasmin Buonarroti was the most rabid of the BABES. She had the zeal of the newly converted. Dan Brown was in clear and present danger.

Naturally, Magill wanted answers to many other nagging questions such as the nature of the connection between P4 and King Billy, and the Edinburgh police force and the second body they talked about, and the Order of Solomon, if there was such a thing. Apparently King Billy was commissioned by P4 and Wee Joe took care of both hits, though the Edinburgh clean-up was outsourced to Auld Reekie's finest. Carlingford O'Connell was the second body, and although the Order of Solomon remained a mystery, Phillips was pretty certain it was one of King Billy's shell companies.

However, there remained the most personal question of all. Why him? Why did he, Simon Magill, need to be involved in an elaborate piece of organisational legerdemain staged to win over a renegade group of P4s?

"I explained this to you before, Simon. Partly because of your accidental association with Brodie, partly because you were in the wrong place at the wrong time, and partly to persuade Aherne that the subterfuge was real. It was the same with Brady and Buonarroti. But the main reason was on account of the Holy Grail, the Sale Greal. I knew you'd be coming for it."

"You have second sight, right?"

"Third sight, Simon. We call it third sight. I can see into the past as well as the future."

"But you didn't foresee Wee Joe's decisive ceremonial intervention."

"No, I didn't. Regrettably. That came completely out of the blue. No one was supposed to die except O'Connell and Brodie. Third sight's imperfect, Simon. Myopic, in fact. We see some things, but not everything. However, I knew for certain you'd ask the right question, Sir Perceval."

The preparation-for-landing announcement dribbled into the first-class cabin of United Flight 1547. Phillips and Magill returned their king-sized seats – big enough for a family of four or a single supersized McDonald's addict – to the upright position. Exasperated, Magill said to his marketing mentor, "But I didn't ask the right question! You told me I'd failed. You said my failure could cost me my life."

"But you didn't fail. You failed the first time I asked you about the secret of business success, but you mentioned it later, accidentally, serendipitously."

"What did I say?"

"I just told you."

"Pardon?"

"Ah, Simon, Simon, Simon. The Irish are lovely people, most of them, but they're awfully obtuse."

"I'm English, Professor Phillips, and true Brits are nothing if not pedantic. What did I say?"

Phillips laughed. "You're famous for your sense of humour too. Correct? The clue was in the statement I just made."

The wheels of the 767 touched down at McCarran with an ominous screech. Magill shouted to make himself heard over the reverse thrust of the roaring engines. "Serendipity. Luck. Accident. Is that the secret of success?"

"No, but it's very, very important. We marketing researchers downplay the importance of sheer chance in business life. The Sony Walkman, *The Simpsons*, Kellogg's Corn Flakes, Ivory soap, the internet, penicillin, dynamite . . . all lucky discoveries, Simon, and there are many more. Barton Brady's *HBR* article was right in that regard. He was a talented man, a sad loss to our profession. But luck's inherently uncontrollable, Simon, so it doesn't really qualify as a managerial success factor."

Magill thought back to his final fateful conversation with Brady. "Yasmin Buonarroti's been lucky all her life, apparently. Maybe it's more manageable than you think, Professor."

"Maybe, Simon, maybe. However, it isn't the Holy Grail of business, the secret of success."

"Secrecy!" Magill yelled. "The secret is secrecy itself!" He was beginning to enjoy testing himself in this guessing game against the guru of gurus. Little did he know that a real test – the test of his life – was less than thirty minutes away.

In response to his enthusiasm, Phillips visibly relaxed. "Almost, Simon, but not quite. Again, secrecy is very, very important. Just think of the so-called secret recipes that help sell all sorts of comestibles: Coca-Cola, Heinz varieties, Kentucky Fried Chicken, Mrs Fields' Cookies, Kellogg's Frosties, Grey Poupon Mustard, Brach's Chocolate Cherries. Think of the gift-giving business, which is based on secrets, surprises and well-I-nevers, as are gift-rich occasions like Christmas, birthdays and Valentine's Day. Think of the self-help management gurus who claim to possess the seven secrets of leadership, efficiency, effectiveness, time management, corporate well-being or, dare I say it, marketing success. People love a good mystery. Humankind is an inherently curious animal. Effective marketers take advantage of this irrefutable fact. But secrecy, though important, isn't the ultimate secret."

Magill raised his palms in defeat, trumped by his elder and better. "I give up. You win. I lose. I'm a failure, I guess."

Laughing, Phillips patted his Wildcats-clad back. "Correct, Simon. Well done. You got there in the end."

"Giving up? Winning? The secret of success is *winning*? Well, there's a shocker, Professor. Hold the front page and nobody leave the room. Lock up your librarians, or your livestock at least."

"No, Simon," she replied with exaggerated asperity. "The secret of success is failure. Business life is basically about *failure*. Hanging on in the face of repeated failure is the trait that distinguishes winners from losers. Although management gurus like me constantly chant the mantra of success – how to attain it, how to sustain it, how to unearth it, how to unleash it – the brutal reality is that the vast majority of business ventures end in failure. Most product launches flop, most innovations implode, most mergers melt down, most CEOs misfire, most R&D founders, most ad campaigns flatline, most long-range forecasts crater. History shows that in business life there is no such thing as untrammelled success, only organisations, brands and leaders that manage to stave off failure for longest.

"History also shows that those who accept failure, learn from failure, and absolutely refuse to be beaten by failure are those who win through in the end. Walt Disney was constantly disparaged by the Hollywood establishment and royally ripped off by perfidious partners. He sank every cent he had into an expensive experimental short, *Steamboat Willie*. Fortunately, the steamboat floated and Walt never looked back.

"Then there's Tide. The world's premier soap powder was once the ugly duckling of the detergent market. Its development caused all sorts of intractable technological headaches. The P&G product police tried to kill it off on numerous occasions. However, a fanatical Proctoid called Dick Byerly refused to let it die. He formed a surreptitious skunk works decades before skunk works got the Tom Peters seal of approval, and eventually won the day in 1947, when the brand was launched to tremendous consumer acceptance. Not only did Tide clean up, it wiped the floor with the competition. It does so to this day. There are countless examples of success through failure, Simon. You yourself have failed several times already, but I'm sure you'll succeed in the end. Maybe the time's right for the relaunch of SimpleSimsonSays.com."

Before grappling with that frightening thought, however, Magill needed to sort out one final issue. "Let me get this clear, Professor. If failure is the secret of business success, then it follows that *your* organisation, which is dedicated to ensuring the failure of ninety-nine percent of marketer endeavours, is actually doing the marketing world a favour! Are you telling me that you're misdirecting the marketing masses for their own good?"

"You have to be cruel to be kind, Simon."

Chapter Forty-Nine

Arms and the Dan

The heat at McCarran's taxi rank was ferocious, both literally and metaphorically. The line ahead was full of Armani-besuited mobpersons who looked as though they were packing more heat than a convention of pizza-oven sales representatives. In Death Valley. Clearly, some kind of family get-together was going down, and there was no way Phillips and Magill could sneak to the head of the line. Concrete footwear is so last year.

Such was the temperature that the petite professor removed her overcoat and revealed her ceremonial costume in all its empurpled glory, not only taking aback innocent bystanders but attracting several admiring comments along "Nice dress, lady" lines. Simon Magill felt underdressed in his Wildcats cut-off.

To pass the time, the Aylesbury Wildcat politely inquired about P4 phillippissimi past and present. It was a transparent attempt to reduce their anxiety levels, which were rising inexorably as forebodings of the challenge ahead loomed ever larger. But Phillips played along, informing Magill that P. T. Barnum was the best of the best. Not only was he a marketer of genius, but he was an incredible raconteur, someone Simon would have thoroughly enjoyed meeting.

"You knew Barnum?" her companion inquired. "Pull the other one, Professor, it's got a bearded lady on."

"I knew them all, Simon. Third sight's a wonderful thing, as near to marketing immortality as makes no difference. It's the means by which we keep track of yestermarketing achievements. The corporeal commercial body passes on, but the craft, the knowledge, the memories are eternal. Most meaningful marketing involves recycling old ideas, despite the prevailing presumption of new and improved. Barton Brady was right about retromarketing as well."

Sensitive to Magill's continuing pain, the prodigious professor lightened the mood with wry tales of P4's most successful marketing misdirections: customer orientation, CSR, *Good to Great* and especially *In Search of Excellence*.

The Desert Cab driver turned to Magill. "Where to, dude?" He was chubby, cheerful and, with his southern slacker drawl, evidently made a very good living from hi-rollers and low-riders alike. "Take your time, dude. I got all day, the meter's running, the aircon in this cab'd freeze the ass off a rattlesnake and I won a Benjamin on the blackjack tables last night. Interesting look you got there, dude. You here for the Elvis impersonator convention? The panda years, right? Nah, I got it now. You're auditioning for Ripley's Believe It or Not. Want me to take you straight there, dude?"

Magill was at a loss. He turned to Phillips for inspiration. "Serendipity Associates' offices, perhaps?"

The pocket-sized professor shook her head. "Possible, but not very likely. I suspect they're heading somewhere symbolic, somewhere more appropriate."

"Can't your third sight help?"

She shook her head again. "You sat at the feet of a master symbologist, Simon. Now's your chance."

Chance, as the late Barton Brady once observed, would indeed be a fine thing. The only problem was that Las Vegas was the world headquarters of chance, the symbological centre of the universe, the home of 1001 marketing attractions if not more, some or none of which might hold the key to their quest. Whatever and wherever it was, Magill surmised, it was likely to be relevant to Dan.

"Driver, is there a theme hotel or attraction devoted to the arts?"

"Sure is, dude. Circus Circus. Hard Rock Hotel. Mandalay Bay's House of Blues. Take your pick. It's Hiram, by the way. Hiram Hecuba at your service. Just call me Hi."

"Hi Hi. I was thinking more of the high arts. Leonardo, Picasso, Stella, Rothko, that kind of thing."

"MGM Grand. Film stars and shit there, dude. Leonardo always stays in the Grand when he's in town. Pacino too. Stiller's more a Four Seasons guy. As for Mickey Rourke, dude's a wack and that's a fact."

Magill wasn't getting through. His English accent and severely split lips were playing havoc with his sibilant diphthongs. "I meant Leonardo da Vinci, the painter, the artist, the thinker, not DiCaprio. I'm thinking painters: Warhol, Matisse, Titian, Goya, Pollock."

"That's the Bellagio, dude. They got an art gallery 'n' shit, though I think it closed a deuce o' years back."

With mounting anxiety, Magill turned to alternative cultural forms. "Literature. Novels. Books," he guessed wildly. "Is there anything with a storybook theme? Fairy stories, even?"

"Sure is, dude. Aladdin? Ali Baba? Excalibur? Check out the Liberace museum as well. Best fairy story in town."

Relief. At last. A breakthrough. "Excalibur! Of course. That's it! King Arthur. The Holy Grail. Lancelot and Guinevere in the Castle of Meleagant." Magill shouted excitedly, "The Excalibur, Hiram, leave no stone unturned!"

"Dude's a wack. Seriously."

The drive from McCarran to the Excalibur took less than ten minutes. As they roared down Tropicana Avenue towards the Strip, Simon could see the pastel towers of the plastic castle looming on his left. On crossing Las Vegas Boulevard, however, he glanced down the kitsch canyon, which seemed decidedly tacky during the afternoon. If ever a city went from ugly daytime duckling to dazzling nighttime swan, it was surely Las Vegas.

Something caught his eye as they turned into Excalibur. It was the Eiffel Tower. "Hold on, Hi. Where's the Eiffel Tower at?"

"That's the Paris, dude. Has a replica of the Louvre museum, an Arc de Triomphe and the Eiffel Tower. Bigger than the original, they say. Newer too."

"That's got to be it," Magill murmured to Phillips. "If she's taking the Danster to a symbolic location of some kind, it can only be Parisian."

On Magill's instruction, Hecuba's cab hung a 360 out of the Excalibur, cruised 500 yards down the Strip, circled the pseudo Arc de Triomphe and slid under the Paris's imitation Art Deco porte cochère. After briefly discussing the most likely destination – the replica Louvre's frontage abutted the casino floor and was way too crowded – the partners in pursuit calculated that Dan Brown's famous aversion to elevators and, presumably, fear of heights were key.

As with most things Las Vegan, the view from the top of the Eiffel Tower is stunning by night, but by day a hot and hazy panorama is the best that can be hoped for. So when Brady and Phillips spilled onto the surprisingly tiny viewing platform, they were the only people there apart from a brown-suited security guard and two conservatively dressed sixtysomething holidaymakers. There was no sign of Yasmin Buonarroti, let alone Dan Brown.

Defeated, Magill turned to Phillips, mumbling "It must have been the Excalibur after all." He rattled the protective metal cage in frustration and gazed forlornly towards the purple encircling hills while waiting for the elevator to reappear.

The pair of sightseers said hello. They too were English, and out of national solidarity Magill struggled to make small talk with Bert and Betty from Basingstoke. They were staying in New York New York, a rollercoaster-wrapped homage to the Big Apple at the junction of Tropicana and the Strip. Oblivious to Magill's distress, Bert happily chatted about the attractions they'd seen: Tom Jones, Cirque de Soleil and an exhibition about the *Titanic*, of all things. Betty was carrying a white plastic bag embossed with the words Bellagio Gallery of Fine Art.

"I'd heard the Bellagio Gallery was closed," Magill observed.

"No, no. We've just come from there," Betty answered. "The permanent display's closed, but they mount temporary exhibitions from time to time. What was it called again, Bill?"

"Masters of the Renaissance, dearest. It was nice to find something original in Las Vegas," he said to Magill. "They even had a da Vinci."

The lanky ginger man turned and stared, open-mouthed, at his companion. Zen-like as ever, Professor Phillips looked back inscrutably and whispered four words. "Ars longa, vita brevis."

Immortalised in the movie *Ocean's Eleven*, the Bellagio Resort and Casino is an oasis of opulence in gimcrack city. Based on an Italian hill village with extravagant Beaux Arts touches, it encircles a replica of Lake Como, whose fountains burst into life, Busby Berkeley style, on the hour and half-hour. However, Simon Magill and his sexagenarian associate didn't have time to take in the show as they hurried over the cross-Strip walkway, struggled through the revolving doors and sped up Via Bellagio, a mosaic-floored monument to the incomparable aesthetic achievements of consumer society – Fendi, Gucci, Hermès, Prada, Dior, Tiffany, Armani – and cut across the marbled casino in search of the fabled art gallery. Nor, for that matter, did they have time to take in the Titians, Raphaels or Caravaggios, let alone the beautifully displayed sketches from Leonardo's priceless notebooks – horses, anatomical drawings and even the Vitruvian Man – courtesy of that postmodern Medici, Bill Gates.

No amount of time, however, would have turned up Buonarroti and Brown. There was no sign of them. The nearest they got was prominently displayed copies of *The Da Vinci Code* in the attached gallery store.

"Strike two," Magill cursed as they exited the store with nothing to show for their labours.

"I attended a conference in the Bellagio once," Phillips said softly to herself.

"Oh really?" Magill replied curtly. His head was spinning with possibilities. Back to the Paris? The Arc de Triomphe? Down the Strip to Excalibur? Across the Strip to the Venetian? Betty said they had art galleries too. Surely she wouldn't have taken him on board the *Titanic*? Mind you . . .

"The conference rooms have very interesting names."

"Really." It could well be *Titanic*. It would be appropriate somehow, if warped, and Buonarroti was nothing if not warped . . .

"They're all named after great artists. Cézanne. Gauguin. Degas. Renoir. Monet. Donatello. Raphael. Da Vinci."

Magill stopped dead in the middle of the ornate, thickly carpeted corridor, forcing swimming pool–bound guests to step around the black-eyed, broken-nosed, purple-teeshirted vulgarian. "There's a da Vinci room? Let's go!"

There are four da Vinci rooms, in fact, situated at the very end of the Grand Patio, opposite the 18-foot windows overlooking the manicured pool area. The first two were empty. The third, and smallest, was empty too. Apart from Yasmin Buonarroti and Dan Brown. Buonarroti was pointing a pistol at the celebrity author, who was spreadeagled face up on a circular wooden table, with arms and legs outstretched, beneath a crystal-dripping chandelier.

"You're just in time, Kate," Buonarroti boomed. "Meet the Vitruvian Dan. He's preparing to meet his maker. But only after he's apologised for his misogynist behaviour. Neat, huh?"

"Yasmin," Phillips said calmly, as if talking to a truculent teenager, "the ceremony was a set-up, an exercise in misdirection. Dan didn't want to be phillippissimus. He's happy to stand down. J. K. Rowling's next in line. You've achieved BABES' aims. There's a P3 position coming up. It's yours. Let's do the right thing and walk away from this. If Dan dies, you die too. There's no way you'll escape the death penalty, not in Nevada, and not when a celebrity's involved. We can sort this out. Let's try to keep calm."

"This isn't about BABES," Buonarroti replied pugnaciously. "It's about *The Da Vinci Code*. Vitruvian Dan's going to die today." She nodded towards two goblets on either side of Brown's splayed body. "One contains fast-acting poison. The other's a slow-acting poison. It's Dan's choice. Rémy Legaludec didn't have a choice in *The Da Vinci Code*. Dan does. But either way he dies."

"If Dan dies," Phillips cautioned, "sales of *The Da Vinci Code* will soar. Premature death is one of the best career moves in the cultural industries. It's a marketing manoeuvre to die for. Literally. Kurt Cobain, Jimi Hendrix, Jim Morrison. Janice Joplin, Sylvia Plath, Virginia Woolf, Rudolph Valentino. Think this through, Yasmin."

"At least there'll be no more Robert Langdon books," Buonarroti spat.

"How do you know he hasn't written dozens already?" Magill retorted. "There could be a long line of Langdon novels waiting to storm the bestseller lists. Posthumously."

Buonarroti turned to her captive, who'd remained silent throughout – understandably, since Las Vegas had forced him to confront the antithesis of everything he admired. For the East Coast aesthete, it represented the noisome abyss of popular culture, the apotheosis of ersatz, the plastic fantastic.

"Are there any more books in the pipeline, Dan?" she asked roughly.

He shook his head.

"What about *The Solomon Key*?" Magill interrupted.

Dan stared at the ceiling. "Writer's block."

"The hardest thing in literature," Buonarroti continued, "is writing a follow-up to a multi-million bestseller. Emer told me that. She's dead thanks to Dan. She's the only person I ever loved. We only met a few days ago but she opened my eyes to so many things. She made me realise I've been wasting my life hustling for business and polishing Barton Brady's ego. Emer means more to me than life itself. She's dead. Brown's responsible. He's going to die." She pulled back the hammer of her Glock. "Take the poison or be shot, Dan. Fast or slow. Take your pick."

"I need a quiet word with you, Yasmin," Phillips said urgently. "Woman to woman. I need to tell you something very important. I'm not trying to trick you, or pull a fast one, but there's a vital fact you need to know."

Buonarroti thought about Phillips's offer for a moment and then nodded curtly. The professor walked slowly round the circular conference table towards the rabid management consultant – no sudden moves – and proceeded to whisper something in her ear. For a moment, Magill thought the imperishable prof had talked her out of it. But Buonarroti shook her head with disbelief and looked as though she was about to burst into tears. "I don't believe you, Kate," she said defiantly. "Time's up, Dan. Take a sip or swallow a bullet."

Magill knew that this was the moment of truth. He thought back to Brady's paean of praise for his former partner and Professor Phillips's advice about asking the right question. "I hear you're a gambler, Yasmin."

"The best. What of it, Magill?"

"How's about a wager?"

"You've got nothing I want."

"But you have something I want. What I want is Dan Brown. If I win, I walk with the Danster. If you win, Dan 'n' I'll knock 'em back together."

"Your death means nothing to me, Magill. I'm not interested in your offer. No deal."

"My death *should* mean something to you. Aherne's killer was my father. He killed her on my instructions. He was my back-up, my heat. I killed your lover, Buonarroti. I foiled your plan." Magill was gambling that Yasmin had left the Norris Center before Wee Joe Monroe was apprehended and that she didn't know the full story of what went on in Belfast.

It worked.

"I could just shoot you where you stand, you sonofabitch."

"You could, but that wouldn't be very sporting, not after you've taken the wager."

"I'm not sure I accepted your wager, Magill. But the thought of you and Brown writhing in agony together kind of appeals to me. So what do you want to do wager-wise – toss a dime, throw a die, cut a deck? I have one here."

"Whatever."

The professor, who had been silent for most of the exchange, spoke up. "Let Dan Brown decide. His life's at stake as well. He has to have an input. It's only proper."

"Fine by me," Magill said.

"What'll it be, Dan?" Buonarroti called. "Coins? Cards? Craps?"

The renowned author sat up, slid off the polished table, composed himself for a second or two and said in his soft yet determined voice, "A riddle."

"Magill," Buonarroti jeered at her English opponent, "I was Noo Yoik's lateral thinking champion from '85 to '89."

"Well then, you've got nothing to worry about. Fire away, Dan!"

Bizarrely, yet appropriately given his fondness for word games of all kinds, Brown painstakingly recited a quirky four-line verse. It was a riddle, he claimed, about the nature of marketing, a puzzle about the marketing code. He spoke up clearly so that both combatants could hear:

See, I send a rhyme excelling
In sacred truth and rigid spelling
Marketing secrets elucidate
For me the speakers will relate.

The air-conditioning system kicked in noisily, though it failed to drown out the ever-present tinkling of the background muzak. Magill recognised Hans Zimmer's theme tune from the *Da Vinci Code* movie. Buonarroti and her ginger opponent stood looking silently at each other for what seemed like an aeon, but couldn't have been more than sixty seconds. The Englishman spoke calmly, remembering his manners.

"Ladies first."

Noo Yoik's lateral thinking champion turned to Kate Phillips, her eyes looking for reassurance. Phillips shook her head. Yasmin took a deep breath. "The obvious answer is secrecy. The secret at the core of marketing is secrecy. Secrecy is the secret of success. There's a trick here, however. There's more to marketing success than secrecy. The secret of success isn't secrecy. It's failure. *Failure* is the key to success. Fail better. Emer Aherne told me that. She said so in her Dan Brown presentation. You've failed, Magill. Get ready to knock them back, boys."

Before Brown could answer, Magill spoke up:

Sir, I will a rhyme construct
By chosen words our group instruct
Cunningly devised endeavour
Try it and remember ever
Widths of circle here you see
Answered now in fateful captivity.

Magill's little recitation was greeted with stunned silence. He tried again, less poetically this time. "Dan, I need a drink, alcoholic in nature, after the Brown logogram involving market's mysteries."

Buonarroti looked askance.

As did Phillips.

But the Danster smiled.

Emboldened, Magill continued, "Can I have a large container of coffee, maybe tea, maybe straight Bushmills instead?"

Buonarroti looked askancer.

As did Phillips.

But the Danster laughed out loud.

On a roll, Magill kept going "For a maid a trick contrived, by nature tough, the Brown survived."

Buonarroti looked askancest.

As did Phillips.

But the Danster clapped his hands with glee. "So you need a drink, Simon, alcoholic in nature? I could do with one myself. I could murder a Bushmills!" He sauntered round the table, wrapped an arm around the lanky Englishman's shoulder and they made their way towards the door. Laughing.

"Aren't you forgetting something, Brown?" Buonarroti yelled, waving her pistol threateningly at the bestselling bookman.

Dan the Man turned to his captor. "He won fair and square. Robert Langdon couldn't have done better. It was pi, Yasmin. Pi is the most mysterious number in the universe, the basis of everything from the wonder of the rainbow, ripples expanding on a pond and DNA's double helix to Heisenberg's uncertainty principle, Riemann's zeta function and Einstein's general theory of relativity. It's more mysterious even than your precious 4Ps, P4, or whatever your malignant organisation's called.

"The riddling rhyme was an example of piphilology, a mnemonic device to help people remember the digits. The number of letters in each word is the key to the puzzle: 3.14159265358979."

Magill and Brown reached the door. "Do you fancy checking out the Old Masters, Dan? They've got a da Vinci or two."

"Don't mind if I do, Simon."

"Guess what's on sale in the gallery store?"

"I can't imagine."

As the cheerful twosome slipped out of the conference facility, a single shot echoed round the da Vinci room behind them.

"Tell me, Dan, where do you get your ideas from?"

Chapter Fifty

Sugar Paddy

The Irish don't need much of an excuse to party, and the closure of Hustler Business School was as good an excuse as any. The accusations of money laundering, though scurrilous and unproven, were sufficiently serious to imperil the entire institution's future. After careful consideration and due process, which took all of three days, the university decided its best interests would be served by the termination of its abortive venture into B-school branding. The award-winning building in Belfast's Titanic Quarter would be reallocated, probably to the urban planning department, and the lecturing staff either offered early retirement or absorbed back into the bosom of the mainstream business faculty. Naturally, no one was sacked, since industrial tribunals would have been, well, awfully messy.

Simon Magill hadn't intended attending the farewell bash. He'd been employed for less than a week, and didn't even have an office to say goodbye to. However, the acting head of school, Ian Kane, said he'd accept Simon's resignation only in person. Magill knew this was blather; he could formally resign by letter and get his P45 posted on. But in order to break Hustler's all-comers' record for the shortest-serving employee – currently held by Phil Kotler, who was appointed sight unseen in the belief that it was the well-known marketing scholar, but turned out to be Philomena, not Philip – Magill was required to hand in his resignation face to face. Simon wanted to see the pudgy rogue again, so what the hell.

The party was in full swing by the time Magill arrived, exhausted and unshaven, from his delayed overnight flight. It was early afternoon when the taxi dropped him off at the architectural abomination. The sinking of the glittering business school, even before it had been officially launched, was the theme of the farewell

379

affair. Rearranged deckchairs were the dominant motif, a string quartet played Ian Kane's signature tune, "My Heart Won't Go On," the Titanic Bar & Grill was the outside caterer – its magnificent centrepiece comprised an ice sculpture of the stricken liner, perfect in every detail – and the newly minted legend that *Titanic* was fuelled by freshly brewed poteen was being tested to destruction. It was women and children first at the bar It was every man for himself when the drink started running out and it became clear that there was insufficient firewater for passengers and crew.

Inevitably, Commodore Ian Kane was resplendent in a made-to-measure naval uniform with white gloves, brass buttons, gold-braid epaulettes and sufficient scrambled egg on his cap to feed everyone in steerage. After regaling the ship's complement with hilarious stories of his recent brush with the law, when he went on hunger strike by devouring every scrap of food in the police station – thereby ensuring that the PSNI would go hungry, not him – the commodore made a stirring farewell speech from a full-sized replica lifeboat that had been towed into the atrium for the occasion.

Simon couldn't help enjoying himself despite the deep-seated weariness in his bones. Two hours later, after chatting affably to numerous people he'd never met before, he sensed that the party was starting to break up. Most of the revellers had decided to continue the wake in the pubs and fleshpots of the nearby Odyssey Omnitron. But just as he was about to join them, Commodore Kane clapped him on the shoulder and said, "Let's do this, Simon. Then we can party like it's 1912."

They made their way to SOS's old office, which fitted splendidly into the nautical theme. When Ian had stopped wheezing from the short walk and finished the rigmarole of lighting up an enormous meerschaum pipe – newly acquired and completely contrary to the building's strict smoking ban – he pulled out a couple of official-looking forms. "Sign at the bottom, me hearty, and you'll secure your official release from Hustler servitude. Remember, if you ever want to come back, we can always find a job in the galleys."

"Rowing?"

"Catering, me lad. I have to maintain my calorie count. Ar-har."

Kane puffed with pleasure on his meerschaum funnel, which belched more black smoke than the *Titanic* at top speed.

Simon signed the forms and sat back in the luxurious leather captain's chair he'd last sat in less than seven days earlier. It felt like a lifetime ago. He handed the documents back to Kane. The commodore reached out to take them, but Magill held on. "Why did you do it, Ian? Why did you set me up?" He was hoping against hope that Kane would deny any involvement, or concoct a characteristically compelling story that would prove his innocence and give Magill something to believe in, even though he knew better.

"How did you work it out?" Kane asked simply.

"Dan Brown," Magill answered. "Phillips said my love of Dan Brown was a key factor in the narrative they invented to get me to Chicago. You're the only person who could have known about that beforehand. I never mentioned it to anyone, and it didn't come up during the job interview. But when you drove me to the airport after the interview I babbled about Dan the Man."

"Yep, it was a pretty good plot," Kane admitted, with a prodigious puff on his funnel. "One of my better ones. Fewer holes in it than *The Da Vinci Code*, that's for sure." He did his cheeky-cherub-chewing-a-honeycomb thing. "The carving under the headstone was a bitch to arrange, especially at such short notice. But it was a nice touch, don't you think?"

"This isn't a bloody joke! Why did you put me through hell, you bastard? What did I ever do to you?"

Kane set his pipe on a lifebelt-shaped brass ashtray. He looked terrible, worse than ever. His face was like lumpy porridge, a satyr gone to seed. "I was under . . . um . . . personal pressure, Simon. I had to do it. I didn't want to. It was a commitment I couldn't break. I tried to help. I covered for you. When the police called after O'Connell's death – when everyone knew you were the last person to see him alive – I arranged a diversion that sent them off in another direction entirely."

"You had King Billy whacked?"

The commodore smirked, shrugged and extended his hands palms up, like a mendicant money-lender.

"That's some diversion, Ian. But it wasn't done for my

protection. You had to make sure the police didn't pick me up because your narrative needed me in Chicago. I'm sure there were other reasons for the hit as well."

A look of infinite sadness fluttered across Kane's porcine features. He seemed more like a raddled roué than a cheeky cherub. "The money laundering was getting out of hand. King Billy was getting greedy. He wanted access to all our clients. He thought he knew it all, thought he was a marketing expert. Everyone's a marketing expert nowadays."

Magill stared at his old friend, whom he'd known for a couple of weeks, tops. "So it was two birds with one stone?"

"You know me, Simon, I'm a double helpings kinda guy."

The captain's chair creaked as Magill stood up to go. But the noise was drowned by another ominous creak. The office door had been opened, with its Hammer Horror sound effects, and a familiar voice carried across the room.

"Hello lover."

He span round, his heart racing and stomach churning. "May Day!" he gulped. She looked even more beautiful than he remembered. She'd removed the ironmongery, restored her hair's natural dark colour and was wearing the sexiest Wren uniform imaginable, complete with beret set at a carnal angle. The sight of her, and the accompanying pain of betrayal, was almost unbearable.

"Hello, Simon," she said pleasantly. "You're looking very well. The new haircut suits you. Makes you look . . . manly."

"Yes, I'm moving on, May."

"I heard." She hung her head, seemingly fascinated by the floor. "I'm . . . I'm . . . I'm sorry you're leaving."

"Well, Ian, I better get going. America's calling. I've got to go back to Aylesbury first, then tidy things up in Edinburgh, and after than I'm off for good."

"Your parents'll be pleased to see you," the chubby commodore said solicitously, while struggling up and extending a hand.

Magill balked, refusing to reciprocate. "I'm keen to talk with my father. We have a lot to discuss. There are bridges to build."

"Can *we* talk before you go?" May Day interrupted.

"Sorry, May, I have a flight to catch."

"It'll only take a few minutes." She looked at him imploringly.

Resolute, Magill started to shake his head, but Ian Kane was already rolling out of the room, practising his nautical gait. He looked like a buoy in a storm. "I'll leave you two to it." The door creaked behind him. A confrontation was unavoidable.

"I love you, Simon."

"You have a strange way of showing it."

May Day suddenly burst into floods of tears. Her arms semaphored frantically, disconcertingly. "I didn't want to. My mother insisted. I begged her to stop. Ultima did too. There was no talking to her, Simon. It was a family matter." She reached out to hold him. He tried to push her away, but she'd wrapped herself around him like an alluring limpet. She felt good – so good – and smelt wonderful.

But Magill remained unmoved. "I could have died, May. A friend of mine did die. The others may have deserved their fate, though I doubt it, but Barton Brady didn't. Eight people were killed on account of your 'family matter.'"

"Relationships are the essence of marketing. You know that, Simon. But blood's thicker than CRM."

Disentangling his tenacious triffid, Magill pushed May Day away. Her beautiful emerald eyes were shining with tears. "Marketing isn't about relationships. It's about the Principal Principle Protracted Protected. You're completely unprincipled, as far as I can make out." He raised his palm like a traffic policeman as she stepped towards him again. "When you came into this room you weren't expecting to see me, were you? You thought I'd gone already, didn't you, May?"

"No, Simon, no! I was looking for you! I wanted to tell you how much I loved you and try to, oh, I don't know, pick up the pieces somehow. Harry the herring gull misses you. The tantric panda's getting lonely . . ."

"Don't waste your breath. I saw Kane's reaction when you called out 'Hello lover.' I saw the look on his face. He's one of your conquests, I bet. You're the person who persuaded him to set me up. Did you tell him you loved him too? Did you burst into tears on cue? Christ, May, the guy's old enough to be your father. He's a cruiserweight to boot . . ."

Her emerald eyes turned cold, hostile, ruthless. "You're no oil painting yourself. Ian Kane's a nice man. Cuddly. Love handles like you wouldn't believe. You're a nice man too. Nondescript but nice. And nice men are . . . um . . . manageable."

"Easily manipulated, you mean."

"I like to think of it as misdirection, *mucker*."

"King Billy as well? Why does that not surprise me?" Magill turned to go. He walked towards the door, only to stop and look back. May Day stood rigid, fists balled by her sides, a ferocious expression on her face. "Gonna kill me, May? Don't bother. I've told the Danster everything, and if I disappear it'll all come out." Simon strolled on but stopped at the door. "One last thing, May, what's your real name?"

Her mouth turned down momentarily, accompanied by a tiny nod of appreciation. She composed herself, straightened her uniform, smiled slightly and looked at him with an "oh why not" expression. "Lucia Buonarroti, if you must know. We're all Buonarrotis. We come from an old Irish–Italian family. Yasmin's from a different branch, but we're closely related. It's funny, she had no idea at all, none whatsoever. But when my mother told her, she couldn't be restrained. She'd no notion of the connection to the cause."

"To Filippo Buonarroti? The conspiracy theorist you mentioned one day? The first phillippissimus after Cagliostro?" Magill felt disgusted, sick to his stomach. "Jesus wept! All of this simply because Dan Brown betrayed the feminist principles of an ancient bloodline he knew nothing about and wanted no part of? It's madness. Get help, woman. Family counselling. Something. Show some grief for your dead mother, if nothing else."

May Day ignored his naïve remark. "Filippo's part of the family line. But he's not the important one. The really important one lived 250 years before Filippo. His name was Michelangelo Buonarroti, though most people know him by his Christian name. Michelangelo was Leonardo da Vinci's greatest rival and sworn enemy. In his day, Michelangelo wiped the floor with Leonardo. Da

Vinci was a dilettante, a charlatan, a showman, a pantomime artist, a ceaseless self-publicist who produced next to nothing. My great-great- great- great- great- great- great- great- great- great- great- great-grandfather really knew how to run a business, deliver the goods, manage production efficiently and, above all, make a profit. He was a much better artist too.

"Until Dan Brown's vile books, which actually describe my distinguished ancestor as an 'ignorant coal heaver,' Michelangelo Buonarroti was widely regarded as superior – *far* superior – to Leonardo da Vinci. But thanks to Damn Brown, the only one anyone talks about is da Vinci, da Vinci, da fuckin' Vinci. Our quarrel with Brown has nothing to do with sexism or feminism. It was about family. He insulted my family, and Irish–Italian families don't take kindly to insults. It was about restoring my ancestor's reputation. BABES didn't stand for Bitches Against Brown's Egregious Sexism. It stood for Buonarrotis Against Brown's Esthetic Stupidity! Blood is thicker than tempera, Simon."

"And ancient family quarrels are more important than love."

"I guess so." She tugged at her beret and set her face bravely, proudly. There were no regrets, none whatsoever, not even for her mother who'd died in the line of familial duty.

Magill opened the office door to its full extent. "This just in, May. Da Vinci was a *much* better marketer than Michelangelo. Mickey may have been a prodigiously gifted artist, but he was a bean counter at heart. Leo was possibly less gifted, as you say. However, his marketing savvy puts Mickey in the shade. And Emer Aherne knew it. She couldn't accept the truth. Don't you know the old saying, May?"

"No, what's the old saying, Simon?" she echoed sarcastically.

"Michelangelo is from Mars, da Vinci is from Venus. Think about it."

"Whatever."

He turned to go. "Your assumed names. May, Day, Ultima, Sullivan, Emer, Aherne. The initial letters form an anagram. It's very apt."

"Really, Simon."

"MEDUSA."

"They were Ultima's idea."

"I thought as much. Medusa had two sisters. She turned men to stone. And got her head chopped off in the end."

"That's the eternal feminine for you, Simon."

"The avenging feminine, you mean."

"Sometimes you have to kill to make things even."

"No, I don't think you do. Forgive and forget. Forgive and forget."

"You forgot something, Mr Forgiveness."

"There's nothing I want to hear from you. I believe in forgive and forget, but not in your case. I've had my fill, thanks all the same."

She smiled at him, siren-like. "The Order of Solomon. I thought you'd have worked it out, especially as Filippo Buonarroti wrote under the pseudonym Abraham Solomon. It wasn't 'order' you heard, Simon, it was 'daughter.' We're the Daughters of Solomon. I told you to listen to things more carefully."

"What's the Solomon connection to Michelangelo?"

"Surely you know my illustrious ancestor's greatest work?"

"Sistine Chapel? St Peter's Basilica? The statue of David?"

"Third time lucky. Who was the offspring of David? You're the son of a minister, Simon. You should know this."

"Solomon. Of course. Neat. Still psycho though. Solomon slaughtered the rival claimants to his throne. Despite his reputation for wisdom, he was as ruthless as his father, the Don Corleone of the Old Testament."

"But he was also someone who the Queen of Sheba respected above all others. He too was in touch with the eternal feminine. Pass it on to Dan. It might help with *The Solomon Key*."

"I doubt it, sister. I very much doubt it."

Chapter Fifty-One

O, Danny Boy

"The proofs, the proofs are calling. I'd better get back to them, Dan."

"OK, Simon, but we need to talk through scenarios for the new Robert Langdon novel."

"Is this the one where he finally gets to bed Sophie Neveu?"

"No! Of course not!"

"Vittoria Vetra?"

"*Simon.* That's quite enough."

"Sophie and Vittoria together, in a steamy *ménage à trois* with Big Bobby?"

"Yeah, baby, yeah!"

Magill couldn't help laughing. "Not that you're a chauvinist or anything, Dan."

"The eternal feminine," the dapper New Englander sighed wistfully. "The eternal feminine. I'm a firm believer in the eternal feminine, Simon."

"Me too, Dan."

As the onshore breezes danced across the balcony of the Danster's Rye Beach mansion, Simon Magill smiled a smile of contentment. He'd left benighted Belfast behind, was reconciled with his father, had recovered from the anguish of his mother's funeral – which was for the best, she'd been all but dead for years – and was dating Assumpta Lynch, an Irish–American angel from Hanover, New Hampshire. It wasn't serious just yet, though Simon was hoping she'd take full-time pity on him. As he told her, there's nothing he'd like more than a happy-as-pi family of 3.141 children (called Pippa, Pierre and Pillow), and a 3.141-legged Irish setter. It was difficult for a girl to resist such an appealing picture of all-American domesticity, Assumpta had said. But she'd try her hardest.

Dan the Man wasn't a hard taskmaster, though his daily routine was, well, nearly as wacko as Jacko's. Up at 4 a.m., sit-ups on the hour, dangling upside-down from the rafters of his study, while maintaining his word count (courtesy of voice-recognition software). Compared to J. D. Salinger, admittedly, the guy was nearly normal, or as normal as any bestselling author nowadays, and he was a delight to work with. Magill took care of the mundane side of the Danster's literary existence – correcting proofs, preparing manuscripts, dealing with publishers and analogous parasites – while the wordsmith got on with the really important stuff: writing. *The Solomon Key* had finally been published to worldwide acclaim, and the artiste was planning four more Langdon novels, making seven in all. Magill suspected that trumping Harry Potter's total sales was the Danster's ultimate ambition, but the objective was never mentioned.

When not working on Robert Langdon's latest adventure, they sat around inventing acronyms, playing Sudoku and trading cryptic riddles. Every so often, Dan would insist on an impromptu piphilology session for old time's sake. The great man could recite 12,000 digits from memory, which was even better than Simon during his pre-teen peak. Not bad for someone in his mid-forties.

Since leaving Hustler, Magill had published a couple of papers on the periodicity of marketing fads, but his heart wasn't really in academia. He aspired to literary accomplishment. He took creative writing classes, submitted short stories to *McSweeney's* (unsuccessfully) and persuaded the Danster to read his amateurish scribblings. The titan was reluctant, in truth. Like all creative geniuses, he was concerned about contaminating his own thought processes – not that he called it contamination. He was much too nice for that. Too polite. However, as the months rolled by, Magill gradually gained Brown's confidence, and every so often they'd toss scenarios around.

One day, after a particularly invigorating session, Simon said, "I've got a great idea for a novel, Dan. It's a thriller."

"Oh yeah, what's the premise?"

"A conspiracy theory at the heart of marketing. Commercial life is controlled by a ruthless secret society called the Priory of Cyan, possibly fronted by an ostensibly innocent publishing house specialising in business books."

The Danster hit the deck of his wooden-floored and -panelled study and started a punishing press-up routine. He was pumping like a piston. "Hmmm. I'm not so sure, Simon."

"It's got sex scenes, Dan. They're pretty short, I grant you, but my creative writing instructor says you should write from personal experience."

"Sex always sells. Even short sex. Better yet if you can include animals. Preferably cuddly. Gerbils, koalas, pandas or some such."

"I've also got my protagonist worked out."

"Let me guess, Simon. It wouldn't happen to be an assistant professor with bright ginger hair?"

"Check."

Pump, pump, pump. One-handed now, without so much as a pant, puff, gasp or wheeze. "The climax wouldn't happen to involve a bestselling author in a theme hotel in Las Vegas?"

"No, no, no. Of course not! How could you think such a thing? She's a marketing-savvy writer of mega-selling children's books and the climax takes place on the topmost turret of Edinburgh Castle."

"Do you think J. K. Rowling will give her permission?"

"Why not, Dan? She gets thrown off, plummets down, pulls out a broomstick and heads off to Hogwarts in triumph. How cool is that?"

Pump, pump, pump. With handclap between each repetition. "Literary agents will be beating a path to your door, Simon."

"Our door, Dan. I was hoping you'd get personally involved. Sprinkle some of that Danster magic dust on it."

The megaselling author suddenly stopped his workout. This was unprecedented. The only time it had happened before was when Dan's gravity boots broke free from their moorings and the literary celebrity plunged head first to the floor, damaging his hands-free headset. "No way, Simon. No way!"

"You could use a pseudonym," Magill insisted. "I was thinking of something like Dan Boyle, Dan Brennan, Dan Brain or similar. Just close enough to the original to give people pause. But not too close, of course."

"Don't like it," Brown said curtly.

"OK, OK, OK. What about Ian Brown, Jan Brown, Stan Brown . . . ? "

"I'm sorry, Simon, it's all too close to home." The Danster stood up, wiping a single trickle of perspiration from his forehead. "However, I've often thought that our Las Vegas face-off has . . . hmmm . . . *literary* possibilities."

"Worth working up?"

"Possibly. Possibly. Maybe somewhere down the line. I still have nightmares about the da Vinci room experience. Perhaps when I've had a chance to come to terms with . . . well . . . hmmm . . . actually . . . hmmm . . . now that you've raised the topic, Simon . . . we'd obviously need to develop or rework it in some way."

"Sure, Dan, whatever you say."

An expectant hush descended on Dan's den. The multimillionaire started to speak, only to fall silent again. He sipped on a Gatorade and stared out of a picture window towards the New Hampshire coastline beyond. After several moments' contemplation, the peerless storyteller spoke up, weighing his words carefully. "There's something I can't get out of my head about our Bellagio . . . er . . . encounter."

Magill chugged a Gatorade too, worn out from watching Brown's brutal routine. "The Vitruvian Dan? The poisoned chalice? The single shot? The look on Buonarroti's face when I worked out the riddle?"

"No, Simon, no. It was something else entirely."

This was the first time they'd ever discussed the unspeakable horrors of that dreadful day. "What was it, Dan?" Magill murmured.

The Danster looked pained, and it wasn't from the push-ups. "I know it's crazy, but I keep wondering what Kate Phillips said to Yasmin Buonarroti before your big gamble. As I recall, she almost burst into tears. I was certain she'd see sense then. But she didn't." He sighed heavily. "I often wonder what Phillips said. Odd, isn't it?"

"I know exactly what was said, Dan."

"How could you? You were further away from them than I was, and I couldn't hear a thing. There was too much noise – the muzak, the a/c, the sound of your knees knocking. Both our knees knocking ... "

"Phillips wrote me a note. I found it in my chinos pocket afterwards. She must have slipped it in on the way up to the Eiffel Tower viewing platform, possibly in the cab. Maybe even on the flight from Chicago. I don't know for sure."

"Really? What did it say?"

"That's the crazy thing Dan. There's no way she could have known this beforehand, not unless she really did have second sight or third sight or whatever it was."

The Danster sat down at his computer terminal, work in progress forgotten. "What did it say, Simon?"

"It said she was going to unsettle Yasmin by telling her that her unborn grandson, Daniel, was deeply ashamed of her. The seer had spoken with Buonarroti's descendant, who was an aspiring author himself, and he said he couldn't and wouldn't forgive his murdering grandmother. By dishonoring the Buonarroti family in that way, she'd condemned them to generations of bad fortune. Daniel himself was living in abject poverty."

Dan looked at him with a tear in his eye. He remembered well what it was like to be a struggling writer. "Do you believe it, Simon?"

"I'm not sure. But the thing that gets me is this. How could she possibly know the conference room confrontation would pan out the way it did? How could she know that family pride, not feminist principles, was the thing that really motivated Buonarroti? I'm at a loss, Dan. I just don't know. What I do know is that it worked. Yasmin Buonarroti, the luckiest gambler in Las Vegas, Noo Yoik's lateral thinking champion, was sufficiently unsettled to let me win the challenge."

"Stranger things have happened."

"Yes, that's true. Though the strangest thing of all is that Phillips's note was wrapped around something. Something significant. Something important."

A broad grin crossed Dan Brown's amiable face. As a gazillion-selling thriller writer, he knew where this was going. "Is it what I think it is, Simon?"

Magill said nothing. Instead he pulled an ancient blue locket from his pocket and held it up by its thin gold chain. It turned slowly in the late afternoon light, reflecting, refracting, remembering.

"You know your theory about the Holy Grail? The one in *The Da Vinci Code*? The one about Mary Magdalene? The one that earned you millions of dollars, worldwide acclaim and a writ or several, including a sizzler from Sir Leigh Teabing?"

"Tell me about it."

"No, but I will tell you that you got it wrong, Dan." Magill let the precious object slither into his left hand. He cupped it in his palm and reached across to his employer. "I think this belongs to you, maestro, with the compliments of P4."

The Danster stared down at the wonderful work of intricately carved lapis lazuli. "I don't want it, Simon. The grail chooses its own recipient. Everyone knows that. It's not mine to want or own. Or even touch. It's yours. It's your responsibility."

Magill slipped the Sale Greal back into his pocket.

"What are you going to do with it, Simon?"

"Dunno, Dan. I was thinking of mailing it to J. K. Rowling, but if the marketing conspiracy book ever comes to fruition, I might give it away as a prize, as a free gift, maybe as part of a tie-in competition. What could be more appropriate for an object of great marketing power? And if it really is the grail, it'll find its way to the right person."

Brown began strapping on his gravity boots in preparation for his next writing session from the rafters. "Given any thought to the tie-in competition?"

"Yes, I have actually. I'll give it to the person who can tell me the real secret of marketing success."

The Danster shook his head vigorously as he struggled with the last of the heavy metal clasps. "That's too easy, Simon. It can only be failure, luck, or secrecy. There's no competition there."

Magill stood up and polished off his Gatorade as he prepared to depart and let Dan the Man get on with his work. "I'm surprised at you, Mr Brown, you being a supposed marketing expert and all that. Failure isn't marketing specific, nor is luck, nor even is secrecy, though it's often employed by marketers. The real secret is something else again. Phillips was misdirecting me with the others. I finally worked out the art of marketing."

"Really?"

"Funnily enough, the clue was in a tiny little wisp of smoke which appeared when Barton Brady hurled the locket onto Phillips's kitchen table and it burst open on impact."

"Interesting."

"Indeed. It encapsulated the essence of marketing."

"Which is?"

"Blowing smoke where the sun don't shine. Marketing, at bottom, involves blowing smoke where the sun don't shine."

"Stick with secrecy, Simon."

Magill laughed and closed the door behind him as the gravity-booted literary genius started another writing session from the rafters. For a second, Simon thought he heard a woman's voice whispering up from the chasms of the earth. But it was only the Danster's soft, lilting New Hampshire accent.

"Renowned marketer Joaquin Sangreal staggered through the vaulted archway of the business school's Grand Gallery. No, no . . . doesn't work . . . hmmm . . . let me see . . . hmmm . . . OK. Take two. The room buzzed with anticipation as the speaker strode towards the imposing podium."

THE END?

Author's Note

As an academic, I feel obliged to refer to my sources and give the reader a "proper" explanation of what I was trying to achieve in *The Marketing Code*. The overall objective of this book is summarised by Ian Kane in chapter 18, when he tells Simon Magill about his aborted literary venture. The present book, like Kane's, is a marketing text written as a novel – a thriller, no less – rather than in the usual bullet-pointed, action-listed, case-studied format.

With this model in mind, I deliberately inverted my principal source of inspiration, Dan Brown's bedazzling blockbuster. Where *The Da Vinci Code* was set in the world of high culture (art, aesthetics), *The Marketing Code* is set in the world of base commerce (marketing, branding); where *The Da Vinci Code* unfolded in delightfully picturesque cities (Rome, Paris, London), *The Marketing Code* unfolds in particularly dangerous cities (Belfast, Chicago, Las Vegas); where *The Da Vinci Code* was predicated on a Cathar/Opus Dei/Priory of Sion conspiracy, *The Marketing Code* relies on a Freemasons/Knights Templar/P2 mixture; where *The Da Vinci Code* is Roman Catholic and makes much of the "sacred feminine", *The Marketing Code* is inherently Protestant and gets in touch with the "sacred masculine"; where *The Da Vinci Code's* hero didn't get the girl along the way, but wished he did, *The Marketing Code's* hero gets the girl but regrets it in the end; where *The Da Vinci Code* was a thriller with a pedagogic subtext, *The Marketing Code* is pedagogy with thrills on top; and, last but not least, where *The Da Vinci Code* was humourless at heart, *The Marketing Code* is humorous at bottom. Well, that was the intention . . .

You may also be interested in some of my specific sources, the ones I drew on in the body of the book. My discussion of *The Da Vinci Code* in the first chapter is indebted to Kent Drummond's excellent chapter in *Consuming Books* (Routledge, London, 2006). Lisa Rogak has written an unauthorised biography, *Dan Brown: The Man Behind The Da Vinci Code* (Robson Books, London, 2005), which is very informative about the Danster's music biz escapades, not least his telephone sex line song, "976-LOVE".

The Edinburgh chapters make use of all sorts of sources, including personal visits to the locations concerned, but I found Ian Rankin's memoir, *Rebus's Scotland* (Orion, London, 2005), particularly helpful on the city's sense of place. Equally helpful was Thomas Cahill's readable study of the early Irish church, *How the Irish Saved Civilisation* (Sceptre, London, 1995). For the history of the Orange Order, see Kevin Haddick-Flynn's excellent *Orangeism* (Wolfhound Press, Dublin, 1999). Haddick-Flynn also discusses Tara, the paramilitary offshoot of the Orange Order which is foreshadowed in Pitcairn Brodie's provocative research report. The relationship between Tara and the paedophile ring in Kincora House is covered by Chris Moore in *The Kincora Scandal* (Marino, London, 1996).

The Las Vegas chapters draw on my own published work, as does Kane's Quantum Theory of Branding, Aherne's Celtic Marketing Concept and Magill's Tripping Point presentation to the apparel executives. I'll spare you the details (though if any tickle your fancy, feel free to get in touch). BTW, you'll be relieved to hear that May Day's herring gull theory of capitalism is as yet unpublished.

It goes without saying that the literature on conspiracy theories is legion. The material on the *Titanic* alone is prodigious and much of it is considerably odder than the stuff I actually included (one involves the curse of an Egyptian mummy – don't ask). For a good general overview of conspiracy theories, see James McConnachie and Robin Tudge, *The Rough Guide to Conspiracy Theories* (Rough Guides, London, 2005). *Secret Societies* by Nick Harding (Pocket Essentials, London, 2005) is also useful, as is Giles Morgan's *The Holy Grail* (Pocket Essentials, London, 2005). Better yet is Richard Barber's *The Holy Grail: The History of a Legend* (Penguin, London, 2005), an exhaustive cultural analysis of the grail legends and associated matters. (This is the book Simon Magill refers to in chapter 46.) As for the Knights Templar, it's hard to beat Piers Paul Reid, *The Templars* (Phoenix, London, 2001), though the wackier side is better represented by Michael Baigent and Richard Leigh, *The Temple and the Lodge* (Arrow, London, 1998).

There's no point listing the literature on Freemasonry, since Masonology is a quasi-academic discipline in its own right. The pro-mason position is typified by John Hamill and Robert Gilbert, *Freemasonry: A Celebration of the Craft* (Angus Books, London, 2004). The anti-mason arguments are itemised in Stephen Knight, *The Brotherhood* (Dorset Press, London, 1986). A book I found particularly useful is *The Shadow of Solomon* by Laurence Gardner (HarperElement, London, 2005). It discusses the admittedly bizarre theories surrounding Irish round towers as well as the Egyptian pyramids' plaster cover, *tcham*.

If you're looking for an insightful analysis of the Ulster Protestant mindset, Geoffrey Beattie is a good place to start. His books *Protestant Boy* (Granta, London, 2004) and *We Are the People* (Mandarin, London, 1993) are very well written, as is *The Faithful Tribe* by Ruth Dudley Edwards (HarperCollins, London, 2000). Equally arresting is Martin Dillon's grisly case study, *The Shankill Butchers* (Arrow, London, 1990). Wee Joe Monroe is a pussycat compared to what the real Butchers got up to. Incidentally, King Billy Solomon is entirely fictitious. Repeat, *entirely fictitious*.

The characters in *The Marketing Code* may be fictitious, but the places are exactly as described. Well, *almost* exactly as described. I took a few liberties for literary purposes. The biggest liberty I took was with Hustler Business School, which doesn't exist, though the building is based on some of the old Harland and Wolff shipyard properties which remain in situ. The café at the Ulster Folk and Transport Museum doesn't sell brown-sauce sandwiches, or at least it didn't last time I was there. The graveyard in Templepatrick does exist and although it's officially described as a Knights Hospitaller facility, I think we can spot misdirection when we see it, right? The Titanic Bar & Grill doesn't claim to serve the stricken liner's final repast, nor does it have passenger lists on display. Actually, it's a very attractive theme restaurant, well worth a visit. The Cheney House in Chicago was vacant for a long time. It's now a bed and breakfast. If you're interested in the gruesome Mamah Cheney story, see Meryle Secrest, *Frank Lloyd Wright: A Biography* (University of Chicago Press, Chicago, 1998). The Bellagio Gallery of Fine Art in Las Vegas does indeed mount temporary exhibitions, though they have never featured the Old Masters, as far as I'm aware. Maybe next year!

Talking of next year, some of you may be interested in the timing of the events described in this novel. I toyed with the idea of including dates and times at the start of each chapter, the way many thriller writers do. But I decided against it in the end. For the record, Emer Aherne's Paris Hotel presentation is delivered on Sunday 8 October 2006. Brodie and Magill meet at the Scott Monument on Monday 9 October 2006. The reconsecration ceremony in Evanston takes place at noon on Friday 13 October 2006. The rest you can work out for yourselves. Before you write, yes, I did consider setting it in 2007, the 700th anniversary of the fall of the Knights Templar. But as Dan Brown's next book is likely to be published by then – though it was originally slated for 2005 – I felt it best to stick with 2006.

Talking of sticking, thank you for sticking with *The Marketing Code*. If you have any comments, I'd love to hear them. I can be contacted via my website www.sfxbrown.com. Paspi perhaps?

Postscript

After finishing *The Marketing Code*, I came across some interesting bits of information, which I feel duty bound to share with you. First, I found out that there really is a concept called Sustainable Marketing, though it refers to the marketing of sustainability and eco-friendliness generally rather than the sustenance of marketing, as such. Second, I'm sorry to report that the Titanic Bar and Grill has shut up shop. I'll spare you the obvious quips about insolvency icebergs, sinking without trace, going down with all kitchen-hands, Save Our Short-order cooks, nearer my cod to thee or, indeed, on-going plans to raise the Titanic Bar and Grill. Third, an architectural purist has pointed out to me that the Masonic building in Arthur Square, mentioned in chapter 18, was built in 1868 and couldn't possibly have been the venue for Ian Kane's 1844 fictional fistfight between Rev. John Carey and General Tom Thumb. But, as Kane's book didn't actually get written, and he would undoubtedly have checked such an important architectural detail, I think we can forgive the cheeky cherub, don't you?

Acknowledgements

Like most literary genres, business books tend to adhere to a standard template. And in my experience, publishers prefer to stick with the proven formula. Cyan, I'm delighted to say, is a wonderful exception to the rule. If Martin Liu hadn't supported my admittedly unorthodox idea of a "management thriller," *The Marketing Code* would never have seen the light of day. I'm enormously grateful for his unstinting encouragement.

I'm equally grateful for the heroic editorial endeavours of Martin's brilliant colleague, Pom Somkabcharti. I've worked with many editors over the years, some more successfully than others, but Pom is quite simply in a league of her own. I can't thank her enough.

Nor, for that matter, can I possibly do justice to all the people who've helped bring *The Marketing Code* to fruition. Alun Richards is an experienced marketer and avid thriller reader. He kept me right on both counts. Hope Schau, a creative writer without parallel, also kept me on the straight and narrow, as did Kent Drummond, whose paper on *The Da Vinci Code* was my original source of inspiration. No less inspirational was my niece, Erin Richards, who spent one summer holiday happily knitting iPod covers, which gave me the idea for Knits Templar. My old friend Kim Lenaghan, broadcaster supreme and covert chick-lit writer, was a constant source of encouragement, not to say merriment. Professor Philip Kotler, the greatest marketing guru of the modern era, took time out of his busy schedule to read and comment on my manuscript. I greatly appreciate his generous comments. Russ Belk, Dawn Iacobucci, Kate Maclaran, John Sherry, Geoff Simmons and Mark Tadajewski also cast their expert eyes over the draft. Thank you all.

Another illustrious academic who warrants a great big thank you is Dr Stephanie O'Donohoe. A stalwart of the University of Edinburgh, she kept me right on the Auld Reekie chapters and, with the aid of her partner, George Harte, she polished up the

Scottish dialogue in chapter 7. Stephanie also arranged for my guided tour of New College, which was brilliantly conducted by Gordon Grant. I'm enormously grateful to Gordon and Stephanie both.

The final person I'd like to thank is Linda, my preternaturally patient wife. Not only has she been nagging me to write a novel for years – although *The Marketing Code* isn't quite what she had in mind – she happily accompanied me on a flying visit to Las Vegas. Most people go to Sin City to see the shows and play the slots. Linda had to put up with someone who spent his time checking sight-lines along the Strip and poking around casino-hotel conference facilities and who, given a choice between Celine Dion at Caesar's Palace and the Tropicana's *Titanic* exhibition, unhesitatingly opted for the latter. You can take the boy out of Belfast . . .